TYNDALE OLD TESTAMENT COMMENTARY

Vo

CW00969401

TOTC

GENESIS

Tyndale Old Testament Commentaries

Volume I

Series Editor: David G. Firth
Consulting Editor: Tremper Longman III

Genesis

An Introduction and Commentary

Andrew E. Steinmann

Academic
An imprint of InterVarsity Press
Downers Grove, Illinois

InterVarsity Press, USA
P.O. Box 1400
Downers Grove, IL 60515-1426, USA
ivpress.com
email@ivpress.com

Inter-Varsity Press, England
36 Causton Street
London SW1P 4ST, England
ivpbooks.com
ivp@ivpbooks.com

InterVarsity Press®, USA, is the book-publishing division of InterVarsity Christian Fellowship/USA® and a member movement of the International Fellowship of Evangelical Students. Website: intervarsity.org.

Inter-Varsity Press, England, originated within the Inter-Varsity Fellowship, now the Universities and Colleges Christian Fellowship, a student movement connecting Christian Unions in universities and colleges throughout Great Britain, and a member movement of the International Fellowship of Evangelical Students. Website: www.uccf.org.uk.

Unless otherwise indicated, Scripture quotations are the author's own translation. Further Bible acknowledgments can be found on pp. xii-xiii.

First published 2019

Image: © Erich Lessing/Art Resource, NY

USA ISBN 978-0-8308-4251-3 (print)
USA ISBN 978-0-8308-9475-8 (digital)
UK ISBN 978-1-78974-090-5 (print)
UK ISBN 978-1-78974-091-2 (digital)

Typeset in Great Britain by CRB Associates, Potterhanworth, Lincolnshire

Printed in the United States of America ∞

InterVarsity Press is committed to ecological stewardship and to the conservation of natural resources in all our operations. This book was printed using sustainably sourced paper.

Library of Congress Cataloging-in-Publication Data
A catalog record for this book is available from the Library of Congress.

British Library Cataloguing-in-Publication Data
A catalogue record for this book is available from the British Library.

P	21	20	19	18	17	16	15	14	13	12	11	10	9	8	7	6	5	4	3	2	1
Y	37	36	35	34	33	32	31	30	29	28	27	26	25	24	23	22	21	20	19

CONTENTS

GENERAL PREFACE

The decision to completely revise the Tyndale Old Testament Commentaries is an indication of the important role that the series has played since its opening volumes were released in the mid-1960s. They represented at that time, and have continued to represent, commentary writing that was committed both to the importance of the text of the Bible as Scripture and a desire to engage with as full a range of interpretative issues as possible without being lost in the minutiae of scholarly debate. The commentaries aimed to explain the biblical text to a generation of readers confronting models of critical scholarship and new discoveries from the Ancient Near East while remembering that the Old Testament is not simply another text from the ancient world. Although no uniform process of exegesis was required, all the original contributors were united in their conviction that the Old Testament remains the word of God for us today. That the original volumes fulfilled this role is evident from the way in which they continue to be used in so many parts of the world.

A crucial element of the original series was that it should offer an up-to-date reading of the text, and it is precisely for this reason that new volumes are required. The questions confronting readers in the first half of the twenty-first century are not necessarily those from the second half of the twentieth. Discoveries from the Ancient Near East continue to shed new light on the Old Testament, whilst emphases in exegesis have changed markedly. Whilst remaining true to the goals of the initial volumes, the need for contemporary study of the text requires that the series as a whole be updated. This updating is not simply a matter of commissioning new volumes to replace the old. We have also taken the opportunity to update the format of the series to reflect a key emphasis from linguistics, which is that texts communicate in larger blocks rather than in shorter segments such as individual verses. Because of this, the treatment of each section of the text includes three segments. First, a short note on *Context* is offered, placing the passage under consideration in its literary setting within the book as well as noting any historical issues crucial to interpretation. The *Comment* segment then follows the traditional structure of the commentary, offering exegesis of the various components of a passage. Finally, a brief comment is made on *Meaning*, by which is meant the message that the passage seeks to communicate within the book, highlighting its key theological themes. This section brings together the detail of the *Comment* to show how the passage under consideration seeks to communicate as a whole.

Our prayer is that these new volumes will continue the rich heritage of the Tyndale Old Testament Commentaries and that they will continue to witness to the God who is made known in the text.

David G. Firth, Series Editor
Tremper Longman III, Consulting Editor

AUTHOR'S PREFACE

When I was first contacted about writing this commentary, I had a moment of doubt – did the commentary editors mean to select me for this privilege? While I had been deeply interested in Genesis for quite a few years and had more recently published a few studies of particular passages in it, I was not prepared for the thought that anyone would want me to write an entire commentary on this most important book of the Old Testament, much less the highly respected Tyndale Old Testament Commentary series and its editors. Nevertheless, when I came to my senses, I gladly accepted the assignment. It has been a joyful task. As every commentary writer knows, one benefits immensely from having to produce such a work – from growth in knowledge of the word of God to new insights gained into its application to faith and life today among God's people.

I am grateful not only for having been chosen to produce this work, but also to those who supported me in it. That includes the librarians in the Klinck Memorial Library at Concordia University Chicago. They assisted me in finding and compiling many publications that I consulted as I studied and wrote. My gratitude also extends to Dr David Firth, whose skilful and expert editorial suggestions helped improve this commentary in ways both small and great. Finally, I would not have been able to do this work as productively and joyfully without the support of my wife Rebecca, who always took an interest in my progress and continuously supported me with her kindly encouragement. Most importantly, to the gracious God of Abraham, Isaac and Jacob, who appeared in the flesh in Christ Jesus as the fulfilment of all the promises in Genesis, belong my everlasting thanks and praise.

Andrew E. Steinmann

ABBREVIATIONS

AB	Anchor Bible
ABD	D. N. Freedman et al. (eds.), *Anchor Bible Dictionary*, 6 vols. (New York: Doubleday, 1992)
ACCS	T. C. Oden (ed.), *Ancient Christian Commentary on Scripture*, 29 vols. (Downers Grove, IL: IVP Academic, 2001)
ANET	J. B. Pritchard (ed.), *Ancient Near Eastern Texts Relating to the Old Testament*, 3rd edn (Princeton: Princeton University, 1969)
AUSS	*Andrews University Seminary Studies*
BA	*Biblical Archaeologist*
BAR	*Biblical Archaeology Review*
BSac	*Bibliotheca Sacra*
CBQ	*The Catholic Biblical Quarterly*
ET	*The Expository Times*
FOTL	Forms of the Old Testament Literature
HUCA	*Hebrew Union College Annual*
IEJ	*Israel Exploration Journal*
JANESCU	*Journal of the Ancient Near Eastern Society of Columbia University*
JBL	*Journal of Biblical Literature*
JBQ	*Jewish Bible Quarterly*
JESOT	*Journal for the Evangelical Study of the Old Testament*
JETS	*Journal of the Evangelical Theological Society*

JM	P. Joüon and T. Muraoka, *A Grammar of Biblical Hebrew* (Rome: Pontifical Biblical Institute, 2006)
JNES	*Journal of Near Eastern Studies*
JNSL	*Journal of Northwest Semitic Languages*
JSOT	*Journal for the Study of the Old Testament*
JSOTSupp	Journal for the Study of the Old Testament Supplement Series
LW	J. Pelikan (ed.), *Luther's Works: The American Edition*, 54 vols. (St. Louis: Concordia, 1955–86)
MSJ	*The Master's Seminary Journal*
NAC	New American Commentary
NCBC	New Cambridge Bible Commentary
NICOT	New International Commentary on the Old Testament
OIMP	Oriental Institute Museum Publications
TDOT	G. Johannes Botterweck, H. Ringgren and H.-J. Fabry (eds.), *Theological Dictionary of the Old Testament*, 15 vols. (Grand Rapids: Eerdmans, 1975–2015)
TLOT	E. Jenni and K. Westermann (eds.), *Theological Lexicon of the Old Testament*, tr. M. E. Biddle, 3 vols. (Peabody, MA: Hendrickson, 1997)
TWOT	R. L. Harris, G. L. Archer, Jr. and B. K. Waltke (eds.), *Theological Wordbook of the Old Testament*, 2 vols. (Chicago: Moody, 1981)
TynBul	*Tyndale Bulletin*
VT	*Vetus Testamentum*
WBC	Word Biblical Commentary
WTJ	*Westminster Theological Journal*
YNER	Yale Near Eastern Researches
ZAW	*Zeitschrift für die Alttestamentliche Wissenshaft*

Texts and versions

| CSB | The Christian Standard Bible. Copyright © 2017 by Holman Bible Publishers. Used by permission. Christian Standard Bible® and CSB® are federally registered trademarks of Holman Bible Publishers, all rights reserved |

ESV   The ESV Bible (The Holy Bible, English
        Standard Version), copyright © 2001 by Crossway,
        a publishing ministry of Good News Publishers.
        Used by permission. All rights reserved

GW   GOD'S WORD®, © 1995 God's Word to the
        Nations. Used by permission of Baker Publishing
        Group

LXX   The Septuagint (pre-Christian Greek version
        of the Old Testament)

MT   Masoretic Text

NET   The NET Bible, New English Translation,
        copyright © 1996 by Biblical Studies Press, LLC.
        NET Bible is a registered trademark

NIV   The Holy Bible, New International Version
        (Anglicized edition). Copyright © 1979, 1984, 2011
        by Biblica. Used by permission of Hodder &
        Stoughton Ltd, an Hachette UK company. All
        rights reserved. 'NIV' is a registered trademark of
        Biblica. UK trademark number 1448790

NRSV   New Revised Standard Version of the Bible,
        Anglicized Edition, copyright © 1989, 1995 by the
        Division of Christian Education of the National
        Council of the Churches of Christ in the USA.
        Used by permission. All rights reserved

SP   Samaritan Pentateuch

TNK   The TANAKH

SELECT BIBLIOGRAPHY

Alexander, T. D. (1997), 'Further Observations on the Term "Seed" in Genesis', *TynBul* 48: 363–367.

Arnold, B. T. (2009), *Genesis*, NCBC (Cambridge: Cambridge University Press).

Backon, J. (2008), 'Jacob and the Spotted Sheep: The Role of Prenatal Nutrition on Epigenetics of Fur Color', *JBQ* 36: 263–265.

Bailleul-LeSuer, R. (ed.) (2012), *Between Heaven and Earth: Birds in Ancient Egypt*, OIMP 35 (Chicago: Oriental Institute of the University of Chicago).

Barnard, H. et al. (2010), 'Chemical Evidence for Wine Production around 4000 BCE in the Late Chalcolithic Near Eastern Highlands', *Journal of Archaeological Science* 30: 1–8.

Bechtel, L. M. (1994), 'What if Dinah Is Not Raped? (Genesis 34)', *JSOT* 19: 19–36.

Berlin, A. (1985), *The Dynamics of Biblical Poetry* (Bloomington, IN: Indiana University Press).

Carmichael, C. M. (1969), 'Some Sayings in Genesis 49', *JBL* 88: 435–444.

Charles, J. D. (ed.) (2013), *Reading Genesis 1–2: An Evangelical Conversation* (Peabody, MA: Hendrickson).

Chisholm, R. B., Jr. (2007), 'Anatomy of an Anthropomorphism: Does God Discover Facts?', *BSac* 164: 3–20.

Clark, W. M. (1969), 'Legal Background to the Yahwist's Use of "Good and Evil" in Genesis 2–3', *JBL* 88: 266–278.

Clifford, R. J. (2004), 'Genesis 38: Its Contribution to the Jacob
   Story', *CBQ* 66: 519–532.
Clines, D. J. A. (1968), 'Meaning of "Let Us" in Gn 1:26', *TynBul*
   19: 53–103.
—— (1997), *The Theme of the Pentateuch*, 2nd edn, JSOTSupp 10
   (Sheffield: Sheffield Academic Press).
Coats, G. W. (1983), *Genesis with an Introduction to Narrative
   Literature*, FOTL 1 (Grand Rapids: Eerdmans).
Collins, C. J. (1997), 'A Syntactical Note (Genesis 3:15): Is the
   Woman's Seed Singular or Plural?', *TynBul* 48: 139–148.
—— (2003), 'Galatians 3:16: What Kind of Exegete Was
   Paul?', *TynBul* 54: 75–86.
Collins, S. (2013), 'Where Is Sodom? The Case for Tall
   El-Hammam', *BAR* 39.2: 32–41, 70–71.
Condren, J. C. (2017), 'Toward a Purge of the Battle of the Sexes
   and "Return" for the Original Meaning of Genesis 3:16b',
   JETS 60: 227–246.
Cross, F. M. (1973), *Canaanite Myth and Hebrew Epic* (Cambridge,
   MA: Harvard University Press).
De Vaux, R. (1978), *The Early History of Israel*, tr. D. Smith
   (Philadelphia: Westminster).
Diffey, D. S. (2011), 'The Royal Promise in Genesis: The Often
   Underestimated Importance of Genesis 17:6, 17:16 and 35:11',
   TynBul 62: 313–316.
Driver, G. R., and J. C. Miles (1952), *The Babylonian Laws*, Volume 1:
   Legal Commentary (Oxford: Clarendon).
Driver, S. R. (1899), *An Introduction to the Literature of the Old
   Testament*, 9th edn, International Theological Library (New
   York: Charles Scribner's Sons).
Foh, S. T. (1975), 'What Is the Woman's Desire?', *WTJ* 37:
   376–383.
Frolov, S. (2012), 'Judah Comes to Shiloh: Genesis 49:10bα, One
   More Time', *JBL* 131: 417–422.
Frymer-Kensky, T. S. (1981), 'Patriarchal Family Relationships
   and Near Eastern Law', *BA* 44: 209–214.
Futato, Mark D. (1998), 'Because It Had Rained: A Study of Gen
   2:5–7 with Implications for Gen 2:4–25 and Gen 1:1 – 2:3',
   WTJ 60.1: 1–21.

Geller, S. A. (1982), 'The Struggle at the Jabbok: The Uses of Enigma in a Biblical Narrative', *JANESCU* 14: 37–60.

Gevirtz, S. (1971), 'The Reprimand of Reuben', *JNES* 30: 87–98.

——— (1975), 'Of Patriarchs and Puns: Joseph at the Fountain, Jacob at the Ford', *HUCA* 46: 33–54.

Goldingay, J. (2010), *Genesis for Everyone – Part 1: Chapters 1–16*, Old Testament for Everyone (Louisville: Westminster John Knox Press).

Good, E. M. (1963), '"Blessing" on Judah, Gen 49:8–12', *JBL* 82: 427–432.

Gordon, C. H. (1977), 'Where Is Abraham's Ur?', *BAR* 3.2: 20–21, 52.

Greenberg, M. (1962), 'Another Look at Rachel's Theft of the Teraphim', *JBL* 81: 239–248.

Griffiths, J. G. (1965), 'Celestial Ladder and the Gate of Heaven', *ET* 76: 229–230.

Grossman, J. (2016), 'Different Dreams: Two Models of Interpretation for Three Pairs of Dreams (Genesis 37–50)', *JBL* 135: 717–732.

Hamilton, V. P. (1990), *The Book of Genesis, Chapters 1–17*, NICOT (Grand Rapids: Eerdmans).

——— (1995), *The Book of Genesis, Chapters 18–50*, NICOT (Grand Rapids: Eerdmans).

Hasel, G. F. (1975), 'Meaning of "Let Us" in Gn 1:26', *AUSS* 13: 58–66.

Heck, J. D. (1986), 'Issachar: Slave or Freeman? (Gen 49:14–15)', *JETS* 29: 385–396.

Hendel, R. (1987), 'Of Demigods and the Deluge: Toward an Interpretation of Genesis 6.1–4', *JBL* 106: 13–36.

Hoffmeier, J. K. (1983), 'Some Thoughts on Genesis 1 and 2 in Light of Egyptian Chronology', *JANESCU* 15: 39–49.

——— (1997), *Israel in Egypt: The Evidence for the Authenticity of the Exodus Traditions* (Oxford: Oxford University Press).

Hoffner, H. A. (1967), 'Second Millennium Antecedents to the Hebrew "ÔB"', *JBL* 86: 385–401.

Holladay, W. L. (2007), 'Indications of Segmented Sleep in the Bible', *CBQ* 69: 215–221.

Houtman, C. (1977), 'What Did Jacob See in His Dream
at Bethel? Some Remarks on Genesis 28:10–22', *VT* 27:
337–351.

Hurowitz, V. (2000), 'Who Lost an Earring? Genesis 35:4
Reconsidered', *CBQ* 62: 28–32.

Johnston, G. H. (2008), 'Genesis 1 and Ancient Egyptian
Creation Myths', *BSac* 165: 178–194.

Kidner, D. (1967), *Genesis: An Introduction and Commentary*, Tyndale
Old Testament Commentaries 1 (Nottingham: Inter-Varsity
Press, repr. 2008).

Kitchen, K. (1966), *Ancient Orient and Old Testament* (Chicago:
InterVarsity Press).

——— (2003), *On the Reliability of the Old Testament* (Grand Rapids:
Eerdmans).

LaBianca, Ø. S. (2003), 'Subsistence Pastoralism', in S. Richard
(ed.), *Near Eastern Archaeology: A Reader* (Winona Lake, IN:
Eisenbrauns), 116–123.

Lang, B. (1985), 'Non-Semitic Deluge Stories and the Book of
Genesis: A Bibliographic and Critical Survey', *Anthropos* 80:
605–616.

Larsson, G. (1983), 'The Chronology of the Pentateuch:
A Comparison of the MT and LXX', *JBL* 102: 401–409.

Lee, C.-C. (2012), 'Once Again: The Niphal and the Hithpael
of *brk* in the Abrahamic Blessing for the Nations', *JSOT* 36:
279–296.

Lessing, R. R. (2007), *Jonah*, Concordia Commentary (St. Louis:
Concordia).

Lessing, R. R., and A. E. Steinmann (2014), *Prepare the Way of the
Lord: An Introduction to the Old Testament* (St. Louis: Concordia).

Leupold, H. C. (1942), *Exposition of Genesis*, 2 vols. (Columbus:
Wartburg; repr. Grand Rapids: Baker, 1982).

McCarter, P. Kyle (1974), 'The Early Diffusion of the Alphabet',
BA 37.3: 54–68.

MacDonald, N. (2004), 'Listening to Abraham—Listening
to Yhwh: Divine Justice and Mercy in Genesis 18:16–33',
CBQ 66: 25–43.

Malul, M. (1987), 'Touching the Sexual Organs as an Oath
Ceremony in an Akkadian Letter', *VT* 37: 491–492.

Martin, T. W. (2003), 'The Covenant of Circumcision (Genesis 17:9–14) and the Situational Antithesis in Galatians 3:28', *JBL* 122: 111–125.

Mathews, K. A. (1996), *Genesis 1 – 11:26*, NAC 1A (Nashville: B&H).

———— (2005), *Genesis 11:27 – 50:26*, NAC 1B (Nashville: B&H).

Maxwell, D. R. (2007), 'Justified by Works and Not by Faith Alone: Reconciling Paul and James', *Concordia Journal* 33: 375–378.

Mendelsohn, I. (1959), 'A Ugaritic Parallel to the Adoption of Ephraim and Manasseh', *IEJ* 9: 180–183.

Millard, A. R. (1966), 'Celestial Ladder and the Gate of Heaven', *ET* 78: 86–87.

Morschauser, S. (2003), '"Hospitality", Hostiles and Hostages: On the Legal Background to Genesis 19.1–9', *JSOT* 27: 461–485.

Murphy, B. (2013), 'The Trinity in Creation', *MSJ* 24: 167–177.

Niehaus, J. (1994), 'In the Wind of the Storm: Another Look at Genesis III 8', *VT* 44: 263–267.

Oblath, M. D. (2001), '"To Sleep, Perchance to Dream . . ." What Jacob Saw at Bethel (Genesis 28.10–22)', *JSOT* 95: 117–126.

Odhiambo, N. (2013), 'The Nature of Ham's Sin', *BSac* 170: 154–165.

Ortlund, D. (2010), '"And Their Eyes Were Opened, and They Knew": An Inter-Canonical Note on Luke 24:31', *JETS* 53: 717–728.

Posnanski, A. (1904), *Schiloh: Ein Beitrag zur Geschichte der Messiaslehre* (Leipzig: Hinrichs).

Provan, I. (2016), *Discovering Genesis: Content, Interpretation, Reception* (Grand Rapids: Eerdmans).

Rendsburg, G. A. (1987), 'Gen 10:13–14: An Authentic Hebrew Tradition Concerning the Origin of the Philistines', *JNSL* 13: 89–96.

———— (2002), 'Some False Leads in the Identification of Late Biblical Hebrew Texts: The Cases of Genesis 24 and 1 Samuel 2:27–36', *JBL* 121: 23–46.

Rickett, D. (2011), 'Rethinking the Place and Purpose of Genesis 13', *JSOT* 36: 31–53.

Rogland, M. (2010), 'Interpreting *'d* in Genesis 2.5–6: Neglected Rabbinic and Intertextual Evidence', *JSOT* 34: 379–393.

Sailhamer, J. H. (2012), 'Genesis', in T. Longman III and D. E. Garland (eds.), *The Expositor's Bible Commentary*, vol. 1 (Grand Rapids: Zondervan).

Sarna, N. M. (1989), *Genesis: The Traditional Hebrew Text with the New JPS Translation Commentary*, JPS Torah Commentary (Philadelphia: Jewish Publication Society).

Sasson, J. M. (1966), 'Circumcision in the Ancient Near East', *JBL* 85: 473–476.

——— (1978), 'Genealogical "Convention" in Biblical Chronography', *ZAW* 90: 171–185.

Seebass, H. (1984), 'Die Stämmesprüche Gen 49:3–27', *ZAW* 96: 333–350.

Shemesh, Y. (2007), 'Rape Is Rape: The Story of Dinah and Shechem (Genesis 34)', *ZAW* 119: 2–21.

Ska, J. L. (1992), 'Sommaires proleptiques en Gn 27 et dans l'histoire de Joseph', *Biblica* 73: 518–527.

Smith, B. (2005), 'The Central Role of Judah in Genesis 37–50', *BSac* 162: 158–174.

Speiser, E. A. (1964), *Genesis: Introduction, Translation, and Notes*, AB 1 (Garden City, NY: Doubleday).

——— (1967), *Oriental and Biblical Studies: Collected Writings of E. A. Speiser*, ed. J. J. Finkelstein and M. Greenberg (Philadelphia: University of Pennsylvania Press).

Steiner, R. C. (2010), 'Poetic Forms in the Masoretic Vocalization and Three Difficult Phrases in Jacob's Blessing', *JBL* 129: 209–235.

Steinmann, A. E. (2002), ''echad* as an Ordinal Number and the Meaning of Genesis 1:5', *JETS* 45: 577–584.

——— (2009), *Proverbs*, Concordia Commentary (St. Louis: Concordia).

——— (2011), *From Abraham to Paul: A Biblical Chronology* (St. Louis: Concordia).

——— (2016–17), 'A Note on the Refrain in Genesis 1: Evening, Morning, and Day as Chronological Summary', *JESOT* 5.2: 125–140.

——— (2017a), 'Jesus and Possessing the Enemies' Gate (Genesis 22:17–18 and Genesis 24:60)', *BSac* 174: 13–21.

————— (2017b), 'Gaps in the Genealogies in Genesis 5 and 11?',
   BSac 174: 141–158.

————— (2017c), 'Challenging the Authenticity of Cainan, Son
   of Arpachshad', *JETS* 60: 697–711.

————— (2017d), *2 Samuel*, Concordia Commentary (St. Louis:
   Concordia).

Stuart, D. K. (2014), '"The Cool of the Day" (Gen 3:8) and
   "The Way He Should Go" (Prov 22:6)', *BSac* 171: 259–273.

Tigay, J. H. (1985), *Empirical Models for Biblical Criticism*
   (Philadelphia: University of Pennsylvania).

Tomasino, A. J. (1992), 'History Repeats Itself: The "Fall" and
   Noah's Drunkenness', *VT* 42: 128–130.

Toorn, K. van der (1990), 'The Nature of the Biblical Teraphim
   in the Light of the Cuneiform Evidence', *CBQ* 52: 203–222.

Tucker, Gene M. (1966), 'Legal Background of Genesis 23',
   JBL 85: 77–84.

Van Seters, J. (1968), 'Problem of Childlessness in Near Eastern
   Law and the Patriarchs of Israel', *JBL* 87: 401–408.

Vergote, J. (1959), *Joseph en Égypte: Genèse Chat. 37–50, à la lumière
   des études Égyptologiques récentes*, Orientalia et biblica lovaniensia 3
   (Louvain: Publications Universitaires).

Vogt, E. (1975), 'Benjamin geboren "eine Meile" von Ephrata',
   Biblica 56: 30–36.

Von Rad, G. (1972), *Genesis: A Commentary*, Old Testament
   Library, rev. edn, trans. J. H. Marks (Philadelphia: Westminster
   John Knox).

Ward, W. A. (1957), 'Egyptian Titles in Genesis 39–50', *BSac* 114:
   40–59.

Wenham, G. J. (1972), '*Betûlāh*, a Girl of Marriageable Age', *VT*
   22: 326–348.

————— (1978a), 'Coherence of the Flood Narrative', *VT* 28:
   336–348.

————— (1978b), 'Lev 27:2–8 and the Price of Slaves', *ZAW* 90:
   264–265.

————— (1987), *Genesis 1–15*, WBC 1 (Waco: Word).

————— (1994), *Genesis 16–50*, WBC 2 (Waco: Word).

Westermann, C. (1985), *Genesis 12–36*, trans. J. J. Scullion,
   Continental Commentary (Minneapolis: Augsburg Fortress).

——— (1986), *Genesis 37–50*, trans. J. J. Scullion, Continental Commentary (Minneapolis: Fortress).

——— (1994), *Genesis 1–11*, trans. J. J. Scullion, Continental Commentary (Minneapolis: Augsburg).

Wieder, A. A. (1965), 'Ugaritic-Hebrew Lexicographical Notes', *JBL* 84: 160–164.

Wilson, R. R. (1977), *Genealogy and History in the Biblical World*, YNER 7 (New Haven: Yale University).

Winnett, F. V. (1970), 'The Arabian Genealogies in the Book of Genesis', in H. T. Frank and W. LaForest Reed (eds.), *Translating and Understanding the Old Testament* (Nashville: Abingdon), 171–196.

Wiseman, P. J. (1985), *Ancient Records and the Structure of Genesis: A Case for Literary Unity*, ed. D. J. Wiseman (Nashville: Thomas Nelson).

Wood, B. G. (2011), 'Hittites and Hethites: A Proposed Solution to an Etymological Conundrum', *JETS* 54: 239–250.

Young, D. W. (1990), 'The Influences of Babylonian Algebra on Longevity among the Antediluvians', *ZAW* 102: 321–355.

Zakovitch, Y. (2005), *I Will Utter Riddles from Ancient Time: Riddles and Dream-Riddles in Biblical Narrative* [Hebrew], Aron sefarim Yehudi (Tel Aviv: Am Oved).

INTRODUCTION[1]

1. Genesis as the foundational book of the Old Testament

Just as every building is supported by a solid foundation, so also the Scriptures as a canon are supported from the start by this book which relates the origin of the world, of sin, of God's promise of redemption and of the people of Israel. The Hebrew title of this book, derived from its first word, *bĕrēšît*, means 'in the beginning', and certainly is appropriate since Genesis relates the beginnings of so many topics found elsewhere in the Scriptures. The English title comes from the Greek designation of the book and means 'origin' or 'source'. Both of these titles are apt descriptions of the book. Most importantly, the book relates the source of God's promise of

---

1. Much of this introduction is adapted from *Prepare the Way of the Lord: An Introduction to the Old Testament* © 2014 R. Reed Lessing and Andrew E. Steinmann. Published by Concordia Publishing House. Used with permission. <www.cph.org>.

the Saviour and traces this pledge through the line of Abraham down to his great-grandson Judah. Thus, Genesis also serves as a foundation for the New Testament and its teaching that Jesus is the fulfilment of God's promises to save humankind from sin and death.

2. Authorship, composition and date

From antiquity the first five books of the Old Testament, commonly called the Pentateuch or, in Hebrew, the Torah (i.e. 'the Teaching'), have been ascribed to Moses. Certainly Moses, as he is presented to readers of Exodus, was qualified to write such a work. The exodus from Egypt took place in 1446 BC when Moses was about eighty years old.[2] Therefore, he lived his early life in Egypt during the eighteenth dynasty, and he was probably in the royal court during the reigns of Ahmose (c.1539–1515), Amenhotep I (c.1514–1494) and Tutmose I (c.1494–1483). During this era Egypt enjoyed great power and international prestige. Contacts with other peoples and cultures were commonplace and would have served to broaden the education of Moses and other princes in the Egyptian court. At this time even uneducated Semitic slaves were writing on the walls of Egypt's turquoise mines at Serabit el-Khadim in the south-west Sinai Peninsula.[3] It would have been even more likely that Moses learned to read and write, and he would have been familiar with the various types of literature that appear in the Pentateuch: historical genealogies, narrative, law codes and speeches.

Moreover, the book of Numbers concentrates on the first and last years of this period, relating few incidents from the other thirty-eight years. During this time Moses could have written the bulk of Genesis–Numbers. Deuteronomy, his last words to Israel, could have been put in written form by someone who listened to these sermons, perhaps Joshua, Moses' assistant, who is portrayed elsewhere as able to write (Josh. 24:26).

---

2. Dates are based upon Steinmann (2011).

3. McCarter (1974: 54–68).

a. Traditional view of the Pentateuch as the work of Moses
i. The witness of the Pentateuch itself

Several passages in the Pentateuch itself indicate that Moses wrote at least a few passages. Yahweh instructed Moses to write an account of Israel's victory over Amalek (Exod. 17:14). Moses recorded God's words to Israel at Mount Sinai (Exod. 24:4). After he smashed the first tablets of the covenant that had been inscribed by the finger of God (Exod. 31:18), Moses wrote a duplicate set (Exod. 34:27). Numbers indicates that at Yahweh's behest Moses maintained the list of campsites that Israel used during their forty years in the wilderness (Num. 33; esp. 33:2). Moses composed the song about God's work for Israel (Deut. 31:22; cf. 32 – 33). Perhaps the most comprehensive statements about authorship of the Pentateuch are found in Deuteronomy 31, where twice we are told that Moses wrote 'this Torah' (Deut. 31:9, 24).

ii. The witness of the rest of the Old Testament

The Old Testament regularly refers to the Pentateuch, and Moses is usually associated with it as its author. Yahweh instructed Joshua to do everything according to the Torah that Moses had commanded (Josh. 1:7). Moreover, this 'scroll of the Torah' was to be Joshua's meditation at all times (Josh. 1:8). Later Joshua built an altar following the instructions in 'the scroll of the Torah of Moses' (Josh. 8:31; cf. Exod. 20:25). Joshua also read every word from this Torah of Moses to Israel, especially the blessings and curses (Josh. 8:34–35; cf. Deut. 11:26, 29; 30:1, 19).

The book of Kings affirms Moses' authorship of the Pentateuch. When David was near death, he instructed Solomon to keep God's commandments that were written in Moses' Torah (1 Kgs 2:3). When he first assumed Judah's throne, Amaziah obeyed the command written in the 'Book of the Torah of Moses' by not executing children of murderers for their fathers' sin (2 Kgs 14:6; cf. Deut. 24:16; 2 Chr. 25:4). Josiah turned to Yahweh 'with all his heart and with all his soul and with all his might' according to 'the Torah of Moses' (2 Kgs 23:25; cf. Deut. 6:5).

The post-exilic books of the Old Testament also testify to Moses' authorship of the Torah (2 Chr. 23:18; 30:16; 35:12; Ezra 3:2; 6:18; 7:6; Neh. 8:1; 13:1). It is noteworthy that Malachi, the last of the Old Testament prophets, quotes God exhorting Israel to remember 'the Torah of my servant Moses' which included the statues and regulations commanded at Horeb (Mal. 4:4; cf. Exod. 20:3–17; Deut. 4:9–10).

iii. The witness of the New Testament

The New Testament recognizes Moses as the author of the Pentateuch. It refers to 'the law of Moses' nine times (Mark 12:26; Luke 2:22; 24:44; John 7:23; Acts 13:39; 15:5; 28:23; 1 Cor. 9:9; Heb. 10:28; cf. John 1:45) and the 'book of Moses' once (Mark 12:26). At times the Pentateuch is simply called 'Moses' (Luke 16:29, 31; 24:27; Acts 21:21). The Torah is frequently quoted with the words 'Moses wrote' (Mark 12:19; Luke 20:28; John 1:45; 5:46), 'Moses said' (Matt. 22:24; Mark 7:10; Acts 3:22; 7:37; 26:22; Heb. 7:14; 12:21), 'Moses allowed' (Matt. 19:8; Mark 10:4) or 'Moses commanded' (Matt. 8:4; 19:7; Mark 1:44; 10:3; Luke 5:14; John 8:5).

In this regard the Gospel of John is most pointed in assigning the Pentateuch's composition to Moses. John 1:17 says 'the law was given through Moses'. Jesus is quoted as ascribing the Torah to Moses, a point his Jewish opponents did not dispute (John 7:19–23). This passage assigns the covenant of circumcision in Genesis 17:1–27 to Moses. Since Genesis is entirely about events before Moses was born, the case for Mosaic authorship of this book is more vulnerable to challenge than for the other books of the Pentateuch. Yet Jesus confidently asserted Moses' writing of the first book of the Torah.

iv. Post-Mosaic additions and glosses in the Pentateuch

Given the witness of the Old and New Testaments to Moses' authorship of the Pentateuch, it is not surprising that the traditional position of both Christians and Jews for most of the last two thousand years has been to affirm the Mosaic origin of these books. Nevertheless, it has long been recognized that the text of the Pentateuch transmitted to us contains a limited number of statements reflecting later editorial additions and changes.

The most evident of these is the account of Moses' death at Deuteronomy 34:1–12. Since this passage ends with a notice that no prophet like Moses had arisen again in Israel (Deut. 34:10–12), it appears that it was added a number of years after Moses had died.

Already in antiquity the rabbis taught that this addition was appended to Deuteronomy by Joshua.[4]

A number of short notices in the Pentateuch appear to be later glosses that were added to explain historical circumstances. Genesis 36:31–43 seems to have been appended sometime after the monarchy was established in Israel: *These are the kings who ruled in the land of Edom before any king reigned over the Israelites* (36:31).

In addition to these notices, it appears that a later scribe updated place names throughout the Pentateuch. This includes the following:

- Dan (Gen. 14:14; Deut. 34:1): This city was called Laish until the tribe of Dan conquered and renamed it (Judg. 18:29).
- Hebron (Gen. 13:18; 23:19; 37:14; Num. 13:22): It is not known when this city, originally called Kiriath-arba (Gen. 23:2; 35:27; cf. Josh. 14:15; Judg. 1:10), was renamed. It was rebuilt in the nineteenth year of Rameses XI (c.1087; i.e. during the latter part of the period of Israel's judges). So perhaps this was the date when it was given a new name. This would also mean that the last words in Numbers 13:22 are also a post-Mosaic scribal updating ('Now Hebron was rebuilt seven years before Zoan in Egypt').
- Rameses (Gen. 47:11; Exod. 1:11; 12:37; Num. 33:3, 5): This city and the surrounding region were not known by this name before the reign of Rameses II (1279–1213 BC). Rameses rebuilt the city of Avaris and renamed it Pi-Ramesses, making it his capital. The region is normally called Goshen in the Pentateuch (e.g. Gen. 45:10; 46:28; 47:1; Exod. 8:22; 9:26).

One other possible place name that could be included is Bethel, which was called Luz before Jacob renamed it (Gen. 28:19). However, it is called Bethel twice before Jacob's day (12:8; 13:3). It is possible that Moses called it Bethel in these earlier passages, since by his day Israel had applied this name to this locale for over four hundred years. On the other hand, it appears that the Canaanites continued to call the city Luz until the tribes of Ephraim and

---

4. Talmud, *Baba Bathra* 14b.

Manasseh conquered it (Judg. 1:23–26). Thus, it is possible that *Bethel* in Genesis is also a later scribal updating (see esp. 35:6).

It is often suggested that the references to Philistines and the region of Philistia (Gen. 10:14; 21:32, 34; 26:1, 8, 14–15, 18; Exod. 13:17; 15:14; 23:31) are other examples of scribal updating in the Pentateuch, since many scholars identify this people with the Sea Peoples who were expelled from Egypt and settled on the coast in south-west Canaan in the twelfth century over three hundred years after Moses. However, the name *Philistine* probably means 'migrant' or 'foreigner' (as it is often translated in LXX). In addition, Genesis 10:14 traces the Philistines' origin to the Casluhim, whereas later sources (Deut. 2:23; Jer. 47:4; Amos 9:7) trace their origin to the related Hamitic people of Caphtor (cf. Gen. 10:14). In Genesis the Philistines are located at Gerar, south-east of Gaza, between Kadesh and Shur (20:1–2; 26:1–6). Moreover, their ruler Abimelech is said to be the *king* (Hebrew *melek*) of Gerar. Later references to the Philistines locate them in the southern coastal plain in five cities: Gaza, Ashdod, Ashkelon, Gath and Ekron, but never in Gerar (Josh. 13:3; 1 Sam. 6:17). In addition, the rulers of these cities are most often called *leaders* (Hebrew *seren*), a term that is never used for Abimelech of Gerar.[5] Thus, it appears that the Casluhite Philistines mentioned in Genesis are not the same as the Caphtorite Philistines mentioned in later Old Testament books. Therefore, the reference to Philistines in Genesis may be speaking of non-Canaanites who came from the Mediterranean to live in the Negev wilderness south-east of the later Philistine settlements on Canaan's coast.[6] Later in Joshua and 1 Samuel the Israelites encountered a related ethnic group also from the west, and they used the same generic designation for this group: Philistines.

With the exception of Deuteronomy 34 and Numbers 12:3, which give no reliable clue as to the date when they could have been added to the Pentateuch, all of the other scribal changes appear to have been made no earlier than the period of the judges. In addition,

---

5. In 1 Samuel the only Philistine ruler called 'king' is Achish, the ruler of Gath (1 Sam. 21:10, 12; 27:2).

6. See also the discussion in Kitchen (2003: 339–341).

Genesis 36:31 cannot be earlier than the establishment of the Israelite monarchy under Saul (c.1049). However, nothing requires them to be later than the reign of David or Solomon, especially since 36:31, when mentioning kings ruling over 'the Israelites', appears to have been written before the division of the kingdom after Solomon's death.

Scholars who accept the Bible's attribution of the Pentateuch to Moses acknowledge that these small changes in the text were made after his day. Nevertheless, they affirm that the Torah as it has come down to us is essentially the work of Moses.

While conservative scholars continue to attribute the composition of the Pentateuch to Moses, Genesis presents the greatest challenge for connecting it with Israel's great prophet. All of the accounts in Genesis take place long before Moses, with the latest event in the book – the death of Joseph – taking place more than three centuries before Moses' birth. Moreover, no statement in the rest of the Old Testament or in the New Testament explicitly connects any passage in Genesis with Moses as its author. Nevertheless, the rest of the Pentateuch presumes knowledge of the narratives in Genesis. For instance, it quotes or alludes to Genesis, assuming that the reader will understand these references as deriving from the Old Testament's first book. Without knowledge of the specific phrasing of these references to Genesis, these allusions often would be meaningless to readers of Exodus, Leviticus, Numbers and Deuteronomy. This is especially true of the accounts of Israel's patriarchs and God's promises to them concerning the land of Canaan and the great nation that would come from them (e.g. Exod. 2:24; 6:8; 32:13; 33:1; Lev. 26:42; Num. 32:11; Deut. 1:8; 6:10; 9:5, 27; 29:13; 30:20; 34:4). Another example is the prophecies of Balaam in Numbers 23 – 24, which reference the patriarchal promises and cannot be fully understood without knowledge of the wording used in Genesis:

Who is able to count Jacob's dust?
(Num. 23:10; cf. Gen. 13:16; 15:5)

Yahweh their God is with them.
(Num. 23:21; cf. Gen. 17:8)

A people rise like a lioness; they rouse themselves like a lion.
(Num. 23:24; cf. Gen. 49:9)

He crouched; he lay down like a lion and like a lioness. Who will
arouse him?
(Num. 24:9; cf. Gen. 49:9)

May those blessing you be blessed and those cursing you be cursed.
(Num. 24:9; cf. Gen. 12:3)

A star will come from Jacob, a sceptre will arise from Israel.
(Num. 24:17; cf. Gen. 49:10)

Such references to Genesis strongly imply that it was available to
readers of the rest of the Pentateuch. Moses must have written
Genesis since he was responsible for the rest of the Torah (see
2 Chr. 23:18; 30:16; 35:12; Ezra 3:2; 6:18; 7:6; Neh. 8:1; 13:1;
Mal. 4:4).

The sources for Moses' knowledge of events before his time are
never directly mentioned in Genesis. They may have included oral
traditions, written records or even direct revelation from God (as
he also revealed the plan of the tabernacle; see Exod. 25:9).

b. The Documentary Hypothesis
i. From doubts about Mosaic authorship to a new theory
Although from antiquity the great majority of Christians and Jews
accepted Moses as the author of the Pentateuch, doubts were
sporadically raised. The Nazarenes, a Jewish-Christian sect concentrated in the Transjordan and mentioned by some church fathers in
the fourth century, rejected Mosaic authorship. The Andalusian
Islamic philosopher Ibn Hazm of Cordova, Spain (AD 994–1064),
believed that Ezra was the primary author of the Pentateuch. In
Reformation-era Germany, Andreas Karlstadt (1480–1541) argued
that if Moses did not write about his death (Deut. 34), then he did
not write any of the Pentateuch.

During the Enlightenment a number of doubts about authorship
arose. In his work *Leviathan* (1651) the English deistic philosopher
Thomas Hobbes held that Moses wrote only those portions of the

Pentateuch that are directly attributed to him, and that the rest of
the Torah was written much later. Benedict Spinoza, a Jewish
philosopher, published a more influential challenge to Mosaic
authorship in 1670. Spinoza noted that throughout much of the
Pentateuch Moses is referred to in the third person. He concluded
that a few portions of the Torah came from Moses' pen, but most
of it was written by Ezra. The Roman Catholic priest and philosopher Richard Simon (1638–1712) argued that the Pentateuch's
several styles combined with chronological difficulties in the text
proved that Moses could not have written it. Instead, it was
composed by a later author who relied on earlier sources.

From the late eighteenth century to the late nineteenth century
a number of theories that denied that Moses wrote the Pentateuch
in whole or in part were developed. Eventually these coalesced
into what has become known as the Documentary Hypothesis,
which continues to be the most popular theory about the origin
of the Pentateuch among many biblical scholars. Proponents of
the Documentary Hypothesis maintain that Genesis is a product
of a process that wove together three sources: the Yahwist
(abbreviated J) who preferred to call God by his proper name
Yahweh; the Elohist (abbreviated E) who preferred to call God by
the Hebrew word for God, Elohim; and the Priestly Writer
(abbreviated P). A fourth supposed source for the Pentateuch,
D, the Deuteronomist, is primarily confined to the book of
Deuteronomy.

Most notable among the supposed P material in Genesis is
1:1 – 2:3. This so-called 'First Creation Account' is placed in opposition to 2:4–25, which is said to give the J-source version of creation
combined with some material from E. Formerly much of the rest
of Genesis was divided between the J and E sources according to
most critics.[7] This theory holds that Genesis, as it has come down
to us, is a product of a final priestly editor during the post-exilic
period. The methods used to isolate these sources and chart the

---

7. In recent decades the existence of much of the E material in Genesis
   has been questioned, and many critics now hold that E is nothing more
   than a supplement to J.

growth of the book of Genesis have always been opposed by conservative scholars, and in more recent decades have been questioned by some critical scholars.

Despite its popularity and influence, source criticism of the Pentateuch has consistently been opposed by conservative scholars. During the second half of the nineteenth century in Germany, E. W. Hengstengberg and his student C. F. Keil defended the Mosaic authorship of the Pentateuch. In England the prominent archae-ologist A. H. Sayce, who had rejected his earlier endorsement of source criticism, pointed out several fallacies in the Documentary Hypothesis. In the USA, William Henry Green of Princeton Theological Seminary noted that the methodology used to identify the four supposed sources of the Pentateuch was inconsistent and at times contradictory. In addition, he also demonstrated that the Documentary Hypothesis did not fully explain the biblical data.

ii. Flaws of the Documentary Hypothesis
One of the major concerns about the Documentary Hypothesis is its subjective nature of identifying the four source documents. Despite the declaration of possessing the 'assured results of higher criticism', none of the alleged documents that make up the Pentateuch have ever been found. Moreover, critical scholars have not been able to agree among themselves as to the content of each document. One scholar may assign a particular verse to E while another scholar assigns it to P. Even more telling is the continued division of the four 'basic' documents into other sources. In Germany, before the Second World War, Noth proposed a G docu-ment that lay behind both J and E. Von Rad divided P into P(a) and P(b). In the early 1920s, the German scholar Otto Eissfeldt claimed to have isolated an L (Lay Source) document within J that preserved the nomadic ideals of the Rechabites (see Jer. 35). In 1927 the American Jewish scholar Julius Morgenstern claimed to have identified a K (Kenite) document that influenced the reforms of Judah's king Asa at the beginning of the ninth century BC. In 1941 Harvard professor Robert Pfeiffer proposed the recognition of an S (Mount Seir) document drawn from texts that were earlier assigned to J and E in Genesis 1:1 – 38:30.

Conservative scholars have argued that the Documentary Hypothesis's view of the growth of the Pentateuch has no parallel in Ancient Near Eastern literature. To counter this, Tigay (1985: 21–52) demonstrated that the *Gilgamesh* epic, a poem from ancient Mesopotamia, was compiled from earlier independently circulated Sumerian stories until it reached its final form in the Neo-Assyrian period (1300–1000 BC). However, Tigay's analysis does not reveal a process similar to the weaving together of various strands (J, E, D and P) as in the Documentary Hypothesis. It simply shows how independent stories were linked together in a serial fashion. At best, Tigay has provided support for form-critical analyses that posit a linking together of stories to produce the theoretical J or E documents.

Another weakness of the Documentary Hypothesis is its reliance upon the use of vocabulary to distinguish various documents. The most obvious use of this criterion is the division of sources based on the divine epithets Yahweh and Elohim. However, source critics also developed extensive lists of words and phrases for each of the four primary source documents. Driver supplies an extensive and often-used catalogue in his Old Testament introduction.[8]

There are numerous problems with using vocabulary in this manner. For instance, two passages from different source documents that are addressing the same subject may use similar vocabulary because of their content. Source critics may view two words as synonyms and assign them to different traditions. Yet two words are seldom exactly synonymous, and their use may be determined by the different nuances in their denotations or connotations rather than by different authorship. Finally, even words or phrases that are assigned to one document may appear frequently in another. The phrase *land of Canaan* is usually said to be characteristic of P (e.g. Gen. 12:5; 17:8). Even so, it appears frequently in passages said to derive from both J and E (e.g. 42:5, 7, 13, 29, 32 [all J]; 44:8 [E]).

_____

8. Driver (1899). Driver does not present a master list of these terms but lists them on a passage-by-passage basis throughout his discussion of the Pentateuchal books on pages 5–102.

In the end, differentiation of the source documents by vocabulary results in a circular argument. A word may be assigned to a
particular source. If that word occurs in a text assigned to a different
source for other reasons, source critics will often claim that it is an
intrusion into the text rather than questioning their assignment of
the vocabulary item in question. Instead, one probably ought to
conclude that the term in question should not be used for source
analysis.

Many scholars have noted that the use of divine names has an
additional weakness: in Ancient Near Eastern literature it is
common for a deity to be referred to by more than one name. This
phenomenon occurs in both Egyptian and Mesopotamian texts.
However, no-one suggests that these texts are compiled from
interwoven source documents.

It appears more likely that the use of divine epithets in the Old
Testament is at least partially due to theme and context. It is
conventional for critics to view Genesis 1:1 – 2:25 as two creation
accounts with the first assigned to P (1:1 – 2:3) and the second being
a conflation of J and E (2:4–25). The more generic name *Elohim* is
often used to emphasize God's general relationship to his creatures,
which explains its use in 1:1 – 2:3. God's proper name *Yahweh*
highlights his covenant relationship with individuals and groups.
Since 2:4–25 focuses on both God's creative activity and his relationship with Adam and Eve, it is not surprising that the compound
Yahweh Elohim is used in this chapter.[9] Therefore, no source explanation is necessary to account for the use of divine names in these
chapters.

Moreover, even critical scholars admit that later redactors may
have changed the particular divine name in some cases. Genesis
22:11, 14; 28:21; and 31:49 are usually assigned to E, yet all use
Yahweh. This has been explained as an example of redactional
activity. If this is the case, how can we be at all certain that the
divine names are any indication of source documents behind
the current text of the Pentateuch?

---

9. Outside of Gen. 2 – 3 the compound *Yahweh Elohim* is rare, occurring
only at Gen. 14:22; 15:2, 8; 24:3, 12, 42.

The identification of duplicate events, often called 'doublets', is another basic method to differentiate sources in the Documentary Hypothesis. These doublets are said to fit into two main categories: the same event may be described in two separate episodes (e.g. Abraham pretending Sarah is only his sister, 12:10–20 [assigned to J]; 20:1–18 [assigned to E]); on the other hand, one account may be said to have resulted from the intertwining of two distinct sources (e.g. the flood narrative, chs. 6–9).

Both of these assumptions present difficulties. For instance, the account in 20:1–18 presupposes that the reader is already familiar with 12:10–20. This is evident from 20:2, which makes no sense unless one has already read 12:11–13. A better explanation, therefore, is that the author of Genesis is relating two different but related incidents, and he wants to highlight Abraham's continued insecurity concerning Sarah and the birth of an heir (cf. 15:1–3; 17:15–19, esp. 17:18).

In the case of intertwined accounts, it is often held that the story of the sale of Joseph in Genesis 37 is such an example. Genesis 37:28 refers to the buyers as both Ishmaelites and Midianites, indicating to source critics that two sources have been conflated. However, Kitchen has shown that 'Ishmaelite' and 'Midianite' are overlapping terms and refer to what is essentially the same group (cf. Judg. 8:22–26).[10] The two terms may have been used by the author for variation. Often it is textual details like this that the source critics use to divide single accounts into doublets when no such procedure is necessary. It often results in ripping apart a text into two accounts so that neither presents a coherent narrative or so that the result is two narratives without literary texture or depth.

Finally, the Documentary Hypothesis is heavily dependent upon two popular philosophical developments of the nineteenth century: the Hegelian philosophy of history and Darwinian notions of evolution. Contemporary historians no longer employ Hegelian historical analysis, since they acknowledge that events and the development of movements and ideas do not follow any such rigid,

---

10. Kitchen (1966: 119, 123).

prescriptive pattern. Moreover, it is impossible to demonstrate that religion evolves in a Darwinian fashion from more primitive forms to more advanced forms. Theological developments are also difficult to predict. Religious groups often revive older movements in new guises or acquire new theological outlooks akin to those discarded long ago. These observations undercut the conceptual and theoretical foundation upon which the Documentary Hypothesis was constructed.

iii. The Documentary Hypothesis as the divide between critical and evangelical views of the origin of the Pentateuch
To this day there remains a divide between conservative Christian and Jewish scholars and their higher-critical counterparts as to the origins of the Pentateuch. The traditional view that Moses was the author of Genesis–Deuteronomy is still maintained and defended. Those who hold this position believe that the witness of the Pentateuch, the rest of the Old Testament, the New Testament and Jesus himself is determinative.

The higher-critical search for the origin of the Pentateuch that occupied scholars in Europe for two centuries and resulted in the Documentary Hypothesis has a chequered history. Even so, it has become the dominant theory in critical scholarship. As noted above, this happened because of the convergence of a number of factors: the popularity of Hegelian philosophy during the latter part of the nineteenth century, the cultural acceptance of Darwinian-like evolutionary approaches to areas beyond biology, and the opinion of many scholars that there are contradictions and inconsistencies in the Pentateuch that cannot be explained if it originated from one author. Each of these assumptions is problematic. Hegel's philosophy has been proven false; Darwinian theories often cannot account for human historical interactions that do not lead inexorably to new and better developments; and what critical scholars see as contradictions and inconsistencies, many evangelical scholars claim are misreadings of the text or mishandlings of its literary features. Where conservatives believe the text can be harmonized, critics assert that the text is being unnecessarily and inappropriately aligned in order to obscure its difficulties.

The majority of critical scholars continue to accept some form of the Documentary Hypothesis despite a vocal minority within their ranks that has argued against it.[11] However, these detractors among the critics are not advocating a return to a Mosaic Torah. Instead, they propose new theories to account for the Pentateuch's completion in the post-exilic era.

The main problems with the Documentary Hypothesis pointed out for over a century by conservative scholars have not been overcome. There is no firm consensus on the exact identification of the sources or on their content or nature. The methods used to isolate sources – vocabulary, content, duplicates, and the like – are problematic, and even some higher-critical scholars have voiced these objections. The supposed source documents – J, E, D and P – remain theoretical with no historical evidence to confirm that they actually existed. Most importantly, the Documentary Hypothesis calls into doubt the veracity of the scriptural witness and the words of Christ himself: 'If you believed Moses, you would believe me, for he wrote about me' (John 5:46).

c. The tôlĕdôt formula and the sources used in composing Genesis

In 1936 Wiseman suggested that the key to uncovering the sources for Genesis lay in the Hebrew word *tôlĕdôt*, meaning generations, family records or descendants. Ten sections of Genesis are marked with the formula [*and*] *these are the family records of* (2:4; 6:9; 10:1; 11:10, 27; 25:12, 19; 36:1, 9; 37:2). Another begins, *This is the book of the descendants of* (5:1). Wiseman posited that the *tôlĕdôt* formula represented the end of a tablet written or commissioned by the man whose name it contained. This corresponded to the common practice in the Ancient Near East of ending a text with a note that recorded the name of the scribe who had written it and the time

---

11. In North America in particular, the Documentary Hypothesis continues to have its defenders. In Europe the theory has morphed into considering most of the Pentateuch as either P material or non-P material, in effect holding that the vast majority of the text of the Pentateuch is a post-exilic composition.

when the tablet was composed. Thus, according to Wiseman, the first source tablet ended at 5:1 with *these are the generations* [or *family records*] *of Adam*.[12]

The major drawback of Wiseman's proposal is that the text that follows each of these *tôlĕdôt* formulas more naturally belongs with the notice than does the material that precedes it. Thus, at 25:19, *These are the family records of Isaac* is followed by accounts about his sons Esau and Jacob (25:20 – 35:29). At 36:1, *These are the family records of Esau* is followed by an account concerning Esau's descendants (36:2–8). Then at 36:9, *These are the family records of Esau, father of the Edomites in the mountains of Seir* is followed by a genealogy of Esau's descendants and a record of Edomite kings (36:10–43). For this reason and others, most scholars have rejected Wiseman's conjecture. Nevertheless, Wiseman correctly drew attention to what appears to be an organizing principle of Genesis: the *tôlĕdôt* formula.

3. Literary features of Genesis

a. Narrowing the focus

Genesis begins with all of creation and ends with the sons of Jacob in Egypt. This broad sweep of Israel's pre-history narrows its focus from the universe to the twelve patriarchs. It begins with creation, focusing on the earth (1:1 – 2:3). Having given this bigger picture, it constricts the reader's view to the creation of humans and their fall into sin (2:4 – 3:24). Next it traces one line of Adam's descendants: the sinful line of Cain (4:1–26). Once it has told the reader about this part of Adam's family, Genesis moves its attention to another son of Adam that Moses wants to spotlight: Seth and his righteous descendant Noah (5:1 – 6:8). This establishes a general pattern for the rest of the book: a wider view is given, then a subsidiary line or lines of descendants are briefly traced, and finally the emphasis is narrowed by placing the focus on the progeny to whom God will extend his favour (see Table 1 on p. 17).

---

12. Wiseman (1985: 79–80).

Table 1 Main lines followed by subsidiary lines in Genesis

Main line	Subsidiary line
Earth (1:1 – 2:3)	
Adam (2:4 – 3:24)	Cain's descendants (4:1–24)
Adam to Noah (4:25 – 5:32)	Sinful humans (6:1–8)
Noah (6:9 – 9:29)	Noah's descendants (10:1 – 11:9)
Shem to Abraham (11:10 – 25:11)	Ishmael's descendants (25:12–18)
Isaac (25:19 – 35:29)	Esau's descendants (36:1–43)
Jacob and his sons (37:1 – 50:26)	

b. God's election by grace

The literary structure of Genesis also highlights the work of God
as the reader follows the increasing attention given to the line from
Adam to Israel. The Almighty created the world and all that is in it
by his all-powerful word (1:1–23). He alone chose to create humans
and endowed them with mastery over the world (2:4–25). When
they sinned, he not only pronounced judgment and banned them
from Eden, but also gave them hope of victory over the tempter
(ch. 3; esp. 3:14–19). Noah walked with God (6:9), but it was
Yahweh's favour that Noah found (6:8) and that rescued humanity
from the deluge. God chose Abram and called him to be the father
of a great nation (12:1–3). Yahweh did not deviate from his choice,
although Abram's faith was less than ideal in trusting that Yahweh
would fulfil his promise (12:11–20; 15:3; 20:1–13). God did not turn
his promise away from Isaac, even when he repeated the deceptive
practices of his father (26:7). Yahweh chose the younger Jacob over
his brother Esau (25:33). Although the sins of Israel's sons Reuben,
Simeon and Levi disqualified them as bearers of the messianic
promise (49:2–7), God's choice of Judah (49:8–12) was not made
because Jacob's fourth-born had always behaved admirably (38:1–
30). Moreover, as Genesis draws to a close, Joseph reminds his
brothers (and also the readers of the book) of Yahweh's plan to
preserve the chosen people of God (50:20).

In most cases God did not choose as humans would have
chosen. Instead, he often chose younger sons over older ones –
Jacob over Esau, Judah over Reuben.

Yahweh's work of choosing Jacob's twelve sons and their
descendants as the people of Israel is also underscored by the
eleven *tôlĕdôt* formulas, which serve to divide the book into twelve
sections: the creation account (1:1 – 2:3) followed by eleven
accounts that progressively lead to the survival of the twelve clans
of Israel in Egypt.

4. Historical and archaeological issues

a. Near Eastern creation accounts
In 1849, among the ruins of the library of Ashurbanipal, the last
great king of the Neo-Assyrian Empire (685–c.627 BC), Austen
Henry Layard discovered an ancient Mesopotamian creation myth
in Nineveh (modern Mosul, Iraq). Named *Enuma Elish* (English
translation: 'when on high') after its first words, the seven tablets
containing the text of this myth were first published in 1876.
Almost immediately scholars proposed that this creation myth
provided the conceptual background for the creation account in
1:1 – 2:3. This connection is still advocated by many, including some
evangelicals (e.g. Walton).

Enuma Elish begins with the divinized primordial waters: Apsû,
representing fresh waters, and Tiamat, representing the oceans.
There is a conflict between Tiamat and the other gods, who reside
in her body. Eventually Marduk engages Tiamat in battle, killing her
and ripping her body into halves which he uses to form the earth and
the sky. Marduk then creates the yearly calendar, the sun, moon,
stars and weather. Marduk also slays Tiamat's son Kingu, and from
his blood mixed with the earth he creates humans to serve the gods.

Some of the alleged parallels to 1:1 – 2:3 are obvious. The
primordial waters and their division between earth and sky are
prominent at the beginning of both accounts (cf. 1:2–8). The creation of the sun, moon and stars and their connection to the
reckoning of time is found in both (cf. 1:14–18). Humans are
formed from the earth in *Enuma Elish*. However, the supposed
parallel for this is not part of the creation account in 1:1 – 2:3, and
is not mentioned until 2:7.

There are several problems, however, with holding that *Enuma
Elish* provides the Near Eastern background for 1:1 – 2:3. For

instance, it is often claimed that Tiamat and the Hebrew word for the primordial waters, *těhôm* (1:2), are cognates. Yet this etymological connection remains controversial. If Tiamat is derived from *těhôm* then the latter should have a Hebrew middle consonant *aleph* and not a *hē*. It also ought to have a Hebrew feminine ending, which it does not. Most now accept that the Hebrew word does not come directly from the Akkadian word, but that both words derive independently from a common proto-Semitic root, *tiham*. Moreover, there is no divine conflict in the Genesis account as in *Enuma Elish* (see below). Most importantly, there is no consensus on the date of the composition of the Babylonian myth. Some date it to the time of the Babylonian king Hammurabi in the eighteenth century BC. Others date it more broadly to sometime in the Kassite Era (eighteenth to sixteenth centuries BC). Still other Assyriologists place it as late as 1100 BC. If the later date is accepted, it would post-date the work of Moses by some three centuries, reversing the direction of dependence from Genesis to *Enuma Elish*.

Recently Johnston (2008) has argued that Genesis is less related to the Assyrian creation myth and is, instead, purposely written to refute Egyptian creation myths. Building on work by A. H. Sayce and, more recently, Hoffmeier (1983), he notes that the general sequence of events from the Old Kingdom (twenty-seventh to twenty-second centuries BC) Pyramid Texts and Coffin Texts is very similar to that of Genesis and that these myths were still current in the Middle and New Kingdom periods (twenty-first to seventeenth centuries BC and sixteenth to eleventh centuries BC respectively). The sequence is as shown in Table 2 on page 20.

A similar sequence is found on the Egyptian Shabaka Stone (inscribed in the eighth or seventh century BC) which preserves the Memphite Theology of the New Kingdom period. One additional parallel from this text with 1:1 – 2:3 is that at the end of creation the Egyptian god Ptah rests at the end of his work, just as God rests at the end of his work at 2:2–3. Intriguingly, Moses (1526–1406 BC) lived during the early New Kingdom period.

Johnston (2008) suggests that 1:1 – 2:3 is a polemic against Near Eastern creation mythology in general and Egyptian mythology in particular. According to this theory, not only would Moses have been relating the correct account of the origin of the world, but he

Table 2 Sequence of events in Pyramid and Coffin Texts and Genesis

Pyramid and Coffin Texts	Genesis 1:1 – 2:3
1. Lifeless watery deep	1. Lifeless watery deep
2. Breath/wind (Atum) moves on the waters	2. Breath/wind of God moves on the waters
3. Creation of light (Atum)	3. Creation of light
4. Emergence of primordial hill	4. Creation of firmament in the midst of the waters
5. Procreation of the sky (Shu)	5. Creation of the sky when waters were raised above the firmament
6. Formation of heavenly waters (Nut) by separation	6. Formation of heavenly waters by separation
7. Formation of dry ground (Geb) by separation	7. Formation of dry ground when waters were gathered
8. Humans accidentally created by tears of Atum	8. Sun and moon created to rule day and night
9. Sun created to rule the world as the image of Re	9. Creation of humans to rule the world as the image of God

was also refuting ancient Egyptian polytheism and creation models which competed against monotheistic faith in Yahweh for the loyalty of Israel after their exposure to Egyptian religion during their long sojourn in the land of the Nile. Therefore, Johnston's argument suggests that Genesis 1 could also be viewed as refuting all Ancient Near Eastern creation myths even without direct knowledge of or reference to the Mesopotamian myths such as *Enuma Elish*.

b. Pre- and post-diluvian genealogies

There are two major genealogies that link Adam to Abraham: the pre-diluvian genealogy from Adam to Noah (5:1–32) and the post-diluvian genealogy from Shem to Abram and his brothers (11:10–26). These genealogies display two unique features: (1) The age of the ancestor is listed. For example, *Nahor lived twenty-nine years and fathered Terah* (11:24). (2) The additional number of years an ancestor lived is also given. For example, *After he fathered Terah, Nahor lived 119 years* (11:25). In addition, the pre-diluvian genealogy includes the total lifespan of each ancestor, such as, *So Seth lived 912 years and then died* (5:8).

Because these genealogies list the age of each ancestor at what appears to be the birth of his descendant, many have attempted to add these numbers together to determine the age of the earth. However, we must exercise some caution in doing this.[13] First, the Hebrew words for 'father' and 'son' can at times denote 'ancestor' and 'descendant'. Moreover, the verb translated *fathered* does not always denote direct fatherhood. The *Theological Wordbook of the Old Testament* notes,

> The word does not necessarily point to the generation immediately
> following. In Hebrew thought, an individual by the act of giving birth
> to a child becomes a parent or ancestor of all who are called a son
> of David and a son of Abraham, *yālad* may show the beginning
> of an individual's relationship to any descendant.[14]

This can be seen in the genealogy of ten generations from Perez to David at Ruth 4:18–22, where the Hebrew word *yālad* is also used. There had to be more than ten generations in this span, given the 837 years between Perez and David. It appears that the author of Ruth purposely omitted some generations so that Boaz would be listed as the honoured seventh person in the genealogy, and David would be in the tenth generation.

In the same way, we should note that in both the pre- and post-diluvian genealogies the highlighted person (Noah, Abram) is in the tenth generation, with each genealogy ending with the birth of three sons (Ham, Shem and Japheth [5:32], and Abram, Nahor and Haran [11:26]). In a study of genealogies that have survived from the Ancient Near East, Wilson (1977) has noted that genealogies tend to be limited to ten generations at most (many are much shorter). Moreover, it is noteworthy that in the pre-diluvian genealogy Enoch, who *walked with God* (5:22, 24), occupies the

---

13. For a discussion of recent attempts to use the genealogies in 5:1–32 and
     11:1–32 to determine the age of the earth and the date of Noah's flood,
     see Steinmann (2017b) where these attempts are shown to rely on
     disprovable theories and suppositions.
14. *TWOT* 1.379; entry 867.

honoured seventh position (cf. Jude 14). Moreover, in the combined genealogy from Adam to Abram, Eber, the eponymous ancestor of the Hebrews, is honoured as the fourteenth generation.

All this suggests that these genealogies may skip any number of generations, making it impossible to assume naively that adding up the years of the pre- and post-diluvian ancestors of Abraham will yield the number of years from the creation of Adam to the birth of Abraham. In a few instances it can be demonstrated that these genealogies list father to son to grandson (e.g. Adam to Seth to Enosh: compare 4:25–26 with 5:3–8; see also Lamech as father of Noah, 5:28; for Terah as father of Abram, compare 11:26 with 11:27–32). However, we cannot be certain that this is the case in every instance in these genealogies.[15]

c. Dating the patriarchs

Using information given in Genesis and knowing the date of the exodus from Egypt, it is relatively easy to establish a timeline for Israel's patriarchs. The most likely date of the exodus is 1446.[16] Jacob and his family entered Egypt 430 years to the day before the exodus (Exod. 12:40–41). Therefore, Jacob entered Egypt on 14 Nisan 1876 (1446 + 430). Jacob was 130 years old when he entered Egypt (Gen. 47:9), so he was born in 2006 (1876 + 130). Isaac was sixty when Jacob was born (25:26), so Isaac was born in 2066. Abraham was 100 years old when Isaac was born (21:5), so Abraham was born in 2166. Thus, the basic dates for this period are:

2166	Abram born (21:5)
2066	Isaac born (25:26)
2006	Jacob born (47:9)
1991	Abraham dies (25:7)
1886	Isaac dies (35:28)
1876	Jacob enters Egypt (Exod. 12:40–41)
1859	Jacob dies (47:28)

---

15. For further discussion, see Steinmann (2017b).

16. Steinmann (2011: 45–65).

Table 3 Detailed chronology of the patriarchs[17]

2166	Abram born (21:5)
2156	Sarai born (17:1, 17)
2091	Abram leaves Haran (12:4)
2081	Abram marries Hagar (16:3)
2080	Ishmael born (16:16)
2067	Abram renamed Abraham (17:1, 21, 24)
2066	Isaac born (21:1)
2029	Sarah dies (23:1)
2026	Isaac marries Rebekah (25:20)
2006	Jacob and Esau born (25:26)
1991	Abraham dies (25:7)
1966	Esau marries (26:34)
1943	Ishmael dies (25:17)
1930	Jacob flees to Paddan-aram (29:15–30)
1923	Jacob marries Leah and Rachel (29:15–30)
1922	Reuben born to Leah (29:32)
1921	Simeon born to Leah (29:33)
1920	Levi born to Leah (29:34)
1919	Judah born to Leah (29:35); Dan born to Bilhah (30:1–6)
1918/1917	Naphtali born to Bilhah (30:7–8)
1917	Issachar born to Leah (30:14–20); Gad born to Zilpah (30:9–11)
1916	Asher born to Zilpah (30:12–13); Zebulun born to Leah (30:14–20); Joseph born to Rachel (41:46)
c.1915	Dinah born to Leah (30:21)
1910	Jacob returns to Canaan (31:38, 41)
c.1902	Jacob goes to Bethel (35:1–15)
c.1901	Rachel dies/Benjamin born (35:16–20)
c.1900	Jacob settles in Mamre (35:27); Judah marries (38:1–2)
1899	Joseph sold into slavery (37:2); Er born (38:3)
1899–c.1889	Joseph serves Potiphar (37:36)
c.1897	Onan born (38:4)
c.1895	Shelah born (38:5)
c.1889–1886	Joseph in prison (39:20)
1888	Baker and cupbearer's dreams (41:1)
1886	Joseph freed from prison (41:46); Isaac dies (35:28)
1885–1879	Years of plentiful harvest (41:47)
c.1879	Er and Onan marry Tamar (38:6–10)
1878–1871	Years of famine (45:11)
c.1878	Judah's wife dies (38:12)
c.1877	Perez and Zerah born (38:27–30)
1876	Jacob's family enters Egypt (Exod. 12:40–41)
1859	Jacob dies (47:28)
1806	Joseph dies (50:22)

17. Steinmann (2011: 67–80).

Abraham was born in Mesopotamia during the end of the Akkadian
Dynasty that had been founded by Sargon the Great. Abraham
would have been in Egypt during the First Intermediate Period
during the overlapping ninth and tenth dynasties. At the end of
the patriarchal period Joseph would have entered Egypt during the
Middle Kingdom period and probably served under the pharaohs
Sesotris I (1920–1875 BC) and his successor Amenemhet II (1878–
1844 BC; see Table 3 on p. 23).

5. Theological themes in Genesis

a. Creation

Genesis' presentation of the creation of the world with humans as
the crown of God's creation (1:1 – 2:3) ranks as one of the most
stirring and majestic passages in all of Scripture. Most striking is
God's use of his spoken word to create (1:3, 6, 9, 11, 14, 20, 24; Heb.
11:3). Unlike the pagan myths discussed above, Genesis emphasizes
that God alone created the heavens and earth and all that fills them
(cf. Rev. 4:11; 10:6). God alone was active in creation of the world,
and this is mentioned particularly often by Isaiah (Isa. 40:26; 41:20;
42:5; 43:7; 45:7–8, 12, 18; cf. Ps. 148:5; Eph. 3:9; Col. 1:16). The
opening section of Genesis also emphasizes that the Almighty
accomplished his creative activity in six days (2:1–3), and that
human beings are the crown of his creation, made in God's image
and likeness (1:26–27; 5:1–2). This image of God with his hands in
the dirt is remarkable; this is no naive theology, but a statement
about the depths to which God has entered into the life of the creation. The parallel here is that of a governing sovereign who cannot
be everywhere present in the realm, but who erects statues of
himself as a witness and reminder of who the real sovereign is. By
analogy, the invisible God has placed human beings in creation so
that, upon seeing the human creature, other creatures are reminded
of Yahweh's rule (cf. Ps. 8:5). This idea is then used of Christ (John
14:9; Col. 1:15) and of Christians (Col. 3:9–10; Eph. 4:22–24).

Also in contrast to the Near Eastern creation accounts, God's
creation was good and perfect, without strife, conflict or contention
(1:4, 10, 12, 18, 21, 25, 31; cf. 1 Tim. 4:4). Critical scholars believe
that, in order to create the world, Yahweh had first to defeat chaos.

Although 1:1 – 2:3 is completely free of any pre-creation combat motifs, John Goldingay believes that, just like other Ancient Near Eastern deities, Yahweh could not create an ordered universe until first he defeated the forces of chaos.[18] This, then, becomes the pattern for future salvific acts.

This understanding of Israel's creational theology goes back to Hermann Gunkel who assumed that prophets like Isaiah employed sea-battle imagery to elicit both protological and eschatological events. In 1895, his book *Schöpfung und Chaos in Urzeit und Endzeit (Creation and Chaos in the Primeval Era and the Eschaton)* argued that the creation account in 1:1 – 2:3 derived from the Babylonian creation epic, the *Enuma Elish*. Gunkel coined the term *Chaoskampf* to describe the motif of a primordial battle between Yahweh and chaos in Genesis 1:2 that derived from Marduk's conquest of Tiamat.

Since Gunkel, Frank Moore Cross shifted the focus of the discussion from Babylonian to Canaanite origins. Following Thorkild Jacobsen, Cross suggested that 'the battle with the dragon Ocean is West Semitic in origin' rather than originally Babylonian, but nevertheless he draws parallels between biblical texts and both Canaanite and Babylonian myths. Whereas Gunkel spoke of *Chaoskampf*, Cross refers more generally to 'the cosmogonic or creation battle with monstrous Sea'.[19] Both of these influential scholars see the 'creational/cosmogonic' conquest of Yahweh over the sea wherever Yahweh exerts his power over water in the Old Testament. In his influential Anchor Bible Genesis commentary published in 1964, Abraham Speiser likewise argues that the Genesis account of creation is the same as the Babylonian creation myth.

Strife and hostility describe our sin-infected world, but this does not mean they were present from the beginning. The universe came into existence by Yahweh's word, not because he defeated primeval agents of chaos. The presence of evil is often explained with dualism, the belief in two eternal powers, one good and one evil. But Moses' description of matter as initially *without form and void*

---

18. Goldingay (2010: 25).
19. Cross (1973: 20–23).

(1:2) does not describe Yahweh's battle over unruly forces to create the world. Evil enters the world in 3:1–24, through the wiles of Satan, after creation is finished. Conflict with the evil one is not connected to creation. To say so is to revert to a mythic Babylonian or Canaanite worldview.

To emphasize that creation was orderly and not the chaotic process visualized by the pagan myths, Genesis presents the six days as a progressive and orderly process organized by God, with the six days paired in two sets of three (see Table 4)

Table 4 The days of creation in Genesis 1

Day 1	Day 2	Day 3
Heavens empty; *light* created	*Expanse of sky* separated from *sea*	*Land* (dry ground) filled with plants
Day 4	Day 5	Day 6
Heavens filled with sun, moon and stars to *light* the sky	*Expanse of sky* filled with birds; *seas* filled with creatures	*Land* filled with animals and people

This schematic pairing of the days, however, is only an approximation of what Genesis demonstrates about God's work, and the parallels are partial and incomplete. Other details in the text of 1:1 – 2:3 demonstrate that there are connections between pairs of days that do not fit into this scheme. For instance, the lights that are created on day four are put in the expanse created on day two. The sea creatures made on day five are put in the sea that was made on day three. Humans were created on day six to rule over animals created on days five and six.[20] Nevertheless, the literary ordering of the six creation days is evident. Yet it would be a false dichotomy to pit the literary features of the text against its chronological features, as some have attempted.

The term *day* is not always used the same way, even in the creation account. In 1:5 and 1:14 what God calls 'day' is the period of daylight as opposed to night-time. Here day is something less than

---

20. Beall in Charles (2013: 133).

a twenty-four-hour day, as the context makes clear. By contrast, in 2:4 the word *day* is used in a phrase to set the temporal context (*in the day* = 'when').

The real question, then, is how to understand the phrases in which *day* is used to demarcate the stages of creation ('day one', 'a second day', and so forth). In the context there are a variety of temporal terms: *start* (i.e. beginning), *evening and morning, day, night, seasons, days* and *years*. All of these terms have their meaning shaped by the context in which they are used. The terms *day* and *night* suggest that these words are being used in opposition to each other and signal what we normally denote by these terms. Thus, the sun – the greater light – dominates daytime, and the moon – the lesser light – rules the night (1:16).

The same is true of evening and morning (1:5, 8, 13, 19, 23, 31). Similarly, *year, seasons* and *years* denote a solar year (365.24218967 days) and its parts (spring, summer, autumn, winter), since the context is the discussion of the way in which these are regulated by the movements of the cosmos (1:14).

In the light of this, the term *day* is used in phrases that designate the stages of creation to mark off a single cycle of daylight and night-time. It seems impossible to argue that all of the other terms are used in their usual sense to denote ordinary evenings and mornings, seasons and years, but that *day* is not. One could, of course, argue this if there were something in the text to suggest it, but lacking that, it is a dubious argument to suggest that *day* means anything other than a single rotation of the earth upon its axis.

Genesis 1:1 – 2:3 is a key passage for later Old Testament and New Testament discussions of the origins of all things and of humans, and of their God-given relationship to all of creation. The commandment concerning the Sabbath refers to the seven days of the creation week (Exod. 20:11). God's creation of humankind affords him the relationship of Father to all people (Deut. 32:6; Mal. 2:10). Moreover, the relationship of man to woman, husband to wife, as partners in sharing dominion over the earth and the responsibility for procreation, was established by God (1:26–29; cf. 2:18–24; Matt. 19:4–6; 1 Cor. 11:8–12).

The Documentary Hypothesis holds that 1:1 – 2:3 and 2:4–25 are two different creation accounts. The first is assigned to the Priestly source (P) during or after the Babylonian captivity, with the second assigned to the Yahwist (J) with additional material from an Elohistic source (E). This theory holds that the two versions have different and even conflicting theological outlooks and goals, as well as different details concerning how creation was accomplished. For instance, in the first creation account animals were formed before humans (1:24–28), whereas in the second one animals were formed after the man (2:7, 19). In the first story humans were created to have dominion over the animals (1:26), whereas in the second they were to work the garden (2:15). In the first account humans as male and female are in the image of God (1:26), whereas in the second they are created to become one flesh (2:24).

However, it is not necessary to view the two accounts as at odds with each other. Clearly, 2:4–25 is not a complete creation account: the existence of the heavens and earth is assumed. There is no mention of the sun, moon and stars. There is no discussion of the creation of sea creatures. Thus, this passage is not a second creation text but an expansion of the description of the creation of humans as male and female.

In addition, the different sequence in the creation of the animals and humans can be explained in complementary ways. For instance, the text relating the sixth day in 1:24–31 may indicate a logical sequence, with humans reserved for last, since they are to be the pinnacle of God's work as reflections of his image exercising dominion on the earth. The text of 2:19 may record the actual sequence once the reader understands the relationship of the man and the woman to the rest of God's creatures.

Moreover, the garden in Eden is introduced to explain the man's occupation and his need for a helper without denying his dominion over the animals or his creation in God's image. Instead, the relation of man to woman as they go about their mutual tasks in the garden is explored. This passage is crucial to understanding marriage as a divinely designed and instituted relationship for mutual comfort and support and for the propagation of the human race. Much of what the rest of the Bible says about marriage and the proper relationship of the sexes to one another is predicated upon this text, especially 2:24 (cf. Matt. 19:4–6; Mark 10:6–8; 1 Cor. 6:16; 7:10–11; 11:8–12; Eph. 5:31, 33).

b. The fall

The fall of humankind into sin occupies a prominent place in Genesis, immediately following the account of God's creation of man and woman (3:1–24). One of the results of sin was increased pain (3:16–17). This would characterize a woman's relationship with her children and a man's relationship to his work. In 6:6 that pain brought grief to God, such that sin even affected him!

The curse upon Adam and Eve for their sin (3:16–19) was not the end of the matter. The consequences of the fall are emphasized throughout the book. The first murder is related immediately after humans are expelled from Eden (4:1–16). Sin's effects accelerate so that whereas Cain was afraid of the consequences of his murderous ways (4:13–14), his descendant Lamech bragged about his homicidal acts (4:23–24). When Adam had another son, that offspring was in his sinful likeness rather than in God's image (5:3). Moreover, several times Genesis directly states that sin had become permanently attached to human nature (e.g. 6:5; 8:21; cf. Job 15:14; Ps. 51:5; Jer. 17:9; Matt. 15:19; Rom. 3:23).

The fall also leads to a renewing, in God's provision of clothing for Adam and Eve, and then a second undoing of creation – the great flood of Noah's day. The land that emerged from the primeval ocean (1:9) is submerged in the great flood, and re-emerges afterwards. Noah is a kind of second Adam, since all subsequent humanity stems from him. Initially judged to be righteous and blameless (6:9), he succumbs to sin in an echo of the fall of Adam and Eve (9:20–27). Whereas Adam's consumption of fruit made him aware of his nakedness so that he tried to cover it up (3:6–7), Noah's drinking wine from fruit of the vine leads him to uncover himself unwittingly, and his sons have to cover him (9:23). In Adam's case the son's behaviour was even more reprehensible than the father's. In Noah's case his son's disobedience leads to dissension among the three brothers. Just as Cain's descendants appear to be the ungodly line in 4:17–24, so Ham's descendant Canaan is cursed by Noah (9:25).

c. God's chosen people

Despite the fact that all humans now carried the stain of sin from birth, God chose some to be his people through whom redemption of the world would come. This first becomes evident in Noah, whose family Yahweh chose to save despite his conclusion that he had to wipe humankind from the face of the earth (6:5–8). From Noah's children, God favoured Shem, and his line is traced to Abram. No reason is given for God's choice of Terah's son – it is simply God's mercy, for Abram would prove to be sinful like the rest of the human race. Yet, despite Abram's failing, God repeats his promise to him seven times (12:1–3 [itself a sevenfold promise]; 12:7; 13:14–17; 15:1–21; 17:1–22; 18:10; 22:15–18). God chose Abram's son Isaac, and Isaac's son Jacob. The choice of this people comes to a climax in Jacob. In addition, the barrenness of Israel's three matriarchs Sarah (11:30), Rebekah (25:21) and Rachel (29:31) highlights the fact that Yahweh

> chooses the foolish things of the world to shame the wise; he chooses the weak things of the world to shame the strong. He chooses the lowly things of this world and the despised things – and the things that are not. (1 Cor. 1:27–28)

The name God gives to Jacob, *Israel*, is a mark of Yahweh's covenant grace. He gives this name to Jacob in order to confirm that the promise given to his father and grandfather now passes to him. It designates Jacob, his children and all their descendants as objects of Yahweh's mercy.

Jacob first receives this name in the momentous wrestling with God (32:24–32). He asks for a blessing before God departs. In that context of blessing, God renames him *Israel*. Here the meaning of the Hebrew name Israel is 'he struggles with God' (32:28). This fits the context, since a wrestling match has just taken place. Because this is meant to be a blessing, one might expect it to denote God's grace (35:10–13; 2 Chr. 9:8; Isa. 11:12; 27:6; 44:21; Jer. 31:31). It is possible that the text includes a double reference in 32:28 in the light of the promises of God repeated to Jacob. A slight variation of the Hebrew word 'Israel' can mean 'El [God] has made right', and the subsequent explanation of the name would be 'Because you are right with God, with men you will prevail'. This is confirmed elsewhere in the Old Testament. The proper noun Jeshurun appears in Isaiah 44:2 and in Deuteronomy 32:15; 33:5, 26, while in Numbers

23:10 Israelites are called 'upright ones'. Jeshurun is linked with the verb meaning to be straight or upright. The *-un* ending is an affectionate diminutive. Jeshurun is parallel with Jacob ('deceiver, liar, trickster') in Isaiah 44:2.

Assuming such a double reference nicely fits the immediate context as well as the wider context of Genesis (6:9; 15:6). This name change indicates an act of mercy and redemption by Yahweh. Formerly, he had the name Jacob, which means 'he deceives'. Now his name is 'God has made righteous'. The deceiver stands forgiven and blessed as an instrument of the promise. It is significant that this act of reconciliation between Yahweh and Jacob accompanies the reconciliation between Jacob and Esau (33:1–19).

Jacob receives the name Israel a second time in 35:10: *God said to him, 'Your name is Jacob, but you will no longer be called Jacob; you will be Israel'* (35:10). The text then includes repetition of the promises of divine favour that God made to Abraham and Isaac: God promises to make his descendants abundant. A great nation and kings will come from him. Yahweh will grant them the Promised Land (35:11–13). In such a context the definition of Israel as 'God has made righteous' would fit well, whereas 'he struggles with God' would not.

After Jacob, Yahweh then carries on the promise not in one person but in the sons of Israel and their descendants, who also have the designation *tribes* or *children* of Israel. Although initially a correlation between the name Israel and the bloodline of Jacob, the term Israel is not inherently an ethnic designation, and belonging to Israel does not require a certain heritage. Rather, the name is a gift available to anyone. This becomes evident not only by the covenant attached to the name but also by the fact that foreigners can become a part of Israel (Exod. 12:48–49; 20:10; 23:12; Lev. 16:29–30; 19:33–34; Deut. 29:11; 31:10–13; Josh. 8:33; Ps. 146:9; Ezek. 47:22–23). Essentially, Israel, then, is the name for the Old Testament people of God and his New Testament people, the church (Rom. 9 – 11; Gal. 3 – 4; and esp. Gal. 6:16).

d. Justification by faith

If Israel is not an ethnic designation, how does one become part of God's people? Genesis addresses this through the subject of justification through faith. Justification involves the declaration of pardon from guilt in an implied courtroom setting. In the Bible, such a declaration comes from Yahweh, who confers this gift upon someone even though by virtue of sin it is not deserved or earned. Justification is received through the gift of faith. Faith contributes nothing to the act of justification – it only receives what God has declared. This pardon is free but comes at a high cost to God who declares it. Forgiveness from the guilt of sin is possible, since the punishment is transferred to the promised Saviour. In this act of justification, the sinner receives the status of being seen by God as completely righteous. This is not the inherent or natural righteousness which Adam and Eve possessed at creation but lost in the fall. Rather, it is an imputed righteousness, which God graciously credits to a person by the merits of the promised seed, Christ Jesus.

Justification through faith in the book of Genesis becomes particularly clear in the life of Abraham. He believes the gracious promise of Yahweh, particularly that in him and his seed all the nations of the earth will be blessed (12:2–3; 17:19; Gal. 3:16). Although Abraham does not have all the details regarding this coming Saviour, he trusts in the gracious plans of God. Through faith in the promise Abraham receives the gift of justification: *Abram believed Yahweh, and he credited it to him as righteousness* (15:6). Especially in this example of Abraham, Paul wishes to make clear that faith does not merit anything before Yahweh. Faith is not a way of earning God's favour. This passive righteousness through faith should not be confused with the active righteousness lived out in a believer's life which is always imperfect in any fallen human. Paul excludes human works in the context of justification. Good works do not precede faith (Rom. 4:3–25; see Heb. 11:8–12). In this way, Paul presents the patriarch Abraham as an archetype of how one may be saved.

While Genesis accentuates justification through faith particularly in the person of Abraham, the book of Hebrews highlights additional persons in Genesis who have this righteousness through faith. Although Genesis says little about Abel, Hebrews indicates that he was righteous through faith: 'By faith he was commended as a righteous man, when God spoke well of his offerings. And by faith he still speaks although he is dead' (Heb. 11:5). Regarding

Noah, after recounting the building of the ark, Hebrews declares: 'By faith, he condemned the world and became an heir of the righteousness that comes by faith' (Heb. 11:7). Thus, not only Abraham but also other persons in Genesis such as Sarah, Isaac, Rachel, Jacob, Joseph and Judah exemplify justification through faith.

6. Genesis as a witness to the promised Saviour

a. The messianic promise

The choice of Israel to be God's people was not simply for their sake, but for the sake of all people. This promise runs throughout Genesis from the first sinners, Adam and Eve, to the last ones in the book – the sons of Israel, especially Judah. God's pledge of a Saviour is traced through the book as it narrows its focus to Jacob and his sons.

Immediately after Yahweh confronted Adam and Eve about their sin he pronounced a curse on the serpent who tempted them. This curse not only condemned Satan for his role in the fall, but it also contained the first glimpse of a promised Saviour who would deliver humans from the curse of sin. God said to the serpent: *I will put hostility between you and the woman, and between your seed and her seed. He will strike at your head, and you will strike at his heel* (3:15).

The woman's seed is often understood to be a collective – the woman's descendants – since this noun can be used in a collective sense. However, C. John Collins has noted that whenever 'seed' is used with singular verbs and adjectives, and especially with singular pronouns, it is not collective but singular.[21] In this text the verb *strike* is singular. More importantly, it is used with a singular pronoun (*hē*), although no pronoun is required by Hebrew syntax in this case. This superfluous use of the pronoun emphasizes that God is promising a particular seed – a single descendant – of the woman who will crush the serpent's head. Therefore, this condemnation of the serpent is also the first gospel promise in the Scriptures, and has been called the 'protoevangelium'. It is humanity's first glimpse of the Messiah.

---

21. Collins (1997).

The word 'seed' is important in Genesis. Alexander has noted that it is used fifty-nine times in the book and only 170 times in the rest of the Old Testament.[22] He also observed that the word conveys the concept that there is a close resemblance between the seed and that which produced it. The descendant is like the ancestor. The seed of the woman would be as human as she was. The keyword *seed* is used throughout Genesis to refer to this original promise of the Messiah as this concept is further developed in the unfolding story of God's people.

Eve understood this promise, as shown in her own words. When Cain was born she named him out of hope that he might be the promised seed from God (4:1). After Cain's sins demonstrated that he was not the expected seed, she said of her son Seth, *God has given me* another seed *in place of Abel, since Cain killed him* (4:25).

Seth's line would lead to Noah, where the promise would be handed down through the line of Noah's son Shem. Following the incident of Noah's drunkenness and Ham's role in revealing his father's shame (9:20–23), Noah prophesied about his sons. A curse was placed on Ham's descendants through his son Canaan (9:25). However, a blessing was given to Shem through Yahweh, his God (9:26). This blessing would be shared with his brother Japheth (9:27) and is traced through Shem's line to Abram (11:10–32).

Yahweh's promises to Abraham, Isaac and Jacob all centred upon the messianic promise. There are several elements to the promises given to Israel's patriarchs, and they are repeated from one generation to the next (see Table 5 on p. 35).

These promises to the patriarchs in Genesis are foundational to the rest of the Pentateuch and are frequently mentioned in the rest of the Old Testament. Their importance and frequency, in that Exodus to Deuteronomy mentions them, has led Clines to claim that the patriarchal promises of God are the theme of the Pentateuch.[23] More importantly, there are two aspects of these promises that ought not to be overlooked. First, they are the flowering of the promises and blessings previously given to Adam

22. Alexander (1997).

23. Clines (1997).

Table 5 Yahweh's seven promises to the patriarchs in Genesis

Promise	Abraham	Isaac	Jacob
Progeny: Become a great nation/ numerous	12:2; 13:16; 17:2; 22:17	26:4, 24	28:14; 46:3
Reputation: Have a great name	12:2		
Messianic seed: Will be a blessing to the nations through his seed	12:3; 22:18		28:14
Protection: Bless those who bless/ curse those who curse; Yahweh will be with him; will be his God/ God of his seed	12:3; 15:1; 17:7–8	26:4, 24	28:15; 31:3; 46:4
Land: God will give the land of Canaan to his seed	12:7; 13:15, 17; 17:8; 22:17	26:3–4	28:13; 35:12
Influence: Father of many nations	17:5–6		35:11
Royalty: Will produce kings	17:6		35:11

and Eve (3:15) and Shem (9:26). Second, all of them are given for the sake of the messianic promise (see John 8:56). The making of Israel into a great nation and the promise of protection was for the purpose of their bringing the Messiah into the world. The land of Canaan was given to the seed of the patriarchs so that Israel would have a homeland that would foreshadow the greater land given to all of Christ's followers (Heb. 11:8–10). Through faith in Jesus people from many nations would become children of Abraham (Matt. 3:9; 8:11; Luke 3:8; John 8:39; Rom. 4:16–17; 9:6–8; Eph. 3:6; 1 Pet. 3:6).

When God brought Jacob down to Egypt he promised him that there he would become a great nation (46:3). While in Egypt all of Jacob's sons would multiply to become a large people. However, before Jacob died, he called his sons to him to prophesy what would become of them and their offspring in the last days (49:1). This included the messianic promise, and the son to whom it would be passed. Reuben, Jacob's firstborn son, was disqualified because of his adultery with his father's concubine (49:2–3; cf. 35:22). Simeon and Levi were rejected because of their double-dealing with the men of Shechem (49:5–7; cf. 34:1–31). Therefore, the messianic promise passed to Judah (49:9–12). He was given the sceptre,

signifying the royal prerogatives of the Messiah (49:10; cf. Mark
15:32; Luke 23:2). More prominently, Judah is depicted as a lion, a
symbol that ever after would be associated with the Messiah (Rev.
5:5). Later, in Balaam's prophecies concerning Israel, blessing for
those who bless the Israelites and curses for those who curse them
are linked to their carrying the messianic promise as the lion (Num.
23:24; 24:9).

Thus, Genesis traces the promise of the Messiah across the
generations as follows:

Eve's seed (3:15) → Shem (9:26) → Abraham (12:2–3 etc.) →
Isaac (26:3–4, 24) → Jacob (28:13–15 etc.) → Judah (49:9–12).

b. The Messenger of Yahweh

Four times in the accounts of Israel's patriarchs a figure called *the
Messenger/Angel of Yahweh* or *the Messenger/Angel of God* appears. The
introduction of this messenger in Genesis prepares for his repeated
appearances in the rest of the Old Testament, where he is
mentioned forty-seven more times. This is no ordinary messenger
of God, for in every book of the Old Testament where he is
mentioned, he is identified as a manifestation of Yahweh himself.

In Genesis 16:7–14 the Messenger of Yahweh appears to Hagar
near the spring on the way to Shur after she had fled from Sarai's
mistreatment (16:7). This Messenger made a promise that only God
can make: *I will surely multiply your seed, and they will be so many that they
cannot be counted* (16:10). Moreover, Hagar realized that she had seen
God (16:13), confirming the identity of this Messenger. Later, when
Hagar and Ishmael were expelled from Abraham's camp, the
Messenger of God called to her and once again promised her
concerning her son, *I will make him a great nation* (21:18).

Yahweh's Messenger also spoke to Abraham to stop him before
he sacrificed Isaac on Mount Moriah (22:11, 15). Once again this
Messenger is clearly identified as God himself when he makes
statements such as *you have not withheld your only son from me* (22:12)
and *I will surely bless you and make your offspring as numerous as the stars
of the sky and the sand on the seashore* (22:17).

Jacob saw the Messenger of God in a dream, in which the
Messenger told him, *I am the God of Bethel* (31:13). Later, near the end

of his life, Jacob would refer to this Messenger in his blessing of
Joseph's sons, Ephraim and Manasseh:

> *The God before whom my fathers Abraham and Isaac walked,*
> *the God who has been my shepherd all of my life to this day,*
> *the* messenger *who has redeemed me from all danger:*
> *May he bless these boys.*
>
> (48:15–16)

Although it does not use the term 'messenger of Yahweh', the
account of Jacob's wrestling with God probably describes another
appearance of this divine Messenger. Jacob called the site of the
wrestling match *Peniel* (i.e. face of God), and said, *I have seen God
face-to-face, and I have been delivered* (32:30).

Clearly, the Messenger of Yahweh is a theophany, an appearance
of God. Such theophanies occur at other vital junctures in the Old
Testament story of Israel. At the burning bush Moses sees the
Messenger of Yahweh who is God calling to him (Exod. 3:2, 4;
cf. Acts 7:30–34). God, who brings his people out of Egypt, is also
this Messenger (Num. 20:16). Yahweh's Messenger appears to the
prophet Balaam and his donkey (Num. 22). He instructs Balaam to
speak only those words which he will give him, which once again
demonstrates that the Messenger is God (Num. 22:35; cf. Num.
23:12, 26; 24:12).

The Messenger of Yahweh appears several times in Judges. In
Judges 2 he admonishes Israel for their unfaithfulness when he says,
'*I* brought you up from Egypt and led you into the land *I* had
solemnly promised to give to your ancestors. *I* said, "*I* will never
break my covenant with you"' (Judg. 2:1). Later, Yahweh's
Messenger appears to Samson's mother and father (Judg. 13). In this
instance, Manoah acknowledges, 'We have seen God!' (Judg. 13:22).

These and other references to the Messenger of Yahweh in the
Old Testament demonstrate God's intimate involvement with his
people. On the basis of statements in the New Testament, many
Christians, beginning with the early church fathers, have recognized
this Messenger as the pre-incarnate Christ. For instance, John's
Gospel says, 'No-one has ever seen God. The only God who is in
the bosom of the Father – he has made him known' (John 1:18).

In addition, the book of Exodus identifies the cloudy pillar that led Israel out of Egypt with the Messenger of God (compare Exod. 13:21–22 with Exod. 14:19). He is the deliverer of his people, and he threw the Egyptian army into a panic (Exod. 14:24). It is no coincidence, then, that when Jesus was transfigured on the mountain and was conversing with Moses and Elijah, he was speaking about 'his *exodus* which he was about to fulfil in Jerusalem' (Luke 9:31). In Jerusalem, through his death on the cross and resurrection, Jesus would lead his people out of the bondage to sin and death just as he had led them out of Egypt's slavery. Before doing any of that, he was the Messenger of Yahweh who promised Abraham and Jacob that they would be his ancestors according to his human nature which he would assume in Mary's womb.

7. Sin and grace in Genesis

As should be evident from the preceding discussion, sin and grace are demonstrated by their constant interplay throughout Genesis. Though humankind fell into sin and deserved to be completely wiped off the face of the earth, in his grace God promised a saviour to Adam and Eve and later saved the entire human race through the preservation of Noah and his family. Though Abraham's faith in God's promise to bless and protect him wavered when he repeatedly deceived others about his relationship with Sarah (12:10–20; 20:1–18), God nevertheless was graciously patient with Israel's first patriarch, and time and again affirmed his promise to him.

In fact, the sins of wilfulness, deception, trickery and lies characterize the patriarchal families throughout Genesis. Isaac repeated his father's deceptive ways (12:11–13) when he lied about Rebekah (26:6–11). Despite God's pronouncement (25:23), Isaac insisted on attempting to give the greater blessing to Esau, leading to Rebekah and Jacob's deception and lying (ch. 27). Laban deceived Jacob, and gave him Leah for a bride instead of Rachel (29:13–30). Rachel misled her father when she fled with Jacob from Paddan-aram (31:30–35). Jacob's sons deceived him into thinking Joseph was dead (37:31–35). When Judah refused to provide a husband for Tamar, his widowed daughter-in-law, she resorted to a ruse in order to bear children for the family line (ch. 38).

Yet despite all of this, God continued to work out his gracious plan for humanity. Through Leah, God would give Judah to Jacob as the bearer of the messianic promise (29:35; 49:8–12). Through the betrayed Joseph, God would preserve his people even though his brothers acted with evil intent (50:20). Through one of the twin sons of Tamar – Perez – God would bring forth a line leading to the great king David (Ruth 4:18–22) and to David's greater son, Jesus (Matt. 1:1–16; Luke 3:23–33).

8. Conclusion

Genesis not only relates beginnings, but it also serves as the foundation for the rest of the Old Testament. Here Moses first teaches about sin and the promise of redemption of the world through the Saviour to come. In its pages readers can see clearly the contrast between their own fallen nature and the great love, grace and faithfulness of God. Themes found first in Genesis grow throughout the rest of the Old Testament until they bud and flower in the New Testament in the person of Jesus, the Christ.

ANALYSIS

1. CREATION (1:1 – 2:3)
A. Day one (1:1–5)
B. A second day (1:6–8)
C. A third day (1:9–13)
D. A fourth day (1:14–19)
E. A fifth day (1:20–23)
F. The sixth day (1:24–31)
    i. The creation of land animals (1:24–25)
    ii. The creation of humans (1:26–27)
    iii. God blesses humans (1:28–31)
G. The seventh day (2:1–3)

2. THE ORIGIN AND SPREAD OF SIN (2:4 – 4:26)
A. The creation of humans (2:4–25)
    i. Setting (2:4–7)
    ii. Synopsis (2:8)
    iii. God plants a garden (2:9–14)
    iv. The creation of man and woman (2:15–25)
B. The fall into sin (3:1–24)

C. The consequences of sin (4:1–26)
  i. Cain murders Abel (4:1–16)
  ii. Lamech exceeds Cain's sin (4:17–24)
  iii. Seth and Enosh (4:25–26)

3. THE FAMILY OF ADAM (5:1 – 6:8)
  A. Genealogy from Adam to Noah (5:1–32)
  B. Noah's righteousness among sinful humanity (6:1–8)

4. NOAH AND HIS FAMILY (6:9 – 9:29)
  A. The flood leads to God's covenant with Noah (6:9 – 9:17)
    i. God's revelation to Noah concerning the flood (6:9–22)
    ii. Noah and his family enter the ark (7:1–10)
    iii. The flood (7:11–24)
    iv. The flood recedes (8:1–14)
    v. Noah leaves the ark and receives the Lord's promise (8:15–22)
    vi. God's covenant with Noah (9:1–17)
  B. Noah's prophecy concerning his sons (9:18–29)

5. THE FAMILY OF NOAH'S SONS (10:1 – 11:9)
  A. Genealogies: Noah's descendants through his three sons (10:1–32)
    i. Introduction (10:1)
    ii. Japheth's descendants (10:2–5)
    iii. Ham's descendants (10:6–20)
    iv. Shem's descendants (10:21–31)
    v. Summary (10:32)
  B. Sin at the tower of Babylon (11:1–9)

6. THE FAMILY OF SHEM: GENEALOGY FROM SHEM TO TERAH (11:10–26)

7. THE FAMILY OF TERAH: ABRAM'S RESPONSE TO GOD'S CALL (11:27 – 12:20)
  A. Terah and his sons (11:27–32)
  B. The call of Abram (12:1–9)
  C. Abram in Egypt: he deceives Pharaoh (12:10–20)

8. THE FAMILY OF TERAH: ABRAM'S FAITHFULNESS REFLECTED IN HIS RELATIONSHIP WITH LOT (13:1 – 14:24)

    A. Abram and Lot separate (13:1–18)
    B. Abram rescues Lot (14:1–16)
    C. Melchizedek blesses Abram (14:17–24)

9. THE FAMILY OF TERAH: YAHWEH'S COVENANT AND ABRAM'S RESPONSE (15:1 – 17:27)

    A. Yahweh's covenant with Abram (15:1–21)
    B. Abram fathers Ishmael by Hagar (16:1–16)
    C. Yahweh's covenant and its sign: circumcision (17:1–27)

10. THE FAMILY OF TERAH: YAHWEH'S REPEATED PROMISE AND ABRAHAM'S RESPONSE (18:1 – 19:38)

    A. Abraham's three visitors (18:1–33)
       i. Yahweh promises Abraham a son (18:1–15)
       ii. Abraham pleads for Sodom (18:16–33)
    B. Lot rescued from Sodom (19:1–29)
    C. Lot's sons by his daughters (19:30–38)

11. THE FAMILY OF TERAH: ABRAHAM RECEIVES THE PROMISED SON (20:1 – 21:34)

    A. Abraham in Gerar: he deceives Abimelech (20:1–18)
    B. The birth of Isaac (21:1–7)
    C. Hagar and Ishmael sent away (21:8–21)
    D. Abraham's covenant with Abimelech (21:22–34)

12. THE FAMILY OF TERAH: THE PROMISE TO ABRAHAM CONTINUED IN ISAAC (22:1 – 24:67)

    A. The sacrifice of Isaac (22:1–19)
    B. News of Nahor's family (22:20–24)
    C. Sarah's death and burial (23:1–20)
    D. Isaac marries Rebekah (24:1–67)
       i. Abraham commissions his servant (24:1–9)
       ii. The servant meets Rebekah (24:10–27)
       iii. The servant obtains Rebekah as a wife for Isaac (24:28–54a)

B. Jacob deceived by Laban (29:15–30)
C. The births of Jacob's sons (29:31 – 30:24)
D. Yahweh blesses Jacob: his flocks increase (30:25–43)

18. THE FAMILY OF ISAAC: JACOB RETURNS TO THE PROMISED LAND (31:1 – 33:20)
A. Jacob leaves Paddan-aram (31:1–21)
B. Jacob and Laban part ways (31:22–55 [MT 31:22 – 32:1])
    i. Laban pursues Jacob (31:22–35)
    ii. Jacob's covenant with Laban (31:36–55 [MT 31:36 – 32:1])
C. Jacob returns to Canaan (32:1 – 33:20 [MT 32:2 – 33:20])
    i. Jacob sends word to Esau of his return (32:1–23 [MT 32:2–24])
    ii. Jacob wrestles with God (32:24–32 [MT 32:25–33])
    iii. Jacob meets Esau (33:1–20)

19. THE FAMILY OF ISAAC: JACOB'S TIME IN CANAAN BEFORE ISAAC'S DEATH (34:1 – 35:29)
A. The rape of Dinah (34:1–31)
B. Yahweh again blesses Jacob at Bethel (35:1–15)
C. Rachel's death (35:16–20)
D. Reuben's sin (35:21–22a)
E. Jacob's sons (35:22b–26)
F. Isaac's death (35:27–29)

20. ESAU'S FAMILY: ESAU'S WIVES AND SONS (36:1–8)

21. ESAU'S FAMILY: ESAU'S FAMILY IN THE MOUNTAINS OF SEIR (36:9 – 37:1)
A. Esau's sons and the chiefs of the Edomite clans (36:9–19)
B. Seir's sons and the chiefs of the Horite clans (36:20–30)
C. The kings of Edom and the chiefs of the Edomite clans (36:31–43)
D. Jacob in Canaan (37:1)

22. THE FAMILY OF JACOB: JOSEPH AS A YOUNG BOY IN CANAAN (37:2–36)
A. Joseph's dreams (37:2–11)
B. Joseph sold into slavery (37:12–36)

23. THE FAMILY OF JACOB: JUDAH'S SONS BY TAMAR (38:1–30)

24. THE FAMILY OF JACOB: JOSEPH IS BLESSED BY GOD IN EGYPT (39:1 – 41:57)
A. Joseph in Potiphar's house (39:1–20)
  i. God blesses Joseph (39:1–6)
  ii. Joseph resists Potiphar's wife (39:7–20)
B. Joseph in prison (39:21 – 40:23)
  i. God blesses Joseph (39:21–23)
  ii. Joseph interprets dreams in prison (40:1–23)
C. Joseph becomes Pharaoh's administrator (41:1–57)
  i. Joseph interprets Pharaoh's dreams (41:1–36)
  ii. Joseph given high rank by Pharaoh (41:37–45)
  iii. Joseph as administrator (41:46–57)

25. THE FAMILY OF JACOB: THE FAMINE BRINGS JOSEPH'S BROTHERS TO EGYPT (42:1 – 45:28)
A. Jacob's sons' first trip to Egypt (42:1–26)
B. Jacob's sons return to him (42:27–38)
C. Jacob's sons return to Egypt with Benjamin (43:1–34)
D. Joseph is reunited with his brothers (44:1 – 45:28)
  i. Joseph accuses his brothers of theft (44:1–17)
  ii. Judah's plea for Benjamin (44:18–34)
  iii. Joseph reveals himself to his brothers (45:1–15)
  iv. Pharaoh invites Jacob and his sons to live in Egypt (45:16–28)

26. THE FAMILY OF JACOB: JACOB'S TIME IN EGYPT (46:1 – 47:27)
A. Jacob goes to Egypt (46:1 – 47:12)
  i. God sends Jacob to Egypt (46:1–7)
  ii. Jacob's family as they enter Egypt (46:8–27)
  iii. Joseph prepares for his family to meet Pharaoh (46:28–34)
  iv. Pharaoh welcomes Jacob (47:1–12)

B. Contrast between Jacob's family and the native Egyptians during the remaining years of famine (47:13–27)
    i. Pharaoh acquires all of the land in Egypt (47:13–26)
    ii. Israel settles in Goshen (47:27)

27. THE FAMILY OF JACOB: JACOB'S AND JOSEPH'S LAST ACTS (47:28 – 50:26)

A. Jacob makes Joseph promise to bury him in Canaan (47:28–31)
B. Jacob blesses Joseph's sons (48:1–22)
C. Jacob's final acts (49:1–33)
    i. Jacob's final blessing for his sons (49:1–28)
    ii. Jacob's final words and death (49:29–33)
D. Joseph's final acts (50:1–26)
    i. Jacob's burial in Canaan (50:1–14)
    ii. Joseph forgives his brothers (50:15–21)
    iii. Joseph's death (50:22–26)

COMMENTARY

1. CREATION (1:1 – 2:3)

Context

Genesis' account of the origin of the heavens and earth not only reveals God's world as he made it for humans to inhabit, but also reveals God himself as the almighty transcendent Creator who was not brought into being but who brought into being all things through his word and will. It serves as the foundation upon which the rest of the book is built, and especially introduces the book's view of humans as a creation of one God who also created the world which humans inhabit.

Comment
A. Day one (1:1–5)

The first five verses of the Bible introduce God's creative acts on the first day. God is elsewhere said to be the creator of heaven and earth (Isa. 40:28; 45:18; see also Isa. 44:24; Jer. 10:16; 51:19; Eph. 3:8–9; Col. 1:16; Rev. 4:11).[1] Therefore, the first verse cannot simply

---

1. This is also affirmed in early Jewish literature outside of the Bible (e.g. 2 Maccabees 7:28).

be a summary of everything else in the chapter but must be a statement of creation of the earth before it was *formless and void* (1:2). God's existence outside of time and space, however, is simply assumed by the author: he created, but he himself has no origin. Moreover, unless one posits an unmentioned (and, therefore, unlikely) gap in time between the creation of heaven and earth and God's activity beginning at 1:3, the creation mentioned in 1:1 is part of the activity that is later summed up by 1:5 as *one day*.

1. *In the beginning* is a statement that locates the creation of space, matter and time when God, including the person of the Son of God, already was (John 1:1–3; 17:5, 24). While some versions attempt to take this phrase as the beginning of a clause completed in verse 3 ('When God first created . . . God said . . .'; cf. NRSV, TNK), there is little support for this, and it could imply that verse 2 is stating that the earth was pre-existent and not part of creation. Most versions as early as the LXX take this as an independent clause (CSB, ESV, GW, NET, NIV) and this verse as a complete sentence. The word for *beginning* (*rēšît*) denotes the initial portion of something.[2] Here it is the initial stage of creation, which is the bringing forth of the raw material of the universe that will be shaped by God's almighty power into a complete and good world.

Created is a word that in Hebrew is used only of God's activity. It occurs six times in this opening account of creation. While at 2:3 it is used as a summary for all of God's activity in this narrative, in the first five instances it introduces new things brought into being: the heavens and earth (v. 1), animate life that is endowed with the *breath of life* (vv. 21, 30) and human beings bearing *the image of God* (v. 27 [three times]). *Created* is in contrast to the Hebrew word for *do* or *make*, which is used throughout this account for making and forming things from already created items or as a general word for God's work (vv. 7, 11, 12, 16, 25, 26, 31; 2:2, 3).

---

2. For example, at 10:10 it denotes the initial extent of Nimrod's kingdom. At Exod. 23:19 and in many other passages it denotes the first portion of the harvest. At Job 8:7; 42:12 it refers to the first part of Job's life. At Jer. 26:1 it designates the first years of Jehoiakim's reign.

2. *Now the earth* places the narrative in a geocentric stance. Everything in the narrative from this point forward will be told from this point of view. However, *formless and void* describes the earth's initial condition. *Formless* (Hebrew *tōhû*) elsewhere is a description of wildernesses (Deut. 32:10; Job 6:18; 12:24; Ps. 107:40; Isa. 45:19) or of a city in ruins (Isa. 24:10; 34:11), or is a word for emptiness (Job 26:7; Isa. 40:17, 23; 41:29; 44:9). *Void* (Hebrew *bōhû*) occurs only with *formless* (Isa. 34:11; Jer. 4:22), and here forms a hendiadys – one concept expressed by two words. This verse is a parenthetical comment that describes the earth as amorphous and waiting to be filled by God's creative activity.

Darkness is not simply the absence of light, but is also a creation of God (Isa. 45:7). So is the *deep* (Hebrew *těhôm*), which signifies the primeval ocean that covered the earth. This word shares a common Semitic root with the word *Tiamat*, the name of the rival of the gods in the Assyrian creation myths. Previously it was argued that this pointed to Genesis borrowing from these Mesopotamian sources, but it is now clear that the Hebrew word and concepts are not derived from or dependent on these pagan myths. Instead, the deep is part of God's created earth which he will shape into the inhabited world.

This verse also contains the first mention of *the Spirit of God*. While the word for *Spirit* could also denote a wind, this phrase occurs fifteen more times in the Old Testament where it always means God's Spirit or a spirit sent from God (i.e. it is not simply a wind).[3] Here the reader's attention is called to God's presence focused on the earth, preparing now for the acts which will transform it into the ideal place for those who will bear his image.

3. *God said* marks the power of God to simply speak things into existence (2 Cor. 4:6; Heb. 11:3; 2 Pet. 3:5). This phrase will be used ten times in the creation account (vv. 1:6, 9, 11, 14, 20, 24, 26, 28, 29). God said that *light* should come into being. Light precedes the

---

3. Only at 1 Sam. 16:15–16, 23; 18:10 is this phrase used for a (harmful)
   spirit sent from God. Elsewhere it denotes God's Spirit of wisdom,
   insight and prophecy (Gen. 41:38; Exod. 31:3; 35:31; Num. 24:2;
   1 Sam. 10:10; 11:6; 19:20, 23; 2 Chr. 15:1; 24:20; Ezek. 11:24).

creation of the sun and other heavenly luminaries. The source of the light is not stated, but elsewhere the Scriptures connect it with God himself in the person of the Word of God, Jesus (John 1:1–5). At the end of all things light will again be provided by God and the Lamb without need of the sun (Rev. 22:5).

4–5. *Good* is the judgment of God on his creation of light. This assessment will be repeated for other creations of God (vv. 10, 12, 18, 21, 25) until all of creation is very good (v. 31). After creating light God *separated* it. This separation is another key aspect of God's creative activity that will be repeated on days two and four (vv. 6–7, 14–18). Here the separation is between light and darkness. The narrative since 1:2 has been geocentric. The separation is implied as being between night and daytime. As the Creator, God has the right also to label his creation of darkness and light as *day* and *night*. The first day's length is summarized by the statement *there was evening and there was morning*, perhaps better understood as 'In summary, there was evening, then there was morning.'[4] The evening and morning are then said to make *one day*. In most versions this is translated *the first day*. However, the Hebrew text contains no article ('the'), and the number is 'one', not 'first'.[5] The beginning of the day is reckoned from evening. This would dictate the way sacred days were celebrated in Israel (Exod. 12:6; Lev. 23:5, 32; Neh. 13:19).

B. A second day (1:6–8)

Since the basic description of the earth as it was originally created highlighted earth's darkness and the deep, that is, the waters

---

4. This type of chronological summary statement is also used in the primeval history genealogies at 5:5, 8, 11, 14, 17, 18, 20, 23–24, 27, 31; 9:29. For instance, at 5:5 the meaning is 'In summary, all the days of Adam that he lived were 930 years, and then he died.' See also the chronological summary statements at Judg. 10:2; 12:7, 9–10, 11–12, 14–15; Ruth 1:4–5; 2 Kgs 11:3. See Steinmann (2016–17).

5. See the analysis in Steinmann (2002) that demonstrates that the Hebrew 'one' is not a circumlocution for 'first' in this context. Also note that the LXX, the oldest known translation of Genesis, translated this as *one day*.

covering the earth, both needed additional creative acts. The darkness was complemented by light on day one. Now on the second day God divides the waters and creates the sky as one item that complements them.

6–7. God's next creative act was to order that an *expanse* be formed between the waters. The Hebrew word for *expanse* (*rāqîaʿ*) is related to the verb meaning 'stretch out' or 'spread out' and is used elsewhere of God's spreading out the heavens and the earth (Ps. 136:6; Isa. 42:5; 44:24). It is also used at Job 37:18 to describe God's spreading out the clouds. Here the expanse is the sky with the upper waters – the clouds – and the waters below the sky – the sea.

8. Once again God labels what he has brought into being, calling the expanse *sky* (CSB; traditionally *heavens*). The repeat of the summary formula for a day (evening and morning) is followed by noting *a second day*. While this is traditionally rendered *the second day*, the Hebrew text contains no definite article here, nor for the third, fourth or fifth days.

C. A third day (1:9–13)

God continues to work with the primeval seas on the third day. Here he orders the waters to part in order to form dry land. Thus, the second and third days create items that contrast with the watery *deep* that was originally part of the earth. The seas are now distinct from both the sky created on the second day and the dry land created on the third day. The seas are now complemented by both sky and land, just as the light became the complement of darkness on day one. The third day also relates a second major work of God: the creation of plants.

9–10. Once more God's creative acts are accomplished by his word. For the last time in the creation account God is said to name his creations: *earth* and *seas*. This first work on the third day is again called *good*.

11–12. God next creates *vegetation* (CSB) which appears to be classified into two types: plants that bear seeds, and trees (plants that bear fruit which contain seeds). *Seed* or *descendant* (when used of humans) is an important Hebrew term in Genesis, occurring sixty-five times, almost one-quarter of its occurrences in the entire Old

Testament. This term reveals God's provision for the continued reproduction of life.

The plants are said to produce seed *according to their kinds*. While this should not be understood narrowly in terms of the modern scientific concept of species, it does reflect God's created order for the world in that the plants produce offspring that share the qualities of their progenitors. For the second time on this day, God saw that what he had created was good, thereby demonstrating two distinct creative acts on one day.

13. The chronological summary formula is repeated again, noting *a third day*.

D. A fourth day (1:14–19)

This day sees the creation of physical light sources (as opposed to the light source on day one). For the first time God's creative word also notes the function that a part of his creation will serve as illumination for an observer having a terrestrial point of view, thereby continuing the geocentric perspective that was first introduced at 1:2. This mention of function already hints that God's ultimate goal was the creation of humans.

The narrative for the fourth day has a strong anti-mythological, anti-polytheistic cast to it. The sun, moon and stars are creations of the one God, not gods to be worshipped. They are assigned functions by the true God (Acts 14:15; 17:24), and therefore are not self-actualizing and autonomous gods.

14–15. According to God's own command, the lights in the sky were explicitly designed for three purposes. One was to distinguish day from night. The second was to serve as signs for the passage of time by marking *seasons*, *days* and *years*. The third purpose was to provide light on earth.

16–18. These verses pay special attention to the two greater lights in the earth's sky, with the stars mentioned only in passing. The text avoids the Hebrew words for sun and moon, since those words could signify the pagan deities associated with these light sources. As with the heavenly lights in general, these lights are said to serve three purposes: to provide light on earth, to be the dominant lights during day and night, and to separate light from darkness, a function that light had been serving since the first day (1:4).

19. The chronological summary formula is repeated again, noting *a fourth day*.

E. A fifth day (1:20–23)

The creation of the first animal life demonstrates God's concern to fill the seas and the skies, the object of his attention on the second day. This life merits God's first blessing.

20–21. The life created on this day is distinct from the plant life created on the third day because it is described as *living creatures*, an expression that applies to all animal life. It is an important description of fish, birds and beasts in this chapter (vv. 21, 24) and again in the account of the great flood (9:10, 12, 15–16).[6] The second use of the word *created* in chapter 1 highlights this new and important aspect of God's creatures.

The sea creatures are described in two categories: *large* or *great sea creatures* and all other creatures in the water. The Hebrew word for the large sea creatures, *tannîn*, is a cognate of the Canaanite word for the sea-dwelling enemy of Baal. Once again Genesis takes an anti-mythological stance by depicting these animals as subject to God. He is able to subdue them (Ps. 74:13–14; Isa. 27:1; 51:9). Elsewhere the word is simply used to denote some kind of land or sea animal (Exod. 7:9, 10, 12; Deut. 32:33; Ps. 91:13; Ezek. 29:3; 32:2).

The creatures of the air are simply described collectively as *winged bird*. The word translated *bird* here can also include flying insects. The verdict of God once again notes the goodness of his work.

22. The Scriptures' first blessing is for the fertility of these newly formed creatures so that they can fill the seas and multiply on earth. God's blessing is not simply a wish, but it endows his creatures with the ability to do what the blessing states.

23. The chronological summary formula is repeated again, documenting *a fifth day*.

---

6. See also 1:30 where it is often translated *breath of life* (CSB, ESV, NET, NIV). The phrase 'living creature' is also used at Lev. 11:10, 46; Ezek. 47:9.

F. The sixth day (1:24–31)

Like the third day, the sixth day sees two creative acts, one pronounced *good* by God (v. 25), and the other *very good* (v. 31). Not only is the sixth day the climactic day of creation, but it also serves to draw two distinctions. One is the distinction between the living creatures created on this day and the previous day. This distinction is highlighted by humans alone being endowed with the image of God. A second distinction is between God and humans. The humans God creates possess his image, but they are not God – unlike God they are to multiply, and they also need God's provision of food just as the living creatures do.

i. The creation of land animals (1:24–25)

24–25. God's command to the earth to produce living creatures is parallel to his command on the third day that the earth produce plants (v. 11). The animals are listed in three broad categories: domestic animals (CSB, ESV, NIV: *livestock*), animals that creep or crawl on the ground (perhaps reptiles and some insects among others), and *wild animals* (GW, NET, NIV, NRSV). Like the plants, the animals are to reproduce *according to their kinds*.

ii. The creation of humans (1:26–27)

26. God's use of the plural *Let us . . . our image . . . our likeness* has been the source of much discussion from earliest times and has generated a number of proposals as to its meaning.[7] Among the more common theories is that God is including the angels or the heavenly court. However, humans are not depicted as sharing the angelic image anywhere in Scripture. Another theory is that this use of the plural depicts God's majesty, though this is without grammatical support.[8] Still another hypothesis is that the plural depicts God's

---

7. Clines (1968) and Murphy (2013) survey the various proposals.

8. The Hebrew verb translated is *let us*, with *us* included as part of the verb's meaning. JM (347, §144e n. 7) remarks that the plural of majesty does not exist in verbs in biblical Hebrew.

self-deliberation.[9] However, this use cannot be demonstrated elsewhere in the Old Testament.[10] Instead, the text clearly depicts God as an inward plurality and outwardly singular – *our image* . . . *his image* (vv. 26–27), and the mention of God's Spirit at verse 2 supports this.[11] While some early Christians took this as a reference to the Trinity, the concept of one God in three persons is only implicit here at best, and is revealed with fuller clarity only in the New Testament.

God's expressed desire is to make *man* (CSB, ESV), or, better stated, *humankind* (NET, NRSV) or *humans* (GW), since immediately God refers to humanity as *them*.[12] They are to display God's image in that they will rule the animals created on days five and six.

God's image in humans is further defined as a *likeness* (see 5:1), indicating that in some respects humans are to be like God. The exact ways in which humans are to be like God are not defined, but later, Adam having a son in his likeness and image (5:3) implies that the image of God was marred by sin but in some sense remains part of every human (9:6; Jas 3:9).

27. The threefold use of *created* emphasizes the high position for which God created humans. Twice they are said to be created in God's image, and once that they were created male and female. This emphasizes that both men and women were the bearers of the image of God.

iii. God blesses humans (1:28–31)

28–30. The second blessing given by God at creation is specifically for humans. It is twofold: the blessing of fertility and of dominion over the animals. Moreover, God provides for humans and animals through plants that are to serve as their food.

31. Finally, God judges his entire creation to be *very good*. With humans at the climax of his creation, this marks the completion of

---

9. Arnold (2009: 44).

10. That is, apart from uses in the early chapters of Genesis. See 3:22; 11:7.

11. Clines (1968: 68–69); Hasel (1975: 65–66); Wenham (1994: 134); Mathews (1996: 163).

12. *Man* is the Hebrew word *'ādām* that is also used as the name *Adam*.

God's work. The chronological summary formula is repeated again, this time emphasizing the conclusion of all of God's creative activity by featuring the first use of the definite article: *the sixth day*, or, more precisely, *a day, the sixth one*.

G. The seventh day (2:1–3)

While the accounts of the first six days follow similar patterns, the seventh day is unique, which may explain why the medieval chapter division intervenes. Nevertheless, there are good reasons for considering it a part of the creation narrative. It is striking that the first use of the *tôlĕdôt* formula (see the Introduction) occurs after the account of God's blessing the seventh day. Moreover, twice in Exodus the seventh day is explicitly connected with the previous six (Exod. 20:11; 31:17).

The uniqueness of the seventh day is that God did no new creative work. That cessation of work marked the holiness of this day and became a model for Israel's need to sanctify the Sabbath (Exod. 16:23; 20:8, 11; 31:14; 35:2; Deut. 5:12; Neh. 9:14; 10:31, 33; 13:22; Isa. 58:13).

At the end of this day there is no refrain like those appended to the other six days. This lack of the refrain is a literary device that sets this day apart and serves to emphasize its holiness.

1. This verse summarizes the previous six days and prepares for the seventh. The completion of God's work covered heaven and earth and *everything in them* (CSB). This last phrase translates the Hebrew 'their army', and is often used to describe the stars.[13] The implication is that God had arranged the contents of heaven and earth with each in its own place and with its own function, just as soldiers are organized into an army.

2–3. The phrase *the seventh day* occurs three times to denote three activities of God. First, by the seventh day, he had completed his work. Second, on the seventh day he *rested* – the word can

---

13. Deut. 4:19; 17:3; 1 Kgs 22:19; 2 Kgs 17:16; 21:3, 5; 23:4; 2 Chr. 18:18; 33:3, 5; Neh. 9:6; Isa. 24:21; 34:4; Jer. 8:2; 19:13; 33:22; Dan. 4:35; 8:10; see Acts 7:42.

mean to cease, and here denotes cessation from work. Finally, God blessed the seventh day and declared it to be holy because he ceased his work of creation. It is interesting to note that Genesis mentions God only ceasing creation. God did not cease all work, and his acts of blessing animals (1:22) and humans (1:28) continued.

Meaning

The creation narrative forms the basis for understanding God's relationship with his creation and its creatures throughout Genesis. It sets the stage for the monotheistic tone of the rest of the book. Moreover, it demonstrates God's right to order and direct the affairs of humans, such as his sending the great flood (chs. 7–9), confusing human languages (11:1–9), striking Pharaoh with plagues (12:17), empowering the aged Sarah to bear a son (21:1–2), building a family for Jacob (29:31 – 30:24) and giving Joseph the ability to interpret dreams (40:8; 41:16). Moreover, the blessings that God places on animals and humans continue throughout the book: through Noah, God saves all living creatures from the flood, and he shows mercy to all nations through Abraham, Isaac and Jacob (18:18; 22:18; 26:4).

Additional note on the seven days of creation

In recent decades the interpretation of the creation week has seen several proposals concerning how the days of creation should be understood, and this is especially true among evangelical Christian scholars.[14] While many evangelicals continue to read the text as setting forth historical days making up an actual week, others have offered contrasting ways to read 1:1 – 2:3. Most of these

---

14. The essays gathered in Charles (2013) present a range of views from American evangelical scholars on how to read 1:1 – 2:24 and, therefore, whether to understand the days as regular (solar) days or simply as some type of literary device for presenting God as the creator of all things without intending the seven days to be understood as the first historical week.

readings of Genesis contain variations and combinations of several proposed interpretations that have circulated for a century or more.

Among these interpretations is the 'framework hypothesis'. This explanation of the six days of creation notes the parallels between the first three days and the last three days (see Introduction). It then posits that this is a literary device to demonstrate God's orderly creation which is, therefore, not intended to be understood literally. Thus, the narrative of the duration of the creation was not intended to depict six actual days. The problem with this use of the framework hypothesis is that it draws a false distinction between the literary aspects of the text and the orderliness of creation as well as the text's chronological features, as if these features cannot coexist in one composition.

Another attempt to explain the six days as figurative is the 'analogical day theory'. This holds that the days are simply an analogy to a week that ends with the seventh day, a Sabbath. God is analogous to a human labourer who does his work in six days and rests on the seventh. The obvious problem with this approach is that later passages in the Scriptures do not state that God's work of creation is 'like six days' followed by a Sabbath. Instead, they state that God did his work of creating the world in six days and then rested on the seventh day, and that Israel are to do the same every week in their work (Exod. 20:11; 31:17). In addition, at Exodus 20:8–11 and 31:12–17 the analogy runs in the opposite direction: the Israelite seven-day working week is compared to God's work of creation, not vice versa. Moreover, it is curious that the provision for the Sabbath year makes no mention of the creation week (Exod. 23:10–11; Lev. 25:1–6, 20–22; Deut. 15:1–3; 31:10–13). There an analogy between the seven days of the Genesis creation and the seven-year cycle of work and rest for the land is obvious, but the Scriptures never make the analogy explicit. If the days were merely analogical, the analogy is more than fitting for the Sabbath-year cycle, but the Scriptures never give voice to such an analogy.

A third approach involves comparing Genesis to the creation myths of the Ancient Near East. Often it is observed that Genesis ought to be read against the backdrop of the generally held ancient views concerning the origin and structure of the universe (i.e. ancient cosmology). While no-one wishes to divorce Genesis from its ancient context, and some rough parallels can be found, it is clear that Genesis is presenting a view of creation that is counter to the most important assumptions of ancient cosmologies from Mesopotamia and Egypt: Genesis is rigidly monotheistic instead of polytheistic; Genesis does not present autonomous entities (gods), but presents creation as subject to the will of the Creator. Genesis, in contrast to the ancient cosmologies, displays God's work as organized into days. This is an important difference and not to be lightly dismissed. The comparison with Ancient Near Eastern creation myths and cosmologies does not demonstrate that these days are to be understood figuratively, and in fact could be pressed in the opposite direction: in contrast to other ancient creation accounts, Genesis' insistence on days places God's work in time, in actual history, and portrays time itself as a creation of the Almighty.

There are compelling reasons for understanding 1:1–31 as depicting six actual, regular days. All six days of creation are defined as the passing of both evening and morning, and the mention of *days and years* on the fourth day (v. 14) refers to normal days and years. The regulations for the Sabbath day are built on the Israelite workday being parallel to God's work at creation (Exod. 20:8–11; 31:12–17) without any hint that the creation days are something other than ordinary days. Like the days enumerated in the refrain *there was an evening and there was a morning, a/the* [number] *day* in 1:1–31, the days in Israel's sacred reckoning begin at sundown in the evening (Exod. 12:6, 18–19; Lev. 23:32; Deut. 16:6; Neh. 13:19–22; Luke 23:54). From this evidence it is hard to escape the conclusion of Basil the Great (c.330–379):

> *And the evening and the morning were one day.* Why does Scripture say 'one day' not 'the first day'? Before speaking to us of the second, the third, and the fourth days, would it not have been more natural to call that one the first which began the series? If it therefore says 'one day', it is from a wish to determine the measure of day and night, and to combine the time that they contain. Now twenty-four hours fill up the space of one day – we mean of a day and of a night ... It is as though it said:

twenty-four hours measure the space of a day, or that, in reality, a day is the time that the heavens starting from one point take to return there. Thus, every time that, in the revolution of the sun, evening and morning occupy the world, their periodical succession never exceeds the space of one day.[15]

---

15. Basil of Caesarea, *The Hexaemeron*, in P. Schaff and H. Wace (eds.), trans. B. Jackson, *St. Basil: Letters and Select Works* (New York: Christian Literature Company, 1895), 8.64.

2. THE ORIGIN AND SPREAD OF SIN
(2:4 – 4:26)

This section of Genesis is marked as the history of the heavens and earth (2:4) and presents the creation of humans and an explanation of how they came into being with the image of God yet no longer possess the inherent holy and righteous nature that God has. Whereas the previous section of Genesis demonstrated that everything God created was *very good* (1:31), this section moves from Adam and Eve possessing the full image of God to humans who have surrendered that image and now only possess a shadow of it in their estrangement from God. One indication of this is the observation made by God himself in later chapters of Genesis that instead of being holy as God is holy, humans are constantly inclined towards evil (6:5; 8:21). As this section closes, some humans are murderous whereas others finally begin to *call on the name of the Lord* (4:26).

A. The creation of humans (2:4–25)

Context
This portion of chapter 2 is often called a second creation account, usually based on the Documentary Hypothesis which assigns the previous section of Genesis to a different source. However, it is

clear that this is not a separate account of creation, but instead offers more detail on the sixth day of creation (1:24–31). This account focuses on the creation of humans, their intended purpose and their relationship to each other as man and woman.

Comment
i. Setting (2:4–7)

These verses give the setting for the account of the creation of humans, describing the earth as it was before human habitation. After the notice that sets this apart as a separate section (v. 4), the next verse notes the need for both rain to make the desert plants grow and a human to till the soil for cultivated plants (v. 5). So God provided the water for the desert plants (v. 6), and humans to cultivate other plants (v. 7).

4. The *account* (GW, NET, NIV) or 'generations' (ESV, NRSV) of the heavens and the earth denotes the first use of the *tôlĕdôt* formula in Genesis (see Introduction). This is the only time that the account is attributed to a thing rather than a person. This formula always introduces a new section of Genesis, and the use of similar statements elsewhere in the Old Testament also indicates this (Num. 3:1; Ruth 4:18; 1 Chr. 1:29). The account is of the *time* (CSB, GW) when they were created. The Hebrew text uses the word that is often translated 'day'. However, like the English word 'day', the Hebrew word can have several meanings depending on context: daytime, a twenty-four-hour period or a general time period. In 1:1–31 the days are defined as *evening and morning* (1:5, 8, 13, 19, 23, 31). Here the context is speaking of a more general era of creation encompassing the first five days of chapter 1.

5. *Shrub of the field* (CSB, NET) refers to plants of the desert wilderness that only sprout and grow after rain (21:15; Job 30:4, 7; see also Job 38:25–27). They had been created on the third day (1:9–13) but had not yet sprouted. *Plant of the field* (CSB, ESV, NET) refers to cultivated plants, especially grains (Exod. 9:22–25). The lack of desert plants could be solved with *rain*, and lack of plant cultivation could be solved with *a man to work the ground.*[1]

---

1. For further discussion, see Futato (1998).

6. To solve the lack of rain, God sent *streams* (NIV, NRSV) or a *mist* (ESV), which is better understood as a rain cloud rising from the earth.² The Hebrew word denotes a rain cloud at Job 36:27, and elsewhere in discussing creation the Scriptures note clouds rising from earth to provide water (Ps. 135:7; Jer. 10:13; 51:16). This rain cloud provided water for the rivers that irrigated the garden (2:10).

7. To solve the lack of someone to cultivate the land, God formed the man. The word *man*, in Hebrew *'ādām*, is not only the name of the first man, but also a play on words with the *ground* or *soil* (Hebrew *'ădāmâ*) from which he was formed. God's intimate involvement in the creation of humans is indicated by the anthropomorphic language of his breathing life into man's nostrils. Man became a *living being*, something he shared with the animals (1:20, 21, 24, 30).

ii. Synopsis (2:8)

This verse is a synopsis of the creation of the garden, which is treated in more detail at 2:9–14, and the placement of the man in the garden, a topic that is expanded in 2:15–25.

8. *Eden* is the area where the garden was placed, and *in the east* locates Eden for the ancient Israelite reader as east of the Promised Land.

iii. God plants a garden (2:9–14)

The garden created for the man included trees and a river. The garden's location is indicated by the four rivers whose mouths (literally, 'heads') converged to form Eden's river. The descriptions of the places where the rivers flowed indicates that the garden was probably in lower Mesopotamia near the Persian Gulf, though this is not certain.

9. The *tree of life* is mentioned several more times in the Old Testament as well as in Revelation. From 3:22–24 it is clear that the tree's fruit could endow humans with immortality. Interestingly, there is no mention of God telling Adam about the tree of life, and Eve later reveals no knowledge of it (cf. 3:2–3).

---

2. Futato (1998: 5–9); Rogland (2010); Wenham (1987: 58).

The *tree of the knowledge of good and evil* has been the subject of much speculation. However, the phrase *good and evil* is often used to denote the ability to decide or determine what is acceptable or unacceptable, legally correct or incorrect, and the fruit of this tree probably bestowed the proclivity to depend on oneself rather than God. It gave the inclination to determine what is morally tolerable or reprehensible independently from God's will. Note that when Solomon prayed for the ability to discern between good and evil, he was granted wisdom (1 Kgs 3:9–12; cf. Gen. 3:6). This explains why later the serpent promised Eve that she would become like God when she ate the fruit of this tree: it was a promise of moral autonomy (3:5).[3]

10–14. *Pishon* and *Gihon* are otherwise unknown. The Gihon is not the better-known spring in Jerusalem that also had this name (1 Kgs 1:33, 38, 45; 2 Chr. 32:30; 33:14). *Havilah* means 'sandy', and probably refers to the Arabian Desert south of Mesopotamia; it may have been associated with one of the descendants of Cush (10:7). The *land of Cush* in the Old Testament often refers to the region south of Egypt. However, here it probably refers to a portion of Mesopotamia later dominated by Nimrod, one of Cush's descendants (10:7–8).[4] *Bdellium* and *onyx* translate Hebrew words whose meaning is not certain.

iv. The creation of man and woman (2:15–25)

This expanded description of the creation of humans as male and female (1:27) notes God's special relationship with humans in that he personally gives them instructions about the trees in the garden. It also emphasizes the intimate relationship between the man and the woman who was formed from part of the man's body: they become one flesh through God's institution of marriage.

15–17. The man was formed before the woman (1 Cor. 11:8–9; 1 Tim. 2:13) and was given the instruction concerning eating fruit from the garden's trees.

---

3. Hamilton (1990: 165–166).
4. Hamilton (1990: 170); Wenham (1987: 65–66).

18–20. God sees the need for the man to have a *helper who will correspond to him* (vv. 18, 20). The word *helper* does not imply inferiority: God is often called a helper for humans (Exod. 18:4; Ps. 10:14; 27:9; 40:17; 118:7). In addition, God simply assumes that the man will provide names for the various types of animals (v. 19), since the man was created in God's image, and God gave names to various parts of creation (1:5, 10).

21–22. God took from the man a *rib* – a word that is used elsewhere to describe a ridge on a hill (2 Sam. 16:13) or panelling on a wall that resembles ribs (1 Kgs 7:3). God's act of bringing the woman to the man completes his act that started with his bringing the animals to him (2:19).

23. *Woman . . . man* forms a play on words both in English and in Hebrew. It is a forceful way of demonstrating that the man recognized the woman as designed especially for him, something that did not apply to any of the animals he had previously seen.

24–25. This is the first logical conclusion in Genesis. It notes the complementary nature inherent in the creation of the sexes. It also defines marriage as God's establishment for the proper relationship of the two sexes to each other (Matt. 19:5; Mark 10:7; 1 Cor. 6:16; Eph. 5:31). Marriage is intended to be permanent as the man is *united with his wife* (GW, NET, NIV). Because they are both perfect, their unashamed nakedness testifies to their ease with each other as creatures of God who are comfortable with the roles he has assigned to them.

Meaning
The creation of humans is carefully laid out in detail in Genesis 2 before moving on to the next section of this longer movement that illustrates sin and its consequences. The reader is shown the need for humans as the crown of God's creation and the caretakers of all he has made on earth. This account of God's design of humans in two complementary sexes who are intended to become one in marriage and to procreate expands on the shorter account of their creation given at Genesis 1:26–31. In this way Genesis presents marriage as a divine gift to humankind intended to benefit the entire earth with its plants and animals. Genesis, therefore, holds that

marriage is not merely a humanly devised convention to be changed
or adapted to new circumstances or conceptions of human
sexuality.

B. The fall into sin (3:1–24)

Context
This chapter pivots from God's good creation to a creation flawed
because of human rebellion. Whereas everything was very good
when God created it (1:31), now sin's effects can be felt in the
botanical realm through man's cultivation of plants (v. 18), in the
animal kingdom (v. 14) and even in the birth of humans (v. 16). In
fact, all of creation was and continues to be affected by human sin
(Rom. 8:20–22).

The narrative of the fall is not to be understood as a parable or
myth. In fact, the New Testament treats Adam and Eve as real
people. Jesus, the second Adam whose life, death and resurrection
reversed the curse on Adam, is a descendant of the first Adam
(Luke 3:23–38). He is the one man who brought life to everyone, in
contrast to Adam whose one trespass brought death to all humans
(Rom. 5:18–19; 1 Cor. 15:20–21). Paul also takes the narrative of
3:1–24 as historical fact, noting even the order of events (1 Tim.
2:13–14).

The origin of sin is the focus of events here. Later Genesis notes
that sin cascades down the generations (4:1–26), that Seth was born
in Adam's image, not God's (5:3), and that even human thoughts are
evil from the earliest age (6:5; see Jer. 32:30). This is developed
further in the New Testament. For example, Paul notes that
'sin came into the world through one man, and death through sin'
(Rom. 5:12). That death, according to Paul, is not simply physical
but also spiritual, since those who live according to the world's
ways and seek to satisfy their inborn desires are dead in their sins
(Eph. 2:1–3).

However, Genesis 3:1–24 is not simply about the effects of sin;
it is also about the compassion of God. He promised that the
serpent's head would be struck (v. 15), destroying the power of
death (Heb. 2:14; 1 John 3:8) and thereby giving life to those who
were dead in their sins (Eph. 2:4–5).

Comment

1. The description of the serpent as *more cunning* or *clever* than all the animals is a Hebrew play on words with Adam and Eve's state of nakedness (2:25): they are 'nude', and the serpent is 'shrewd'. They will seek to be wise (v. 6), only to realize they are *naked* (v. 7). The serpent's first cunning act is to question what God actually said, thereby raising doubt.

2–3. Eve repeats God's instructions about eating fruit, but adds that they are not to *touch* the fruit of the tree of knowledge. This addition to God's word – perhaps a production of Eve's logic about the fruit – signalled to the serpent Eve's vulnerability to his logic.

4–5. The serpent gives voice to the first open contradiction of God: *You will not die.* He then proceeds to claim to have knowledge of God's thoughts, and he portrays those thoughts as selfish: God wants no-one to be *like God knowing good and evil* (see comment on 2:9).

6. Eve's observation of the fruit attributed to it three properties: it was *good for food, delightful to look at* and *desirable for obtaining wisdom* (csb). She ate and gave some to Adam to eat. Adding to the scene's drama, it is told without reported conversation, though later God will allude to Eve's words to Adam (v. 17).

7. The result of eating the fruit was that the couple had their *eyes opened*, not to see with wisdom (cf. v. 5) but to behold their nakedness, which they were anxious to cover. Ironically, the rest of Scripture treats fallen humans as having closed eyes in spiritual matters. Eyes blinded by sin can only be opened by God's action (21:19; Num. 22:31; 24:3, 15; 2 Kgs 6:17, 20; Pss 119:18; 146:8; Isa. 35:5; 42:7; Luke 24:31; Acts 26:18).[5]

8–11. Adam and Eve's next encounter with God takes place during the *evening breeze* (csb, nrsv), literally the 'wind of the day'.[6]

---

5. See the discussion in Ortlund (2010) of the opening of the Emmaus disciples' eyes as a sort of reverse parallel to Adam and Eve's fall.

6. Recent suggestions that this phrase actually means 'in the wind of a storm', signalling God's wrath and causing Adam and Eve to hide, are without warrant. See Niehaus (1994); Stuart (2014: 259–265). The knowledge of guilt alone was enough to drive the pair to hide from God.

The confirmation that Adam and Eve now knew good and evil is provided by the fact that they *hid*, indicating that they knew their choice of good ran counter to God's notion of good. Their guilt-ridden actions – making clothes of fig leaves and hiding – were questioned by God.

12–13. Adam is the first human to speak with God, but when he does so, it is to blame Eve for the transgression and also to imply that the entire situation is God's fault, since it was caused by *the woman that* you *gave me* (v. 12). Not wanting the blame to lie with her, the woman seeks to shift it to the serpent (v. 13).

14–15. Since the blame has been shifted to the serpent, God first addresses him. Of the three who defied God, only the serpent is directly cursed. While the curse is often understood as the serpent being made to move on his belly, it ought to be noted that the other judgments of God do not transform the basic nature of either the woman or the man: the woman was always the one to bear children through labour (v. 16),[7] and the man was always intended to labour with the soil (v. 17). Therefore, the curse most likely did not transform the locomotion of snakes. Instead, that locomotion will now be subject to futility: he will ingest *dust*, the raw material that was used to make Adam (2:7) and the dust that will be left as a result of human death (v. 19). The curse also involves the relationship between the serpent and the woman, the two whose actions began this narrative. Hostility will mark their relationship and the relationship of their offspring (literally, 'seed'). While the woman's *seed* is often understood as a collective singular to denote all of her descendants, Collins has recently demonstrated that because the following pronoun, *he*, is singular, the woman's seed refers to a particular descendant who will strike the serpent's head (Matt. 1:23; Gal. 4:4–5).[8] This passage was called the 'protoevangelium', the first gospel, by early Christian interpreters.

16. God moves next to the person who shifted the blame to the serpent. No curse is explicitly mentioned here, nor any explicit

---

7. Note that Eve was *created* female (1:27).

8. Collins (1997); see also Steinmann (2017a) as well as the discussion of the messianic promise in the Introduction.

reason for the fact that the consequences of sin will lead to labour pains. The Hebrew word for *pain* here is the same word that describes Adam's painful labour as a result of the curse on the soil (v. 17). Yet despite the difficulty of labour, the woman will continue to *desire* the love, companionship and intimacy of marriage to her husband. In recent times some have understood this desire to be a desire of the woman to dominate her husband, based on the use of the same word at 4:7.[9] However, 4:7 contains very difficult Hebrew and is not a reliable guide to understanding this term.[10]

17–19. The man, like the serpent, is told the reason for God's judgment on him: *Because you listened to your wife*. Adam – not Eve – had heard God's instruction (2:17–18). He instead chose to listen to his wife. The curse on the earth would bring Adam misery for the rest of his life as he toiled to provide food for himself and his family. The judgment on him, and therefore on all humans, is that they will return to the *dust* from which Adam was formed.

20. Adam's choice of a name for his wife is explained by the fact that she would be the mother of all humans. In Hebrew the name *Eve* sounds like the word for 'life', and may derive from the same root. This is an act of faith on Adam's part. He heard the promise of victory over the serpent through a descendant of the woman, such that the curse of death would be temporarily abated so that she could bear children.

21–24. The end of the narrative features a number of acts of God which can be viewed as further judgment on Adam and Eve but which are also acts of divine compassion: God provides clothes, and by restricting their access to the tree of life and banishing them from the garden, he prevents humans from living for ever in a permanent state of estrangement from their creator. The *cherubim* are mentioned elsewhere in the Old Testament in association with God's throne and presence (Exod. 36:35; 37:7–9; Ezek. 1:5; 10:15). Since God is the source of life, restricting access to the tree also

---

9. Arnold (2009: 70); Hamilton (1990: 201–202). This was first proposed by Foh (1975).

10. Condren (2017). Condren favours translating the word as 'return (to one's original place)' instead of *desire*.

restricted access to eternal communion with God. This access was
restored in Christ (Rom. 5:1–2; Eph. 3:11–12).

Meaning
This account of the first human sin introduces a prominent theme
that will run throughout the rest of the Genesis narrative: humans
– even the best of humans – are infected by sin and subject to its
effects. The continuation of the Genesis story in the next chapter
will demonstrate these effects. The situation, however, is not viewed
as irredeemable. God promised a seed of the woman who would
overcome the serpent. Adam's name for his wife, *Eve*, testified to
his belief that God is a God of life who can overcome the most
dreadful effect of sin, namely death. The divine compassion shown
to Adam and Eve as they are banished from the garden introduces
the overriding theme of Genesis: God's love for humanity that will
ultimately lead to his choosing Israel as bearers of the promised
blessing for all nations.

C. The consequences of sin (4:1–26)

Context
This chapter is in the form of two genealogies that begin with
Adam (vv. 1–24 and 25–26) and include several expansions that
explain something about some of the generations (vv. 17, 19–24,
25–26). The longest expansion is the account of the murder of
Abel (vv. 2–16). As the expansions of these genealogies demonstrate, the point is not simply to trace various lines from Adam, but
to show the sorrowful history of the now-sinful human race. The
chapter begins with murder, but ends with people calling on God,
their only refuge in a sin-filled world.

Comment
i. Cain murders Abel (4:1–16)
The murder of Abel clearly demonstrates how quickly sin had
become ingrained in humans as a result of Adam and Eve's
rebellion. More importantly, the author's account of God's interaction with Cain portrays God as patiently and mercifully dealing
with Cain despite the heinous nature of his crime.

1. *Knew* (NRSV, ESV) is used of Adam's sexual relationship with Eve. The result was Cain, whom Eve named. The name *Cain* sounds like 'got' in Hebrew. Eve acknowledged God's blessing in providing her son, since she got him *with the Lord*. Perhaps she thought that this was the promised seed (3:15).

2-8. The birth of a second son is described in much more summary fashion (v. 2). His name, *Abel*, is also the Hebrew word for 'vapour' or 'breath'. Like a vapour, Abel will quickly be gone from the narrative (Ps. 144:4; Job 7:16).

The two sons' livelihoods account for their distinct offerings. Both animal and grain offerings were acceptable to God according to the laws in Leviticus. However, God did not accept both sons' offerings. The difference is to be found in their attitude in making the offerings. Cain simply brought some of his harvest, perhaps signalling that his offering was pro forma (v. 3). Abel, however, offered the *firstborn* and the *fat* (v. 4). Offering the firstborn exhibited faith that God would provide for the birth of more animals, and the fat of the animal was seen as the richest and most desirable part, displaying the esteem and respect that Abel had for the Lord.

Cain's anger, which showed even on his face, led God to intervene (vv. 6-7). He warned Cain of sin's desire for him, thereby giving Cain opportunity to repent.

The report of the murder begins with Cain speaking to his brother (v. 8). While the MT does not state what Cain said, the ancient versions add, 'Let's go out to the field.'[11]

9-16. Immediately the author transitions to God's confrontation of Cain. God's questions about Cain's sin mirror his questions to Adam concerning the first sin.[12] Cain's famous reply *Am I my brother's keeper* [or *guardian*]? was intended to say that Cain was not responsible for his brother's whereabouts. However, it has an ironic quality because Cain did have responsibility for his brother's death.

The shed blood of Cain is treated as a living witness issuing an appeal for justice (v. 10), leading to God's first curse directly on any human (v. 11). God's curse has two consequences for Cain: he will

---

11. SP, LXX, Syriac, Vulgate.

12. Note especially *Where is your brother?* (v. 9) versus *Where are you?* (3:9).

no longer successfully farm the ground, and he will wander the earth (v. 12). However, in his unrepentant guilt, Cain sees twice as many consequences: banishment from the soil, hiding from God's presence, wandering the earth and fearing human retribution (v. 14). Despite Cain's attitude, God showed him some mercy by vowing sevenfold vengeance on anyone who killed Cain (v. 15). The choice of seven may be symbolic, suggesting a complete and perfect retribution (Pss 12:6; 79:12; Prov. 6:31). The mysterious mark on Cain to prevent anyone from harming him is never explained. The author is careful to note that Cain left God's presence (v. 16). God did not abandon Cain, but the unrepentant Cain produced his own estrangement from God. The place east of Eden where Cain wandered is called *Nod*, Hebrew for 'wandering'.

ii. Lamech exceeds Cain's sin (4:17–24)

The interrupted genealogy of Adam continues with Cain's son and a line leading down to Lamech. This is the first of three linear genealogies in the early chapters of Genesis (see 5:1–32; 11:10–26).[13] In each case the final generation segments into the children of that final generation (4:22; 5:32; 11:26). Interestingly, Lamech, who is featured at the end of this genealogy that starts with Adam, is the seventh generation listed. This produces an interesting contrast between the murderous braggart Lamech and the godly Enoch, who is also listed seventh after Adam (5:21–24).[14]

17. Though Cain was condemned to wander, he built a city in honour of his son. This may be a further indication of Cain's unrepentant defiance of God and his curse by seeking a permanent residence. The name *Enoch* may derive from the Hebrew root that means 'to train' or 'dedicate', which would be most appropriate in this context. Three others in Genesis bear this name: a son of Jered (5:18–24), a son of Midian (25:4) and Reuben's eldest son (46:9).

---

13. A linear genealogy follows one particular line. The genealogies in 10:1–32 are segmented. That is, they follow multiple lines of several descendants from one person.

14. On the importance of the seventh position in biblical genealogies, see Sasson (1978).

18. Four generations are presented in summary fashion to link Enoch to Lamech. Starting with Adam, this makes Lamech the seventh generation listed. This important placement will also mark Seth's descendant Enoch (5:21–24).

19. The first mention of polygamy comes with the description of Lamech. While God provided only one wife for Adam and blessed marriage on the basis of two partners forming one flesh (2:24), and although monogamy is held up as the ideal in the New Testament (1 Tim. 3:2, 12; Titus 1:6), Lamech took two wives, indicating his proclivity to defy God in keeping with the attitude of his ancestor Cain.

20–22. Each of Lamech's sons is described as *the father of* a certain activity. Like the English word *father*, the Hebrew word can indicate a number of relationships other than that of biological father. In this case it attributes to each son the establishment of a particular enterprise. *Naamah* is the first sister mentioned in the Bible.

23–24. Lamech's short poem demonstrates the progress and magnification of sin among humans. Whereas Cain feared retribution for his murder of Abel, Lamech revels in his murderous action by claiming to enjoy a magnification of the vengeance from seven to seventy-seven. Jesus may have had this passage in mind when speaking to Peter about a forgiving heart – the godly opposite of Lamech's attitude (Matt. 18:21–22).

iii. Seth and Enosh (4:25–26)

25–26. While sin was being magnified through one line of Adam, another line had started. The brief genealogy here will be extended in the next chapter. The inclusion of this short three-generation genealogy is to demonstrate the godliness of a second line from Adam. Like the name *Cain* (v. 1), the name *Seth* is followed by a play on words, since in Hebrew it sounds like the word translated *given* (v. 25). Despite the disappointment in Cain, Eve's faith in God's providence is displayed by her statement about having a replacement for Abel. Seth's son is named *Enosh* (v. 26). This is another word for 'man', and therefore is similar in meaning to the name of his grandfather Adam. The final note demonstrates that although sin was now rampant on earth, there remained some who sought to be reconciled to God as *they began to call on the name of the Lord.* This

phrase is used later in Genesis to describe worship by Abraham and
Isaac (12:8; 13:4; 21:33; 26:25). Since *Lord* in Hebrew is God's name
Yahweh, this describes a close and familiar relationship with God.

Meaning
The account of the heavens and the earth (2:4 – 4:26) demonstrates
God's love for humans as the crown of his creation. He specially
formed man from the ground and breathed into him the breath of
life (2:7). He instituted marriage for the well-being of human society
(2:24). Even after Adam and Eve's rebellion, God lovingly promised
a deliverance from the serpent (3:15), provided them with clothes,
kept them from living for ever in their sinful state (3:21–24) and
blessed them with children (4:1, 25).

Yet this narrative also shows how the result of human rebellion
is estrangement from God. They no longer have access to Eden's
garden. Sin tumbles through human generations producing
heinous crimes like murder and something even more deadly –
defiance of God. Because of their estrangement from God,
humans are also estranged from each other, and conflict and strife
become part of human existence: conflict between the serpent and
the woman (3:15), strife between the woman and the man (*he will
rule over you*, 3:16), conflict between the man and the ground
(3:17–19), strife between brothers (4:8) and conflict among all
humans (4:23–24).

However, in the midst of this chasm between God and humans
there is hope, since humans can plead to God for mercy by calling
on his name. Much of the rest of Genesis is about God seeking to
bridge the gap between himself and sinful humankind, as shown
in the stories of the lives of Noah, Abraham, Isaac, Jacob and
Joseph.

Additional note on the knowledge of the name Yahweh in Genesis

Beginning at 4:26, Genesis reports that long before Yahweh
appeared to Moses in the burning bush (Exod. 3), people knew God
by his name (e.g. Gen. 9:26; 15:2; 24:12, 50; 26:22; 28:16), and they
used it in worship of him. This name of God is Yahweh, often

rendered 'LORD' with small capitals in English Bibles to distinguish it from the Hebrew word for 'Lord' or 'master'.

Proponents of the Documentary Hypothesis have argued that Exodus 3:13–15 and 6:2–3 contradict this by stating that God's name was unknown generations before Moses. The strongest evidence appears to be from Exodus 6:2–3: 'Then God spoke to Moses, telling him, "I am the LORD. I appeared to Abraham, Isaac, and Jacob as God Almighty, but I was not known to them by my name "the LORD"' (CSB). Thus, the Documentary Hypothesis argues that behind the various books of the Pentateuch are different sources, some of which attribute worship of God by his name to a time before Moses while others claim that the name Yahweh was unknown until God revealed it to Moses.

Despite these claims, this theory runs counter to the clear witness of the book of Genesis and also involves a misunderstanding of what Moses was told by God at the burning bush and later in Exodus. At the burning bush there is no claim that the patriarchs and others did not know God's name. In fact, Exodus 3:16 assumes that the Israelites in Egypt will recognize the name as connected with Abraham, Isaac and Jacob when Moses asserts that Yahweh has appeared to him. Exodus 4:30–31 confirms this. The only person in Exodus who does not recognize Yahweh is Pharaoh (Exod. 5:2).

A closer look at Exodus 6:3 reveals what God meant when he told Moses that he was not known to Abraham, Isaac and Jacob by his name Yahweh. Elsewhere, similar statements about knowing God's name Yahweh do not introduce a name which was not previously known or experienced by anyone. Instead these passages describe the recognition of the *significance* of the name (e.g. 1 Kgs 8:41–43; Ps. 83:16–18; Isa. 52:6; Jer. 16:21). Thus, the name itself might have been well known to worshippers of God long before God explained its significance to Moses from the burning bush (Exod. 3:14–15).

Another clue to this is the contrast between the name Yahweh and the title God Almighty (Hebrew *El Shaddai*) at Exodus 6:2–3. There God said to Moses, 'I am the LORD' (i.e. I am Yahweh). This simple statement without any explanation of the name's meaning expects the hearer to understand its significance. This basic

proclamation is never made to the patriarchs.[15] However, God did
say to Abraham, 'I am God Almighty' (Gen. 17:1–2; 35:11), revealing
his power to give Abraham many descendants. Thus, Abraham
knew God as God Almighty: that is, he understood the significance
of that particular title for God. However, God did not reveal the
significance of his name *Yahweh* until he first spoke to Moses.

---

15. God says to Abram, 'I am Yahweh who . . . ' (15:7) or to Jacob,
   'I am Yahweh, the God of your fathers' (28:13), but never simply 'I am
   Yahweh.' The addition in both cases of the descriptive phrase after the
   name is another indication that the patriarchs knew the name, but not
   its significance.

3. THE FAMILY OF ADAM (5:1 – 6:8)

Context

The previous section of Genesis noted the contagion of sin from its inception through to later generations. It ended, however, on a note of hope with the line of Seth calling on the name of the Lord. Would this godly line overcome the effects of sin? This next section of Genesis sadly demonstrates that despite several godly members of Seth's line – notably Enoch and Noah – sin would still infest the world. When God could find only one righteous man, it would lead to God taking drastic action.

The genealogy follows a formula that varies only slightly for some members. In general a progenitor is mentioned as living a certain number of years when he generated a descendant. Then we are told he lived a certain number of years after that and had sons and daughters. Finally the total number of years the person lived is given with the ominous note *then he died*, a reminder of God's words at 2:16–17.

There are three modifications to this formula: for Adam, for Enoch and for Lamech. In addition, Noah's formula is

incomplete and will not be completed until his story is ended at
9:28–29.

Finally, it ought to be noted that two people share names with
persons in Cain's line: Lamech (5:28–31; see 4:19–24) and Enoch
(5:21–24; see 4:17).

Comment

A. Genealogy from Adam to Noah (5:1–32)

This genealogy spans eleven generations from Adam to Noah's
sons. However, the focus is on Noah, the tenth person in the
genealogy (see 6:8).

1–2. These verses begin with the second *tôlĕdôt* formula. It varies
from the others by mentioning a *record* (NET, TNK) or *written account*
(GW, NIV). Traditionally translated 'book', the word refers to any
written record.

The balance of these verses adopts language from the description of the creation of humans at 1:26–28. Since Adam had no birth
to describe in this genealogy, this sketch accounts for his unique
origin as a direct creation of God and for his and Eve's initial
holiness, since they were in the likeness of God. Together they were
called *man* (CSB, ESV, TNK), *humankind* (NET, NRSV) or *humans* (GW).
In Hebrew this word is the same as Adam's name.

3. Adam's section in the genealogy is unique in noting that Seth
was born *in his likeness, according to his image,* thereby drawing a
distinction between Adam's initial holiness and Seth's initial sinful
condition. This distinction is achieved by the overall setting of this
statement. It follows a demonstration of what Adam's children
were like in that Cain murdered Abel (4:1–16) and Lamech bragged
to his wives about killing a young man (4:23–24). In addition, it
precedes the account of the corruption of all humankind and the
pervasive nature of human sinfulness that led to God's destruction
of the earth by floodwaters (6:1–8). The intervening genealogy
tracing Seth's descendants down to Noah's time (5:1–32) serves to
link the sinfulness before the genealogy (4:1–16, 23–24) to the
sinfulness after it (6:1–8). In this way it indicates that the image of
Adam in Seth's line was the corrupt image that also permeated the
rest of humanity, since all persons were sinful (6:5).

4–5. The rest of the information about Adam sets the pattern for all of the other men listed in this genealogy: we are told how long he lived after fathering Seth (800 years), that he fathered other sons and daughters, and his age at death (930 years).

6–11. This genealogy reveals its purpose in its choice of which son of Adam it follows. By choosing Seth, the son whom Eve saw as a replacement for Abel (4:25), it draws a direct contrast between the sinful line of Cain and this more godly line of Sethites. *Enosh*, though seldom mentioned elsewhere in the Scriptures (see 1 Chr. 1:1; Luke 3:38), is also important because his name marks this as the godly line of Adam's descendants (cf. 4:26).

12–14. The name *Kenan* may be a variation of the name *Cain*.

15–17. The name *Mahalalel* is Hebrew for 'praise of God' or 'praising God'.

18–20. Perhaps the least prominent man in this genealogy is *Jared*, whose name may mean 'slave'.

21–24. The godly *Enoch* occupies the honoured seventh position in the genealogy (Jude 14; see discussion on 4:17–24).[1] Enoch's life is different in that he is said to have *walked with God*, suggesting a particularly close and intimate relationship with his creator. The form of the Hebrew verb signifies that Enoch walked back and forth – that is, he continually and habitually walked with God. Only one other person is said to have walked with God: Noah (6:9). Instead of reporting Enoch's death, the text says he *was not because God took him*, testifying to his life of faith (Heb. 11:5). The only other person to have escaped death is the prophet Elijah, whose transport to heaven is described in vivid and dramatic terms (2 Kgs 2:11). The hope of Christians who await Jesus' promised descent from heaven is that they, too, will be taken without death to be with the Lord (1 Thess. 4:17).

25–27. The name *Methuselah* may be derived from the Akkadian for 'man of Shelah', perhaps a reference to a place. Two persons in Genesis are named *Shelah* (10:24; 11:12–15).

28–31. *Lamech*'s life contains an additional note concerning his naming of *Noah*, whom he hoped would *bring us relief*. Lamech

---

1. On the importance of the seventh position in biblical genealogies, see Sasson (1978).

mentions the *painful labour* that is the plight of humans – using the same word that God used twice at 3:16–17 to describe the lot he assigned to Eve and Adam. The name *Noah* means 'rest' but contains sounds similar to the word for *bring us relief.* Perhaps Lamech was hoping that Noah would be the long-expected fulfilment of God's promise concerning the crushing of the serpent's head (3:15).

32. The ten-generation linear genealogy ends with an eleventh segmented generation listing all three sons of Noah. The English text may give readers the impression that these three sons were triplets, all born when Noah was 500 years old. However, from the information at 7:6 and 11:10 it is clear that Shem was born when Noah was 502 years old. Therefore, the notice probably means Noah was 500 years old when God promised to bless him with sons, and he eventually had three.

B. Noah's righteousness among sinful humanity (6:1–8)

This short note on the wickedness of humanity and God's reaction to it serves as a bridge from the end of the genealogy to the account of God's saving Noah and his family from the great flood. It demonstrates how corrupt humanity had become and foregrounds Noah's favoured status with God in the context of God's regret in making humans. While God determines to wipe humankind and other creatures from the face of the earth (v. 7), his favour towards Noah signals that this will not result in a complete end to life on earth (v. 8).

1–3. After a brief note on the setting for this short narrative – the time when humankind began to multiply – the births of *daughters* are highlighted. In contrast to the daughters of mankind, the *sons of God* are introduced. This phrase has been interpreted in three different ways.

The oldest-known interpretation is found in ancient compositions such as 1 Enoch and the book of Jubilees, as well as in a number of the early church fathers. It is also widely held among modern scholars, especially those who believe that this account is based on mythology from the Ancient Near East. This position holds that the sons of God are angels, and cites Job 1:6; 2:1 where this phrase is used to describe members of God's heavenly court. However, this interpretation is not without problems. It introduces angels into Genesis with hardly any prior discussion of them apart from the cherubim who guarded the way to the tree of life (3:24). Moreover, in the New Testament Jesus clearly teaches that angels do not marry (Matt. 22:29–30; Mark 12:24–25; Luke 20:34–36). It could also be added that although the Scriptures at times speak of angels appearing as humans, they never depict them as having bodies that function like those of humans: they do not eat, drink or sleep. It is hard, therefore, to conceive of them mating as humans do.[2] Moreover, Hendel has noted that 'The sexual mixing of gods and mortals is unattested elsewhere in West Semitic lore', thereby casting doubt upon the supposed mythological background behind this text.[3] Finally, it ought to be observed that this intermarriage of the sons of God and daughters of mankind contributes to God's judgment on humanity (vv. 3, 5–7). Since these marriages were initiated by the sons of God, it seems incongruous that God would judge humankind on the basis of what angels did.

Another opinion, popular among ancient Jewish sages beginning in the second century AD and advocated by some contemporary scholars, proposes that *the sons of God* refers to human judges or rulers. The marriage of the sons of God to the daughters of mankind is, then, a reference to aristocrats intermarrying with commoners. This interpretation primarily relies on Psalm 82:1, 6–7 where judges are called 'gods' and later 'sons of the Most High'. It is, however, difficult to fathom why God would have judged human marriages that crossed societal boundaries as demonstrating human depravity (v. 3), or why this would have made him regret creating humankind (v. 6).

---

2. Note that the resurrected Jesus ate to demonstrate to his disciples that he was not a spirit (Luke 24:37–43). Angels, however, are spirits (Heb. 1:14), and in the New Testament fallen angels are often called 'evil spirits' (Luke 7:21; 8:2; Acts 19:12–16) or 'unclean spirits' (Matt. 10:1; 12:43; Mark 1:23, 26–27; 3:11, 30; 5:2, 8, 13; 6:7; 7:25; 9:25; Luke 4:36; 6:18; 8:29; 9:42; 11:24; Acts 5:16; 8:7).

3. Hendel (1987: 16, n. 16).

A third interpretation is that *the sons of God* refers to the faithful worshippers of God. This position, held by some church fathers, such as Augustine, and also by the Reformers, such as Luther and Calvin, is most likely correct. It ought to be especially noted that the line of Seth is explicitly connected with those who called on the name of the Lord (4:26). God's faithful people in Seth's line were epitomized by figures such as Enoch, Lamech and Noah. The daughters of men, then, would have been the rest of humankind who were not faithful, as exemplified by the line of Cain, especially Lamech. The contrast between Lamech and Enoch, both listed seventh after Adam in their respective genealogies, may hint at this distinction. The same could be said of the comparison of the two Lamechs (4:19–24; 5:28–31). Nevertheless, the intermarriage mentioned here is not simply between the line of Seth and the line of Cain. Instead, the two lines exemplify the difference between the faithful and the unfaithful, which probably accounts for the more general characterization *sons of God/daughters of mankind* instead of the specificity of *sons of Seth/daughters of Cain*.

While the exact phrase 'the sons of God' is not used in the Old Testament for faithful believers, the concept is present. At Deuteronomy 32:5 Israel, who ought to have been faithful but had become corrupt, are rejected as God's sons. Psalm 73:15 refers to the faithful as 'the generation of your [i.e. God's] sons'. Hosea 1:10 calls Israel 'sons of the Living God'. This is extended in the New Testament where several passages refer to believers as 'God's children' (John 1:12; 11:52; Phil. 2:15). Given the contrast between defiance of God in the line of Cain and faithfulness in the line of Seth that is present in the immediate past context, this interpretation has much to commend it.

Furthermore, since the intermarriage of the sons of God and daughters of mankind led God to conclude that humanity was corrupt, later parallels are also instructive. God forbade the Israelites to intermarry with the pagans in the land of Canaan because of the danger of them or their children abandoning God (Deut. 7:1–4). The subsequent history of Israel's experience with apostasy resulting from intermarrying with pagans as recounted elsewhere in the Old Testament bears this out (e.g. Judg. 3:1–6; 1 Kgs 11:1–13; Ezra 9:1–15; Neh. 13:23–28).

Finally, it ought to be noted that the actions of the sons of God mirror Eve's actions when she disobeyed (v. 2; see 3:6): they *saw* the daughters of men, judged them to be *beautiful* (literally, 'good') and *took* them as wives. The parallel is striking and invites the reader to see the sin of the sons of God as similar to the sin of Eve. Both forfeited a close relationship with God and as a result brought divine wrath not only on themselves but also upon all humanity.

The consequence of God's observation of humanity's corruption is a withdrawal of his *Spirit*. The Spirit of God took an active interest in creation at the very beginning (1:2), but now God is withdrawing his Spirit because humans are *flesh* (ESV, NRSV) or *mortal* (NET, NIV). This word was last used at the creation of Eve (2:21, 23, 24) to confirm that she was an appropriate female counterpart to Adam. Now it is used to denote human corruption that leads to mortality. It also indicates something that humans share with animals, since throughout the account of the flood, humans and animals together will be called *flesh* (6:12, 13, 17, 19; 7:15, 16, 21; 8:17; 9:4, 11, 15, 16, 17).

The consequence of God's withdrawing his Spirit from humans and their flesh is that *their days will be 120 years*. The meaning of this statement has been debated. One theory is that this refers to the reduction in the lifespan of humans. Before the flood men were living in excess of 700 years (Enoch's life was foreshortened, 5:24). A lifespan of only 120 years would be a considerable reduction. The problem with this interpretation is that the human lifespan does not decrease to 120 years. Only a few exceptional persons live that long or slightly longer (e.g. Abraham, Isaac, Jacob, Moses, Aaron). Instead, a full life comes to be seventy or eighty years (Ps. 90:10).

More likely, the 120 years refers to a grace period before God would pour out his wrath on humankind. God is patient and forbearing, and he postpones his judgment to allow for repentance. This will not be the last time he does this. For instance, Jonah's message to the great Assyrian city implied the same: 'In forty days Nineveh will be demolished!' (Jon. 3:4, CSB).

4. The enigmatic *Nephilim* are mentioned as having been inhabitants of the earth when the sons of God were marrying the daughters of mankind. The intermarriage did not affect the Nephilim, since they were also around afterwards. While the author assumes that his readers will know something about the Nephilim, we can only guess as to who they may have been. Later at Numbers 13:33 ten of the spies that Moses sent to Canaan claim that the Nephilim are still living in Canaan centuries after the flood. While their report ought to have been received sceptically as an exaggeration on a par with modern urban legends, it does reveal that the Israelites in Moses' day believed that the Nephilim were characterized by being excessively tall. This may have led the LXX to translate *Nephilim* as *giants* here in Genesis. We are also told that the daughters of men bore children who were *mighty heroes of old, the famous men* (NET). However, we are not given any clue as to how they gained their fame. Again, the writer assumes his original audience would have understood.

5–6. These verses speak about the Lord's observations regarding humans and are heavily laden with anthropomorphic language to describe God: he *saw, regretted* and *was grieved* in his *heart*. The total domination that sin had over humans and their thoughts from the earliest age aroused not only God's wrath but also his deep disappointment in every person's attitude and actions. Most pointedly, the word translated *grieved* (v. 6) has the same root in Hebrew as the *painful labour* that characterized the plight of sinful humans (3:16, 17; 5:28). Human sin brought sorrow not only to humankind, but also to God.

7–8. God's disappointment led him to resolve to wipe out not only humankind but also the animals which had been placed under human care and authority (1:28). Yet humans were not completely irredeemable. Noah found God's favour, an indication of Noah's faith in God's promise first given to Adam and Eve that he would overcome the serpent who had led them into sin (3:15). This, however, is more of a comment on God's gracious nature than it is on Noah's merit.

Meaning
The trajectory of sin sketched in the previous section of Genesis (2:4 – 4:26) did not have an exception in the more faithful line of Seth. Instead, though Enoch, Lamech and Noah proved faithful, they were still subject to sin. It is noteworthy that Noah is not said to have earned God's favour but to have found it (v. 8). He, too, was

part of humanity and subject to the same futility attributed to all other people (v. 5). From this point forward no sinful act by Noah or any of his descendants ought to surprise the readers of Genesis. Noah's drunkenness (9:21) as well as the repeated duplicity of Abram (12:10–20; 20:1–18), Isaac (26:7–11), Jacob (27:1–40), Laban (29:13–30) and Joseph's brothers (37:31–36) ought not to astonish anyone in the light of what God observes even among his most faithful antediluvian worshippers.

Yet there is something else that should not be unexpected in the balance of the book of Genesis: God's mercy and patience with those who find favour from him. Here he waits 120 years before dispensing his wrath on humanity and animals. Later he will unwearyingly deal with patriarchs who display doubt in his promises and whose behaviour is less than godly. Ultimately, this portion of Genesis is less about the line of Seth than it is about God. He is stricken in his heart over fallen humanity, yet he is full of compassion. Here we see what God later declared about himself to Moses:

> The LORD – the LORD is a compassionate and gracious God, slow
> to anger and abounding in faithful love and truth, maintaining faithful
> love to a thousand generations, forgiving iniquity, rebellion, and sin.
> But he will not leave the guilty unpunished, bringing the fathers' iniquity
> on the children and grandchildren to the third and fourth generation.
> (Exod. 34:6–8, CSB)

Additional note on the ages of the persons in the genealogies of Genesis 5 and 11

The long lifespans of the persons in the genealogies in 5:1–32 and 11:1–32 have been noticed since antiquity. With the exception of Enoch, whom God took, no person listed in 5:1–32 lived less than 777 years, and the average, including the foreshortened life of Enoch as well as Noah who died after the flood, was 702 years. In 11:1–32 the lifespans after the flood are shorter, ranging from Shem's 600 years to Nahor's 148, and averaging 290 years. Clearly, Genesis views a change after the flood that reduced the lifespans of humans. But how are the long ages of the genealogies to be explained?

Comparison of these genealogies has been made to the Sumerian King List, a document from southern Mesopotamia that lists the kings of the city Sumer and neighbouring dynasties, their supposed reign lengths and the locations of the kingship. It also knows of a flood and of longer lifespans for the antediluvian kings as compared with the post-diluvian kings. However, the years attributed for the various kings before the flood are vastly larger than those of 5:1–32, ranging from 43,200 years to 18,600 years.[4] Superficially, the Sumerian King List is parallel to the genealogies in 5:1–32 and 11:1–32. However, at best it can be said that the Sumerians also preserved a tradition concerning a great flood before which people lived longer lives.

Some have resorted to treating the Genesis genealogies as legendary, and therefore the numbers as artificial. Others believe that the lifespans were exaggerated in order to magnify the blessing of God.[5] Yet the rest of Scripture treats the antediluvians as historical persons (e.g. Noah is assumed to be an actual historical figure at Isa. 54:9; Matt. 24:37–38; Luke 3:36; 17:26–27; Heb. 11:7; 1 Pet. 3:20; 2 Pet. 2:5). This argues that the accounts of these men, including their ages at death, are to be taken seriously.

Some have attempted to justify the large numbers by claiming that they were calculated on a sexagesimal (base sixty) system that makes them appear inflated.[6] However, the sexagesimal system fails to explain adequately the particular ages listed in 5:1–32.

Thus, there exists no reliable justification for the longer lives of the antediluvians and the reduced lifespans of the post-diluvians. The difference may have been environmental, with a change in the climate due to the flood gradually shortening lives afterwards. On the other hand, their lifespans may simply have been due to God's design and providence before and then after the flood. In addition, the long lives of the genealogies continue into the lives of Abraham (175 years, 25:7), Isaac (180 years, 35:28), Jacob (147 years, 47:28), and several of Jacob's sons, including Joseph (110 years, 50:22).

---

4. Hamilton (1990: 252).

5. Westermann (1994: 353–354).

6. E.g. Young (1990).

Beyond Genesis, Moses lived 120 years (Deut. 34:7) and Aaron 123 years (Num. 33:39). Both Moses and Aaron seem to have been exceptions in their era, probably due to God's blessings on them. Yet nowhere do the Scriptures hint that the lifespan of either is not to be understood literally.

4. NOAH AND HIS FAMILY (6:9 – 9:29)

Like the previous two sections of Genesis, this one also begins with a *tôlĕdôt* formula. It is also framed by mention of Noah and his three sons (6:9; 9:18–29). The notice of Noah's death that sums up the years of his life is similar to the formula used in the previous section's genealogy (5:1–32). So, in a sense, this brings to a close the narrative that began with creation. By the end of this section the original creation has been destroyed by a flood, and the narrative is now on the cusp of a new beginning that will start with the sons of Ham, Shem and Japheth repopulating the earth under the first covenant of God with humans (9:8–17). This will happen with a new blessing of fertility similar to the one given to Adam and Eve (1:28–30). However, there will be important differences on the renewed earth. Instead of being charged with ruling the animals, humans now will deal with creatures who fear them, but still remain under their authority (9:2). As plants provided sustenance for people before the flood (1:29), they will remain a part of the human diet, but the animals will also become food. This is a section of transition – from the original created order to a new order that is similar, but different in key ways. It will also be a transition from longer days on earth for humankind to shorter lifespans. Finally, it will be a transition for those who remain faithful to their Maker. Previously God had provided them with the promise of Eve's descendant who would crush the serpent's head (3:15); now they will also live in hope in the God of Shem (9:26).

A. The flood leads to God's covenant with Noah (6:9 – 9:17)

In this account of the flood the active individuals in the narrative are God and Noah. Noah's sons are only mentioned in the introductory verses (6:10) and when they enter the ark with Noah (7:13). This passive role for Noah's sons serves to put the focus on God's relationship with Noah, a relationship that saves not only humanity but also all animal life. This culminates in God's first covenant with humans and also with all the living creatures that were with Noah.

The flood also acts as a kind of new creation. As at the beginning the earth was covered with water (1:2), so again it will be covered with water. Out of the first creation came life that enjoyed God's blessings to reproduce and fill the earth (1:22, 28). Out of this judgment on corrupt life comes a renewing of the earth that confirms the earth's cycles of years and days (8:22), renews the blessing of fertility (9:1) and establishes God's covenant never again to destroy all life with a flood (9:9–11). However, in God's revulsion of the violence that marred the antediluvian world, he confirms a staunch commitment to human life and establishes capital punishment as appropriate to enforce a respect for all persons' lives (9:4–5).

i. God's revelation to Noah concerning the flood (6:9–22)

Context
The *account* (GW, NET, NIV) or *generations* (ESV, NRSV) of Noah is the third *tôlēdôt* formula in Genesis, marking the fourth major section. There is a brief but expanded description of Noah's relationship with God (v. 9; see v. 8), a reminder about his sons (v. 10; see 5:32) and a new description of God's observation about the wickedness on earth and his resolve to judge it (vv. 11–13; see vv. 5–7). This time, however, God's determination to judge the earth is voiced to

Noah, followed by a description of the ark that is to be made and a promise of God's covenant with all living creatures whom Noah is to take on the ark with him (vv. 14–21).

Comment

9. Noah is described in three ways, all of which point to his relationship with God. He was *righteous*, the first man to be described this way. Later, 15:6 reveals that righteousness is not something earned by sinful humans but is credited to them through faith. This, of course, is key to Paul's understanding of the gospel in the New Testament (Rom. 4:1 – 5:1; Gal. 3:6–9) and is also how Noah became righteous (Heb. 11:6–7). However, faith that receives God's righteousness is evident in the way a person lives (Jas 2:21–24), so a second description of Noah is that he was *blameless* among his contemporaries. This word does not denote absolute sinless behaviour, since Noah himself was capable of sin (9:21). Rather, it is used to speak of humans who live a life of integrity that seeks to have one's deeds match one's faith. It is how God later called Abram to live (17:1). Thus, it speaks to the outward manifestation of faith, and can also be used to describe the unblemished appearance of sacrificial animals (e.g. Lev. 1:3, 10). Finally, Noah, like Enoch before him (5:22, 24), *walked with God*, that is, he continually and habitually maintained a relationship with the Lord.

10. Almost immediately after the description of Noah we are told about his three sons who are always listed in the order *Shem, Ham and Japheth* (6:10; 7:13; 9:18; 10:1; 1 Chr. 1:4).

11–12. The statement of the earth being *corrupt in God's sight* (literally, 'before God') stands in contrast to God's view of the earth when he completed its creation (1:31). *Corrupt* is a key word in these verses, repeated three times, and then a fourth time at verse 13 (translated as *destroy*, csb). The corruption is defined further by the permeation of *violence* throughout the world. This word denotes 'cold-blooded and unscrupulous infringement of the personal rights of others, motivated by greed and hate and often making use of physical violence and brutality'.[1] To make the contrast with

---

1. *TDOT* 4:482.

God's perfect creation, verse 12 begins *God saw*, a phrase used at 1:31 when God saw that his work was very good. The tragedy of sin and its consequences is made all the more palpable for the reader who is invited to see the sin-filled world from God's perspective.

13. God's instructions to Noah are in two parts, each with a short prologue (vv. 13, 17–18) followed by instructions (vv. 14–16, 19–21). This prologue reveals to Noah that an end is coming for *all flesh* (ESV, NRSV), that is, 'every [living] creature' (CSB, NET). God first offers evidence for his decision: the *violence* that fills the earth (see v. 11). Then he tells Noah that he will *destroy* all creatures along with the earth. In Hebrew this word has the same root as *corrupt* in verses 11–12.

14–16. The instructions tell Noah to build an *ark* (v. 14). In Hebrew this word is used again outside the flood narrative only at Exodus 2:3, 5 for the vessel in which Moses was placed. It probably was derived from the Egyptian word for 'box'. *Gopher wood* is mentioned only here in the Old Testament. It probably refers to a type of cedar or pine. The ark was to have *rooms* (v. 14), literally 'nests', a quite appropriate term for places where animals would reside. The *pitch*, another word used only here, apparently was used to caulk the seams between wood beams. The dimensions of the ark are given in cubits, the length of a forearm. Many modern translations convert this to modern measurements assuming 18 in. or 45 cm per cubit. The word often translated *roof* (v. 16) is another word that occurs only here in the Old Testament. Some commentators believe it is actually a word for 'window'. No matter what the meaning, there appears to be a cubit between it and the top of the sides of the ark, perhaps indicating either that the roof provided an overhang or that there was a type of clerestory window to allow light to enter the ark. The instructions provided for only one *door* in the ark's side but for three *decks* within.

17–18a. The second prologue finally introduces God's means of judgment: a *flood*. The Hebrew term is used only here and at Psalm 29:10 where this flood is referenced. It appears to be a term for the collecting of the waters, since the term is not used in the flood account after 7:17 as the flood waters were rising. God's intent is to destroy every creature with *the breath* [literally 'spirit'] *of life*. This term, though different in Hebrew, is probably synonymous with the breath of life given to animals and humankind at creation (1:21; 2:7; see 7:22). To emphasize his judgment, God plainly states that everything on earth will die. Since the Hebrew verb *die* is not used of plants in the Old Testament, this refers only to animals and humans. In contrast, God promises to make a *covenant* with Noah. This is the first use of this term in the Old Testament. The covenant itself is made after the flood following Noah's complete obedience to God's instructions (9:9–11).

18b–21. The second set of instructions to Noah begins in the second part of verse 18 and involves what should be allowed to occupy the ark. The only humans allowed in the ark were Noah and Noah's wife, sons and son's wives. Peter noted that these eight persons were saved by water (1 Pet. 3:20). The instructions also include a male and female pair of all *living creatures* (v. 19). The types of animals are specified according to the types at creation (v. 20; see 1:20–25) according to their kinds (1:21, 24, 25), signalling the intent to repopulate the earth after the flood just as it was populated after God created animals. In addition, God told Noah that the animals would come to him to be brought into the ark.

Proponents of the Documentary Hypothesis believe that there is a contradiction between the pair of animals mentioned here and the seven pairs of clean animals mentioned at 7:2, indicating two distinct sources that were woven together to create the flood account. However, there is no need to explain the difference in these verses as a contradiction. Instead, here God is giving the general instructions, and later when the ark was finished he would clarify and expand on those instructions to include enough of the clean animals and the birds to allow for both the survival of the species and sacrifices (8:20). Moreover, all animals entered the ark paired, male and female, even those that were in multiple pairs. Therefore, this general statement is true, just not as detailed as later (7:2–3).

Finally, Noah was to take *food* into the ark. To this point all food was derived from plants (1:29–30).

22. The chapter ends with a note that *Noah did* what God commanded. The form of this verse is similar to later notices when persons faithfully followed God's instructions (e.g. Exod. 7:6, 10, 20; 12:50).

Meaning
Once again, the earth is corrupted, but not irredeemable. Noah –
though a sinner (see 9:21) – continued to walk with God as his
ancestor Enoch had done (5:22; 6:9). The next step in that
redemption is portrayed by the obedience of Noah. The mention
of his three sons points to the future repopulation of the earth
following the flood, as do the animals that were to be taken aboard
the ark (6:19–20).

ii. Noah and his family enter the ark (7:1–10)

Context
These verses begin with God's instructions to Noah the last week
before the flood and rain, and with a notice of Noah's obedience
(vv. 1–5). Then a summary of Noah's entry into the ark with his
family and the animals is given (vv. 6–10). This account of the entry
will be expanded with more detail at the beginning of the account
of the flood (vv. 11–16).

Comment
   1. While earlier the reader was told that Noah was righteous
among his contemporaries, here the Lord tells Noah that he alone
is righteous before the Lord. The wording is careful. It does not say
that Noah was righteous to his contemporaries, and, like other
descendants of Adam and Eve, he was sinful. Nevertheless, he was
righteous before God by faith (see comment on 6:9).
   2–3. The instructions for which animals to take are now given in
more detail (see 6:19–20). The land animals are in two classes: clean
and not clean.[2] The clean animals were to be taken into the ark in
seven pairs. Some understand the text to mean simply seven of each
kind of clean animal (e.g. NET). However, the text says *seven, seven, a
man and his wife* for the clean animals and *a pair, a man and his wife* for
the rest of the animals. Therefore, it is clear that seven pairs are
intended. All the birds were to be taken into the ark in seven pairs,

---

2. Note that God does not label some animals 'unclean' (which is a different
   Hebrew word), but simply the opposite of clean.

literally 'seven, seven, male and female'. The purpose of this was to allow for *offspring* (CSB, ESV, NET; literally 'seed'). It would appear that the distinction between animals that were clean and that were not clean had to do with sacrifices, not with the later distinction of animals that the Israelites could eat (clean) and those that could not be eaten (unclean). Meat was not allowed to be part of the human diet until after the flood (see 1:29; 9:3).

Recently, however, it has been proposed that the pre-diluvian human diet consisted of vegetable matter *and* meat from domestic livestock and that there were carnivorous animals before the flood.[3] There are several problems with this theory, however. One concerns 1:29–30, where God explicitly gave plants to humans and all animals (*everything having the breath of life in it*, CSB, NET, NIV), but made no mention of giving animal flesh as food to any living creature. Thus, to theorize that domestic animals were part of the human diet (or that some animals were carnivores), one must assume that God was explicit about eating plants but for some unfathomable reason simply did not mention eating meat from domestic livestock. Another problem concerns feeding the obligate carnivores on the ark.[4] The logistical problem with Noah stocking and preserving enough meat for such animals would have been overwhelming, and most (if not all) of it would have spoiled in the first weeks on the ark. Certainly there were not enough of the clean animals (who came on the ark in seven pairs) to feed the carnivores for an entire year. This theory concerning meat in the pre-flood diet also requires that the phrase *every moving creature that lives* at 9:3 be a reference only to wild land animals or only to animals that were both wild and non-predatory.[5] Such an assertion is based on the premise that the word for *moving creature* (Hebrew *remeś*) always denotes 'wild animal' or 'non-predatory wild animal'.[6] However, it ought to be noted that the

3. Provan (2016: 121–124).

4. Obligate carnivores are those animals, such as felids (cats) or canids (dogs, wolves, coyotes, foxes, jackals, etc.), whose diet *requires* meat.

5. Provan (2016: 124).

6. The noun *remeś* can mean 'wild animal', especially when it is used in contrast to 'livestock' (Hebrew *běhēmâ*; cf. 1:24–26; 6:7, 20; 7:14, 23; 8:17;

phrase *every moving creature that lives* is unique to 9:3. The modifying phrase *that lives* thereby designates animals in general (as opposed to plants, which are never characterized in the Old Testament as having life).[7] Therefore, it is best to conclude that Genesis depicts humans (and animals) as strictly herbivorous before the flood.

4. Apparently God allowed *seven days* for Noah to bring all the animals into the ark before the start of the deluge. In addition, the Lord told Noah that the flood would involve *forty days and forty nights* of rain (see also v. 12). The mention of days and nights may have been to emphasize continual rain. Elsewhere the inundation is said to have lasted forty days, probably meaning days inclusive of both daytime and night-time (v. 17).

5. After God's instructions are concluded we are simply told that Noah complied. The wording is similar to the second part of 6:22.

6–7. The summary of Noah's entry into the ark begins with Noah's age of *600 years* at the beginning of the flood (v. 6). Later his age will be given with more specificity (v. 11). The waters are specifically given as the reason for Noah and his family's entry into the ark, perhaps signalling that they came into the ark with the final animals just as the rain and flood began (v. 7).

8–9a. The types of animals that Noah took into the ark are listed in four categories, which appears to combine the statements at

---

1 Kgs 4:33 ('reptiles', csb); Ps. 148:10; Ezek. 8:10). However, it can also be used to mean all land animals (as can *běhēmâ*; cf. Pss 36:6; 49:12, 20; 73:22; 147:9; Eccl. 3:18–19, 21). Note Gen. 8:19 which characterizes the living creatures that came off the ark as existing in two categories: *all the moving creatures and all the flying creatures*, and then redefines these two categories as *every creature that moves* [Hebrew *rōmēś*] *on the earth*. Clearly, the domestic animals that boarded the ark and that God commanded Noah to take off the ark (7:14, 21; 8:1, 17) are included in the term *moving creature* in this verse. Otherwise one must conclude that domestic livestock did not come off the ark.

7. That is the necessary construal of the relative phrase *that lives*. It is unlikely that it means moving creatures that are living as opposed to moving creatures that are dead, as if God was implying that Noah leave behind the carcasses of wildlife that died while on the ark.

verses 2–3 and 6:20: animals that are clean, animals that are not clean, birds and crawling animals. They entered two by two (literally 'two, two'), male and female, wording that accommodates both the clean animals and the birds (seven pairs) as well as the rest of the animals (one pair).

9b–10. Once again, the author emphasizes that Noah followed God's command (v. 9b). Then he notes the seven days after God's instruction (v. 10). This is the reverse of the wording in verses 4–5 and forms a frame around Noah's compliance to God's instructions.

Meaning

God's instructions to Noah are carefully preserved in this part of the flood narrative to emphasize God's concern that the creatures he created be preserved. In addition, the text twice more underscores the fact that Noah complied with God's directives. This demonstrates to readers that Noah was what God knew him to be: the most faithful man in his generation and the proper choice for preserving life on earth.

iii. The flood (7:11–24)

Context

This beginning of the flood narrative proper treats two topics: an expanded account of the entry of Noah and his family into the ark at the beginning of the flood (vv. 11–16) and the rise and crest of the flood (vv. 17–24).

Comment

11–12. The *six hundredth year, second month* and *seventeenth day* of Noah's life is the first of five specific dates given in the flood narrative to mark important milestones (see Table 6 on p. 99).

The flood had two sources of water: the *springs of the great deep* and *the windows of heaven* (v. 11), both expressed with metaphorical flourishes also employed elsewhere in the Old Testament (Isa. 24:18; Amos 7:4; Mal. 3:10). The *deep* was last mentioned at the beginning of creation (1:2). Two different passive verbs are used: the springs *burst open* (literally, 'were split') and the windows *were*

Table 6 Dates given in the flood narrative

Reference	Event	Year	Month	Day
7:11	Flood began	600	2	17
8:4	Ark came to rest	[600]	7	17
8:5	Tops of mountains visible	[600]	10	1
8:13	Water dried up	601	1	1
8:14	Land dried	[601]	2	27

opened. Both passives point to God's activity in bringing the deluge
on earth. The inundation of the land from waters below and above
that were separated on the second day (1:6–8) is a reversal of God's
work on the third day (1:9–13). The *forty days and forty nights* of rain
(v. 12) fulfilled God's earlier word to Noah (v. 4). Just as Noah did
everything God commanded, so God did everything he had said he
would do. The word for *rain* is the Hebrew word denoting the heavy
winter rains in Palestine.

13. *Shem, Ham and Japheth* are mentioned by name only here in
the flood narrative. All of the men are mentioned by name, while
the four wives remain unnamed. It is from this verse that Peter
could mention eight people saved from the flood (1 Pet. 3:20), since
neither Noah nor his sons practised polygamy.

14–16. While the types of animals that came into the ark mimic
the animals created on the fifth and sixth days in 1:20–31, the flying
animals are carefully defined as both *birds* and *all winged creatures*
(v. 14).[8] The connection to 1:20–31 is made especially through the
mention of each type of creature *according to its kind*. We are told
that *all flesh* came into the ark by *pairs* (v. 15; literally, 'two, two') and
male and female of all flesh (v. 16). This emphasizes Noah's faithful
execution of God's instructions (see 6:19), while also noting that
God preserved life, though he had resolved to destroy all flesh
(6:12–13). This preservation is emphasized as God shut them in
the ark.

8. The Hebrew specifically says *every flying creature* [Hebrew *ʿōp*] *according
to its kind*, *every bird* [Hebrew *ṣippôr*], *every wing*.

17–20. The last use of the term *flood* occurs with the notice of the rising waters during the *forty days* of rain that lifted the ark so that it floated above the mountains (vv. 17–19). The waters are said to have been 15 cubits above the mountains. Since the ark was 30 cubits high, this probably indicates that the ark's draught was 15 cubits (v. 20). Thus, the water rose high enough to lift the ark at least 15 cubits over the highest peak.

21–24. Verses 21–22 emphasize the death of all life and employ six terms used in the creation narrative for days five and six: crawling animals, birds, livestock, wild animals, swarming animals and humans. All of these contained *the breath of the spirit of life* (CSB), a phrase that expands on the phrase *breath* [literally 'spirit'] *of life* in this flood narrative (6:17; 7:15, 22). In contrast, verse 23 emphasizes God's act of preserving Noah and all the lives with him. Finally, we are told that the waters inundated the earth for 150 days (v. 24). This probably includes the forty days of rain, since these 150 days are the same as the 150 days of 8:3. They account for the five months from the entry of Noah into the ark (v. 11) to the ark coming to rest (8:4). Thus, the waters rose for forty days, crested, and then dropped for 110 days until they were low enough for the ark to come to rest in the Ararat Mountains.

Meaning
This account of the saving of Noah's family and the animals in the ark not only reveals God's compassion towards his creatures, but also demonstrates his wrath against sinful humanity. While the faithful Noah survived with all the life on the ark, the rest of the world perished (7:21–23). Even the earth's animals, which are amoral creatures, incapable of sin against God, were affected by the consequences of the tide of sin which had overwhelmed the earth.

iv. The flood recedes (8:1–14)

Context
The receding of the flood is recalled in two stages. First the waters subsided until the ark came to rest (vv. 1–4). Next, Noah sent out birds from the ark to determine when it was safe to leave the ark (vv. 5–14).

Comment

1–3. While 'remember' can at times be used of recalling something, the Hebrew word also has other connotations. That God *remembered* (v. 1) does not imply that he had forgotten about Noah or that he had to recall Noah's situation. Instead, this expression notes God's faithfulness to his promise, especially when he delivers his people from trouble or provides for them (19:29; 30:22; Exod. 2:24; Num. 10:9; Luke 1:72). At times 'remember' can be used of people's faithfulness to God and his covenant (Exod. 20:8). Because God remembered he sent a *wind* to dry the waters. This signals a transition to a sort of recreating of the earth, since God's Spirit was present over the waters at creation (1:2), and the word for *wind* is also the word for *Spirit*.

Now the *springs of the deep* and the *windows of heaven were closed* and the *rain was stopped.* Like the beginning of the inundation, at the end of the deluge the action associated with the sources of water is described in the passive voice, implying that they are under God's control (v. 2; see 7:11).

4. The ark *rested,* the first of several plays on words with Noah's name in the flood narrative. The ark's location was *on the mountains of Ararat.* This is a Hebrew expression that means 'one of the mountains in Ararat'.[9] Ararat is the region known in antiquity to the Assyrians as Urartu. It is a mountainous region in Armenia in south-west Turkey and north-west Iran surrounding Lake Van. Today one of the mountains in that region is often called Mount Ararat, owing to a tradition stemming from the eleventh to twelfth centuries AD.[10]

5–9. When Noah could see the tops of neighbouring mountains he opened a window in the ark, which apparently allowed him to see more of the landscape as well as observe the birds he would send out. He first sent out a *raven* and then a *dove.* The raven flew *back and forth,* the Hebrew text indicating that it went out from the ark and returned, apparently roosting on the ark but not returning to Noah.

---

9. Similar expressions are found elsewhere when Hebrew uses a plural for an indefinite singular. For example, 21:7 ('sons' means 'a son', i.e. Isaac) and Judg. 12:7 ('the cities of Gilead' means 'one of the cities of Gilead').
10. *ABD* 1.352–353.

This behaviour continued for two months until the water dried up from the land (see v. 13). Ravens are carrion eaters, so it could sustain itself without Noah feeding it. The dove, on the other hand, found no place to land, literally no 'resting place', a second play on Noah's name in this chapter. So the dove returned to Noah in the evening. Doves and pigeons feed on seeds, fruits and plants. The return of the dove told Noah that plant life had not yet sufficiently recovered.

10–11. One week later Noah sent the dove out again and this time it brought back a newly sprouted *olive leaf*, indicating that plants were beginning to grow again.

12–13. Noah waited another week before sending the dove out a third time. When the dove did not return, Noah knew that sufficient plant life was growing to support the dove. This prompted him to open the ark's cover to observe that the water was gone and the ground was drying.

14. Exactly one year and ten days after Noah and his family entered the ark the land had dried and they could leave the ark. This is often assumed to be 370 days, with the year reckoned as 360 days, since the 150 days of the flood appear to span exactly five months (compare 7:11 and 8:4). However, of this we cannot be certain. For instance, the ancient Egyptian civil calendar contained twelve months of thirty days each but then added an additional five days at the end of the year to approximate a complete solar year. Under that scheme Noah would have been on the ark 375 days.

Meaning
God's providence and care for his creation is highlighted in the opening of this part of the flood account when God *remembered* Noah and the creatures on the ark. The receding of the floodwaters, the result of God's action precipitated by his remembering, brings hope to a narrative that had sounded a foreboding note by stating that only Noah was left (7:23).

v. Noah leaves the ark and receives the Lord's promise (8:15–22)

Context
The end of the time on the ark is told in two parts. First God speaks to Noah, and Noah responds by leaving the ark (vv. 15–19). Next,

Noah responds to God's mercy by offering a sacrifice, and God reacts to Noah's sacrifice (vv. 20–22).

Comment

15–17. Like Noah's entrance into the ark, his exit comes in obedience to God's instructions (see 7:1). Although Noah had determined that the land was dry, he faithfully waited for God's guidance before venturing back into the world. With him were to come the animals which God promised would *swarm . . . be fruitful and multiply*, thereby restoring vibrant life to the world.

18–19. The exit from the ark is reported, and for the only time the animals are said to move *by groups* (NET) instead of pairs. The word when applied to humans signifies *clans* or *families* (see CSB, ESV, NRSV).

20. Noah's response to God's favour in saving his family was to build an *altar*. Though sacrifices had been mentioned earlier in Genesis (4:3–4), this is the first in a series of times when God's faithful people in Genesis would build an altar (12:7–8; 13:18; 22:9; 26:25; 33:20; 35:1, 3, 7). The sacrifices consisted of every kind of clean animal and bird that Noah had taken onto the ark, an indication of his thankfulness for God's deliverance. This is the first and only mention of a *burnt offering* in Genesis. In the Mosaic law the burnt offering in which the entire animal was consumed on the altar was used both for a voluntary offering for sin (Lev. 1:4; 5:10; 9:7) and for thanksgiving (Lev. 22:17–25; 23:18; Num. 10:10; 15:1–11).

21. Using highly anthropomorphic language, the author tells us that God smelled a *pleasing aroma*. The Hebrew word for *pleasing* is another play on words with Noah's name. It implies that God also found rest.[11] God's response was to resolve never to *curse the ground* because of human sinfulness and never again to *destroy* the living creatures. Note that the reference to human inborn sinfulness is similar to the description of humans before the flood (6:5).

---

11. In his lectures on Genesis to his students at Wittenberg, Luther translated the phrase as 'an odor of rest' and stated that 'at that time God rested from his wrath' (*LW* 2.116).

22. God's vow to preserve the cycles that sustain life on earth is presented in poetic form using merisms, pairs of opposites that together signify a whole. First comes *seedtime* (autumn in Palestine) *and harvest* (spring), indicating the yearly agricultural cycle. Then this cycle is called *cold and heat*, followed by *summer and winter*. Note that those two pairs are essentially the same but arranged in opposite order. The final pair signifies a solar day, *day and night*, and hearkens back to the first day of creation with the first darkness and light (1:5).

Meaning

Noah's trust in God is indicated by his patience in waiting for God's instruction to leave the ark rather than simply using the evidence gathered from his release of birds as an indication that it was safe to disembark (8:6–11). Noah acknowledged God's undeserved providential care for his family and the animals by offering a sacrifice. His worship was prompted by God's action and was not – like worship among the ancient pagans – an attempt to curry divine favour. Noah knew that God had already shown him favour. God also rewarded Noah and his descendants for his humble gratitude as shown in the sacrifice: God vowed never to destroy the earth again with a flood and always to provide the yearly cycle that permits food to grow for man and beast.

vi. God's covenant with Noah (9:1–17)

Context

Following the previous revelation of God's thoughts, this section discloses God's words to Noah. It is arranged in two speeches. The first (vv. 1–7) contains instructions to Noah about what he and his family are to do. The second (vv. 8–17) is about what God will do for humankind. This second speech has two subsections. It begins with God's covenant (vv. 8–11) and continues with the sign of the covenant (vv. 12–17). Both speeches are framed by similar opening and closing statements (vv. 1 and 7; vv. 8–11 and 17).

Comment

1–3. God's blessing is given to Noah and his sons (v. 1). The inclusion of Noah's sons looks forward to the main feature of the blessing: future generations that will *fill the earth*. The blessing is identical to the beginning of the blessing on Adam and Eve at 1:28. This is another connection between the flood account and the creation narrative. However, what follows is distinctly different. God is not recreating the earth; he is transforming it from its antediluvian state to a new post-diluvian existence. The new relationship between humans and animals is an indication of this. Now animals will have *fear and terror* (CSB) of humans (v. 2). This phrase is used elsewhere in the Pentateuch to denote the fright God will bring upon the Canaanites when Israel comes into the Promised Land (Deut. 11:25). The list of animals that will experience this trepidation is similar to the lists of animals Noah took with him on the ark (see 6:20; 7:8; 8:17, 19). However, it also includes *fish*. The reason for this fear is that the animals are now given *into your hand* (v. 2) and may be eaten (v. 3). The phrase *into your hand* not only signifies authority (see CSB, NET) and control (see GW), but also the power of life and death (14:20; Deut. 19:12). Therefore, humans are allowed to eat *every living creature*. The dietary distinction between clean and unclean animals for Israelites came about later as part of God's covenant with them as given through Moses. Note also that this new permission to eat animals is explicitly contrasted with God's previous instructions about food which included only plants (see 1:29–30).

4–6. Though humans are now allowed to eat animals, the restriction on eating *blood* would remain a reminder of the sanctity of life among all of God's living creatures. This is later clarified by Moses' instruction to Israel that blood was to be drained from an animal before its meat was eaten (Deut. 12:16–23). An even higher sanctity is afforded to human life. Both animals and humans will be held accountable for taking a human life (v. 5). While the authority to hold animals accountable is not discussed, God granted human society the authority for capital punishment. The wording of this grant is particularly memorable because of its structure involving only six words in concentric parallels:

Whoever sheds the blood of **humans, by humans** his blood *will be shed.*
(v. 6)

The reason for this heightened sanctity for human life is because it bears God's image (see 1:27). However, the authority for punishing the taking of human life is not given here to individuals, but to society. This is discussed also in the New Testament by Paul (Rom. 12:19; 13:1–5).

7. God ends his blessing with language similar to that of its beginning. However, the *fill* of verse 1 is expanded for explanation: *spread out* [literally 'swarm'] . . . *and multiply*.

8–11. God's words to Noah and his sons continue with ratification of the covenant by a sign. God had promised to establish a covenant with those who went into the ark (6:18). Now he establishes it with those who came off the ark (vv. 9–10). God promises that there will never again be a *flood* and reiterates this for emphasis (v. 11).

12–16. The establishing of the covenant comes with a *sign* that will confirm its validity not simply for those who came off the ark, but for all future generations who will see it (v. 12). Three times God mentions his *bow* in the *clouds*. The connection is clear: the rainclouds will bear the sign that will cause God to *remember* his covenant. Once again this expression notes God's faithfulness to his promise (see comment on 8:1–3). Signs are often associated with God's covenant. For instance, circumcision is a sign of his covenant with Abraham and his descendants (17:10–14), and the Sabbath was a sign of God's covenant with Israel (Exod. 31:13–17). In every case the sign is primarily for the humans who receive the benefit of God's grace. Here, though God will see the sign and remember, the comfort derived from the sign is for humans.

17. God ends his covenant promise with words similar to those that began it.

Meaning

The blessing for Noah and his sons mirrors his original blessing on Adam and Eve (9:1, 7; cf. 1:28). His placing the animals under Noah's authority mirrors the invitation to Adam and Eve to rule the animals (9:2; cf. 1:28). Then his permission to eat meat mirrors his original grant of plants for food (9:3–6; cf. 1:29). In this way Genesis presents the flood not only as a destructive force that extinguished life but also as a creative force that brings a new order to the world. It also ushers in the first of God's covenants mentioned in Scripture. This covenant was designed to provide encouragement and comfort to Noah and his descendants. Whenever they see the rainbow, they can be assured that God still remembers his promise to every living creature.

Additional note on Noah and the flood account

The account of the flood is one of the best-known incidents in Genesis and through the centuries has been discussed and studied closely. In modern times questions have been raised concerning a number of features of the text, including its connection to Ancient Near Eastern flood myths as well as its own coherence and its depiction as a deluge. The major concerns raised over the centuries about this unique event are discussed in this note.

a. Noah in the Bible and ancient Jewish literature
Though Noah is depicted as faithfully executing God's instructions, there is little else shown us about him before or during the flood. His words are not reported, and the only actions he undertakes apart from carrying out God's instructions are in association with the sending of birds from the ark (8:5–14).

Despite this dearth of information about Noah, his actions clearly commend him as a godly man. His righteousness that led to the saving of the lives of his family was noted by Ezekiel, who grouped him with the godly Daniel and Job (Ezek. 14:14, 20). Isaiah compares God's covenant with Noah to his future covenant with his people (Isa. 54:9–10).

In the New Testament, Noah's trust in God is held up as one of the great examples of faith in the Scriptures (Heb. 11:7). His faithful actions condemned the world, and through his faith he inherited righteousness from God. Peter notes that Noah received God's protection, and calls him a 'preacher of righteousness' for his faithful acts in building the ark and saving the seven members of his family (2 Pet. 2:5; see 1 Pet. 3:20).

Extra-biblical Jewish literature also celebrated Noah's righteousness, but began to add exaggerated and speculative claims about him and his life. Sirach 44:17 calls Noah 'perfect and righteous', noting his vital role in keeping humanity alive by preserving a remnant. Wisdom 10:4 notes that when the earth was flooded because of human sinfulness, the wisdom of God saved humanity by steering 'the righteous man by a worthless piece of wood' (i.e. the ark). In Jubilees, Noah's righteousness is lauded and exaggerated in the following ways:

1. He alone was accepted by God among humankind (Jubilees 5:19).
2. Noah's righteous heart was accepted on behalf of his sons, who were also saved (Jubilees 5:19).
3. Noah made the ark exactly according to God's instructions (Jubilees 5:22).
4. His offerings to God are enumerated as ox, goat, sheep, kids, salt, turtledove and a young dove (Jubilees 6:3).
5. Noah and his sons took an oath not to eat blood and made a covenant with the Lord (Jubilees 6:10–11).

Noah is described in 1 Enoch as a paragon of blamelessness, love and uprightness (1 Enoch 67:1). However, the ark is said to have been provided for him by the angels. Moreover, 1 Enoch quotes Noah as claiming that his grandfather Enoch revealed heavenly secrets to him (1 Enoch 68). A later section of 1 Enoch, known as the Book of Noah, relates a legend concerning Noah's birth, portraying him as a newborn whose hair was white as snow and whose eyes emitted light that lit an entire room.

Clearly, Noah's role in Genesis shows him to be a pivotal person in the history of God's people. The rest of Scripture lauds his righteousness and his role as one through whom God preserved life on earth. Noah's pivotal role in Genesis led to his being incorporated into much more speculative Jewish literature that also invented exaggerated claims about him and his acts. Nevertheless, while modern persons often think of Noah only in connection with the ark, it is clear that his life and righteous behaviour were often seen as a model for those who followed him in the faith.

b. Genesis 6 – 9 and Mesopotamian flood myths
Stories of ancient floods are found in many cultures, and were often viewed as the classic example of human catastrophe. These have

often been compared to Genesis.[12] However, the closest parallels to the biblical account are found in Mesopotamian flood traditions, especially the eleventh tablet of the *Epic of Gilgamesh* and its earlier form in the *Atrahasis* story. In addition, there is a fragmentary Sumerian flood story. While there are a number of striking parallels between these and Genesis 6:1 – 9:29, there are significant differences, including the names of the hero of the story (Ziusudra [Sumerian], Utnapishtim [*Gilgamesh* and *Atrahasis*]) and the reason for the flood. In the Babylonian versions the flood is decreed by a divine council of gods. In the *Atrahasis* version this is to silence humankind which has grown so active and noisy that the gods cannot sleep. However, one of the gods who favours the hero warns him and gives him instructions for building a ship. The reason for constructing the ship, however, is to be a guarded secret, and anyone enquiring as to its purpose is to be put off through the hero's dissembling responses.

While at one time many scholars asserted that the Genesis account was derived from *Gilgamesh*, it is now widely recognized that at best Genesis and *Gilgamesh* may testify to a common Semitic tradition. Among the parallels are the following:

1. Both Noah and the Babylonian hero, Utnapishtim, are told of the impending flood by a sympathetic deity. In Utnapishtim's case this is the god Enki, a rival to Enlil.
2. Both are given directions for constructing a wooden vessel sealed with pitch.
3. Animals are taken on board each vessel.
4. On each vessel a door is closed before the flood.
5. The vessels both come to rest on a mountain.
6. Both Noah and Utnapishtim send out birds to determine whether the land is dry.
7. Noah and Utnapishtim offer sacrifices after surviving the flood.
8. Both Noah and Utnapishtim are given blessings by a deity.

---

12. See Lang (1985) for a survey of such studies.

While these general parallels seem impressive, the differences in details demonstrate completely different orientations of the stories. The Genesis account is thoroughly monotheistic, whereas *Gilgamesh* is in keeping with Babylonian pagan polytheism. In Genesis only Noah's family and the animals board the ark, which is stocked with provisions of food. However, in the Babylonian version the hero's family is joined on the ship by both craftsmen and animals, and it is stocked with food and valuables.

Other differences are easily seen simply from a survey of the Babylonian epic. The god Enlil has previously attempted to destroy humankind three times by a plague and two droughts before convincing the other gods to send a flood. Enki then warns his worshipper, the hero of the story of the flood. In contrast to the seaworthy design of the ark in Genesis, the ship in *Gilgamesh* is a cube, 120 cubits on each side, which would have had little success in surviving a cataclysmic flood. In addition, it has seven decks in contrast to the ark's three decks. In the Babylonian version the flood lasts a mere six days. On the seventh day the hero opens a window to see land. The ship comes to rest on Mount Nisir, which is often identified as a mountain in modern Kurdistan. After waiting seven days, the hero releases three birds: a dove and a swallow, both of which return to the ark, and then a raven, who does not return. Since the raven apparently found a place to land, the hero decides to leave the ark. He offers a sacrifice to the gods, and the gods swarm around it, since they are famished from lack of sacrifices to eat. The blessing on the hero is eternal life. The gods, in contrast, have learned their lesson and realize the value of humans. They persuade Enlil to desist from any further attempts to extirpate humans from the earth, though the gods take steps to limit human population growth. Most notable among these is the work of the mother-goddess Nintu, who brings a measure of infertility to women.

More importantly, the theology of the Babylonian myths will surely strike many modern readers as shallow and insipid. Genesis' great themes of human wickedness and mortality, the tension between God's wrath directed at sin and his graciousness shown to a sinful but faithful Noah, and his covenant with all life show the Mesopotamian myths to be bland, hackneyed and trite in comparison.

A common view among scholars today is that the Mesopotamian myths and the Genesis account share a common origin and present two different literary perspectives on the same event. If this is the case, Genesis can be seen to reflect that tradition faithfully, whereas the Mesopotamian myths are hopelessly corrupted. The Genesis account is completely consistent with the message of the book as a whole: that God has given a gracious promise to humankind to rescue it from sin through a descendant of Eve (see 3:15), and that promise will not be abandoned but will continue through Noah, his son Shem (see 9:26) and on to Abraham, Isaac and Jacob.

c. The Documentary Hypothesis and the flood narrative

Advocates of the Documentary Hypothesis often point to 6:1 – 9:29 as a prominent example of the benefit of literary criticism in determining the sources behind the present text of the Pentateuch. Supposedly two sources are woven together in these chapters: the Yahwistic (J) and the Priestly (P) (see discussion of the Documentary Hypothesis in the Introduction). A number of criteria are used to determine which portions of the flood account originally derived from J or P. It is claimed that J exclusively used *Yahweh* (*the Lord* in most English versions) as the divine name, depicted the animals on the ark as seven pairs of each of the clean animals and birds and one pair of the unclean animals, and had the forty days of rain that followed seven days of waiting for the flood. On the other hand, P supposedly uses only *Elohim* (*God* in most English versions) as the divine name, knows only of the animals on the ark in pairs, has the waters rise for 150 days and fall for 150 days, and makes the flood last somewhat more than one year.

There are a number of problems with this analysis, however. The mention of the seven pairs of clean animals and birds appears to be a more specific instruction confined to 7:2–3, whereas the rest of the account simply refers to pairs of animals (6:19–20; 7:9, 15). To avoid a pedantic and tedious account, the author may have simply reserved the details of seven pairs to one explanation and used a more general characterization elsewhere.

Moreover, the structure and coherence of the entire flood story argues that it is not the result of an editorial stitching together of disparate sources, but a finely crafted single literary composition. Wenham (1978a: 337–339) demonstrates that 6:10 – 9:19 is characterized by a long series of concentric parallels (a chiasm or palistrophe). For instance, at the end of the flood narrative (9:1–19), *Shem, Ham and Japheth, the ark, the flood, the covenant* and *food* are mentioned in the exact reverse order to that found in the opening scene (6:10–21).

Another indication of coherence of the entire account is the order in which groups of days are given:

7 days of waiting for the flood (7:4)
7 days of waiting for the flood (7:10)
40 days of rain (7:17)
150 days the waters prevail on the earth (7:24)
150 days the waters subside (8:3)
40 days the ark rested on the mountain before Noah opened the window (8:6)
7 days between the first and second sendings of the dove (8:10)
7 days between the second and third sendings of the dove (8:12)

Since some of these time periods overlap, Wenham notes that 'some of the references to time in the flood appear to have as much a literary as a chronological function. They underline the symmetry of the flood's rise and fall, thereby enhancing the structure of the palistrophe.'[13] It is unlikely that this is the work of a later editor who was simply weaving together two separate sources. However, even if that is what happened, he has done it so skilfully as to obscure his source material, subjugating his sources to his own final text. If that is the case, any source analysis that relies on divine names and numbered groups of days is likely to be simplistic and highly questionable.

In addition, we ought to note that the flood account follows a literary pattern that is evident elsewhere in Genesis: a subject is

---

13. Wenham (1978a: 339).

introduced and then later given in expanded form. For example, 2:4–24 is an expansion on the sixth day of 1:24–31. In 6:1 – 9:29 we see this in several places (see Table 7, with the supposed sources noted in parentheses).

Table 7 Literary pattern of the flood account

	Introduction	Expanded explanation
God's judgment on sin	6:5–8 (J)	6:9–13 (P)
God's covenant with Noah	6:18 (P)	9:8–17 (P)
Animals on the ark	6:19–20 (P)	7:2–3 (J)
Entry into the ark	7:6–10 (P & J)	7:11–16 (P & J)
God's blessing for the earth	8:22 (J)	9:1–7 (P)

Note that if the source analysis is correct, then sometimes J expands on P but at other times P expands on J or on itself. Even less likely, the two accounts of the entry into the ark would have us believe that the editor's knitting together of sources produced both an introduction and an expanded explanation. The likelihood that all of these introductions and expanded explanations can be explained by source analysis is very low. It is much more probable that the account derives from a single authorial hand.

Finally, Wenham (1987: 168–169) notes that certain elements of the flood tradition are missing from either J or P in the classic analysis. J does not contain the building of the ark, the ark resting on a mountain, nor the exit from the ark. On the other hand, P omits any command to enter the ark, the closing of the ark's door, the opening of the ark's window, the sending out of birds, and Noah's sacrifice and God's reaction to it. All of these are found in the Mesopotamian flood legends and it is strange that J or P omits them, yet, when combined, the Genesis account resembles the broad outlines of the Mesopotamian texts. While Wenham noted this, he continued to employ the classic source terminology, though in his assignment of sources he differs noticeably from the classic Documentary Hypothesis. It is much more consistent and in keeping with his observations to conclude that there are no theoretical J and P sources behind the flood narrative in 6:1 – 9:29.

B. Noah's prophecy concerning his sons (9:18–29)

Context

The final part of the history of Noah's family that began at 6:9 relates Noah's drunkenness and its aftermath. Noah, like Adam, is the progenitor of the entire human population on earth (vv. 18–19). The text also contains other interesting parallels between Noah and Adam.[14] Noah was a *man of the soil* (v. 20), a subtle allusion to Adam who was formed from the soil (2:7). Immediately after readers are told that Noah was a man of the soil, they read that Noah *planted* a vineyard. Earlier, after God formed Adam from the soil, his next act was to plant a garden. After Noah drank *some of the wine* he sinned in becoming drunk, and his nakedness was revealed (vv. 21–22). Adam also partook of some fruit (3:12) and sinned, thereby revealing his nakedness (3:7). In both cases the nakedness required someone else to cover it (v. 23; 3:21).

The parallels extend also to Noah's sons. Like Adam who had two godly sons, Abel and Seth, and one ungodly son, Cain, so Noah's sons Shem and Japheth are accounted as godly and receive his blessing whereas Ham is seen as ungodly. Cain's sinful act led to his descendant Lamech's sinful arrogance (4:19–24). So also the curse uttered by Noah will fall on Canaan, ancestor of several peoples of the land of Canaan whose great sinfulness is condemned (10:15–19; 13:13; 15:16; 18:20; Lev. 18:3, 24–30).

This last narrative about Noah, then, is not simply a strange story about Noah's drunkenness and his sons' actions. Instead, it prepares the reader for the next stage of the Genesis narrative on a renewed earth that is still beset by human sin but also by the hope that can come only through the blessing that derives from the God of Shem (v. 26). Thus, a new literary pattern emerges in Genesis: after each covenant given by God, sin will continue to be highlighted as the central problem of the human condition, even for those who receive the covenant promises. Yet God will remain faithful to his promises and continue with his plan to redeem humans from the curse of sin and death.

---

14. See Tomasino (1992).

Comment

18–19. The recounting of Noah's sons who came off the ark is intended to connect this new narrative with the end of the flood account. *Canaan* is mentioned here and in verse 22 in anticipation of the curse (v. 25). It also indicates that this incident took place some years after the preceding flood account, since Canaan was the youngest of Ham's sons, all of whom were born after the flood (10:1). The brief notation concerning Noah's sons as the progenitors of the population of *the whole earth* connects forward to 10:1–32 and also connects Noah to Adam, since both were individual men whose offspring would fill the earth.

20–21. Noah is the only person in Scripture to be characterized as a *man of the soil*. This not only refers to his viticulture, but also connects him to Adam, the man who was formed from the soil. While wild grapes may have been harvested before this, we are told that he was *first to plant a vineyard*. This correlates with archaeological evidence for the oldest-known winery, which is in Armenia, part of the region of ancient Ararat.[15] In Noah's drunken state he *uncovered himself*. While commentators have at times sought to excuse Noah's inebriation, often offering the suggestion that, as the first vintner, he may not have been aware of the effects of wine, the Scriptures are unanimous in condemning overconsumption of alcohol (e.g. Job 12:25; Ps. 107:27; Prov. 23:21; Rom. 13:13; 1 Cor. 6:10; Gal. 5:21; Eph. 5:18; 1 Pet. 4:3). Moreover, the pairing of inebriation and nudity at Habakkuk 2:16 and Lamentations 4:21 shows it to be extremely shameful. Noah's drinking *some wine* to the point of insobriety is no more to be excused than Adam's attempt to justify his eating *some of the fruit* of the tree of the knowledge of good and evil (3:12).

22–23. Through the centuries there have been a number of suggestions concerning the exact nature of Ham's sin.[16] Some have taken it to be either that Ham took advantage of his father's drunken state to have sex with Noah or with his mother, Noah's wife. These rely on the phrase *saw . . . naked* which is used at

---

15. Barnard (2010).

16. A convenient summary can be found in Odhiambo (2013).

Leviticus 20:17 to speak of illegitimate sexual relations between
siblings. However, there the seeing is mutual. Nor can this be connected to the common Hebrew phrase for incest – to uncover
someone's nakedness (see Lev. 18:6–19) – since Noah uncovered
his own nakedness. Another suggestion is that Ham took voyeuristic
pleasure in seeing his father naked. However, there is no suggestion
of this in the text itself. Instead, Ham's sin was in not honouring his
father by demonstrating discretion and loyalty. Though his father's
shame was exposed, he did nothing to respect his father by
concealing it from others. This is evident in the contrasting action
of Shem and Japheth, who *covered their father's nakedness* and took
extraordinary measures so that they *did not see* his nakedness.

24–25. We are not told how Noah *learned what Ham had done to
him.* Here we also learn that Ham was Noah's youngest son. Noah's
reaction was to place a curse on Canaan. This is the first mention
of a curse by a human. There has been much discussion as to why
the curse was placed on Canaan and not on Ham. Ancient Jewish
sages noted that God had blessed all three sons of Noah, such that
Noah would have been unable to bring a curse on what God had
blessed (see Num. 22:12).[17] This would explain why Noah avoided
cursing Ham, but does not account for his cursing Canaan among
all of Ham's sons (see 10:6). Instead, it ought to be noted that
Noah's curse and his blessings (vv. 26–27) are prophetic, and this
curse directs the reader forward to the promise of the subjugation
of the land of Canaan to Abraham and his descendants.

In the past the curse on Canaan was used to justify enslaving
peoples who were considered to be the descendants of Ham. This
horrible misuse of this passage ignores not only the fact that the
curse was not placed on all of Ham's descendants, but also that
the Scriptures themselves point to Israel's occupation of Canaan
as the fulfilment of Noah's words.

26–27. In contrast to the curse on Canaan, a blessing is given to
the Lord, the God of Shem. This unexpected wording – the blessing is
placed on the Lord instead of directly on Shem – presumes that
Shem already had a dedication to Yahweh, thereby highlighting the

17. *Genesis Rabbah* 36:7.

relationship between God and Shem as well as Shem's descendants, especially Abraham, Isaac and Jacob. Only because of God's gracious and merciful favour towards Shem's progeny can they claim any blessing for themselves. For this reason the church fathers as well as the Reformers understood this blessing as an extension of the promise to Eve (3:15).[18] While the ultimate messianic import of this blessing could not be seen apart from the later blessings on Abraham, Isaac, Jacob and Judah, and as revealed fully in Jesus Christ, one ought not thereby to reduce this simply to a mundane promise to Shem's descendants concerning their possession of the land of Canaan or the like.

Noah's utterance that God will *extend Japheth* forms a play on words, since both involve the same consonants in Hebrew.[19] Japheth's blessing is tied to Shem and comes through his presence in *the tents of Shem*. This ultimately points forward to the blessing on Shem being extended to the nations, including even the descendants of Ham (Isa. 2:2–3; 19:23–24; Mic. 4:1–2; Matt. 8:11). Note that both the blessings on Shem and on Japheth include the statement that *Canaan will be his slave*. This places in sharp relief God's blessing on those who trust in him in contrast to his wrath poured out on those who instead reject the Lord and defile themselves (e.g. Lev. 18:24).

28–29. The last two verses in chapter 9 note Noah's death using a modified form of the formula for the end of lives as found in the genealogy of Adam's son Seth (Gen. 5). There are two important adjustments to the formula. One is that Noah's final days are counted following the flood rather than following his being a progenitor of descendants. The other is the absence of any mention of other sons and daughters, thereby pointing to Ham, Shem and Japheth as the only progenitors of the post-diluvian populations of the earth.

---

18. E.g. *LW* 2.178–185.

19. In fact, it is likely that the proper noun *Japheth* was pronounced *yapht* in pre-exilic Hebrew. This would make an exact phonological match for the verb *extend*.

Meaning
The history of Noah's family that encompasses the flood, Noah's
drunkenness and his prophecy concerning his descendants begins
a second phase of God's creation, linking the end of the original
earth's human and animal descendants to the beginning of a
renewed earth. As such it is an important bridge between the
antediluvian world and the world which would be inhabited by
God's chosen people Israel. Through the flood it closes out the
earth's original created state yet also brings forth a transformed
earth from the waters that covered it, just as the first state of the
world came forth from the waters of the deep. However, this
changed earth will still be inhabited by sinful humans, and the
promise to crush the serpent's head through a descendant of Eve
(3:15) will now be reintroduced through Noah's son Shem (9:26).

Moreover, this section of Genesis foregrounds both God's
wrath against sinful humans and his mercy to sinners who trust in
him as Noah did. Noah's faithfulness in exactly and unerringly
following the Lord's instructions concerning the ark, his family and
the animals testifies to his faithfulness to God who was faithful and
merciful to him. Yet even the faithful Noah would err in consuming
too much wine. This tension between God's people as both pious
followers of the Lord and sinners like the rest of humankind is first
clearly portrayed in Noah but is the same tension that will be seen
in Abraham, Isaac, Jacob and Jacob's sons.

5. THE FAMILY OF NOAH'S SONS (10:1 – 11:9)

At first glance the section called the family record (*tôlĕdôt*) of Noah's sons appears to contain two disparate items: the nations descended from Shem, Ham and Japheth, and the account of the Tower of Babylon. The so-called Table of Nations (10:1–32) demonstrates the interrelationships and geographical distribution of the nations in and near the Ancient Near East. It repeatedly mentions that the peoples *spread out* (10:5, 18, 32) and that each of the nations had *their language* (10:5, 20, 31). Thus, it appears to be a self-contained unit, bounded on either end by similar introductory and closing statements (10:1, 32). Yet it also anticipates the account of the confusion of languages and scattering of nations mentioned at the end of the Tower of Babylon account (11:9). For instance, the only biographical information given in the Table of Nations is that of Nimrod, whose kingdom began at Babylon (10:10). Also, the only explanation for a person's name in the Table of Nations is that of Peleg, during whose days *the earth was divided*, that is, the nations were scattered, each to its own territory (10:25). This explanation of Peleg's name

involves wordplay, since it sounds like the Hebrew word for
'divided'. The only other obvious wordplay based on a name is
found in the Tower of Babylon narrative, where the city is called
Babylon (Hebrew *bābel*), since God *confused* (Hebrew *bālal*) human
languages there (11:9).

The Table of Nations and the Tower of Babylon story are also
connected by common vocabulary, such as *scatter* (10:18; 11:4, 8, 9),
land of Shinar (10:10; 11:2), *build* (10:11; 11:4, 5, 8), and the word for
earth/world or *land/country* which is used fifteen times in this section.
It is used eight times with the meaning *earth/world* (10:8, 25, 32; 11:1,
4, 8, 9 [twice]) and seven times with the meaning *land/country* (10:5,
10, 11, 20, 31; 11:2).

Chronologically speaking, these two sections of the family
record of Noah's sons are in reverse order. Three times in the Table
of Nations readers are told that each group had its *own language*
(10:5, 20, 31), though this did not come about until God confused
the languages at Babylon (11:9). Interestingly, the Table of Nations
speaks of the people having their *own languages*, and the Hebrew
word for *languages* is 'tongues'. However, the Tower of Babylon
account also speaks of the world having one language which God
confused. Here the Hebrew word for *language* is 'lip'. Thus, Moses
has constructed a pun which implies that confused lips lead to
different tongues.

Together, these two accounts concerning the nations that came
into being after the flood link back to the previous section through
the mention of Noah's sons (10:1, 32). By locating Abram's family
among the nations of the ancient world, they look forward to the
next section of Genesis, the genealogy from Shem to Abram
(11:10–26). It is interesting to note that in the nations descended
from Shem (10:21–30), the descendants of Joktan are discussed.
However, the descendants of his brother Peleg are not. Instead, that
is left to the next section of Genesis, where we learn that Abram is
descended from Shem through Peleg. Between the descendants of
Shem in the Table of Nations and the descendants of Shem as
given in Abram's ancestry falls the Tower of Babylon narrative.
Thus the scattering of the peoples and the confusion of human
languages is framed as a pivotal event in the history of the earth's
repopulation following the flood.

A. Genealogies: Noah's descendants through his three sons (10:1–32)

Context

This section, the Table of Nations, deals with the descendants of Noah's three sons. It is divided into three main subsections, one for each son. They are framed by similar statements of introduction and conclusion. All three sections begin with the statement 'X's sons' (vv. 2, 6, 22), though the section treating Shem's sons is prefixed by a statement calling attention to his descendant Eber (v. 21). In addition, each section closes with a similar statement about the descendants' *lands*, *language*, *clans* and *nations* (vv. 5, 20, 31). While Noah's sons are always listed in the same order – Shem, Ham, Japheth (5:32; 6:10; 7:13; 9:18; 10:1; see 1 Chr. 1:4) – the Table of Nations works in the opposite order, probably to show the geographic relationship to the original home of Abram. Japheth's clans are the most remote. Ham's clans are closer and interact with Abram later in Genesis. Of course, the descendants of Shem are the closest, with Abram coming from a branch of the clans of Shem.

This genealogy is not intended to list all of the peoples of the world. Instead, it is crafted to present the most important nations in the Ancient Near East that are not part of the line that preserves God's promise of a Saviour. For instance, none of the nations descended from Peleg are mentioned. Among Ham's sons, no descendants are listed for Put, although there are extensive lists for the other three sons. Instead, it appears that the Table of Nations is concerned only with nations in and around the Ancient Near East that might come into contact with the bearers of God's promise, Abraham, Isaac, Jacob, and the nation from him, Israel. In addition, this genealogy sometimes mentions individuals, such as Nimrod, Peleg and Eber, while at other times it mentions nations or at least the name of an ancestor who gave his name to the nation descended from him.[1]

---

1. This can be seen in the Hebrew text with proper nouns that end in the singular gentilic ending *-î*, roughly equivalent to English *-ite*, or the plural gentilic ending *-îm*, roughly equivalent to the English *-ites*.

Often these names were then associated with a region where these nations presumably settled.

The crafting of the table can be seen in the fondness of its use of the number *seven* and its multiples, tying this repopulating of the earth back to God's original work of creation in six days plus a day of resting from the work of creation. The phrase *sons of* occurs fourteen times. Japheth's descendants include two groups of seven: his descendants (v. 2) and the descendants of his descendants (vv. 3–4). Among Ham's descendants, Cush has seven descendants (vv. 6–7) and so does Mizraim (vv. 13–14).[2] Moreover, there are seventy descendants of Noah's sons in the Table of Nations: fourteen from Japheth, thirty from Ham and twenty-six from Shem. This is probably intended to match the seventy descendants of Jacob who accompanied him to Egypt (46:27; Exod. 24:9; Num. 11:24). Later, all Israel would be represented by seventy elders (Exod. 24:9; Num. 11:24). According to Moses, God established the nations corresponding to the number of the children of Israel (Deut. 32:8).

Comment

i. Introduction (10:1)

1. This is the fourth *tôlĕdôt* formula in Genesis, and the only one said to be about someone's sons. In the Table of Nations the phrase *Noah's sons* occurs only here and at verse 32.

ii. Japheth's descendants (10:2–5)

The shortest list of descendants is the one pertaining to Japheth. This is probably because they lived furthest from Israel.

2. *Gomer* most likely refers to the Cimmerians. This nation is mentioned in both Assyrian and Greek texts. They occupied land north of the Black Sea. Eventually they were driven south and settled in Cappadocia in Asia Minor.

---

2. The Philistines are not included, since the text is ambiguous as
   to whether they were descendants of Ham (see comment on
   vv. 13–14).

Magog cannot be identified with any certainty. From what is said at Ezekiel 38:2; 39:6 they probably occupied land far north of the Promised Land.

Madai refers to the Medes who lived north-east of the Tigris River (2 Kgs 17:6; 18:11; Isa. 13:17; 21:2; Jer. 51:11; Dan. 5:28; 6:8, 12, 15; Acts 2:9).

Javan is the Ionian Greeks who settled in southern Greece and western Asia Minor (Isa. 66:19; Ezek. 27:13). Later in the Old Testament this becomes a general name for all Greeks (Dan. 8:21; 10:20).

Tubal and *Meshech* are usually mentioned together in the Old Testament (1 Chr. 1:5; Ezek. 27:13; 32:26; 38:2–3; 39:1). They lived in central and eastern Asia Minor. In Assyrian texts they are known as *Tabali* and *Mushki*.

Tiras is not mentioned elsewhere in the Old Testament except for 1 Chronicles 1:5, which is dependent on this passage. Some have associated the name with ancient Thrace in Europe directly north-west across the Bosporus from Asia Minor. Others associate them with the Tyrrhenians who eventually settled in Tuscany in Italy and are known today as the Etruscans.

3–4. *Ashkenaz* is usually identified as the Scythians, who originally inhabited the Russian steppes north and east of the Black Sea. Later they drove the Cimmerians southwards and probably settled in Media.

Riphath is otherwise unknown.

Togarmah appears to be associated with Javan, Meshek, Tubal and Gomer, and probably occupied land to the far north or north-east of Palestine (Ezek. 27:13–14; 38:3–6).

Elishah is probably a clan that settled on Cyprus, which was known to the Assyrians and Babylonians as *Alashia*.

Tarshish, though often mentioned in the Old Testament, is difficult to identify. Lessing (2007: 70–73) makes a strong argument that this is Tarsus on the south-central coast of Asia Minor.

Kittim were located on Cyprus and probably associated with the town Kition. Elsewhere in the Old Testament this name is used to refer to the western extremes of the known world.

Dodanim is unknown. However, this may have originally read *Rodanim* as at the parallel at 1 Chronicles 1:7. In both passages the

LXX reads *Rodanim*.[3] This would be most reasonable, since it would refer to the island of Rhodes in the Aegean Sea, placing them in the same general area as Elishah, Tarshish and Kittim.

5. The *coastland peoples* (CSB, ESV, NRSV) probably refers to all of the descendants of Japheth, many of whom appear to have been located in or around the Mediterranean and Black Seas.

iii. Ham's descendants (10:6–20)

Ham's descendants make up the longest list among these three. As in the other lists, the names of the descendants came to signify the lands where they settled.

6. Ham's sons are associated with locations in north-east Africa. *Cush* is Nubia (classical Ethiopia), located south of the second cataract of the Nile.

Mizraim is the Hebrew name for Egypt.

Put is disputed, but probably refers to a portion of Libya. This makes the most sense, since the list of Ham's sons appears to move in a south-to-north direction.

Canaan is the territory west of the Jordan River, including Palestine, Lebanon and portions of Syria. Its boundaries are reported in verse 19.

7. Cush's sons are connected to locations in Africa and Arabia. *Seba* appears later as an important trading centre (Ps. 72:10; Isa. 43:3), but its location is unknown.

Havilah is also unknown, though 25:18 and 1 Samuel 15:7 suggest that it is somewhere on the Arabian Peninsula. The name also occurs in the line of Shem (v. 29).

Sabtah and *Sabteca* are unknown, but some have suggested connections with places in Arabia.

Raamah is often suggested as being in southern Arabia, and at Ezekiel 27:22 it is associated with Sheba.

Raamah's's sons *Sheba* and *Dedan* may be the Arabian tribes known for commercial trade (1 Kgs 10:1–13; Ps. 72:10, 15; Isa. 60:6;

---

3. The confusion may have come about by the confusion of the Hebrew letters corresponding to *d* and *r*, which are very similar to each other in all Hebrew scripts of all periods.

Ezek. 27:15). Abraham also had grandsons named Sheba and Dedan, so we cannot be certain which pair were the Arabian traders (25:3). However, Sheba and Dedan are mentioned with Ephah, another grandson of Abraham, at Isaiah 60:6, making it unlikely that Cush's sons Sheba and Dedan were the Arabian traders.

8–12. Unlike the persons listed in Ham's line, Nimrod does not lend his name to a place or an ethnic group. The short narrative about him identifies him as the first imperial ruler and a champion hunter. His name is associated with the founding of important ancient cities in Mesopotamia. The meaning of the saying about him as a *mighty hunter before the Lord* is much discussed. Many take it simply as a superlative, indicating a very mighty hunter. His kingdom is said to have begun in middle and lower Mesopotamia.

Babylon is a very ancient city, dating at least as far back as the third millennium BC.

Erech, known as Uruk to the Babylonians, is modern-day Warka.

Akkad was the home of a powerful kingdom under Sargon I in the twenty-fourth century BC, but has never been located.

No ancient city has been identified as this *Calneh*, though a different Calneh in Syria is mentioned in Amos 6:2 and Isaiah 10:9.

The area of these cities is called *Shinar*, a word that is not used in ancient Mesopotamian documents but is in documents from Egypt and the ancient Hittite empire. It may be derived from an old pronunciation of Sumer.

The next cities mentioned are all located in upper Mesopotamia. *Asshur* is a city in ancient Assyria and lends its name to the region. *Nineveh* was the most important city, dating to around 4500 BC. Its ruins are near modern Mosul.

Rehoboth-Ir means 'city plazas' and may have been a part of greater Nineveh.

Calah, modern Nimrud, was first settled in the early third millennium BC. In the ninth century BC it functioned as the capital of the Assyrian Empire.

Resen, though said to lie between Nineveh and Calah, has never been located.

13–14. Mizraim's descendants are largely unknown. Some have attempted to identify the *Ludim* with the Lydians of Asia Minor, but this is unlikely, since all of these peoples seem to be located in or around Egypt. *Lehabim* are the Libyans. *Naphtuhim* are likely people from middle Egypt near Memphis.[4] *Pathrusim* are the people of Pathros, that is, Upper Egypt (Jer. 44:1, 15; Ezek. 29:14; 30:14).

The *Casluhim* may be people from Lower Egypt.[5] Casluhim are said to be *from where the Philistines come*. This may simply be a note of where the Philistines lived before coming to south-western Canaan. Thus, it may imply that the Philistines mentioned in Genesis are actually Casluhim, Egyptians from the Nile Delta. It is often suggested that the references to Philistines and the region of Philistia (10:14; 21:32, 34; 26:1, 8, 14–15, 18; Exod. 13:17; 15:14; 23:31) are examples of scribal updating in the Pentateuch, since many scholars identify this people with the Sea Peoples who were expelled from Egypt and settled on the coast in south-west Canaan in the twelfth century over three hundred years after Moses. However, the name *Philistine* probably means 'migrant' or 'foreigner' (as it is often translated in the LXX). In addition, 10:14 traces the Philistines' origin to the Casluhim, whereas later sources (Deut. 2:23; Jer. 47:4; Amos 9:7) trace their origin to the related Hamitic people of *Caphtor*. In Genesis the Philistines are located at Gerar, south-east of Gaza between Kadesh and Shur (20:1–2; 26:1–6). Later references to the Philistines locate them in Canaan's southern coastal plain in five cities – Gaza, Ashdod, Ashkelon, Gath and Ekron – but never in Gerar (Josh. 13:3; 1 Sam. 6:17). Thus, it appears that the Casluhite Philistines mentioned in Genesis are not the same as the Caphtorite Philistines mentioned in later Old Testament books. Therefore, the reference to Philistines in Genesis may be speaking of non-Canaanites who came from the Nile Delta to live in the Negev wilderness south-east of the later Philistine settlements on Canaan's coast.

The last people mentioned here are the *Caphtorim*, peoples from Crete. They may be descendants of Mizraim who left Egypt and colonized Crete.[6] The reference to Philistines and a region called

4. Rendsburg (1987: 91).

5. Rendsburg (1987: 91–92).

6. Rendsburg (1987: 92–96).

Philistia in the Pentateuch may be speaking of these non-Canaanites who came from the Mediterranean to live on Canaan's coast.

15–19. The most detail is given for the Canaanites, probably in view of the promise of the land of Canaan given to Abraham, Isaac and Jacob later in Genesis. *Sidon* is also the name of the most prominent Canaanite city on the Levantine coast in Moses' day. Later, it would be supplanted in importance by Tyre.

Heth is the ancestor of a people called Hittites in many English versions. However, this is not the Anatolian Hittites whose homeland was in modern-day Turkey but a Canaanite group to which some persons named in the Old Testament belonged (e.g. Ephron, Zohar, Uriah; see 23:7–8; 2 Sam. 11).[7] Since members of this ethnic group are often called *sons of Heth* in the Hebrew text, it might be better to call them *Hethites*.[8]

Jebusites were the Canaanite inhabitants of Jerusalem, which was also called Jebus (Josh. 18:28; Judg. 19:10).

Amorites, *Girgashites* and *Hivites* are often mentioned in lists of the peoples of Canaan (e.g. 15:19–21).

Arkites inhabited the Lebanon coast, including the city of Irqata, and the *Sinites* probably lived nearby in a town called Siannula mentioned in Ugaritic and Assyrian texts.

Arvadites lived in Arvad (modern Ruad), an island city marking the northernmost point of Phoenicia. It is mentioned in the Amarna Letters, Assyrian inscriptions and Ezekiel 27:8, 11.

Zemarites probably inhabited the city of Sumur mentioned in the Amarna Letters and Assyrian texts as lying south of Arvad. Its exact location is unknown.

Hamathites lived in Hamath (modern Hama) on the Orontes River in Syria. It was the northernmost city in Canaan.

---

7. Wood (2011).

8. As, for instance, is done consistently in CSB. See CSB at Gen. 15:20; 23:3, 5, 7, 10, 16, 18, 20; 25:9–10; 26:34; 27:46; 36:2; 49:29–30, 32; 50:13; Exod. 3:8, 17; 13:5; 23:23, 28; 33:2; 34:11; Num. 13:29; Deut. 7:1; 20:17; Josh. 3:10; 9:1; 11:3; 12:8; 24:11; Judg. 3:5; 1 Sam. 26:6; 2 Sam. 11:3, 6, 17, 21, 24; 12:9–10; 23:39; 1 Kgs 9:20; 15:5; 1 Chr. 11:41; 2 Chr. 8:7; Ezra 9:1; Neh. 9:8; Ezek. 16:3, 45.

The mention of the Canaanites scattering at later times forms a literary connection between the Table of Nations and the next narrative, which mentions scattering of humankind from the Tower of Babylon (11:8). This scattering of the Canaanites probably refers to their moving south from Sidon into Palestine so that they were resident there when Abram arrived (12:6).

The borders of Canaan (v. 19) are given first from north (Sidon) to south (Gerar and Gaza). Then the eastern border is defined by the Cities of the Plain: Sodom, Gomorrah, Admah and Zeboiim. The phrase *as far as Lasha* is somewhat enigmatic, since its location is unknown.

20. The summary verse tells the reader four ways in which this list of Ham's descendants is organized: by *clans . . . languages . . . lands . . . nations* (cf. v. 31).

iv. Shem's descendants (10:21–31)

Since Shem's descendants include the line of descent that bears the promise of God through Arpachshad, Shelah, Eber and Peleg, it is treated last.

21–22. Shem is called *Japheth's older brother*, making him the eldest of the three sons, since Ham was the youngest (9:24). While some have argued that the text should be understood as saying that Japheth is the eldest brother, Hebrew grammar precludes this. Shem is called the ancestor of *all the sons of Eber*. Presumably this anticipates the labelling of Eber's descendants as *Hebrews*, which apparently is derived from Eber's name (14:13; 39:14, 17; 41:12).

Elam is east of Mesopotamia in modern south-west Iran. While the Elamites did not speak a Semitic language, they are said to have descended from Shem.

Asshur is the name for Assyria in upper Mesopotamia.

Arpachshad was traditionally connected with Babylon, but this is uncertain.

Lud has in the past been identified as the ancient Lydians who lived in western Asia Minor and were called *Luddu* by the Assyrians. However, since this would mean that Lud was very distant from the rest of the Shemite nations, some have disputed this identification.

Aram was ancient Syria. It is important in Genesis for its connection with Abraham, Isaac and Jacob (11:28–32; 25:20; 28:5;

31:18, 20–24). Aram is also the name of one of Abraham's grand-nephews (22:21).

23. Only two lines of Shem are traced beyond the first generation. One is that of *Aram*. Aram's sons are difficult to identify. *Uz* is probably in western Arabia but is difficult to locate, since there were two other men with this name. One was a nephew of Abraham (22:21) and the other a descendant of Esau (1 Chr. 1:42).

24. Many of the descendants of Arpachshad are difficult to locate, but most seem to have inhabited the Arabian Peninsula or lower Mesopotamia.

25. Eber's two sons are mentioned, but only *Joktan*'s descendants will be expanded in the following verses. *Peleg*'s name forms a play on words with *divided*. While the meaning of *in his days the earth was divided* is disputed, it most likely refers to the scattering of nations and confusing of languages at Babylon (11:1–9). While the word for *scatter* (11:8) is not the same as *divided*, the word for *divided* is used at Psalm 55:9 for confusing someone's speech, making it likely that we are told that Peleg was alive when God confused the languages of humankind.

26–30. A few of Joktan's sons can be associated with known places, but most are probably associated with Arabia.

Sheleph has been associated with the Yemenite tribes called *Salf* or *Sulf*.

Hadoram is the area of Hadramaut east of Yemen.

Yerah is also the Hebrew word for 'moon'. The moon was a major deity worshipped in South Arabia.

Uzal is probably *Azal*, the ancient name for Sanaa, the capital of Yemen.

Ophir was known as a source of fine gold in antiquity (1 Kgs 9:26–28; Ps. 45:9). While places such as South Africa or India have been proposed for this, it is more likely that it was located on the Arabian Peninsula.

Havilah is mentioned at 2:11 as another source of gold. It probably was a location somewhere in the north-east corner of the Arabian Peninsula.

Verse 30 gives the boundaries of the area where the descendants of Joktan settled. However, none of the landmarks mentioned can be identified with certainty.

31. This summary for Shem's descendants matches the summary for Ham's descendants (v. 20)

v. Summary (10:32)

32. The summary verse for the Table of Nations not only repeats wording from the introduction (v. 1), but also adds that these names came to represent nations. The final sentence links the Table of Nations to the next section which explains how the nations came to be spread out on earth.

Meaning

As is often the case in Genesis, genealogical lines that are subsidiary to the line bearing the messianic promise are treated first before moving on to give a more detailed account of those who are entrusted with carrying forward God's pledge of a redeemer. In this case the descendants of Noah's three sons who settled throughout the Ancient Near East are treated. Shortly hereafter the line leading to Abram, the great patriarch of Israel, will be set forth in more detail (11:10–26).

B. Sin at the tower of Babylon (11:1–9)

Context

Having given an account of the nations scattered around the Ancient Near East, Genesis now tells how that dispersal happened. Thus, these nine verses contain an account of what happened *before* the situating of the nations. That explains why the world had one language and vocabulary as this story opens (v. 1), but the Table of Nations mentions that each nation had its own language (10:5, 20, 31).

This narrative begins and ends with *the whole earth* (vv. 1, 9), marking it off as a distinct section. Wordplay figures prominently in this storyline. The most obvious is the play between *Babylon* (Hebrew *bābel*) and *confused* (Hebrew *bālal*). In addition, the people say *let us make bricks* (Hebrew *nilběnāh*), but God says *let us confuse* (Hebrew *nābělāh*). For Hebrew readers this would have also reminded them of the word for 'folly' (Hebrew *něbālâ*). This wordplay is used to highlight the human folly of those who think they can assume God's prerogatives for themselves. However, it also emphasizes God's protection of humans in keeping them from becoming arrogantly comfortable in their sinful ambitions. His confusing of the languages prevented humans from permanently being estranged from him because of their complete reliance on their sinful achievements.

Comment

1–2. The opening note about a single *language and vocabulary* (CSB) sets this narrative chronologically before the Table of Nations (10:1–32). We are told that people migrated *eastward* (NET, NIV), probably moving from the region of Ararat into Mesopotamia. Some English versions translate this as *from the east*, but that is unlikely. Similar Hebrew wording is used at 13:11 where the meaning is definitely that Lot moved eastward. The *plain* that they found apparently was *Shinar*. At 10:10 the major cities of Shinar are identified as Babylon, Erech, Akkad and Calneh.

3–4. The intentions of these people are revealed in two thoughts they express. The first is that they ought to make bricks. The note about bricks in place of stone and asphalt in place of mortar compares Mesopotamian building materials with those used in Palestine in antiquity. The second thought they express is about the building of a city and *a tower with its top in the heavens*. This is ominous, since the last mention of city building was at 4:17 where Cain built a city, thereby defying God's intent that he be a wanderer on the earth. The description of their plan and its ultimate demise is strikingly similar to Jeremiah's later prophecy about Babylon:

> Even if Babylon should ascend to the heavens
> and fortify her tall fortresses,
> destroyers will come against her from me [i.e. God].
> (Jer. 51:53, CSB)

The purpose for this city is to *make a name* for themselves which will keep them from being scattered. Once again defiance of God is expressed, since God had given a blessing for humans to spread throughout the earth (9:7). Interestingly, the actual work of building the city and tower is not mentioned. This is the author's way of demonstrating that the builders were trying to be like God, who can simply speak and bring about what he intends. So we are told their words, but not about the actual undertaking of construction.

5–7. Ironically, though the aspiration was to have a tower with its top in the heavens, God had to *come down* to see it. The Lord observes that they have begun their building project as *one people* with a common language. This allows that *nothing they plan to do will be impossible for them.* Since already before the flood God has observed that every human thought is always evil (6:5), the Lord is concerned about the potential for great human sinfulness if he does not take action to hold these plans in check. The solution is: *let us confuse their language.* Destroying the city and the tower which could have been rebuilt would have been futile. However, by constructing language barriers between the nations, collective sin would be restrained. This is the third and last time in Genesis that God's inner thoughts are portrayed in the first person plural (see 1:26; 3:22).

Just as the builders' words about their intentions to build are left to portray their act of building, so God's words about his intention to confuse human language are left without a description as to how he accomplished it. God is able simply to think or speak and make it come about, but the humans had to actually build to bring about their intentions (see v. 5).

8–9. The consequences of God's actions are portrayed in two verses. The city's construction was brought to a halt by God's scattering the builders over the face of the earth. What they had hoped to avoid (see v. 4) was triggered by their own folly. The city was called Babylon, and Moses connects this to the word for *confuse.* This is an ironic twist on the city's name which later Babylonians would claim to mean 'gate of God'. A further irony is that the builders wanted to make a name for themselves. They accomplished that, but it was a mocking name – Babylon, a city of confusion.

It should be noted that this summary of God's acts to halt the collective defiance of the builders is framed by the statement *from there the Lord scattered them over the face of the earth* (vv. 8, 9). This is not only an act of judgment and punishment, it is also designed to satisfy the mandate to fill the earth (9:1) as well as to limit human possibilities for collective efforts that lead to arrogant folly and sin.

Meaning

The Table of Nations and the Tower of Babylon account at first blush appear to be vastly different in both style and content. However, the two are designed to be complementary. The Table of Nations shows the fulfilment of God's blessing on Noah and his sons as their descendants fill the earth. However, the Tower of Babylon story shows that humans resisted God's blessing and arrogantly sought to prevent being scattered across the globe. Yet God's plan for a renewed earth after the flood would not be thwarted. His scattering of the nations was part of his greater plan to call someone from the line of Seth to bear his promise first given to Eve. Thus, this family record of Noah's sons (see 10:1) connects the antediluvian plan of God for reversing the curse of sin to the next section – the tracing of the promised line of Seth through Eber's son Peleg to Abram (11:10–26) – and prepares us for Abraham, the most important bearer of that promise in Genesis, his son Isaac and his grandson Jacob.

At the same time the Tower of Babylon account emphasizes that the flood did not provide a cure for human sin and hubris. In fact, the city of Babylon would come to symbolize faithless society and its sins, arrogance and rebellion against God. Isaiah will portray Babylon as wilful, self-righteous and comfortable in sinful luxury. Yet God will judge it (Isa. 47:8–13). While the first builders of Babylon sought to make a tower that reached into heaven, in Revelation Babylon would be used as a symbol of humans and their societies whose sins are piled as high as heaven (Rev. 18:5). Because of this sinful nature of fallen humans, God would not only scatter humankind and confuse its language, he would also keep his promises to Eve, Abraham, Isaac and Jacob so that at Pentecost the language barriers between nations could be overcome by the power of God's Holy Spirit (Acts 2:1–40). The gospel of Jesus Christ transcends human language through the living and active Word of God (Heb. 4:12). It unites people from all the scattered nations into one people of the God of Abraham, Isaac and Jacob (Matt. 8:11), redeemed from Adam's sin and filled with the Spirit so that they can sing with one voice in praise to the Lord, their Redeemer and Creator (Eph. 5:18–20).

Additional note on the literary structure of the primeval history (1:1 – 11:9)

From creation to the scattering of the nations at Babylon, Genesis presents a sort of pre-history leading up to the patriarchs of Israel. This primeval history is often depicted as more legendary than real. However, Genesis is presenting the sweep of history that prepares for the detailed account of God's choosing and creating one special nation to bear his promise to all of humankind. As such, it displays God's work in time in two panels that parallel each other, and does so as actual historical events. The first panel depicts the created earth and the subsequent corruption of it by sin. The second panel depicts the earth renewed through the flood and repopulation of it, though sin remains a curse.

These two panels are arranged in parallel fashion, presenting five major themes presented in the same order in each panel as Genesis prepares for God's final creative act in this book: the bringing forth of a new nation, Israel (Isa. 43:1, 15). These five themes in two panels are shown in Table 8.

Table 8 The five major themes presented in two parallel panels

Panel 1	Panel 2	Theme
Creation (1:1 – 2:25)	Flood (6:9 – 9:17)	Beginnings: A created/renewed world
Fall into sin (3:1–24)	Noah's nakedness (9:18–24)	Sin leads to human nakedness that needs to be covered
Cain kills Abel (4:1–16)	The curse of Canaan (9:24–29)	Sin affects the next generation
Cain and Seth's genealogies (4:17 – 5:32)	The Table of Nations (10:1–32)	Descendants of one man (Adam/Noah)
Intermarriage of the faithful and the unbelieving (6:1–8)	Tower of Babylon (11:1–9)	Human arrogance and God's judgment

This two-panel literary design is purposeful, as shown especially by the placement of the Table of Nations and Tower of Babylon in reverse chronological order so that the five themes can be present in the same order in both panels. The complete primeval history is designed to demonstrate the need for God's chosen people and his wisdom in choosing sinners to bear his promise, since there is no cure for a sin-infested world apart from God's promise and plan as worked out through them in the nation of the Saviour for all people, Israelite and non-Israelite alike (1 Cor. 12:13–14). All that is left is to connect the primeval history to the story of Abraham, Isaac and Jacob. That will be accomplished in the next major section of Genesis, the genealogy from Shem to Terah and his sons.

6. THE FAMILY OF SHEM: GENEALOGY FROM SHEM TO TERAH (11:10–26)

Context

This brief family history (*tôlĕdôt*) of Shem connects the primeval history to the patriarchal narratives that will occupy most of the rest of Genesis. It explores one line of Shem that had not been treated in the Table of Nations (10:1–32), the line beginning with Shem going through Eber and his son Peleg (10:25) and ending with Abram and his brothers. It is similar to the genealogy from Adam to Noah (5:1–32) both in form and in the fact that it ends with a generation of three brothers (5:32; 11:26). Together these two lines trace the promise of God to crush the head of the serpent (3:15) from Eve's son Seth to Noah and his son who was the next bearer of the promise, Shem (9:26), and on to the most important recipient of God's gracious promise in Genesis, Abraham.

In form this genealogy is strikingly similar to the one in 5:1–32. Yet there is a key difference, as can be seen in the recurring formulas in the two genealogies:

Genesis 5	And [Person A] lived [X] years and generated [Person B]
	And [Person A] lived after he generated [Person B] [Y] years
	And he generated sons and daughters
	And all the days of [Person A] were [X + Y] years, and he died.
Genesis 11	And [Person A] lived [X] years and generated [Person B]
	And [Person A] lived after he generated [Person B] [Y] years
	And he generated sons and daughters.

The final note of the total years and death is conspicuous by its absence in 11:10–26. The absence of this death notice is a reminder of God's promise of patience with humankind after the flood (8:21–22). After the folly of the Tower of Babylon there was no worldwide calamity. Instead God used the scattering of the nations to fulfil his desire that the earth be populated (9:1). Death would still affect all people, but the absence of the death notice brings a hopeful note to the rest of Genesis. Readers are now prepared to focus on the promise of God to Abraham, Isaac and Jacob that *in you all the nations of the earth will be blessed* (18:18; 22:18; 26:4; 28:14).

This genealogy stands at the head of the patriarchal history of Genesis and initiates a pattern that will last until the end of the book: shorter genealogies will alternate with longer patriarchal narratives, as shown in Table 9 on p. 138.

Therefore, this genealogy is both backward- and forward-looking, but of these two, the view towards the future is the greater light for readers.

Comment

10. *Two years after the flood* has caused problems for interpreters. Genesis 5:32 appears to place Shem's birth when Noah was 500 years old, and 7:6 places the flood when Noah was 600 years old. So this verse would place Shem's birth when Noah was 502 years old. One proposed solution is that 10:21 should be read as if Japheth was Shem's older brother so that 5:32 mentions the age of Noah

Table 9 Alternation of shorter genealogies
with longer patriarchal narratives

Genealogy of Shem:	**'This is the family history of Shem'**	11:10–26
Abraham as God's chosen one:	'This is the family history of Terah'	11:27 – 25:11
Genealogy of Ishmael:	**'This is the family history of Ishmael'**	25:12–18
Jacob as God's chosen one:	'This is the family history of Isaac'	25:19 – 35:29
Genealogy of Esau:	**'This is the family history of Esau'**	36:1–43
Joseph and Judah:	'This is the family history of Jacob'	37:2 – 50:26

when the first of his three sons, Japheth, was born. However, this is a questionable way to understand 10:21. Perhaps the best we can say is that the Hebrew verb for 'father a son or descendant' is not to be understood as one would in English. For instance, at 10:15 it is used of Canaan fathering Sidon, who appears to be a person (as his firstborn), but it is also used of Canaan fathering nations such as the Amorites. Thus, the exact action taken by Noah when he was 500 years old is not clear to us.

The birth of Arpachshad demonstrates Shem's faith in God's blessing as he is fulfilling the mandate to fill the earth (9:1) soon after the flood. This sets the tone for the entire genealogy as leading up to God's blessing on Abram.

11. This note of Shem's remaining life (500 years) and death sets the pattern for the rest of the notices in this genealogy. Note that unlike in the pre-diluvian genealogy (5:1–32), the age at death is not listed.

12–15. The LXX includes another person in the genealogy at this point – Kainan (as a son of Arpachshad). However, this is most certainly a secondary addition to the text.[1] These ancestors of

---

1. Steinmann (2017c).

Abram – *Arpachshad* (vv. 12–13) and *Shelah* (vv. 14–15) – are of little prominence in the rest of Scripture.

16–17. *Eber*, though of seemingly little significance in this genealogy, is an important ancestor of Abram since his name was used to characterize his descendants as Hebrews (cf. *all the sons of Eber*, 10:21)

18–19. *Peleg* played a prominent role in the Table of Nations, since the division of the earth happened in his lifetime (10:25). This perhaps is also emphasized by the sudden reduction in human lifespan at this point. Eber lived 464 years (vv. 16–17), and before him Shelah lived 433 years (vv. 14–15). However, Peleg lived only 239 years, and the next two generations will experience similar lifespans.

20–23. *Reu* (vv. 20–21) and *Serug* (vv. 22–23) are two of the more obscure persons mentioned in Scripture, appearing elsewhere only in genealogies (1 Chr. 1:25–26; Luke 3:35).

24–25. *Nahor* is listed two generations before Abram, who will also have a brother by this name.

26. The genealogy ends with three sons of one man, *Terah*. This matches the antediluvian genealogy from Adam to Noah and his three sons.

It appears as if Terah had triplets, *Abram, Nahor and Haran*, when he was seventy years old. However, this is not the case. After Terah's death at 205 years of age, Abram was called by God to leave Haran (12:1–4). At that time Abram was seventy-five years old, implying that Abram was born when Terah was 130 years old. The date was 2166 BC.[2] Perhaps another brother was born when Terah was seventy. Or, as noted in the comment on verse 10, it may be that the Hebrew verb for fathering children is not well understood.

Meaning

The genealogy of Shem completes the line from Adam to Abram, at which point the pace of the narrative in Genesis slows. The two genealogies of this line (5:1–32 and 11:10–26) combine to point the reader to God's promise. To subtly demonstrate this, the two

---

2. Steinmann (2011: 67).

genealogies highlight important members of this descent from Adam using the numbers ten and seven. The righteous Noah is the tenth generation listed after Adam, and Abram is the twentieth. Enoch, who walked with God, is the seventh, and in the combined genealogies Eber, the eponymous ancestor of the Hebrews, is the fourteenth.[3] From Eber to Abram are seven generations, counting inclusively. The blessed son of Noah, Shem, is in the middle of these generations, and Abram is ten generations after him. All these are purposeful arrangements of the genealogical information that most likely skips over some unnamed ancestors in order to foreground these righteous men.[4]

Moreover, the genealogy starts again with Shem to trace this line, instead of starting with Peleg where this line diverges from the other descendants of Shem (10:25). By doing this, Moses has created an implied pun with the Tower of Babylon narrative. There the builders sought to make a name for themselves (11:4). They failed to achieve a good reputation, but the real name comes in the promised line of Shem, whose name means 'Name'. God had already provided a name in the promised line of the Saviour to come. Thus, this genealogy looks forward to the man to whom God would promise a *great name*, Abraham (12:2).

---

3. On the importance of multiples of the seventh position in biblical genealogies, see Sasson (1978).

4. Genealogies that are selective (i.e. they skip some generations) are common in the Scriptures. See Steinmann (2017b). This, of course, implies that one cannot use the ages of the persons mentioned in these genealogies to determine the date of the flood or the age of the earth.

7. THE FAMILY OF TERAH: ABRAM'S RESPONSE TO GOD'S CALL (11:27 – 12:20)

Context

A new long section of Genesis begins with the family history (*tôlĕdôt*) of Terah and extends until 25:11. For the purposes of this commentary, this family history will be split into seven sections.

Having traced the promised line of humankind from Shem to Terah and his sons, this new history, though labelled the family history of Terah, will concentrate on only one of his sons, Abram. It begins with a short description of Terah's sons and grandson Lot and how they came to be living in Haran before Terah's death. Following this we are introduced to Abram through God's call to him and his response, which occupies all of chapter 12. We see Abram's response as a great act of faith in leaving Haran for Canaan (12:1–9), but then see it as a failure of faith as he leaves Canaan on his own and travels to Egypt (12:10–20). This will begin Abram's struggle that is in some way paradigmatic of the life of all believers – moments of great trust in God and moments of weakness and doubt. It will climax in Abraham's greatest test, after which the promise quickly moves on to Isaac in the next generation (22:1 – 24:67).

Comment
A. Terah and his sons (11:27–32)

This short section introduces the family of Terah and explains their lives before God called Abram to leave Haran.

27. The introduction to the family of Terah is marked by his mention here and again at the end in verse 32. The list of sons connects this with the previous genealogy of Shem but also includes Terah's grandson Lot in anticipation of his importance in later narratives (13:1 – 14:24; 19:1–38).

28. Haran's death is important for understanding Lot's attachment first to Terah (v. 31) and later to Abram after Terah's death (12:4–5). *Ur of the Chaldeans* is most often identified with the city in lower Mesopotamia with this name. However, there are good reasons to believe that the Ur mentioned here is a city in the area of Haran, probably modern-day Sanliurfa in Turkey near the Syrian border.[1] First, Abram calls Haran *my native land* (24:7, CSB; see also ESV, TNK) or more precisely 'the land of my birth'. This phrase when used elsewhere always signifies one's native land, not a region to which one emigrated (31:13; Ruth 2:11; Jer. 22:10; 46:16; Ezek. 23:15). Second, a tablet from ancient Ebla speaks of an Ur in the land Haran.[2] Third, the Ur in lower Mesopotamia was a Sumerian city, and the Chaldeans did not penetrate this area until about 1000 BC, making it unlikely that it would have been called 'Ur of the Chaldeans' by Moses.[3]

29. It appears that Abram and Nahor were younger than their brother Haran and married after his death. Apparently neither Abram nor Nahor had children at this time (see 22:20–24). Abram's relationship to his wife Sarai is not mentioned. Elsewhere we learn that she was his half-sister (20:12), but this is hidden from the reader at this early juncture in Genesis. Sarai was ten

----

1. Historically this city has borne many names. In Hellenistic times it was called Edessa or Callirrhoe.

2. Gordon (1977).

3. One might argue that this is a later interpretive gloss. See the discussion of later updating of the Pentateuch in the Introduction.

years younger than her husband, placing her birth in 2156 BC (17:1, 17).[4] Nahor married his niece Milcah. The reason for mentioning Milcah's sister Iscah is not obvious, since this is the only statement about her in the Bible. There was a strong attachment to family in this clan, as exhibited by endogamy – marrying one's relative (see also 24:1–4; 29:13–30). Genesis preserves the information about the patriarchs' endogamy – especially Abram's marriage to his sister, which was later forbidden in the law of Moses (Lev. 18:9; 20:17; Deut. 27:22), and Jacob's marriage to two sisters (Lev. 18:18). This testifies to the antiquity and reliability of the information in Genesis.

Sarai means 'princess' and may be a reference to Šarratu, the wife of the moon god Sin in the Mesopotamian pantheon. *Milcah* means 'queen' and may be a reference to Malkatu, the daughter of Sin. If this is the case, then the gods worshipped by Israel's ancestors (Josh. 24:2, 15) might have been especially associated with the cult of the moon or astral deities in general.

30. Sarai's plight is quickly summarized. This, of course, would have been a major source of anguish and even conflict in Abram and Sarai's marriage. Barrenness often caused bitterness in the lives of women in antiquity, and the Old Testament contains other examples (Judg. 13:2–3; 1 Sam. 1:2–8; Isa. 54:1). Abram and Sarai's lack of children is in contrast to Haran's having two daughters and one son and sometime later children being born to Nahor's wife Milcah and his concubine Reumah (22:20–24).

31–32. The intention of Terah to go to Canaan is not explained, but it does presage Abram's later move to Canaan at God's behest after Terah's death (12:1–9). There is no mention of Nahor's accompanying his father, but he eventually moved to the same area (24:10). The death notice for Terah not only supplies the missing lifespan data from the previous genealogy, but also notes that he did not complete the move to Canaan, having settled in Haran (often spelled 'Harran'). Haran is on the Balih River some 20 miles (32 km) south-east of modern Edessa (ancient Urfa).

---

4. Steinmann (2011: 71).

B. The call of Abram (12:1–9)

2091 BC

The narrative pace of Genesis slows at the beginning of this chapter. In contrast to the fast pace of centuries from Adam to Terah, the storyline extending over fourteen chapters focuses on Abram's life and relationship with God who calls him to be the bearer of the promise that will be a blessing to all nations. This chronicle of the favour of God begins in 2091 BC,[5] Abram's seventy-fifth year, with his call to leave his father's house in Haran.

1. The Lord's first and last words to Abram begin with an imperative: *Go* and *Take* (22:2). Here a triple reference to the place from which Abram is to go is included: county, homeland, father's house. God's last instructions contain a triple mention of whom Abram should take: your son, your only son whom you love, Isaac. Abram is to go to the land which Yahweh will *show* him. The reference to the land is vague, though formerly the goal of Terah's move from Ur was Canaan, the land God will promise to Abram. In addition, at 15:7, God states that he brought Abram out of Ur to give him the land of Canaan, thereby implying that Canaan as a destination was revealed to Abram (and perhaps Terah) before they left Ur. At this point he is not promised the land of Canaan, but that is certainly implied. Yet, as Hebrews 11:8 points out, Abram did not know what his destination would be. Perhaps what God had revealed before Terah's death was not the destination for Abram by himself. The next verses will explain how God showed Abram the land: he travelled from north to south through the land – Shechem (v. 6), between Bethel and Ai (v. 8), and finally to the Negev (v. 9). Later, God will command Abram to travel throughout the land which God will give him (13:17).

2–3. These two verses present seven statements to Abram that explore the aspects of God's blessing. The first three and the fifth and sixth statements are promises of what God will do. The fourth statement is about Abram, and the seventh about all peoples on earth:

---

5. Steinmann (2011: 72).

1. *I will make you a great nation* (God's promise).
2. *I will bless you* (God's promise).
3. *I will make your name great* (God's promise).
4. *Be a blessing* (an imperative, here expressing an invitation to Abram).
5. *I will bless those who bless you* (God's promise).
6. *I will curse those who treat you with contempt* (God's promise).
7. *All the peoples of the earth will consider themselves blessed through you* (the peoples' reaction).

The promise of a great nation is ironic in the light of the notice of Sarai's barren state at 11:30, but by being placed first, it is foregrounded as the most important blessing. Much of the story of Abram will revolve around having an heir to produce this nation.

The promise of a great name is also somewhat ironic in the light of the previous attempt by people to make a name for themselves at Babylon (11:4). The true privilege of a great name can only be conferred by God. In the Old Testament there are only three 'great name's. In addition to Abram, we note that David was promised a great name (2 Sam. 7:9; 1 Chr. 17:8). More importantly, God's name is great (Josh. 7:9; 1 Sam. 12:22; 2 Sam. 7:26; 1 Kgs 8:42; 1 Chr. 17:24; 2 Chr. 6:32; Pss 76:1; 99:3; 138:2; Jer. 10:6; 44:26; Ezek. 36:23; Mal. 1:11). There are two implications of this grant of a great name. First, since God's name is the ultimate great name, Abram here is being adopted as God's son. Second, as shown by David receiving a great name, this promise bestows royal title on Abram. This is reinforced later in Genesis when it is promised that kings will come from Abram and Sarai (17:6, 16), and the Hittites recognize Abraham as prince (23:6).

The fourth statement is often taken to be a promise and translated as a passive: *you will be a blessing* (CSB, ESV, GW, NIV). However, the Hebrew verb is an imperative – *be a blessing* – which can be used not only for commands but also for invitations. Here God is inviting Abram to receive the previous three blessings and thereby become a blessing to others. As such it offers a transition to the next promises of God which focus on Abram's relationships with others.

The fifth and sixth statements are paired as polar opposites. God promises that Abram's blessings will become blessings to others who look favourably on him and protection from those who are hostile. This is summarized later as God being Abram's shield (15:1).

The seventh statement reveals the reaction of peoples to Abram and the blessing he brings. Traditionally, this has been translated passively: 'all peoples . . . will be blessed' (CSB, ESV, GW, NIV), though because of the form of the verb in Hebrew some have taken it to be reflexive: 'all peoples . . . will bless themselves' (TNK) or 'all [peoples] . . . will bless one other' (NET). However, it is probably best to understand the reflexive form here as an indirect reflexive with an estimative force: *all peoples . . . will consider themselves blessed.*[6] In this case, the passive construction in English (and Greek: see Acts 3:25; Gal. 3:8) more closely approximates the intended meaning of the Hebrew verb than does a strictly reflexive translation.

4–6. Not only does the text emphasize that Abram went as the Lord told him, but it also makes a point of noting that Lot accompanied him, mentioning him twice (vv. 4–5). Thus, Abram's departure from his *father's house* is somewhat incomplete, since Lot will continue to be with him for some time. The conditions to God's command were not completed until Lot later separated from Abram (13:1–13). At that point God reiterated his promise to Abram (13:14–17). Abram's age is given for the first time here and will also be noted at other important junctures (16:16; 17:1, 24; 21:5; 25:7). This helps the reader to understand the patriarch's trust in God in that he is already seventy-five years old and without a son as heir. Presumably Lot was his heir until they later parted company (13:8–13). We are also told that Abram had become wealthy while in Haran, having acquired possessions and slaves that he brought with him to Canaan. His first stop is at Shechem, a place that will play an important role in the lives of later patriarchs (33:19; 34:2–26; 35:4) and in Israelite history (Josh. 24; 1 Kgs 12). Shechem was located between Mounts Ebal and Gerizim and today lies just east of the modern city of Nablus.

The *Oak of Moreh* is mentioned only here. However, 'Oaks of Moreh' (plural) associated with the same general area are mentioned

---

6. Lee (2012).

at Deuteronomy 11:30. The specific type of tree denoted by the
Hebrew term is disputed, but most modern versions understand it
to be an oak tree, either the Tabor oak (*Quercus ithaburensis*) or the
common evergreen oak (*Quercus calliprinos*). However, many commentaries take it to be a terebinth (*Pistacia palaestina*). The name *Oak
of Moreh* means 'Oak of the Teacher', which may imply that the
peoples of the land used this tree for divination. If that is the case,
then this tree may also be mentioned at Judges 9:6, 37, where it is
called 'the Oak of the Pillar at Shechem' and 'the Diviners' Oak'. In
any case, it seems that the *Oak of Moreh* is probably referenced again
at Genesis 35:4 and Joshua 24:26, though the name *Oak of Moreh* is
not used in either passage.

The mention of the Canaanites being in the land not only forms
a connection with the Table of Nations (10:15), but also prepares
the reader for the patriarchs' interaction with several Canaanite
peoples, such as the sons of Heth (often translated *Hittites*; 23:3–20;
25:9–10; 26:34; 27:46; 36:2; see 10:15), the Amorites (14:13; 48:22)
and the Hivites (34:2; 36:2).

7. The Lord's theophany at *Shechem* is the first of eight times in
Genesis where it is said that *Yahweh appeared* or *God appeared* to a
patriarch.[7] God's manifestation explicitly confirms the implied
promise of the land of Canaan as the possession of Abram's
descendants (see v. 1). This statement unites the two great temporal
foci of the promises to the patriarchs: descendants and land. Both
foci are the intermediate steps in the fulfilment of the great salvific
promise of blessing for all peoples.

Abram's response is worship: he built an altar, an echo of Noah's
altar built in response to God's delivering him from the waters of
the flood (8:20). Altar-building (and presumably sacrifice) is an act
of worship in response to the Lord's actions. It is mentioned three
more times for Abram (v. 8 [Bethel]; 13:18 [Hebron]; 22:9 [Mount

---

7. The other places where the phrase *Yahweh/God appeared* is found in the
text are 17:1; 18:1 (to Abram); 26:2, 24 (to Isaac); 35:1, 9; 48:3 (Jacob).
Apparently 35:1 counts Jacob's dream at Luz/Bethel as an appearance
of Yahweh, although 'appeared' is not used of God in the account of
the dream (28:12–15).

Moriah]), once for Isaac (26:25 [Beersheba]) and once for Jacob (35:7 [Luz/Bethel]). Thus, the author again uses the sacred number seven when noting the instances of altar construction in Genesis. Building an altar as a response to a theophany will continue in Israelite history (Exod. 20:24; Judg. 13:16; 1 Kgs 3:15).

8–9. The report of Abram's move to the area of Bethel is fairly extensive. It mentions him pitching his tent there, implying an extended period of time spent in this place. The mention of both Bethel and Ai not only further defines Abram's residence, but also presents two names of places that derive from later events. Bethel was named by Jacob. Its former name was Luz (28:19). Ai means 'ruin', a name that most likely derives from Joshua's sacking of the city (Josh. 8). The use of these two names cannot date from Abram's day, and Ai cannot date from Moses' time. Most likely these names were later scribal replacements for the Canaanite names of these towns in order to make the text more intelligible for later readers.

Abram's extended stay at Bethel led to his building another altar where he would *call on the name of the Lord*, suggesting regular formal worship of God. This phrase connects Abram to the godly people before the flood who worshipped Yahweh (4:26).

Abram's journey eventually continued southward to the Negev in the southern portion of the land between the Judean hills and Kadesh Barnea. By this point Abram has seen the land from north to south – God has shown him the land (cf. v. 1).

C. Abram in Egypt: he deceives Pharaoh (12:10–20)

c.2088 BC

While the previous account of Abram in Canaan demonstrated his trust in God, this narrative shows his doubts about God's promises. God had guaranteed that those who blessed Abram would be blessed and those who cursed him would be cursed. Had Abram trusted this promise he would have had no fear of being killed in Egypt (v. 12), would not have resorted to subterfuge (v. 13), and would not have involved Pharaoh and Sarai in an adulterous relationship (v. 19). Yet despite Abram's lack of confidence in God's pledges, God remained faithful to Abram. He struck Pharaoh's house with pestilence to protect Abram's marriage (v. 17) and he allowed Abram to become richer (v. 16; see 13:2). The blessing depends on God's promise, not on Abram's behaviour.

The account is presented in three scenes: Abram's move to Egypt, including his conversation with Sarai (vv. 10–13), the entry into Egypt when Sarai is taken into Pharaoh's household (vv. 14–16) and the Lord's action leading to Pharaoh's rebuke of Abram (vv. 17–20).

10–13. While Abram's move to Canaan was prompted by God's word, his move to Egypt was triggered by an acute *famine in the land* (v. 10). The famine is mentioned twice within one verse, suggesting that the only consideration given by Abram for the move was the famine's severity. Each of the patriarchs would migrate because of famine (26:1; 42:5; 47:11–13). The absence of God's instructions to leave Canaan is not commented upon by the author. However, an ominous note is sounded by Abram basing a decision on temporal observation rather than divine mandate. The Hebrew text suggests that Abram intended to settle in Egypt for some time as a resident alien.

Abram's plea to Sarai has four elements:

- Observation: Sarai is a beautiful woman (v. 11; see vv. 14–15).
- Supposition: the Egyptians will kill Abram but let Sarai live (v. 12).
- Request: *Say you are my sister* (v. 13).
- Intended result: things will go well for Abram, and he will be allowed to live (v. 13).

Each of these four elements calls for some comment.

Sarai's beauty appears to modern readers to be exaggerated. She had to have been sixty-five years old when the family left Haran (compare 12:4 with 17:17). After some time in Canaan, she would have been somewhat older, but probably was somewhat shy of seventy. However, it ought to be noted that standards of beauty vary from culture to culture, and this statement ought not to be understood according to modern notions of beauty. In addition, Sarai would live 127 years, so at sixty-five to seventy years old she may still have been quite attractive, especially given the blessing of longevity that was characteristic of the patriarchal families.[8]

No reason is given as to why Abram would have presumed that the Egyptians would kill him and take his wife. He is depicted as making no such assumption among the Canaanites, though he would make the same assumption later among the Philistines when he would again engage in the same deception (20:11). However, 20:13 implies that Abram made this assumption and the resulting request that Sarai claim she was his sister wherever they went from the time they left Haran.

Sarai's reply to the request is not reported, but given the subsequent turn of events, it appears that she was complicit in Abram's duplicity. The statement was not, strictly speaking, a lie, since Sarai was Abram's half-sister (20:12). However, at this point the reader has not been told this information about Sarai, since when Abram later revealed his sibling relationship when speaking to the Philistine king Abimelech, he was offering a rather lame excuse for his dishonesty. There is no way of excusing Abram's action: he deceived Pharaoh, and he did not trust God's promise to protect him (12:3).

The results that Abram intended did come about: he fared well (v. 16) and he was not killed. However, there is no hint in the text that the results justified Abram's means to those ends. Moreover, he was immediately expelled from Egypt when his deceit was discovered. This worked contrary to his reason for entering Egypt in the first place, thereby calling into question his judgment in the matter of Sarai and in his decision to leave Canaan.

14–16. Abram's perception of Sarai's beauty was shared by the Egyptians (v. 14). In fact, while Abram described her as *beautiful* (v. 11), they saw her as *very beautiful*. She was so comely that word got to Pharaoh about this woman through his officials (v. 15). The use of the title *Pharaoh* for the king of Egypt did not gain currency until Egypt's eighteenth dynasty, around 1500 BC. Before this it

---

8. Abram lived 175 years (25:7); Isaac lived 180 years (35:28); Jacob lived 147 years (47:28); Joseph lived 110 years (50:22); Levi lived 137 years (Exod. 6:16).

retained its original meaning, 'great house' (= 'palace'). Therefore, the use of this term here displays evidence of Moses' own milieu in the fifteenth century BC. The taking of Sarai into Pharaoh's household implies that she became part of his harem and one of his wives, as Pharaoh explicitly admits in verse 19.

Abram was favoured by Pharaoh with property, including *camels*. The mention of these pack animals has led some to posit that Genesis is a late composition, dating to the first millennium BC, on the theory that domesticated camels were not known in Egypt and Palestine until that time. However, there are a number of problems with this contention. Evidence for the early domestication of camels is far-reaching. They were used in Iran as early as the twenty-seventh century BC and in the Indus Valley by the twenty-third century. Moreover, dromedary camels were domesticated earlier than this, possibly in the first centuries of the third millennium BC.[9] While widespread use of camels in Palestine is not documented before 1400 BC, the patriarchs' use of camels obtained either in Egypt (probably as a luxury item) or in Mesopotamia, as well as their use in caravans passing through Canaan, is not an indication of anachronisms in Genesis.[10]

17–20. While we are not told the nature of the plagues visited upon Pharaoh's household, there is a foreshadowing of the later plagues in Exodus. In this case God used the plagues as a warning to Pharaoh, a form of indirect divine revelation. Nonetheless, God holds Pharaoh responsible for adultery, even when it was committed

---

9. LaBianca (2003: 120) notes, 'There seems to be general agreement among experts about the domestication of the one-humped camel or dromedary – possibly in Somalia – sometime during the third millennium B.C.E.'

10. See 12:16; 24:10–11, 14, 19–20, 22, 30–32, 35, 44, 46, 61, 63–64; 30:43; 31:17, 34; 32:7, 15; 37:25. LaBianca (2003: 121) states, 'It is a curious fact, in this regard, that as far as the Levantine countries are concerned, the camel does not appear to have played a very significant role either as a herding animal or as a transport animal before 1400 B.C.E.' Note that this statement does not rule out camels in Palestine; it only says that their role was not significant before 1400 BC.

unknowingly. In the Old Testament sinners are held accountable even for unwitting sins, as demonstrated later by the laws on sacrifices in Leviticus.

Pharaoh's rebuke of Abram is scathing (vv. 18–19) and directly blames him for involving the Egyptian king in adultery (v. 19). This may have contributed to Sarai's continued barrenness, as God did not open her womb for many more years. This was as a demonstration that Isaac was not Pharaoh's child. Note that in the case of Abimelech taking Sarai just before Isaac's birth (20:1–18), the reader is pointedly told that Abimelech did not have sexual relations with her (20:4), prior to the birth of Isaac.

It is noteworthy that Abram had no reply to Pharaoh. His silence places an exclamation point on his conduct. His actions were morally reprehensible, even to the Egyptians. He lied about his relationship to Sarai, he put his wife at risk, he accepted property gained under false pretences and he behaved completely selfishly, putting his welfare before his wife's well-being. For this he was sent away from Egypt, and his plan to escape the famine in Canaan thoroughly backfired. Nonetheless, he was allowed to keep the property he amassed in Egypt, perhaps because Pharaoh feared further plagues should he have confiscated Abram's ill-gotten gains.

Meaning
These opening portions of the life of Abram as follower of Yahweh initiate themes for much of what is to come later. Genesis 11:27–32 introduces persons important for the remaining narrative of Abram's life and the life of Isaac: Abram, the barren Sarai, Lot and Nahor (22:20–23; 24:15–29). The beginning of the Abram narrative, 12:1–9, sets the tone not only for the rest of Abram's life with God, but also for the rest of Genesis. Here Abram receives God's promise and responds in faith. This promise becomes the heritage of Isaac, Jacob and Jacob's sons. Moreover, the promise is given not simply for the sake of Israel, but for the entire human race. The blessing for Abram will bring blessing to all nations (Jer. 4:2; Acts 3:25; Gal. 3:8). Even Israel's enemies such as Egypt and Assyria will join in sharing the blessing (Isa. 19:24). Like Abram, they will *call on the name of Yahweh* (12:8; Zeph. 3:9), and those who share Abram's faith will be like Abram, who left his homeland and looked for a

new place, 'a city . . . whose designer and builder is God' (Heb. 11:8–10).

But Abram's life was not simply a straight line of ever-increasing faith. As the very next incident in his life demonstrates, he, like all believers, struggled with the challenges of life. These challenges led him to rely on cunning and deception rather than simply trusting that God would keep his promise of blessings and curses on those who interacted with Abram (12:3). Moreover, Abram's deception introduces a family trait that is found throughout Genesis. Abram will also deceive Abimelech concerning his relationship with Sarai (ch. 20), and Isaac will similarly mislead the king of Gerar about Rebekah (26:7–11). Rachel and Jacob will conspire to trick Isaac (27:1–40). Laban will dupe Jacob into marrying Leah (29:13–30). Rachel will deceive Laban (31:22–35). Simeon and Levi will use cunning and duplicity to deceive and kill the inhabitants of Shechem (34:8–29). Jacob's sons will deceive him about Joseph (37:31–35). The sinful inclination that God observed to be part of every human is no less a part of the patriarchal family (6:5). In fact, this sinful tendency to deception is shown in bold relief by comparing the foreign monarchs with the patriarchs in the wife/sister stories in Genesis (12:10–20; 20:1–18; 26:7–11). The kings are more concerned about morality than is either Abram or Isaac.

Nevertheless, God's commitment to his promise overrides human weakness. The promise to Abram will be repeated in similar terms to Isaac and then to Jacob. Ultimately, the story of Abram and his descendants is not about their transgressions, but about God's grace. His commitment to rescue humankind from sin and death moves the narratives to point ever forward to God's unfolding promise in Genesis and the rest of Scripture.

8. THE FAMILY OF TERAH: ABRAM'S FAITHFULNESS REFLECTED IN HIS RELATIONSHIP WITH LOT (13:1 – 14:24)

Context

When God first called Abram, he told him to leave his native land and his father's household (12:1). Abram partially obeyed, leaving Haran and travelling to Canaan, but taking with him a member of his father's household – Lot. Even this partial obedience, however, was temporary, since Abram took it upon himself to leave Canaan for Egypt. Now that Abram is restored to the land that God had shown him (13:1; see 12:7), his second act of obedience – cutting the ties to his father's household – comes in Genesis 13 as Lot and Abram separate. Abram will rescue his nephew when he is captured (14:11–16) and he will plead for Sodom, where Lot is living (18:16–33), but their parting will come in this chapter. After this, Genesis will never again depict direct interaction between Abram and Lot. They will remain relatives, but will be separated by distance – Abram at Hebron (13:18) and Lot in Sodom (13:12). Moreover, the text places distance between them for the reader by making 13:8–9 the last recorded words spoken by Abram to his kinsman Lot. Yet Abram's familial ties to Lot will continue a while longer when he rescues Lot from captivity (14:1–16). After securing Lot, he provides for his return to Sodom.

Comment
A. Abram and Lot separate (13:1–18)

c.2087 BC

Yahweh's original promises to Abram implied the gift of the land – *go . . . to the land I will show you* (12:1) – but they explicitly focused on two intertwined promises: Abram would have descendants (i.e. a great nation, 12:2), and he would be the bearer of the messianic promise – he would be a great blessing (12:2) and all peoples would be blessed through him (12:3). This account of the parting of the ways of Abram and Lot focuses on one facet of God's promises to Abram: the promise of possession of the land of Canaan as a place for Abram's descendants (12:7; 13:14–17). The promise of the land becomes the focus of this chapter as Abram returns from Egypt to the land of Canaan. Thus, 13:1–18 is tied back to 12:1–9 especially through the emphasis on the land. It is also linked forward to Abram's concern for an heir to receive God's promises (15:1–21). Between these is situated the remnant of Abram's former association with the house of his father: Lot. Lot's situation between the possession of the land and the birth of an heir is a test for Abram: will he make the final break with his father's household?[1]

1–4. The mention of Abram's return to Canaan contains three geographic references. His re-entry comes as he arrives in the Negev in the extreme south of the land. This southernmost and driest part of Canaan was characterized by more settlement during the Middle Bronze Age than in later eras, making Abram's presence there quite plausible. He then moved on from place to place until he came to Bethel in the centre of Canaan, the second geographic reference. Then we are specifically told that he went to the place

---

1. Rickett (2011) notes the connection between the promise of the land and the final separation of Abram from his father's household as a central theme in 13:1–18.

between Bethel and Ai where he had built an altar, where he again called on Yahweh's name (see 12:8).

It is interesting that Lot is mentioned last among the people and things that came out of Egypt with Abram (v. 1; contrast 12:5). Already the text is placing some distance between Abram and his nephew.

Abram's wealth is also noted. Presumably, much of this came from Pharaoh (see 12:16). The Hebrew text contains a play on words between Abram's previous time in Canaan when the famine was severe (Hebrew *kābēd*) and this time when Abram was wealthy (also Hebrew *kābēd*). Abram's wealth was not only in cattle, but now included silver and gold (v. 2). This is the first mention of precious metals as a sign of wealth. Previously 2:11–12 noted the land of Havilah as a source of fine gold, but Abram is the first person mentioned in the Pentateuch as possessing gold.

5–7. Lot's wealth is mentioned as he is introduced into the narrative as a rival to Abram for the land. The text emphasizes this when it says he *also* had flocks, herds and tents. We are told that they *lived together* but their possessions made them unable to *live together* (v. 6). 'Living' or 'dwelling' is a key term throughout this chapter: other peoples lived in the land (v. 7); Abram would live in Canaan, and Lot near Sodom (v. 12); Abram would live at Hebron (v. 18).

The quarrelling was not between Abram and Lot, but between their herdsmen – probably slaves – and they appear in the narrative as surrogates that express the tension between these two now-wealthy men. There is a touch of irony in the note that Canaanites and Perizzites were living in the land. They could occupy the land together, but Abram and Lot could not. Perizzites are mentioned for the first time here in the Pentateuch; they will be mentioned twenty-two more times in the Old Testament. In Genesis they appear again in 15:19–21 amidst a list of ten ethnic groups occupying the land that God promised to Abram. They are again paired with the Canaanites at 34:30.

8–9. Abram takes the initiative to offer a solution to the friction between the two households. He notes that as *relatives* or 'kinsmen' they ought not to engage in strife with each other (v. 8). By characterizing Lot as a relative (the Hebrew word is the regular word for 'brother'), Abram is at once noting their obligation to live together peacefully (see Ps. 133:1). At the same time, he is not treating Lot as his heir, but trusting in God's promise to grant him heirs. Lot will be called Abram's relative twice more in the next chapter (14:14, 16).

Abram's offer to allow Lot to choose from *the whole land* (v. 9) not only is generous, but also displays his faith in God's promise to give his offspring the land. Lot's choice is not the determining factor; God's promise is.

10–13. From a hill in the vicinity of Bethel one could look out over the land to the east and see the southern end of the Jordan River as it entered the Dead Sea. The fertile area north of the Dead Sea is the area called *the Plain of the Jordan* (vv. 10–11; see 1 Kgs 7:46; 2 Chr. 4:17) and, therefore, was the area in which the five Cities of the Plain were located. The Cities of the Plain traditionally were thought to have been located south of the Dead Sea due to the mention at 14:10 of bitumen pits in the Siddim Valley where the kings of the Cities of the Plain battled the invaders from Mesopotamia. While there are some bitumen deposits on the northern side of the Dead Sea, they are most abundant to the south.

However, the indications in Scripture are that these cities were in the Jordan Plain north of the Dead Sea. The evidence includes not only this passage but also 1 Kings 7:46 and 2 Chronicles 4:17, where Succoth (modern Tell Deir Alla) is associated with the Jordan Plain. Moreover, this area is often simply called 'the Plain'. According to Deuteronomy 34:3 this region extended from Jericho west of the Jordan River to Zoar on the east side of the Jordan. Other references to 'the Plain' also appear to be to the Plain of the Jordan and reinforce this (Gen. 19:17, 25, 28–29; 2 Sam 18:23).[2] This area is compared to *the Garden of the Lord* (that is, Eden) and to Egypt. All three places had one prominent feature in common: major rivers flowed through them.

The reference to the description of the Plain as *before the Lord destroyed Sodom and Gomorrah* not only implies a later change in the Plain's appearance but also assumes that the reader is already familiar with the destruction of those cites even before reading

---

2. See Wenham (1987: 207) and especially Collins (2013).

Genesis 19. However, the mention of the destruction of those cites also rings a much more ominous note. Like Eve, Lot observed the attractiveness of one of the options, and then made a choice that would end in his being surrounded by sin (vv. 10, 13; cf. 3:6). While Canaan where Abram settled (v. 12) was a place that often in Scripture is characterized as a hotbed of idolatry, Lot's living near Sodom put him close to a place of intense evil: the men are described as *wicked, sinning greatly against Yahweh* (v. 13).

14–18. With Lot's departure God once again repeated his promise to Abram, this time filling it out in more detail than in 12:7. Now *this land* becomes *this land that you see*, and God promises it not simply *to your descendants* but *to you and your descendants for ever* (v. 15). This fuller promise may signal that Abram – with the departure of the last remnant of his father's household – has finally fulfilled all of the conditions placed on the promise when God first called him (see 12:1). Yahweh also uses enhanced language to describe Abram's promised offspring. They will be *like the dust of the earth* (v. 16). As God makes clear, this metaphor indicates a countless number of progeny. Abram as the owner of Canaan is now instructed to travel around it as a kind of inspection of the property he will be acquiring (v. 17). In response to this command, Abram left the area of Bethel and the altar he had built there and travelled to Hebron, where he built another altar (v. 18). Hebron will be important in the story of Abram's possession of the land. It is here that he will first obtain the Canaanites' recognition that he holds title to a portion of Canaan – the cave at Machpelah (23:1–20).

While elsewhere Mamre is the name of a place just north of Hebron (23:17, 19; 25:9; 35:27; 49:30; 50:13), the oaks apparently were on the property of a man by that name (14:13, 24), after whom this place would be named.

B. Abram rescues Lot (14:1–16)

c.2097–2084 BC

This account of Abram's military action taken to save Lot – the only report of Abram as a warrior – serves two purposes. First, it reinforces the difference between Lot's choice of a land in which to dwell and Abram's living in the land God gifted to him. Second, it is a test of Abram's true separation from Lot, the last remnant of his father's household (see 12:1). Would Abram take Lot back into the Promised Land after this debacle? Clearly Abram does not. Although Abram rescued his relative, the text is careful to place distance between him and Lot. There is no reported dialogue between them, and Lot is simply included in the list of property and people of Sodom and Gomorrah that Abram liberated from the four Mesopotamian kings (14:16; cf. 14:11–12). Later Abram returned these possessions and people – including Lot – to the king of Sodom (14:21–24; cf. 19:1). While Abram remained loyal to his kinsman, he valued God's promise of the land of Canaan, and therefore did not violate the condition God had placed on that promise.

The antiquity of Moses' source for this material is shown in that five times he stops to explain to his readers names of places that have changed: *Bela* is now *Zoar* (14:2, 8; see 19:20–22); the *Siddim* is the *Dead Sea* (14:3); *En-Mishpat* is now *Kadesh* (14:7); the *Shaveh Valley* is now *King's Valley* (14:17). In addition, he apparently used an updated reference for the area of the eastern Negev, calling it *the territory of the Amalekites* (v. 7), a people who came to occupy this region several generations after Esau.

1–4. These verses describe the subjugation of the five Cities of the Plain by Chedorlaomer for twelve years, c.2097–2086 BC. Since the aggressors in this first part of the account were the four Mesopotamian kings, they are listed first. *Amraphel* appears to be a Semitic name (v. 1). He was king of *Shinar*, which is Babylon (cf. 11:2; Zech. 5:11). The name *Arioch* has parallels in names found in upper Mesopotamia at Mari and Nuzi, and we should probably locate *Ellasar* in that region. *Chedorlaomer* is an Elamite name, matching his depiction as king of Elam, while *Tidal* is a Hittite name borne by several later kings from the eighteenth to the thirteenth centuries.[3] *Goiim* ('nations') is an unusual designation for Tidal's realm.

Each of the five subjugated kings is associated with one of the Cities of the Plain (v. 2). The names of *Bera* ('in evil') of Sodom and

3. Kitchen (2003: 320).

Birsha ('in wickedness') of Gomorrah appear to be purposely modified in order to remind the reader of the extreme sin of those cities. The only city whose king is not named is *Bela*, which would be known as *Zoar* ('little place') after Lot fled there (see 19:20–22). Ironically, this is the only city to later escape destruction when God destroyed Sodom and Gomorrah. *In the thirteenth year they rebelled* (v. 4), probably meaning that these cities, and perhaps others in the region, refused to pay tribute to Chedorlaomer.

5–7. *In the fourteenth year*, that is, c.2084 BC, the four allies from Mesopotamia came to enforce their hegemony over the region. From the list of places they defeated, it appears that the rebellion was not confined to the Cities of the Plain, but also included cities throughout the Transjordan. The cities listed as conquered before the battle in the Siddim Valley show the initial route of the Mesopotamians to have been from north to south along the King's Highway. *Ashtaroth Karnaim* was in Bashan (v. 5). It is modern Tell Ashtarah in southern Syria near the ancient site of Karnaim (modern Tell Sa'd).[4] The *Rephaim* survived until as late as the end of the fifteenth century when their last king, Og, was defeated by Israel (Deut. 1:4; 3:11, 13). The site of *Ham* is unknown, but it must have lain south of Ashtaroth Karnaim on the way to the next city conquered. The *Zuzim* may be the same as the Zamzummim, the Amorite name for the Rephaim (Deut. 2:20). *Shaveh Kiriathaim* ('plain of Kiriathaim') is probably a location near the later Moabite city of Kiriathaim whose location is now unknown (Num. 32:37; Josh. 13:19; Jer. 48:1, 23; Ezek. 25:9).[5] *Emim* appears to be the Moabite name for the southern Rephaim who were later displaced by the Moabites (Deut. 2:20–21). The southernmost place on the itinerary is the home of the *Horites* in the *mountains of Seir* all the way to *El Paran*, which is Elath on the Gulf of Aqabah (v. 6).[6] Twentieth-century scholarship tended to identify the Horites with an Indo-European people in the Ancient Near East known as the Hurrians whose native land was in Anatolia and northern

---

4. *ABD* 1.491.
5. *ABD* 4.85.
6. *ABD* 2.423.

Mesopotamia. However, this identification is unlikely, since the names of the Horites listed at 36:20–30 are Semitic names, not Indo-European names.

Next the army turned north-west and defeated *En Mishpat*, the older name for *Kadesh* in the Desert of Paran west of Edom (v. 7; cf. Num. 13:26; 20:16). Moving eastwards, the allies defeated the territory later occupied by *Amalekites*, a people who would be named after Amalek, the grandson of Esau (36:11–12, 15–16). Before engaging the five kings from the Cities of the Plain, the army conquered the *Amorites* at *Hazazon Tamar*, later called En Gedi (2 Chr. 20:2), on the western shore of the Dead Sea.

8–12. It appears that the army next turned northwards towards the Siddim Valley on the north shore of the Dead Sea, and that the five kings of the Cities of the Plain tried to cut them off before their cities could be attacked. Note that in this case the five kings are mentioned first, marking them as the initiators of the battle (vv. 8–9).

Interestingly, the result of the battle is not directly stated. Instead, we are told how the defeated armies fled (v. 10). The kings of Sodom and Gomorrah *fell into* the bitumen pits. English translations make it appear as if these kings inadvertently stumbled into the pits and were killed. However, the king of Sodom was still alive after Abram rescued Lot, suggesting that he did not die (14:17). This seeming discrepancy disappears when it is noted that the Hebrew verb denotes not only falling, but also deliberately lowering oneself. It is used this way of dismounting a camel (24:64) or from a chariot (2 Kgs 5:21). Thus, it appears that these kings hid in the pits in order to escape, while the rest of the defeated troops *fled to the mountains*. In the meantime, the victorious army sacked Sodom and Gomorrah, taking goods, food and people, including Lot (vv. 11–12).

13–16. For the first time in the Bible someone is called a *Hebrew* (v. 13). This term is derived from Abram's ancestor Eber (10:24–25; 11:14–17) and is an ethnic designation that is most often used in the Old Testament either by non-Israelites to describe Israelites or by Israelites when they are identifying their ethnicity to non-Israelites. Note that it serves to contrast Abram's ethnicity with that of *Mamre the Amorite*. Mamre is mentioned only here and possibly at 13:18 and 18:1, and his brothers Aner and Eshcol are mentioned only in this chapter (vv. 13, 24). Elsewhere, these are names of places. Mamre is associated with Hebron. Eshcol is a valley near Hebron (Num. 13:23–24; 32:9; Deut. 1:24). Aner is a city that would eventually lie in the territory of Manasseh and would be given to the Levites (1 Chr. 6:70).

Apparently Abram had made some sort of agreement with the three Amorites that allowed him to live in the vicinity of Hebron and perhaps obligated all the parties to a mutual defence. It was likely that Abram's allies were more than willing to join him in the rescue effort, since the Mesopotamians had attacked their fellow Amorites in Hazazon Tamar (14:7).

Abram's contribution to the expeditionary forces included *318 trained men* (v. 14). The word describing these men (*ḥănîk*) occurs only here in the Old Testament, but is also known from the Egyptian Execration Texts and is used to denote a Palestinian overlord's retainers.[7] The description of them as *born in his household* marks them as slaves who had grown up in Abram's household (17:12, 13, 23, 27; Lev. 22:11; Jer. 2:14). *Dan* was the city in northernmost Canaan originally called Laish but later renamed after the Israelite patriarch of the same name. Its use here is probably due to a post-Mosaic updating of the place name, since Moses could not have known the city by this name.

The tactic of splitting the men into several units and attacking by night enabled this smaller force to defeat a larger one (v. 15). Gideon would use similar tactics when attacking the Midianite coalition (Judg. 7:15–23). *Damascus*, one of the world's oldest continuously inhabited cities, is first mentioned here. The routed Mesopotamians fled towards home and Abram pursued them past Damascus to *Hobah*, whose location is unknown. The mention of the recovery of property and people (v. 16) highlights Lot and his property, just as Lot's capture by the Mesopotamians was also highlighted (14:12).

C. Melchizedek blesses Abram (14:17–24)

c.2084 BC
When Abram was returning from his victory over the Mesopotamians, he was met by two kings: Melchizedek and the king

---

7. *TWOT* 1.301.

of Sodom. This section provides a contrast between these two in order to show how God kept his promise to Abram: *I will bless those who bless you* (12:3).

17. Abram's return took him through the *Shaveh Valley*, which is identified as the *King's Valley*. The meaning of *Shaveh* is unknown, though the suggestion that it means 'ruler' would fit the context well.[8] The King's Valley is mentioned at 2 Samuel 18:18 and appears to be near Jerusalem, perhaps where the Hinnom and Kidron Valleys converge south of the City of David. The arrival of the king of Sodom must mean that he had heard of Abram's victory and was hoping to use this as an opportunity to repatriate some of his people who had been captured (see v. 21).

18–20. The presence of *Melchizedek* is explained by the fact that Abram was in the vicinity of *Salem* (v. 18). This is the first mention of Jerusalem in the Bible, and this shorter name for the city is used again in Psalm 76:2 in association with Mount Zion. Moreover, a priest 'like Melchizedek' is associated with Zion in Psalm 110. Interestingly, this is the only mention of Jerusalem in the Pentateuch. Since the historical setting of this chapter is the late third millennium BC, this is also the earliest-known historical reference to Jerusalem. Outside the Bible, the earliest surviving references to Jerusalem are from Egypt (as Rusalimim, c.1850 BC) and the Amarna texts from fourteenth-century Egypt (as Urusalim).[9]

Melchizedek is called *king of Salem* and *priest to God Most High* (Hebrew *'ēl 'elyôn*). The God worshipped by the patriarchs is often characterized as God (i.e. Hebrew *'ēl*) followed by a descriptor: God Everlasting (Hebrew *'ēl 'ôlām*, 21:33), God Almighty (*'ēl šadday*, 17:1; 35:11; 48:3) or God, the God of Israel (*'ēl 'ĕlohê yiśrā'ēl*, 33:20). While the Canaanite pantheon's supreme god was also called El, the pagan god is not in view here, as Abram makes clear when he equates Yahweh with God Most High (v. 22).[10]

---

8. Wieder (1965: 160–162).

9. *ABD* 3.751.

10. Note that 21:33 equates God Everlasting with Yahweh, and 17:1 equates God Almighty with Yahweh.

The provisions that Melchizedek provided for Abram and his men – *bread and wine* – indicate Melchizedek's graciousness. This is further underscored by the blessing which he pronounced (vv. 19–20). It was a double blessing. The first was a general blessing on Abram from God Most High who is called *Possessor* [or 'Creator'] *of heaven and earth.* The Hebrew verb *qnh* normally means 'acquire' or 'possess', but based on the similar verb in Ugaritic, some argue that it here means 'create'.[11] No reason is given for his invoking God's blessing on Abram. None of the things Abram has done – such as leaving his homeland for Canaan, separating from his father's household and rescuing Lot – merit God's blessing, which is freely given to Abram at his call.

The second blessing is upon *God Most High who has handed your enemies over to you.* God's actions merit a blessing – praise for God who deserves all the credit for military victory (Deut. 20:3–4; Pss 44:3, 7–8; 144:9–10; Prov. 21:31).

Following this blessing we are told that Abram gave Melchizedek *a tenth of everything*, that is, one-tenth of all the goods that he had captured (cf. Heb. 7:2). Thus, Melchizedek who blessed Abram was himself blessed (cf. 12:3).

21–24. This scene opened with the king of Sodom and now returns to him. He is as ungracious as Melchizedek was gracious. His words begin with a demand: *Give me the people* (v. 21). Abram was entitled to claim everything he had rescued – people and property. The king of Sodom was willing to lose the property, but not the people.

Abram gets the last word in this episode. He swore before the God whose blessing he had just received: *the Lord, God Most High* (v. 22). He refused even the smallest, most insignificant portion of the spoils of battle such as *a thread or sandal strap* (v. 23). While he received the blessing from the king of Salem, he did not want to give the selfish king of Sodom any excuse for claiming that Abram's blessing of riches came from him. Yet, recognizing the help he had received from his allies, he allowed them to claim their shares (v. 24).

---

11. See e.g. Mathews (2005: 150) as well as CSB, NET, NIV. ESV has 'possessor'.

Meaning

This section of Genesis serves as a bridge between Abram fulfilling the requirements of God's call and the important concern that will follow: how God will fulfil his promise to make Abram a great nation. This shows the first stage of God's promise to Abram: the granting of the land. Upon his return from Egypt, he will never again leave the land God has pledged to give him.

Throughout 13:1 to 14:24 Abram is the major actor, and Lot is mostly passive. No words by Lot are recorded here, and his only act is to choose to live in the Valley of the Jordan near Sodom. Lot is distanced from Abram not only by his moving across the Jordan River to the east, but also in the mind of the reader who is drawn to Abram and his courageous acts: the offer to let Lot have the first choice of land, and the rescue of Lot from the forces of Chedorlaomer and his allies. Abram maintains loyalty with his father's family while also separating from it.

Abram's encounter with the king of Sodom and Melchizedek rounds out these narratives and brings several important themes to the foreground for later narratives. First, the contrast between the king of Sodom's ungraciousness and Melchizedek's generous greeting and blessing begins to illustrate the statement that the people of Sodom were very wicked (13:13). The king of Sodom shows no gratitude for what Abram has done. He only makes demands of the patriarch. This lack of gratitude is only the tip of the iceberg as far as Sodom's sins are concerned. Yet the reader is now prepared for greater sins from the Sodomites in 19:1-29.

Melchizedek not only graciously provides food and drink for Abram's retinue, but also, in his capacity as priest of God Most High, he blesses Abram and God. This blessing emphasizes God's work and mentions no merit on Abram's part. God did not call him because of anything he had done, and God's favour remained on him even when he had departed from the land of promise and when he had deceived Pharaoh in Egypt. This is a reminder that God's greatest blessings – those that have come to us through the promise given to Abram and that have ultimately been fulfilled in Jesus – also come to us without any merit on our part (Rom. 3:23–24; Eph. 2:8–9; 2 Tim. 1:9).

9. THE FAMILY OF TERAH: YAHWEH'S COVENANT AND ABRAM'S RESPONSE (15:1 – 17:27)

Chapter 15 relates God's covenant with Abram (v. 18). Previously God had given Abram his promises (12:1–3; 13:14–17), but now for the first time Yahweh makes this a binding covenant between himself and Israel's great patriarch. The promises were conditional: Abram was to leave his father's household and to go to the land that God would show him (12:1). He was to travel around the Promised Land to see what God was giving him (13:17). Abram fulfilled those conditions in chapter 13 with the departure of Lot, and he had received God's blessing through the priest Melchizedek. Now that Abram has fulfilled the conditions placed upon him, God comes to him with unconditional promises (15:1, 14–16) and seals them in a binding agreement: a covenant (15:18–21).

However, Abram continues to experience doubt as to God's promise. He accepts Sarai's suggestion that the promise can be fulfilled through Sarai's slave girl Hagar (16:1–4). This attempt to manipulate God's promise leads only to misery for both women and, therefore, also for Abram (16:4–9). Yet God remains true to his promise to bless Abram's progeny and even extends that blessing to Abram's descendants through Hagar (16:1–12; 17:20). Still, the covenant with Abram needs to be restated (17:1–8), since Hagar's child is not the chosen son who will inherit God's promise (17:18, 19, 21). However, everyone in Abram's household will come under the blessings God has pledged as long as all the males in the family are circumcised (17:9–14, 23–27).

In some respects, this is the high point of the Abraham narratives. It is the only place where Abram is explicitly said to have believed God's promise (15:6). Moreover, Abram is only the second person in Genesis explicitly to be accounted righteous by God (15:6; see Noah at 7:1). It is also the place where Abram's concern about having an heir is first voiced (15:2), and, with the exception of 19:1–38, this concern will occupy every chapter from 15:1 through to 22:24.

A. Yahweh's covenant with Abram (15:1–21)

Context
c.2083 BC
In this chapter the promise of a descendant is ratified by a covenant ceremony where God not only guarantees his promises but also lays out for Abram what will happen in future generations until the pledge concerning the land of Canaan is first fulfilled.

Comment
    1. *After these things* is a phrase used in Genesis to indicate a new narrative. Similar phraseology is used at 22:1, 20; 39:7; 40:1; 48:1.[1] *The word of the Lord came* is a formula used for a revelation to one of God's prophets. It is used most frequently in Jeremiah and Ezekiel. Here Abram is the first prophet to receive such revelation, which comes in a *vision*. Later God will call him a prophet (20:7), the only person so designated in Genesis.

    God's opening words, *do not be afraid*, are often used by God to allay the fears of his people. They will occur again at 26:24 and 46:3.

---

1. Outside Genesis, similar phrases occur at Josh. 24:29; 1 Kgs 17:17; 21:1; Esth. 2:1; 3:1.

By placing these words first, Yahweh is demonstrating that he understands Abram's concern before it is expressed (see v. 2). God is Abram's *shield*. God as his people's shield and ultimate protector is a repeated theme elsewhere in the Old Testament (Deut. 33:29; Pss 3:3; 18:2; 28:7). The promise that *your reward will be very great* is general enough to encompass all of Yahweh's previous promises to Abram – numerous descendants, a great name, blessings and the land of Canaan.

2–3. For the first time Abram engages God in dialogue, voicing his concern over what God can give him – implying that the only thing Abram feels he is lacking is a child and heir, and that his servant *Eliezer of Damascus* will inherit instead (v. 2). It is often assumed that Eliezer is the unnamed steward of Abram's household mentioned at 24:2. The phrase *heir of my house* is difficult, since the words translated *heir* occur only here.[2] However, considering that in verse 3 Abram restates his concern that *you have given me no offspring* and that *a member of my household will be my heir*, it is most likely both verses are referring to Eliezer as Abram's heir.

4–6. God replies by assuring Abram of an heir, *one who comes from your own body* (v. 4). This phrase always means a direct physical descendant in the next generation – a son (25:23; Ruth 1:11; 2 Sam. 7:12; 16:11; 2 Chr. 32:21; Ps. 71:6; Isa. 48:19; 49:1). Therefore, God states in the most forceful way that Abram will have a son.

To emphasize that this son would be the first in a line of many descendants, God told Abram to look at the sky and count the stars (v. 5). This vision, therefore, came at night – a common time for divine revelations in Genesis (15:17; 26:24; 28:11–13; 31:11–13; 46:2). The comparison of the number of descendants to the number of stars will become a frequent way of referring to God's people in the Pentateuch (22:17; 26:4; Exod. 32:13; Deut. 1:10; 10:22; 28:62).

Verse 6 is, perhaps, the most important verse in Genesis from the viewpoint of the New Testament. It sets forth a relationship

---

2. Several other understandings of this phrase have been suggested. For a discussion of these in detail, see Hamilton (1990: 420–422) and Mathews (2005: 164–165).

between Abram's faith – he *believed the Lord* – and God's action – *he credited it to him as righteousness*. Thus, this passage clearly states that faith was the instrument through which God's credit of righteousness was received.

Paul uses this verse twice to teach that righteousness before God is not a matter of human effort, but is received through faith apart from any good works (Rom. 4:3; Gal. 3:6). Of course, through the centuries there has been a struggle to reconcile Paul's use of this verse with James's quotation that appears in a discussion of Abraham's works (Jas 2:21–24, esp. 2:23). However, it ought to be noted that James is speaking of Abraham being justified by works in contrast to mere claims of being righteous (Jas 2:14, 24). When the word 'justified' is used as a contrast between words and works, 'justified' means 'demonstrated to be righteous', and this is why James also points to Abraham's willingness to sacrifice Isaac as an act flowing from his faith (Jas 2:21; cf. Gen. 22:1–19).[3] However, Paul does not contrast actions and words as demonstrating one's righteousness; instead, he contrasts faith and actions as ways to be viewed as righteous before God. In Paul's case he is using 'justified' in its meaning 'declared to be righteous'.[4] Therefore, there is no discrepancy between Paul and James. Paul's teaching is focusing on how one is viewed as righteous before God: it is purely through faith that one receives God's declaration of righteousness. James, in contrast, is speaking of how one's righteousness is demonstrated to human beings: it can only be seen by other persons through one's outward actions that are motivated by faith.

7–10. Yahweh continues his reassurance to Abram by identifying himself as the God who brought Abram out of Ur in order to grant him possession of the land (v. 7). This is a proclamation of God's gracious activity in Abram's life. A nearly identical declaration of Yahweh's gracious activity is found in the preface to the giving of the commandments from Sinai: 'I am the Lord your God who brought you out of the land of Egypt' (Exod. 20:2).

---

3. This is the *demonstrative* use of the verb 'justify' (Greek *dikaioō*).

4. This is the *forensic* use of the verb 'justify'. For these different uses of this word, see Maxwell (2007).

Abram, however, was looking for greater assurance that he would possess the land (v. 8). In the midst of his great faith, he still remained a frail human who sought a sign from God to bolster his trust. Asking for a sign is not necessarily an expression of unbelief or belief beset by doubt (though it may be that; see Gideon at Judg. 6:33–40). Here it is faith seeking a visible guarantee through which God directs the believer to greater trust. In a similar way Moses sought God's visible presence to go with Israel to reassure them (Exod. 33:14–16).

The visible sign of God's covenant promise comes in the form of a ceremony involving animal carcasses (vv. 9–10). The splitting of all the animals except the birds, which were probably too small to split, was part of a ceremony that accompanied the pledging of a covenant. Such a ceremony is mentioned at Jeremiah 34:18–19. It is also probably reflected in the Hebrew idiom for making a covenant: 'to cut a covenant'. When the parties to the covenant passed between the divided animals, they were pledging to keep the terms of the covenant. If they failed to do so, they were symbolically invoking the fate of the animals on themselves: they, also, would be cut in two. Since God would pass between the animals, and since God cannot be divided, Abram would have absolute assurance that God would keep his promise.

11–16. Abram had to guard the carcasses from birds of prey all day until sundown, when a *deep sleep* enveloped him (vv. 11–12). The word for *sleep* here is the same word used to describe the sleep that Adam experienced when God made Eve (2:21). The terror that descended on Abram was a realization that he was in God's presence (cf. Exod. 15:16).

God first spoke to Abram and described the way that his descendants would come to possess the land (vv. 13–16). The description begins with Israel's time in Egypt as resident aliens, culminating in the oppression described in Exodus 1. The exodus itself would not only bring judgment on Egypt but also bestow possessions on Abram's descendants – a clear parallel to Abram's own exit from Egypt (12:16–20). Yet it is clear that Abram himself would not have possession of the land in his lifetime. Instead, he would die a peaceful death and be buried at an old age – presumably in the Promised Land (cf. 25:7–10). Since Abram would not receive the land himself, it is clear that he 'was looking forward to a city . . . whose designer and builder is God', as the writer to the Hebrews says (Heb. 11:10). Faithful people such as Abram 'desire a better place – a heavenly one' (Heb. 11:16, CSB).

God mentions Abram's descendants as being in Egypt *four hundred years* (v. 13). Since the actual time in Egypt was 430 years (Exod. 12:40–41), here God is likely speaking in round numbers. Israel are also depicted as returning to the Promised Land *in the fourth generation*. Often these two are reconciled by claiming that the word *generation* as used in this verse means a lifetime.[5] Since the patriarchs lived well over one hundred years each, it is argued that four generations was a meaningful way of expressing four hundred years to Abram. The problem with this argument is that the Hebrew word for 'generation' never carries the meaning of an entire lifetime elsewhere. More likely, the fourth generation is counted from the time of the oppression by the Egyptians to the return to the land. Thus, the oppression began in the lifetime of the generation that included Moses' parents, then Moses, and the exodus generation – the generation of Moses' sons Gershom and Eliezer (Exod. 18:3). That generation died in the wilderness (Num. 32:13), and the next generation entered the land.

The reason for this delay in taking the land is revealed at the very end of Yahweh's speech: *the iniquity of the Amorites has not yet reached full measure*. Thus, Israel's later conquest of the land was not only a way of keeping the promise to Abram, it was also a way of God serving his justice and judgment on the pagan inhabitants of Canaan for their abhorrent practices.

17–21. When complete darkness came that evening God appeared as *a smoking fire pot and a flaming torch* (v. 17). This is reminiscent of the appearance of God in the smoke and fire of the pillar that led Israel through the wilderness (Exod. 13:21–22). The pledge of the covenant came as God passed through the fire. It united the two concerns expressed by Abram: the promise of offspring and the possession of the land. The boundaries of the land are given from south to north (v. 18). The *brook of Egypt* is

---

5. Hamilton (1990: 435–436); Kidner (1967: 136); Mathews (2005: 174–175).

the Wadi el Arish in the northern Sinai (Num. 34:5; Josh. 15:4). The northern extent of the land, the *Euphrates*, was reached only during the reigns of David and Solomon (1 Kgs 4:21). The land is also described by noting its inhabitants (vv. 19–21). This list of ten is the longest Old Testament list of ethnic groups in Canaan. It does not mention later inhabitants of the land such as Moabites or Ammonites (19:37–38), but does include earlier inhabitants such as the Rephaim (cf. Deut. 2:9–11, 20–21). This attests to the antiquity of this list and its relevance to Abram in the late third millennium.

Meaning

Through most of the first part of the Abram narrative the tension revolves around the patriarch's desire for a son. God had promised to make Abram a great nation, and in this chapter he reinforced that by promising him a great reward (15:1). Immediately, however, Abram questioned what reward God could give him if he had no heir. With nothing other than God's promise of many offspring illustrated by the stars in the sky, Abram believed God. This is one of the high points of the entire story of this great father of Israel. Its use at multiple points in the New Testament demonstrates the importance from antiquity of this chapter for the history of God's people. The covenant ratification ceremony, which came *after* Abram believed God, reinforced the inviolability of God's promise and added to it the promise of the land of Canaan (15:18–21).

B. Abram fathers Ishmael by Hagar (16:1–16)

Context

2081–2080 BC

Between two statements of God's covenant to Abram concerning his numerous offspring (see 15:4–5; 17:3–8, 19), Sarai proposes a way for Abram to have a child. The giving of Hagar to Abram and the birth of Ishmael is a misguided attempt to induce God's promise through human effort. Nevertheless, God will remain faithful to his promise and even bless Hagar with many descendants, since her son will also be Abram's. In this way God shows himself faithful to his promises even when human beings doubt those promises and feel the need to take matters into their own hands.

Comment

1. The new story begins with a short description of circumstances that inform the reader about the story (v. 1).[6] The two pertinent pieces of information are Sarai's continued infertility (cf. 11:30) and her ownership of an Egyptian slave girl, presumably obtained years before in the land of the Nile (cf. 12:16). While some scholars would draw a distinction between the word used for slave girl here and another Hebrew word for a female slave, there appears to be little difference between the two words.[7]

2–3. Sarai suggests a solution to the problem of childlessness. She begins by blaming God for her inability to bear a child (v. 2). Her statement is one of despair despite God's promise, and her viewpoint is self-centred. Her desire is that Abram should help her *build a family*, an implied play on words since the Hebrew words for 'build' and 'son' sound similar. A wife presenting a slave girl to her husband in order to provide him with children is a widely attested custom in the Ancient Near East and was not viewed as illegitimate in that culture.[8] However, there are indications that Moses the narrator is subtly expressing God's disapproval. We are told that Abram *listened to* Sarai. The wording of this phrase matches only Adam's listening to Eve at 3:17. Moreover, *Sarai, Abram's wife, took Hagar . . . and gave her to Abram, her husband* (v. 3). This statement is closely parallel to Eve's act at 3:6 when she gave Adam the fruit of the tree of the knowledge of good and evil.

Hagar now became Abram's second *wife*, given to him by Sarai her mistress (v. 3). The chronological note that this happened after

---

6. Beginning a new narrative with a circumstantial clause is common in Genesis (e.g. 3:1; 4:1; 21:1; 24:1).

7. The word used here is frequently used as a counterpart to a male slave (Hebrew *šipḥâ*: 12:16; 20:14; 24:35; 30:43; 32:6; Deut. 28:68; 1 Sam. 8:16; 2 Kgs 5:26; 2 Chr. 28:10; Esth. 7:4; Eccl. 2:7; Isa. 14:2; Jer. 34:9–11, 16; Joel 3:3). The other Hebrew word for a female slave is also frequently used in the same way (Hebrew *'āmâ*: Exod. 20:10, 17; 21:7, 20, 26–27, 32; Lev. 25:6, 44; Deut. 5:14, 21; 12:12, 18; 15:17; 16:11, 14; 2 Sam. 6:20; Ezra 2:65; Neh. 7:67; Job 31:13).

8. Frymer-Kensky (1981); Van Seters (1968).

a decade in the land of Canaan may explain Sarai's exasperation: she had waited for the promise for what she may have thought was more than an acceptable period of time. Note that Hagar was given no choice in the matter.

4–6. Hagar's resulting pregnancy leads to a reversal of sorts. Proverbs 30:21–23 notes the intolerable consequences of a slave girl replacing her mistress, and Hagar's new attitude illustrates the problem: now the slave girl looks with contempt on her mistress Sarai (v. 4), and Sarai blames Abram for the strife between the two women (v. 5). Abram is quoted for the first time in this chapter: he calls Hagar *your slave* instead of his own wife, and grants Sarai power over her. Hagar is now *in your* [Sarai's] *hands* (v. 6), instead of, in Sarai's words, *in your* [Abram's] *embrace* (literally, 'bosom', v. 5). When Sarai says *May the Lord judge between me and you*, she may have been implying that Abram had encouraged Hagar's insolence.

Sarai's mistreatment of Hagar and Hagar's fight from her is a mirror image of Israel's exodus from Egypt. Here the Hebrew mistreats the Egyptian and the Egyptian flees. In the exodus the Egyptians mistreat the Hebrews and the Hebrews flee. The words for *mistreat* and *flee* used in verse 6 are used in Exodus to describe Israel's situation (Exod. 1:12; 14:5; 22:21; 23:9).

7–8. The first appearance of *the Messenger/Angel of the Lord* in Genesis is to Hagar (see discussion in the Introduction). The setting is the spring on the way to *Shur* (v. 7), the southernmost route from Canaan to Egypt that ran from Beersheba to the Bitter Lakes by way of Kadesh Barnea. Shur is the name of the wilderness in the north-western Sinai Peninsula. The Messenger refers to Hagar as *slave of Sarai*, not as the wife of Abram. In reply to the Messenger's question, Hagar honestly admits that she was fleeing her mistress Sarai.

9–10. The Messenger's instruction that Hagar should return to Sarai and submit to her authority appears harsh (v. 9). However, two things should be clearly understood. First, while God did not create humans for the bondage of slavery, he expects obedience to human authorities, even to slave masters when slavery is practised (Eph. 6:5–6; Col. 3:22; Titus 2:9; 1 Pet. 2:18). Therefore, Hagar's insolence was not endorsed by God, though Sarai's mistreatment of Hagar was also wrong (Eph. 6:9; Col. 4:1). Second, and more importantly, the Messenger extends the promise given to Abram to Hagar's descendants. By returning to Abram's household, Hagar and her child will receive the blessing of many offspring. Here the Messenger identifies himself as God: I *will greatly bless* . . .

11–12. The Messenger now proceeds to the first annunciation (announcement of an impending birth) in the Bible. Such announcements often include the giving of the child's name, frequently adding an explanation of the name (17:19; 18:9–15; Judg. 13:3–7; Isa. 7:14–17; Matt. 1:20–21; Luke 1:11–20, 26–38). In this case the boy was to be named *Ishmael*, meaning 'God hears'. The Messenger explains *that the Lord has heard your cry of affliction* (v. 11).

The Messenger also describes Ishmael's later life. He will be like a *wild donkey*, a species that inhabits the wilderness (v. 12). This implies that Ishmael and his descendants will have a nomadic desert lifestyle. In addition, the Ishmaelites are predicted to have contentious relations with others. Finally, it is said that Ishmael will live *near his relatives* or *in opposition to his relatives*. The Hebrew phrase is ambiguous. However, this phrasing is repeated at 25:18 where we are told that the Ishmaelites settled in the northern Sinai Peninsula, south of their Israelite kinsmen who lived in Canaan.

13–14. At this point, Hagar displays her recognition that the Messenger is an appearance of Yahweh, and she becomes the only person in the Old Testament to name God. The name *El-roi* means 'God sees me', and Hagar marvels that she has seen God who sees her (v. 13). The well at that place took its name from Hagar's name for God: *Beer-lahai-roi*, 'the well of the living one who sees me'. It apparently was located somewhere north of Kadesh. Bered, mentioned only here, has not been located.

15–16. Three times in these two verses Ishmael is called Abram's son, and three times we are told that Hagar bore him. In addition, Abram gives him the name that God chose. While Sarai's scheme was to build up her family (see v. 2), the text makes clear that this son is not reckoned to be Sarai's in any way. Ishmael is the son of Abram and Hagar. The distinction will become important in God's determination of which child of Abram will inherit the blessing (see 17:18–20). Thus, these last verses of this chapter link forward to the next narrative concerning the covenant connected with circumcision.

Meaning

Coming on the heels of Abram's great moment of faith in God's pledge to make him the father of many people, this chapter portrays an all-too-flawed human attempt by Abram and Sarai to fulfil God's promise by taking matters into their own hands. Abram fathered a son, but the manner in which it was accomplished introduced tension into his household caused by the friction between Sarai and Hagar. Ironically, the most vulnerable person in the episode is the woman who provided Abram with his son: Hagar, a slave girl. Yet, as we are reminded repeatedly in the Scriptures, God is especially attuned to the cry of the powerless, the downtrodden and the defenceless. He comes to Hagar's aid, making an appearance to someone who is both a woman and not among God's chosen people – both rare events in the Old Testament. Not only for Abram's sake, but also for Hagar's benefit, God promises to bless this child even though – as the reader will later learn (17:18–19) – he is not the child of the promise.

Additional note on polygamy in the Old Testament

Scripture teaches that monogamy was God's original design for humankind. In the beginning God created Eve as the helper for Adam and blessed them in their marriage (1:27–28). And in what is probably the narrative's first logical conclusion in Genesis we are told: *Therefore a man will leave his father and his mother and cling to his wife, and the two will become one flesh* (2:24). This statement pre-supposes that one man will have only one wife and suggests that the marriage union in some sense restores the unity that existed before the woman was created from the man's flesh (2:21–23).

However, any reader of Genesis is immediately confronted by the problems in the families of Abraham and Jacob caused by friction among their multiple wives. To most who are only casually acquainted with the Old Testament it is clear that several other prominent men were polygamous: Gideon, David and Solomon all had multiple wives. In addition, the following men had more than one wife:

- Lamech (Gen. 4:19–24)
- Esau (Gen. 28:9; 36:2, 6)

- Elkanah (1 Sam. 1)
- Ahab (1 Kgs 20:2–7)
- Jehoiachin (2 Kgs 24:15)
- Jerahmeel (1 Chr. 2:26)
- Ashhur (1 Chr. 4:5)
- Shaharaim (1 Chr. 8:8)
- Rehoboam (2 Chr. 11:21)
- Rehoboam's sons (2 Chr. 11:23)
- Abijah (2 Chr. 13:21)
- Jehoram (2 Chr. 21:14, 17)
- Joash (2 Chr. 24:3)
- Zedekiah (Jer. 38:23)

Therefore, at least twenty Israelite men, including two of Israel's patriarchs, are portrayed as polygamous. We probably ought to assume that most, if not all, of the kings of Israel and Judah practised polygamy, since it was common in the Ancient Near East, and nine of the twenty Israelite polygamists named above were kings. During antiquity in the Ancient Near East, royal polygamy was common, and the Old Testament notes that foreign kings such as Belshazzar (Dan. 5:2, 3, 23) and Xerxes (the husband of Esther) were polygamous.

Polygamy was not simply an Old Testament practice. It was also extant in New Testament times, though no man in the New Testament is specifically portrayed as having more than one wife. Josephus, however, notes that Herod the Great had multiple wives.[9] He also notes that both King Monobazus of Adiabene and his son Izates had several wives.[10]

Polygamy in the Ancient Near East was not only a marital practice; it was also intertwined with economic and political expediencies. Unmarried women without fathers or husbands – often widows – were likely to be poor, since they normally did not inherit, nor did they commonly own land (although there were exceptions;

9. Josephus, *Jewish War* 1.477, 480, 562–563; Josephus, *Jewish Antiquities* 17.19.

10. Josephus, *Jewish Antiquities* 20.17–20, 85, 89.

see Num. 27:1–11; 2 Kgs 8:1–6; Job 42:15). In order to be provided with food and shelter, such widows might remarry, and in some cases it would be marriage to a man who already had a wife. Poor men who could not support their entire households might sell their daughters as concubines to men who sought a wife (Exod. 21:7–11). Often the purchaser was a rich man who could afford a second wife. Kings often married many wives to solidify relationships with powerful families within their kingdoms or for political alliances with other kingdoms (as is implied in the case of Solomon, 1 Kgs 11:1–3).

There is no indication anywhere in the text of the Bible that any of these polygamous men's marriages beyond the first marriage were invalid; that the polygamous men were not in reality married to any wives other than their first wife. These were all marriages. In fact, one searches in vain in the Scriptures for a general prohibition of polygamy. Even concubines were considered to be wives (e.g. Gen. 37:2), though of a lesser status than wives for which one paid a bride price. Therefore, it would be wrong to state that polygamous marriages in the Old Testament or even such marriages as found in some cultures today were or are not marriages.

However, we should not conclude that polygamy has God's full approval or that it is not somehow contrary to his design for men and women. The Scriptures show by both negative and positive examples that God's design for marriage is monogamy. When God first created marriage, since it was *not good for the man to be alone* (2:18), he formed one woman to be his wife (2:22). His design is that *the two* [a man and a woman] *will become one flesh* (2:24).

The Pentateuch contains laws specifically addressing cases of polygamy. Exodus 21:7–11 contains laws about a daughter who has been sold as a slave and is to be married to her master or to her master's son. Exodus 21:10 regulates what may become a polygamous relationship in such circumstances: 'If he takes an additional wife, he must not reduce the food, clothing, or marital rights of the first wife' (CSB). In addition, Deuteronomy 17:14–20 contains laws limiting Israelite kings. Since it was common in the Ancient Near East for kings to practise polygamy, Deuteronomy 17:17 limits the king to a few wives, not many: 'He must not acquire many wives for himself so that his heart won't go astray' (CSB). Solomon was an example of a king who broke this law and whose heart did turn away from God (1 Kgs 11:1–8). Finally, Deuteronomy 21:15–17 regulates the granting of inheritances in polygamous circumstances. It assumes that in most cases a polygamous man will have only two wives:

> If a man has two wives, one loved and the other unloved, and both the loved and the unloved bear him sons, and if the unloved wife has the firstborn son, when that man gives what he has to his sons as an inheritance, he is not to show favoritism to the son of the loved wife as his firstborn over the firstborn of the unloved wife. He must acknowledge the firstborn, the son of the unloved wife, by giving him two shares of his estate, for he is the firstfruits of his virility; he has the rights of the firstborn. (CSB)

All of these laws anticipate problems precisely because of polygamy. None of the problems they address would exist in the family of a monogamous man. This in itself is a subtle indictment of the social, economic and political systems that made polygamy acceptable or sometimes even preferable for the woman. We ought to remember that not all of the Pentateuchal laws were given by God to show his approval of practices that the laws tolerated. For instance, Jesus himself declared that the Pentateuchal law on divorce was not given because God approved of divorce, but because some Israelites in the hardness of their hearts did not live in marriage as God had originally intended (see Deut. 24:1–4; Matt. 5:31–32; 19:3–12; Mark 10:2–12).

In addition, the Old Testament often demonstrates the problems that can arise within polygamous families. There can be friction and jealousy among the several wives. Examples include Sarah and Hagar (Gen. 16:4–6; 21:8–21), Rachel and Leah (29:31 – 30:24), as well as Hannah and Peninnah (1 Sam. 1:4–7).

There can also be friction and tension among the children of different wives. Ishmael's behaviour towards young Isaac led to him and his mother Hagar being expelled from Abraham's household (Gen. 21:8–10). Joseph's half-brothers by the concubines Bilhah and Zilpah must have resented the fact that he was placed over them by Jacob (37:2). In the book of Samuel we encounter problems among

David's children from different mothers. Amnon's rape of his half-sister Tamar is the first of these incidents (2 Sam. 13:1–22). This led to Absalom's hatred of Amnon and eventually to his murdering Amnon (2 Sam. 13:23–33). This rivalry among children from different mothers continues into the book of Kings, where we learn of Adonijah's attempt to take the throne before David could place Solomon on it (1 Kgs 1:5–27). By these negative examples Scripture demonstrates that polygamy is far from the ideal marital practice.

The ideal of monogamy is also upheld in the New Testament when Paul instructs both Timothy and Titus that one of the qualifications of pastors and deacons is that they be 'the husband of one wife' (1 Tim. 3:2, 12; Titus 1:6).[11] As leaders in the church, they are to demonstrate God's ideal in marriage.

We should also note that one of the great pictures of God's relationship to his people is that of a husband to a wife, and this is always depicted as a monogamous relationship.[12] This metaphor is employed both in the Old Testament, where Israel is Yahweh's wife, and in the New Testament, where the church is the bride of

---

11. These statements have been interpreted in various ways. Some have understood them to deny the pastoral office and the diaconate to unmarried men. However, if that were the case, Paul himself would have been disqualified (1 Cor. 7:8). Others have argued that it disqualifies men who remarry after being widowed, but this would contradict the principles about marriage Paul cites at 1 Cor. 7:39. The most likely meaning is that a pastor or deacon must have no more than one wife, which definitely rules out having more than one wife at a time and may also forbid pastors from divorcing faithful wives and then remarrying (which could be construed as serial polygamy).

12. Ezekiel 16 pictures Yahweh as marrying only one sister, personifying Jerusalem, but then later Ezekiel 23 speaks of Yahweh's marriage to two sisters, who represent Samaria and Jerusalem. The two sisters reflect the division of the kingdom into northern Israel and southern Judah, which was the result of the apostasy of Israel's northern tribes. Originally Yahweh chose and redeemed Israel from Egypt to be his one people – his only bride. The resulting two wives was an indictment of Israel's unfaithfulness, not a choice by God to have two wives.

Christ. In Ephesians 5:22–33 Paul sees Christian marriage as a reflection of the relationship between Christ and his church. Christ is the only Saviour, and he has only one bride and body, the church, comprised of all who believe in him. Thus, the Christian ideal for marriage is monogamy, and faithful Christians who aspire to marriage and wish to please God ought to shun polygamy.

C. Yahweh's covenant and its sign: circumcision (17:1–27)

Context
2067 BC
God's promise that Abram would have an heir was confirmed more than fifteen years before his appearance to Abram in this chapter (cf. 15:1–21). In the meantime Sarai had proposed a solution by giving Hagar to Abram to have a child for her. That did not work, and Ishmael would never be considered Sarai's child. Now, thirteen years after the birth of Ishmael, God reaffirms and expands his covenant to Abram (17:4–8), granting a blessing also to Ishmael (17:20), but insisting that the heir will come through Sarai (17:15–16, 19, 21). God's covenant is now not simply with Abram but also with his descendants. Therefore, the perpetual sign of the covenant is circumcision on the eighth day of life for Abram and his male offspring (17:9–14).

Comment
1–2. Abram is now ninety-nine, which means that thirteen years have passed since Ishmael's birth (v. 1; cf. v. 25). This is the second of three times when we are told that Yahweh appeared to Abram (see also 12:7; 18:1). In Genesis the language of God appearing to someone is only used with the patriarchs.[13]

When Yahweh appeared to Abram this time he identified himself as *God Almighty* (Hebrew *'ēl šadday*). This name for God occurs also at 28:3; 35:11; 43:14; 48:3; Exodus 6:3; Ezekiel 10:5. At Genesis 49:25 he is simply *the Almighty* (Hebrew *šadday*), a name for God that occurs frequently in Job and in several other places in the Old

---

13. See 26:2, 24 (Isaac) and 35:1, 9, 48 (Jacob).

Testament. While *Almighty* is an ancient understanding of this name, its meaning is debated. What is clear is that in Genesis this name of God is always associated with God's promise of children and fertility.

Here Abram is invited by God to *live* [literally 'walk'] *in my presence and be blameless*. This is somewhat reminiscent of Enoch and Noah, who *walked with God* (5:22, 24; 6:9). The connection to Noah is particularly strong since he is the only other person in Genesis to whom the adjective *blameless* is applied. This word denotes integrity in one's actions. 'Walking in God's presence' will be used by Abram to describe his relationship to God (24:40). Later it will be used by Jacob to characterize his father's and his grandfather's relationship to God (48:15). This emphasis on Abram's life with God flows out of his faith that was reckoned to him as righteousness by God (15:6). In fact, walking blamelessly is connected to righteousness and blessings upon one's children in Proverbs (Prov. 20:7).

After inviting Abram to walk in his presence, God then offers a covenant that will bind him to Abram and will guarantee him an extremely great number of descendants (v. 2). The phrase *extremely great* is used three times in this chapter to describe the multiplying of Abram's descendants, including those through Ishmael (cf. vv. 6, 20).[14]

3–6. Abram's response to God's invitation is to prostrate himself before the Lord as a sign of his respect (v. 3). While Yahweh had previously promised Abram that he would be the father of a great nation (12:2), here for the first time he promises that Abram will father *a multitude of nations* (v. 4). The shift may be due to Ishmael. Although Ishmael is not the child of the promise, God nevertheless, for Abram's sake, will bring a great nation from him (see v. 20).

God's change of the patriarch's name to *Abraham* signifies his promise and also serves as a play on words with his description of Abram as *father of a multitude of nations* (v. 5). While there are previous instances in Genesis of a play on words associated with the giving

---

14. This is quite significant since *extremely great* (Hebrew *mĕ'od mĕ'od*) occurs only twelve times in the entire Old Testament.

of a name, this is the first instance of a person being renamed. The name *Abram* means 'father (is) exalted', but *Abraham* apparently means 'father of a multitude'.[15]

The new name is further explained to signify that not only nations will come from Abraham, but also kings (v. 6). This will be important also in the renaming of Sarai (cf. v. 16). This pledge to Abraham will be repeated in different words to Jacob, where fertility, descendants and royalty will again be joined together in a single promise (35:11).[16] That Israel would eventually have a king is occasionally mentioned elsewhere in the Pentateuch (49:10; Num. 24:17; Deut. 17:14–20; 28:36).

7–8. God next confirms his covenant not only with Abraham, but now for the first time with *future offspring throughout their generations*. The covenant entails Yahweh being their God (v. 7). That is, they are also invited into the same relationship, walking in God's presence as Abraham did (cf. v. 1). For Old Testament examples of Abraham's descendants doing this, see David (Ps. 56:13), Hezekiah (2 Kgs 20:3; Isa. 38:3) and an unnamed psalmist (Ps. 116:9).

For the third time God notes that this covenant promise includes the land where Abraham is living, which God now specifically identifies as Canaan (v. 8; cf. 12:7; 15:18). The land is called Israel's *permanent possession*, but this is immediately followed by the statement *I will be their God*. This is not simply a restatement of the previous verse. Instead, it is qualifying the promise of Canaan as a permanent possession: it will be that only as long as Yahweh is Israel's God. When Israel rejected God to worship the gods of the Canaanites, the people were removed from the land (see Deut. 28:58–63; 1 Kgs 14:15–16). Although they were eventually restored, the Jews were removed from the land again after rejecting God and his Christ (see Luke 10:16; 21:24; John 1:11).

9–14. God's third speech goes on to specify what Abraham is to do to seal this covenant. The centrality of circumcision as a covenant obligation is signalled by the use of the words *covenant* and *circumcise*, each occurring six times in these verses.

---

15. *TWOT* entry 04.0b.
16. Diffey (2011).

God emphasizes that these instructions are not simply for Abraham but for all of his descendants by mentioning them twice before revealing the sign of circumcision (vv. 9–10). Four provisions apply to circumcision:

1. It applies to *every one of your males* (v. 10) – not only those born in the household but also slaves purchased from outsiders (v. 12).
2. It is a *sign of the covenant* between God and Abraham (v. 11), a *permanent covenant* (v. 13).
3. Circumcision on the eighth day of life is to be observed *throughout your generations* (v. 12).
4. If a male is not circumcised, he *will be cut off from his people* since *he has broken my covenant* (v. 14).

God does not state for whom circumcision is a sign. Clearly, a few signs in the Old Testament are a reminder for God. The rainbow reminds God of his promise to Noah (9:12–17). The blood on the lintels and doorposts in Egypt was a sign for God to pass over the Israelites' houses (Exod. 12:7–13). However, other divinely instituted signs were for God's people. For instance, the Sabbath was a sign for Israel that God had set them apart from other nations (Exod. 31:12–17). Likewise, God commanded Israel to wear tassels on the corners of their garments as a reminder of his commands (Num. 15:37–40). While scholars often debate whether circumcision was a sign for God or for Abraham and his descendants, it is likely that by being left unstated for whom the sign functioned it was intended as a sign for all parties to the covenant.

Another much-discussed provision is that of a male who is uncircumcised being *cut off from his people*. It is not clear who will be responsible for removing such a person from the people. Similar provisions for cutting someone off from the people that occur frequently in the divine legislation in Exodus, Leviticus and Numbers do not clarify this. Was this something God would do or was it something the people were to do, a sort of ex-communication? Most likely, this would be God's action. That is, a male who was not circumcised would nullify God's obligations under the covenant, as the phrase *he has broken my covenant* implies (v. 14).[17]

Circumcision was not, in itself, unique to Israel. Other nations in the Ancient Near East practised it, but usually as a rite for men coming of age or in anticipation of their marriage.[18] What is unique to Israel is the practice of circumcision on the eighth day (one week after birth, counting the days inclusively). Thus, this rite in Israel did not focus on human action that prepared men to father children, but emphasized God's covenant that promised fecundity and fertility to Israel. Long before an Israelite male was mature enough to father children, he would be circumcised and brought into the covenant that pledged many descendants to come.

15–16. The Lord's attention now turns to Sarai, whose name is changed to *Sarah* (v. 15). These are two variations of the same name, both meaning 'princess'. Yet the change is significant since she will not only have a son, but will also be the mother of nations and kings (v. 16). To emphasize the seriousness of this promise God twice says *I will bless her.*

17–18. Once again Abraham prostrates himself before God. But this time his sign of respect is undone by his laughter and his thoughts. Abraham's assertion that a 100-year-old man and a ninety-year-old woman cannot produce a child (v. 17) is reasonable for humans, but it demonstrates doubt in God's ability to bring life from those who are 'as good as dead' (Heb. 11:12). While he does not speak his thoughts to God, he tries to steer God in another direction, exclaiming, *If only Ishmael would live in your presence!* This statement on the surface appears to be simply a father's plea on behalf of the son whom he loves. However, in the context of Abraham's thoughts, it takes on a darker meaning by signifying doubt that God can keep his promise.

19. God's reply is insistent to the point of naming the yet-to-be-conceived child *Isaac* just as he had named the embryonic Ishmael

---

17. Hamilton (1990: 474–475); Wenham (1994: 25).

18. Sasson (1966). Note that Jer. 9:25–26 lists Egypt, Edom, the Ammonites, Moab and unnamed desert tribes among nations who practised circumcision.

(see 16:11). The name is in one sense a rebuke of Abraham, demonstrating that God knew his thoughts and had heard his laughter, since the name *Isaac* derives from the word for 'he laughed'.[19] However, it is clear that God will get the last laugh: he will grant Abraham and Sarah a son, and that son will receive the same *permanent covenant* and same promise of descendants that God has given to Abraham.

20–22. To address the legitimate fatherly love of Abraham for Ishmael, God says, *I have heard you*, a play on the lad's name that also affirms that the Lord understands Abraham's attachment to his son by Hagar (v. 20). Ishmael will receive several promises from God summarized in the statement *I will bless him*:

1. God will make him fruitful and multiply him.
2. Ishmael will father twelve tribal leaders (25:13–16).
3. He, too, will become a great nation.

One thing is lacking, however, from the blessing on Ishmael: God's permanent covenant will not be with him. Instead, God will confirm his covenant with Isaac (v. 21). Nevertheless, it is clear that Ishmael is not disqualified from the covenant because of his sinfulness or any other inadequacy. Yahweh blesses him and loves him as one of his creatures and also for Abraham's sake. However, God is insisting that the choice of the covenant line from Abraham will be his and his alone. This same sovereign choice of God will be evident also in the choice of Jacob over Esau despite Isaac's desires.

Isaac, God promises, will be born in one year's time. Already this is what Abraham had understood about God's promise sealed with circumcision. He was ninety-nine years old at this time, yet he presumed that he would be 100 years old (and Sarah, who was ten years younger, would be ninety) when God claimed that he would become a father to Sarah's child (see v. 17). Thus, God's promise and the attached rite of circumcision were enough to convince

---

19. In Hebrew the word for 'and he laughed' is comprised of five letters. The name *Isaac* is identical except that it omits the first letter.

Abraham that the time God had repeatedly spoken about was near, only a year away.

Usually nothing is said about God ceasing to speak or leaving (v. 22). The narrative usually just moves on to the next event. Here, however, is a clear indication of the end of God's words. This clear demarcation between God's visible presence and his absence prepares readers to understand the next verses which relate Abraham's immediate keeping of the covenant. Abraham's actions were not supervised by God. They were Abraham's own outward expression of his inward acceptance of God's promise.

23–27. Verse 23 is a summary of Abraham's activity in response to God Almighty's invitation to live in his presence (cf. v. 1). The details follow in the next verses: Abraham's age (v. 24), Ishmael's age (v. 25), then the circumcision of all the household's males, including Abraham and Ishmael (vv. 26–27). The twice-stated *that same day* (vv. 23, 26) alerts readers to Abraham's renewed faith in God's promise.

Meaning

Like 15:1–21, 17:1–27 is about God's covenant, but these two chapters highlight different aspects of Abram's righteousness. While 17:1–27 emphasizes the outward sign of the covenant, 15:1–21 highlights the inward nature of faith that receives God's promise – the circumcision of the heart (Deut. 10:16; 30:6; Jer. 4:4; Rom. 2:29). Chapter 15 accentuates God's imputed, passive righteousness that was Abram's by faith (15:6), while 17:1–27 underscores Abram's active righteousness of obedience (17:1, 23–27).

Between these two chapters we are told of Sarai's impatience with God's promise and Abram's acquiescence to her suggestion of a way to provide an heir to God's promise. Therefore, between two chapters demonstrating Abram's great faith we learn that Israel's patriarch also had moments of weakness. Like his earlier unfortunate decision to leave Canaan for Egypt (12:10–20), his taking of Hagar as his concubine brought unintended consequences – in this case, strife within his household as Hagar showed disrespect to her mistress Sarai and Sarai mistreated Hagar, causing her to flee. Nevertheless, God remained faithful to his promise despite Abram's missteps of doubt. Yahweh went so far as to extend his promise to

Abram's son Ishmael, even though the boy was not part of God's plan to make Abram into a great nation.

God's covenant in this portion of Abram's story focuses on the second stage of the promises made to him by God. The first stage, 12:1 – 14:24, highlighted the granting of the land of Canaan. Now this earlier part of God's pledge to Abram is tied to the promise of descendants who will inherit the land (15:18–21; 17:7–8). Thus, these chapters revolve around the promise of an heir, beginning with Abram's anxiousness caused by Sarai's infertility (15:3) and ending with Abraham demonstrating trust in God's promise by circumcising his entire household (17:23–27).

The climax of God's covenant concerning Abram's heirs is emphasized by the signs given to him as reminders: the change of his name to Abraham and of his wife's name to Sarah. Most importantly, the sign of circumcision will be a reminder not only to Abraham, but also to future generations. Circumcision, however, was not merely an outward sign. From what is said about it in 17:1–27 and in the rest of Scripture, circumcision also applied God's promise to the circumcised child and his entire household. With an Israelite boy's circumcision God's promise incorporated him into God's people. Moreover, the promise came to the entire household, including the females as well as the circumcised males. This, in fact, highlights that the most important circumcision was not the cutting away of the foreskin, but the circumcision of the heart (Deut. 10:16; 30:6; Rom. 2:28–29). This internal circumcision was for both males and females. It was for every Israelite who shared Abraham's faith and clung to God's promise. It continues to be that for all – even the uncircumcised – who believe and to whom, like Abraham, God credits their faith as righteousness, who become Abraham's true sons (Rom. 4:1–11; Gal. 3:6–7; cf. Gen. 15:6). Under God's new covenant in Christ Jesus there is now no longer any distinction between Jews and Gentiles, males and females, slaves and free (Gal. 3:28) – the very distinctions highlighted with the institution of circumcision among Abraham's family.[20]

---

20. Martin (2003).

10. THE FAMILY OF TERAH: YAHWEH'S REPEATED PROMISE AND ABRAHAM'S RESPONSE (18:1 – 19:38)

With God's covenant sealed though the circumcision of Abraham and his household, Yahweh pays one last visit to Abraham before the birth of Isaac. Two very important questions are answered in 18:1 – 19:38: how will Sarah finally receive the news of her impending pregnancy? And what will become of Abraham's remaining closest family tie, his relationship to his nephew Lot, in the light of a new family relationship that will be even closer – that of his son and heir?

The first part of 18:1–33 addresses the first question. Previously Sarah had doubted that she was part of Yahweh's promise to Abraham and had taken steps to provide him with an heir through her slave girl Hagar (16:1–16). In the next chapter, God had emphasized that the heir of the promise would be a son born to Sarah (see 17:19) Now in chapter 18 God and two angels visit Abraham with the promise of a son through Sarah and specifically ask Abraham about her, involving her in the conversation (18:9, 15). Here Yahweh emphatically assures the couple that Sarah will have a son within the year (18:14).

The second question is addressed by the remainder of chapter
18 and all of chapter 19. Abraham pleads for Sodom, since that is
where Lot has chosen to live. However, Abraham does not take
direct action to rescue Lot as he had done previously (14:1–16).
Instead, the patriarch learns of God's mercy through his conversation with God as judge of the whole earth, and then leaves Lot's
future in God's hands. Lot, who has not come under the covenant
of circumcision, proves to be a most fallible man, despite being a
righteous person before God (see 2 Pet. 2:7). Perhaps a consequence of the lingering effects of living in the depravity of
Sodom, Lot's drunkenness and his seduction by his daughters will
lead to the births of Moab and Ben-ammi. The relationship
between Abraham and Lot would for ever be made distant by

Table 10 Parallels between Genesis 18 and 19

Genesis 18	Genesis 19
Abraham sitting in the entrance of his tent (18:1)	Lot sitting in the city gateway (19:1)
Abraham goes to meet the three men (18:2)	Lot stands to greet the two men (19:1)
Abraham bows (18:2)	Lot bows (19:1)
Abraham's invitation (18:3)	Lot's invitation (19:2)
wash your feet (18:4)	*wash your feet* (19:2)
then you can go (18:5)	*early tomorrow go on your way* (19:2)
Bread is baked (18:6)	Bread is baked (19:3)
Sarah laughed (18:12, 13, 15)	Lot's would-be sons-in-law thought he was joking (19:14)[1]
Outcry against Sodom is great (18:20–21)	People's great outcry against the city (19:13)
sweep away the righteous/the city (18:23, 24)	*you will be swept away* (19:17)
spare the whole place (18:26)	*I'll grant your request* (19:21)[2]
Do = destroy [the city] (18:25, 29, 30)	Do = destroy [the city] (19:22)

1. In Hebrew the same verb root is used for *laughed* and *joking*.
2. In Hebrew the same verb root is used for *spare* and *grant*.

Lot's bad choices: first to live in the condemned city of Sodom and then to allow himself to be plied with wine to the point of incapacitation of consciousness (19:33, 35). The subsequent difference between Abraham's heirs and the descendants of Lot is foreshadowed by the very different origins of Isaac and Lot's sons. One will be born as the result of God's promise and act; the others will stem from the immoral, incestuous acts of Lot and his daughters.

Chapters 18 and 19 are connected to each other, and a number of striking parallels between the two chapters tie them together (see Table 10 on p. 190).

These parallels demonstrate that there is an authorial intent to tie these two narratives together so that readers will compare and contrast them. In both chapters righteous men offer hospitality to strangers. (18:1–8; 19:1–3). However, Abraham's hospitality is completed, whereas Lot's is interrupted by the lascivious behaviour of the men of Sodom (19:4–5). In both, someone does not believe what is reported about God's intended actions: Sarah laughs (18:12), and Lot's potential sons-in-law think he is joking (19:14). In 18:16–33 Abraham learns about God's mercy to the righteous and the wicked although the outcry over Sodom's sins is great. In contrast, in 19:1–38 Lot witnesses God's judgment against the wicked but his rescue of his own family.

A. Abraham's three visitors (18:1–33)

Context

2067 BC

Chapter 18 divides easily into two parts. The first centres on God's restatement of the promise of a son for Abraham and Sarah, and Sarah's reaction. The second part focuses on Abraham's plea for Sodom that highlights God's role as merciful judge of all the earth.

Comment

This visit is the last time that Genesis speaks of Yahweh appearing to Abraham (v. 1; cf. 12:7; 17:1), making it the climax of God's continuing promises and pronouncements to the patriarch and the occasion of the most specific ones: that a child will be born within a year, and that God will execute his judgment on Sodom.

i. Yahweh promises Abraham a son (18:1–15)

1. The setting of God's appearance is described in detail. Abraham is once again at *the oaks of Mamre*, outside Hebron (cf. 13:18; 14:13). Moreover, Abraham is in *the entrance of his tent*, apparently taking advantage of the cool shade, since this theophany took place *in the heat of the day*.

2–5. In this case God's arrival involves what appears to be *three men* (v. 2); this is the only place in Scripture where a trio of heavenly guests is depicted. Apparently this is Yahweh (v. 22) and two angels (19:1) who appear to Abraham and seem to catch him unaware of their arrival. Abraham's running to them and bowing down is the beginning of his showing them hospitality – even though he did not know at that moment that they were God and his angels (cf. Heb. 13:2).

Abraham apparently spoke to the one whom he perceived to be the leader of the three, calling him *My lord*, a polite form of address akin to English 'sir'. His invitation is for them to relax for a while with him. It was customary in antiquity for a good host to provide water for guests to wash their feet, which was normally done when stopping on a journey or entering a house (19:2; 24:32; 43:24; Judg. 19:21; 2 Sam. 11:8; Song 5:3). As here, male hosts did not wash the feet of their guests, but provided water for them to wash their own feet. When guests' feet were washed by someone else, it was a task reserved for women or slaves (1 Sam. 25:41; Luke 7:38, 44; 1 Tim. 5:10). This is what made Jesus' washing of his disciples' feet so extraordinary (John 13:5–14).

Abraham also offers them a *bit of bread* (or 'food') for refreshment.[3] Then, in typical Near Eastern indirect phraseology used when speaking to strangers, he said, *This is why you passed your servant's way*. In essence, Abraham is expressing his pleasure at serving as their host.

---

3. The Hebrew word often translated *bread* can also be used in a more general sense for any food.

6–8. Abraham's provision for his guests is more than a little snack. Instead, he provides a sumptuous feast. His instructions to Sarah indicate that she was to use *three measures* (or 'seahs') of flour, about 21 quarts or 20 litres (v. 6). He himself picked out a choice calf and added curds and milk to the feast (vv. 7–8). As host, Abraham himself did not eat, but stood observing his visitors, ready to provide for any of their needs or requests. The tree under which they ate was presumably one of the oaks of Mamre mentioned earlier.

9–10. Either after or during the meal the guests enquire about Sarah's whereabouts (v. 9). This is the first hint that these are no ordinary guests, since they not only know that Abraham is married, but they even know the name of his wife – the name that Yahweh bestowed on her previously (cf. 17:15). Sarah, as a proper Near Eastern matron, did not mingle with the male visitors, but was in the tent as the men ate their meal. The answer to their question – *in the tent* – obviously was intended to include her in this conversation, and later the text clarifies that she was indeed part of it because she was *listening at the entrance of the tent* behind Abraham (v. 10).

Knowing that Sarah can hear their dialogue, Yahweh now gives Abraham and Sarah the most specific version of the promise of a son: he will be born *in a year's time*. The Hebrew phrase is an idiom, literally 'as the time of living', and is used only in this chapter and in 2 Kings 4:16–17, both times in connection with the promise of the birth of a son.

11–12. Verse 11 is a parenthetical comment that provides background information not only about the advanced ages of the couple but also that Sarah was past *the age of childbearing*. Again, a Hebrew idiom is used: literally 'the path of women' had ceased. This is a reference to the cessation of menstruation.[4]

Sarah found the statement by Yahweh so startling and incredible that *she laughed to herself* (v. 12). She saw no possibility of becoming pregnant, referring to herself as *worn out* and wondering whether she would *have delight* from her aged husband. The delight here

---

4. Note that a similar phrase is used at 31:35 where Rachel refers to her menstruation as 'the road of women'.

probably refers to sexual pleasure and is a Hebrew noun related to the word *Eden* (cf. 2:8, 10, 15; 3:23–24; 4:16), and elsewhere used of luxury items (2 Sam. 1:24; Ps. 36:8; Jer. 51:34).[5]

13–14. God preserved Near Eastern etiquette in confronting Sarah over her laughter and scepticism by addressing Abraham (v. 13). Yahweh paraphrased the first part of Sarah's statement as *Can I really bear a child when I'm old?* However, out of deference to his host he made no mention of Abraham's advanced age.

God's rhetorical challenge rebukes Sarah's unbelief: *Is anything impossible for the Lord?* (v. 14). In this statement he also reveals his identity: he is Yahweh who can do what he has stated. In his mercy to the couple – and indeed to all people (cf. v. 18) – he does not withdraw his promise because of Sarah's disbelief, but repeats it, noting that he will *come back*, and this will result in Sarah bearing a son in about a year's time.

15. Sarah's fear led her to deny laughing – breaking with the rules of propriety as she spoke directly to the Lord. While fear led to the lie, this also demonstrated that Sarah now believed the promise and understood who the one making the promise was (cf. Heb. 11:11). In his forbearance God did not vent his wrath on her for contradicting him. He simply but firmly contradicted her and set the record straight.

ii. Abraham pleads for Sodom (18:16–33)

16. To signal a shift in the narrative the conversation abruptly ends and the scene's location changes with the men's departure from the vicinity of Abraham's tent to a place overlooking Sodom, with their gracious host Abraham seeing them off.

17–19. The narrative now gives us God's thoughts as he contemplates revealing his next actions. It begins with a question: should Yahweh reveal his plans (v. 17)? The reasons for revealing his plans begin with God's promises, which are related in a modified version of 12:2–3. Here is the only place in Genesis with a reference to Abraham's descendants as a *powerful nation* (v. 18). Abraham's

---

5. Note that the related verb occurs at Neh. 9:23 where it refers to enjoying the abundance of the land.

importance, however, is worldwide as all nations *will be blessed through him*. The Hebrew verb is not passive, as implied by many English translations, but reflexive with an estimative emphasis: they 'will consider themselves blessed' (cf. 12:3).[6] God then notes a purpose for his choosing Abraham: *he will command his children . . . to keep the way of the Lord by doing what is right and just* (v. 19). Instruction of children would be later commanded of Israel (Exod. 12:25–27; Deut. 6:1–7) and was important for passing on godly wisdom (Prov. 1:8; 3:1; 6:20).

God's way of doing what is right and just will be illustrated in this chapter and Abraham will learn more about it when he pleads for Sodom. Yahweh states that through these things he will *fulfil to Abraham what he promised*

20–21. These next words of the Lord must have been said aloud, since Abraham's subsequent plea for Sodom assumes that Sodom may fall under God's judgment. Two items demonstrate God's omniscience: he knows about the outcry because of Sodom and Gomorrah, and he knows that the sins of those cities are *very serious* (v. 20). The sins of these Cities of the Plain are described by Ezekiel as pride and haughtiness, having plenty but not taking care of the poor and needy, and committing abominable acts before God (Ezek. 16:49–50; cf. Lev. 18:5–30).

God then states that he will investigate whether the acts of the people of Sodom and Gomorrah justify the outcry he has heard (v. 21). This seems to contradict the notion that God knows everything. However, it should be borne in mind that at this point God is assuming the role of judge for the purpose of revealing his actions to Abraham.[7] In this anthropomorphic role of judge he would assemble the evidence in order to render a verdict.

22–25. As the men *went towards Sodom*, Abraham *was standing before the Lord* (v. 22). Here is an indication that one of the men was God himself. The other two will eventually be identified as angels (19:1). The Masoretes believed that the text originally said that God stood before Abraham, but that it was corrected by scribes to place

---

6. Lee (2012).

7. Chisholm (2007: 6–11).

Abraham before God in order to avoid the irreverent thought that God was inferior to Abraham. However, from 19:27 and from LXX it would appear that the text may have always had Abraham standing before God.

For the first time in Scripture, a man initiates a conversation with God. Abraham's longest part of the conversation is his initial plea. He is probing how God would be a righteous judge if the righteous and wicked are both destroyed when God punishes the cities. He begins with a rhetorical question: *Will you really sweep away the righteous with the wicked?* (v. 24). Here Abraham assumes that God already knows of the sins of Sodom and Gomorrah – that is, Abraham understands that God knows about the wicked men of Sodom and is going to vent his wrath on them. He is seeking, however, to spare any who may not deserve God's fury, knowing that God loves the righteous even while executing his wrath on the wicked (Ps. 146:8–9). He cannot conceive of God punishing fifty righteous persons with the wicked despite the grave sins of the rest of the inhabitants, so he asks for everyone to be spared (vv. 24–25). His statement culminates with his appeal to God as *judge of the whole earth* (v. 25).

26–32. God's reply is short and to the point, and all his subsequent replies will be similar (vv. 26, 28, 29, 30, 31, 32). The conversation now moves very quickly with Abraham asking in turn for the entire city to be spared if forty-five, then forty, then thirty, then twenty and finally just ten righteous persons are found there. In all but one case (v. 29), Abraham is careful to note his lowly status before the earth's judge: he is dust and ashes (v. 27; cf. Job 30:19; 42:6), and he begs God not to be angry for his repeated requests (vv. 30, 32).

The question is sometimes raised as to why Abraham stops at ten righteous.[8] However, it ought to be obvious that by this point Abraham has learned of God's overwhelming love for his righteous people. He is now convinced that God the judge will do what is right and that the righteous will not suffer the same punishment as the wicked.

_____

8. MacDonald (2004); Mathews (2005: 230).

33. The conversation having ended with God getting the last word, the scene shifts location again. The Lord went on his way, presumably to Sodom and Gomorrah, and we are told that Abraham returned *to his place*, presumably his tent at the oaks of Mamre.

Meaning

Once again God reassured Abraham that he would have a son, this time specifying that he would be born within a year. Sarah's laughter exhibited her doubts, but Abraham demonstrated his faith in pleading for Sodom. While Abraham had for many years been anxiously occupied with his need for an heir, he also remembered his nephew Lot. Certainly his plea for Sodom was primarily motivated by the possible destruction of his kinsman. Yet he pleaded for any who might be righteous although living in that wicked city. Such persons would have been his brothers and sisters in faith even if they were not related to him by blood. So also Christians pray for each other, even for those they may never have met (Eph. 6:18). The narrative is now prepared to turn to focus on Lot for the last time.

B. Lot rescued from Sodom (19:1–29)

Context

2067 BC

The account of the destruction of the Cities of the Plain focuses on Lot, who had previously chosen to live there (13:10). God had shown Abraham that he would not punish the righteous with the wicked, and this account shows that to be true in a way that even Abraham did not envisage. Because of the sinful acts of their inhabitants, God did not spare Sodom, Gomorrah, Admah or Zeboiim (19:28–29; Deut. 29:23). However, God spared Lot and his family, and for Lot's sake he spared Zoar.

Comment

1–3. Sodom was too far away from Hebron for the angels to have walked there by nightfall. Therefore, the arrival of the two angels in Sodom *in the evening* is a confirmation of their heavenly origin (v. 1). Lot's presence in the gate to the city shows that he had become a respected member of the community. Like Abraham, when he saw these strangers he immediately bowed down and extended hospitality to them (cf. 18:2–4), offering them lodging (v. 2). Their initial refusal is puzzling, since cities were considered safer lodging than the countryside, and a house safer than the city square. We are told, however, that Lot *urged* them to accept (v. 3). The same Hebrew verb will be used later when the men of Sodom *pressure* Lot (see v. 9).

Lot *prepared a feast* for them, but it featured *unleavened bread*, a rather plain food for a feast. In fact, this is the only place in the Scriptures where the words *feast* and *unleavened bread* occur together.

4–8. The complete corruption of the city is shown by the comprehensive description of the men who surrounded Lot's house: *both young and old from the end of the city* (v. 4). Their demand is that Lot send out his guests *so we can have sex with them* (v. 5) – literally, 'so that we may know them'. In Genesis *know* is frequently a euphemism for sexual relations (cf. 4:1). Some have tried to argue that the demand of the Sodomites was not sexual, but simply an insistence that they be able to understand who it was that was staying in the city with Lot.[9] This is belied by the fact that Lot begs them not to do *this evil* (v. 7) and then offers his daughters *who have not been intimate* [literally, 'have not known'] *a man* (v. 8). Clearly, Lot understood their request as sexual in nature.

While Lot courageously went outside and shut the door behind him to protect the others in his house, it is shocking that Lot chose to offer his daughters up to abuse. While it is true that he had an obligation to the guests who had *come under the protection of [his] roof* (v. 8), this does not excuse his willingness to expose his daughters to the depraved mob. It would seem that Lot, who addressed the crowd as *my brothers* (v. 7), was more concerned with identifying with the city than with fulfilling his vocation as father.

9–11. The mob's reaction is to press their case and classify Lot as an outsider (v. 9). They reject his judgment that their proposed act is evil and seek to force their way into his house. The angels

9. E.g. Morschauser (2003).

not only had to rescue Lot (v. 10), but also struck the Sodomites with *blindness* (v. 11). The Hebrew word is sometimes translated 'a blinding light' and occurs only here and at 2 Kings 6:18. In both instances it is a temporary blindness that makes those struck blind unable to find what they are seeking. In an interesting contrast, the book of Acts portrays Paul struck by a blinding light (Acts 9:1–9) which allowed him to see Jesus and be filled with the Holy Spirit (Acts 9:17).

12–14. With Lot safely in his house, the angels urge him to get his family out of Sodom (v. 12). They explain the urgency, repeating God's reason for the impending destruction (v. 13; cf. 18:20) and their mission. Lot left the house to warn his sons-in-law *who were going to marry his daughters*, but their reaction was not to take his words seriously (v. 14). The sons-in-law were also blinded – not by the angels, but by their own sin which rejected God's judgment (Luke 17:28–29).

15–16. Travel was not normally attempted at night, so at dawn as the sky lightened the angels urged Lot to escape the city's punishment (v. 15). Lot's hesitation is not explained (v. 16). Perhaps he was reluctant to leave his property behind. Yet the text emphasizes that it was the Lord's compassion that made the angels lead his family outside the city despite his dawdling (v. 16).

17–22. Lot was instructed to run to the mountains and escape the Plain, making clear that God intended to destroy all five Cities of the Plain (v. 17). They were quickly to go directly out of the Plain without even looking back. Lot's pleading acknowledged the angels' kindness, but claimed that he would not be able to arrive in the mountains before the destruction fell from the Lord onto the Plain (vv. 18–19). His plea for the small city to be spared was not, like Abraham's pleas to God, for the sake of any righteous persons who may have lived there, but rather for his own benefit. His statement that it was only a small city implied that Yahweh would be sparing only a few wicked people so that he, a righteous man, could survive there.

Lot's request was granted, and one of the angels told him to hurry, since he could not destroy the Plain until Lot had reached safety (vv. 21–22). It appears that God had previously instructed the angels to ensure Lot's survival. A final note tells us that this city, formerly known as Bela (see 14:2), came to be called Zoar: its name sounds similar to the word Lot used to describe it as *small*.

23–26. Lot arrived at Zoar – the small city – by sunrise (v. 23), just in time for God to rain fiery sulphur, destroying the entire Plain. The extent of the annihilation is made clear by noting the obliteration of *the inhabitants of the cities and whatever grew on the ground* (v. 25). Lot's wife became part of those destroyed as she ignored the angel's instructions not to look back (v. 26). Perhaps she was from Sodom, since she was not mentioned previously.[10] She became a warning to those who would later flee Jerusalem's destruction by the Roman armies (see Luke 17:31–33).

27–29. The final note on the destruction sees the scene shift back to Abraham at the oaks of Mamre where his conversation with Yahweh took place (v. 27). Abraham's looking down towards Sodom and Gomorrah (v. 28) serves as a bookend together with Abraham's visitors looking over Sodom (18:16) to mark the beginning and ending boundaries of the narrative about God's judgment on the evil of the Cities of the Plain. The smoke rising from the land *like the smoke of a furnace* emphasizes God's presence as the judge who meted out this punishment. His fearful presence would be accompanied by the same smoke on Mount Sinai (Exod. 19:18). Finally, it is noted that Lot was saved because *God remembered Abraham* (v. 29). While Abraham did not explore the complete depths of God's compassion on his righteous people (he stopped at ten righteous persons, 18:32), God nevertheless took Abraham's plea for Sodom and Gomorrah to the extreme by extracting Lot before the firestorm fell on the Jordan Plain.

C. Lot's sons by his daughters (19:30–38)

Context
2067–2066 BC
This is the last story about Lot in Genesis. The account serves to tell us about his descendants, who will also disappear from the

---

10. Mathews (2005: 242).

narrative. Moab will be mentioned again only as a geographical marker (36:35), and Ammon will not be mentioned at all.

Comment

30. Lot's fear of Zoar – perhaps because its citizens are as wicked as Sodom – leads him into the mountains with his daughters. Ironically, this is where the angels had initially directed him to go (19:17). Having lost all of his great wealth which had earlier brought about his move away from Abraham (13:8–13), Lot is reduced to living in the humblest of conditions.

31–33. The elder daughter, Lot's *firstborn*, devises a plan so that she can bear a child (vv. 31–32). Her assertion *Our father is old* is not a judgment on his virility, but probably a belief that he is too old and now too poor to be able to find them suitable husbands; therefore, *there is no man in the land to sleep with us* (literally, 'come into us', v. 31). Lot's intoxication recalls Noah's drunken state (v. 33; cf. 9:21). However, in this case Lot's children use it in a much worse way to take advantage of him without his knowledge. Having seen how he was willing to allow them to be sexually abused in Sodom (v. 8), they now are not above taking sexual advantage of their father.

34–35. The elder daughter urges her sister to repeat her act, and the parallel language serves to paint the younger daughter as being as depraved as her sister.

36–38. The two sons born from these incestuous unions are given appropriate names: *Moab* probably means 'from father', and *Ben-ammi* means 'son of my people'. Apparently neither daughter is ashamed of her actions. Instead, by the choice of the names of their sons they enshrine what they have done.

Meaning

When Abraham left Haran after the death of his father, Lot came with him despite God's instruction for Abraham to leave his father's household entirely behind (12:1). Abraham's only reminder of his ties to his father's family had been through Lot. Although they had parted ways once (13:8–12), Abraham had come to Lot's rescue when he was captured (14:13–16). Now Abraham would have to consider two family issues: God's promise of a son, and the danger in which Lot had placed himself. Here we encounter Genesis' final contrast between Abraham's family as defined by his father's descendants, and his new family to be established through his own descendants.

Abraham learned from his guests – Yahweh and two angels – that he was on the verge of having a son by Sarah as the Lord had promised. Despite Sarah's doubts, the visit of Yahweh and his angels drew Sarah into a closer relationship to God and his promise. Abraham and Sarah would become parents together and establish their longed-for family. Moreover, this family would produce Abraham's great descendant Jesus and be the way in which *all families of the earth would consider themselves blessed* through Abraham (18:18).

Meanwhile, Lot was living in Sodom, and God was about to destroy that city. God revealed this to his chosen servant Abraham so that he could learn more fully *what is just and right* and teach his children *the way of the Lord* (18:19). Abraham's plea for God to consider sparing Sodom and Gomorrah was not built around his familial ties with Lot but was founded in an appeal to God to have compassion for the sake of the righteous among the wicked in those cities. Surely Abraham realized that Lot was in danger, but his maturing faith understood that God was concerned about all of those who, like Abraham, had been reckoned righteous through faith (15:6). If Lot was among them, God would count him along with the other righteous persons in the city. Abraham's humble boldness in repeatedly asking God to consider sparing the cities for the sake of fewer and fewer righteous persons shows his trust in God as a judge who was both just and compassionate. Thus, Abraham became an example to all who believe, showing future generations that God's most important way of relating to them is through his gracious mercy (Exod. 34:6). That mercy would ultimately be found in Abraham's promised great descendant, Jesus (John 1:14; 1 Pet. 1:3).

The account of the Lord's angels rescuing Lot and destroying the Cities of the Plain draws a contrast between Abraham and his nephew. Lot was a righteous man, but he had placed himself among the unrighteous. This environment corrupted his family. Although in his compassion God spared Lot and his family, Sodom's wicked environment affected his entire household: Lot disgracefully offered his daughters to be sexually abused by the men of Sodom (19:8); Lot's wife paid with her life when she looked back to Sodom, apparently longing for it and its evil ways more than for escape from destruction (19:26); and Lot's daughters, who had lived in Sodom with its wicked practices, including its sexual sins, would themselves commit sexually immoral acts to further their own desires (19:30–38). Lot, therefore, also is an example to all believers – but a negative one – warning of the sinful ways that can become ingrained in the lives even of those to whom God has granted faith (cf. 2 Pet. 2:7–8).

11. THE FAMILY OF TERAH: ABRAHAM RECEIVES THE PROMISED SON (20:1 – 21:34)

This section is centred on Abraham's two sons. It tells of the birth of Isaac and of the expulsion of Hagar and her son Ishmael. The story of the early part of Isaac's life is paired with the account of the later part of Ishmael's life (21:20–21). After this Ishmael will play no large part in the rest of the Genesis narrative. His genealogy will be briefly summarized (25:12–18), and he will only be mentioned in passing (28:9; 36:3). Instead, the narrative will begin to focus on Isaac, Abraham's son of the promise.

Framing the accounts of Abraham's sons are two encounters with Abimelech (20:1–18; 21:22–34). While these may seem to be unrelated to the stories concerning Abraham's sons, they are connected to threats posed to God's promises to Abraham. In the first encounter, Abimelech takes Sarah as his wife, threatening the promise of a son to Abraham and Sarah. In the second encounter, Abraham has a well he has dug seized. In the end, Abimelech acknowledges Abraham's right to the well at Beersheba, his first permanent possession of any part of the land that Yahweh has promised him. Therefore, the first signs of the fulfilment of

God's pledges to the patriarch are presented together in the same context.

A. Abraham in Gerar: he deceives Abimelech (20:1–18)

Context

2067 BC

There have been challenges to the authenticity of this account. Critics have charged that this wife/sister story is a doublet – that is, it is a twice-told story that essentially repeats the plot of Abraham in Egypt (12:10–20).[1] Supposedly these two accounts are simply different versions of a tradition about Abraham deceiving someone about his relationship with Sarah. However, this depends largely on the assumption that a person would not make the same error twice – an assumption that experience tells us is false.[2] In addition, there are indications that the author of this chapter knew about the earlier story and so is not incorporating an independent tradition but instead relating a second actual lapse by Abraham into deception concerning Sarah. For instance, Abraham's words in 20:2 are obscure unless one has already read 12:11–13. The patriarch's words at 20:13 reference his call by God (12:1), showing that the author of this chapter expected his reader to know the setting of the previous wife/sister story. The description of Abraham as a prophet (20:7) fits well as building on the narrative of his intercession for Sodom (18:16–33, esp. 18:17; cf. Amos 3:7), whereas the earlier wife/sister story fits better in the earlier context.

Comment

1–2. Abraham's travels took him to the extreme south of the land between Kadesh Barnea and the Wilderness of Shur in the north-western Sinai Peninsula (v. 1). From there he went northwards to Gerar, which appears to have been located on the south-western edge of Canaan (cf. 10:19). Once again Abraham resorted to representing Sarah as his sister instead of his wife (v. 2) – though

---

1. One could also add the similar act by Isaac (26:7–11).

2. Kidner (1967: 148).

this time the ruse is not explained, since the author expects readers to remember Abraham's doing this in Egypt (see 12:10–13).

The name *Abimelech* is mentioned for the first time in this story, and this king will reappear later to interact with Abraham at 21:22–32. About ninety years later another king of Gerar named Abimelech will interact with Isaac (see 26:1–33). This may indicate either that it was a popular family name for this dynasty of kings or that Abimelech (meaning 'my father is king') was a throne name given to the kings of Gerar.

As a result of Abraham's deception, Abimelech took Sarah to be one of his wives. Unlike the pharaoh who had previously taken Sarah (see 12:15–16), Abimelech does not seem to have tried to give Abraham any goods in exchange for permission to take his putative sister.

3–7. God's appearance to Abimelech warns him of his impending death because of his taking another man's wife. The threat probably comes not only because of the potential adultery but also because Abimelech appears simply to have used his high position to commandeer the woman (v. 3).

The narrative is careful to tell the reader that Abimelech had not yet consummated his intended union with Sarah. His reply to God understands the threat as being to his entire people, not simply to him (v. 4). Abimelech proclaims his innocence twice – both before and after citing words from both Abraham and Sarah claiming to be brother and sister (vv. 4–5).

God's reply acknowledges Abimelech's claim of not knowing the marriage relationship he had violated, and that the Almighty himself had kept Abimelech from sinning with Sarah (v. 6). This statement shows that God's mercy extends even to those who are not his people, for it not only spared Abimelech and his city, but also preserved inviolate the relationship of Abraham and Sarah from whom would come the line leading to the Saviour. When Isaac was born, there would be no doubt that he was the son of Abraham.

With God's instructions to return Sarah to her husband he tells Abimelech that Abraham is a *prophet* who will *pray* for him so that he will live instead of dying (v. 7). These are the only uses of the words *prophet* and *pray* in Genesis. However, the concept of Abraham as a prophet has already been presented: he is the Bible's first interceding prophet (18:22–33).[3] Moreover, God revealed his thoughts and plans to the patriarch (18:17–21; cf. Amos 3:7). The intercession would be effective to spare both Abimelech and his people, confirming the king's assumption that more persons than he would have been punished by God for his indiscretion.

8–10. Abimelech's report to his court was probably meant to warn everyone in his city of the dangers of taking advantage of Abraham. It had the intended effect: *the men were terrified* (v. 8). However, Abimelech was not afraid to confront Abraham. He properly castigated him for his lies (vv. 9–10). But his final question to the patriarch seeks understanding: *What made you do this?* (v. 10).[4]

11–13. Abraham's reply is quite telling. He thought *there is no fear of God in this place* so they would kill him because of his wife (v. 11). This is a clear parallel to his motives for carrying out this same deception earlier in Egypt (12:12), although this time he does not mention Sarah's beauty. Her advanced age, by her own admission, made her less desirable (18:12). Abimelech's motive for taking her probably had more to do with seeking to align himself with a rich alien resident than with lust for Sarah. Yet lack of mention of giving her brother Abraham any bride price for her cast suspicion also on Abimelech that partially confirmed Abraham's fears.

Abraham also revealed that claiming to be brother and sister was not a complete fabrication. They shared the same father, though had different mothers. He claimed to have adopted this subterfuge wherever they lived (vv. 12–13). Whether Abraham is exaggerating about this is hard to say. The Scriptures, however, reveal only two times when Abraham resorted to this ploy.

This statement reveals a tendency among Israel's patriarchs to marry close relatives – a practice known as endogamy and later outlawed in the legislation given to Moses (Lev. 18). However, it was frequent among Terah's descendants: Nahor married his niece Milcah, Isaac married his second cousin Rebekah, and Jacob married his cousins Rachel and Leah. One motive for this endogamy

---

3. For other intercessory prayers of the prophets see Jer. 11:21–22; Amos 2:12–13; 7:16–17.

4. Literally, 'What did you see that you did this?'

appears to have been to insulate the family from Canaanite influences (cf. 24:2–4; 26:34–35).

14–16. Now, having taken Sarah and been forced by God to return her to Abraham, Abimelech finally offers him the equivalent of a bride price in animals and slaves (v. 14). In addition, he allowed Abraham to remain in his land – perhaps to keep an influential prophet nearby (v. 15; contrast 12:19–20).[5] Finally, he also paid an enormous penalty of 1,000 shekels to demonstrate that Sarah was returned inviolate.[6] Considering that Abraham paid 400 shekels for the cave at Machpelah (23:15–16), this was an extraordinarily large sum. Nevertheless, Abimelech also showed his resentment over the matter by telling Sarah that he was giving it *to your brother*, avoiding calling Abraham her husband (v. 16).

17–18. Although Abraham prayed and interceded for Abimelech's household, we are pointedly told that it was God's action, not Abraham's intercession, that brought healing (v. 17). Moreover, it was Yahweh's work that had made everyone in Abimelech's household infertile, and this was specifically because of *Sarah, Abraham's wife* (v. 18). Once again, despite the patriarch's bad behaviour, God was faithful to his promise to protect Abraham (cf. 12:3; 15:1).

Meaning

God's protection of Abraham is presented in this chapter but not in a way that excuses Abraham's repeated sin of deceiving others about his relationship to Sarah. Abraham offered Abimelech a flimsy excuse for his duplicitous portrayal of Sarah as his sister: that Sarah actually was his half-sister. Abimelech threw that attempt at self-justification right back at Abraham, telling Sarah to give the silver he gave to her to her *brother*. The entire narrative highlights a recurrent failing of Abraham: he did not fully trust God to curse those who treated him with contempt (12:3). In this way readers are reminded of their own weaknesses that may lead them to repeat a particular shameful behaviour, and are called instead to find integrity in their behaviour by trusting in God's promises (1 Cor. 10:13).

---

5. Mathews (2005: 258).

6. That is, about 25 lb or 11.5 kg of silver.

B. The birth of Isaac (21:1–7)

Context

2066 BC

The birth of Isaac highlights God's word of promise by using various words for speaking. God *said* (v. 1) and *promised* (twice, vv. 1, 2). He also *commanded* (v. 4). Thus, the birth account of Isaac emphasizes God's work through his word, just as Genesis 1 emphasizes his work of creation through the words he spoke. In response, Sarah *said* (v. 6) words of human expression: *laugh* (twice, v. 6) and *told* (v. 7).

Comment

1–2. These first two verses focus on what God did for Sarah. Yahweh kept his promise and *came to Sarah*. The Hebrew verb, often translated 'visited', denotes having a focused interest in someone or something. It will be connected with future mothers, such as when the Lord gave children to Hannah (1 Sam. 2:21). A Greek verb with a similar denotation is used in the New Testament to note God's gift of a son to Elizabeth (Luke 1:68). The timing of Sarah's pregnancy and Isaac's birth is signalled by two markers: Abraham's old age (v. 2; cf. 17:17; 18:11) and the *appointed time God had told him* (v. 2; cf. 17:16; 18:10–14).

3–5. The focus now shifts to what Abraham did in keeping with God's instructions. First, he named his son Isaac (v. 3; cf. 17:19). Note the triple designation of this son who would be the bearer of the messianic promise (v. 3): [1] *his son* [2] *who was born to him,* [3] *the one Sarah bore to him.* A similar triple designation will later emphasize that Isaac is the promise-bearer when Abraham is commanded to sacrifice him (22:2): [1] *your son,* [2] *your only son,* [3] *whom you love.* Second, he *circumcised* Isaac when he was eight days old, making him the first infant child to be circumcised under God's covenant (v. 4; cf. 17:12). Finally, Abraham's age at fatherhood – 100 years old – fulfils God's pledge despite Abraham's earlier doubt (v. 5; cf. 17:17).

6–7. The narrative now shifts back to Sarah and her joy in finally becoming a mother. Her faith now acknowledges that *God made me laugh* and even anticipates others laughing with her in her delight (v. 6). Laughter not only names Isaac (= 'he laughs') but also has been a leitmotif in the anticipation of this couple's parenthood at

an advanced age (17:17; 18:12–15). The incredulity expressed by
Abraham and Sarah's earlier laughter is now expressed by Sarah's
rhetorical question: *Who would have told Abraham that Sarah would nurse
children?* (v. 7). The answer is: no-one – except God! His work
allowed Sarah to bear a son for the aged patriarch.

C. Hagar and Ishmael sent away (21:8–21)

c.2063 BC

Now that Genesis has covered Isaac's birth, the author moves to
tell readers about the rest of Ishmael's life, beginning with the
circumstances under which he and Hagar were expelled from
Abraham's household. This procedure is in keeping with the overall
method of relating events in Genesis: first ancillary lines of descent
are narrated (in this case Ishmael), then the major line of descent is
resumed (the end of Abraham's life and the marriage of Isaac).

8. The next few years are summarized in saying *the child grew*. It is
impossible to say how old Isaac was when he was weaned, although
if 2 Maccabees 7:27 is any indication, he may have been about three
years old. The feast probably celebrated the end of infancy and
beginning of childhood. Considering the high infant mortality rate
before the rise of modern medicine, this was an important
milestone for the family.

9–10. Sarah observed *the son of Hagar the Egyptian whom she had
borne to Abraham mocking* (v. 9). Nowhere in this story is Ishmael
mentioned by name, allowing the narrative to distance him from
Sarah and eventually from Abraham. *Mocking* is from the same root
as the word *laughter* and the name *Isaac*. Since in this form the word
can take on several nuances, commentators have understood it in a
number of different ways.[7] However, at Galatians 4:29 Paul
understands Ishmael as persecuting Isaac, so the meaning is likely
to be *mocking*, a meaning that also applies at 39:14, 17.[8]

---

7. See the discussions in Hamilton (1995: 78–79) and Mathews (2005: 268–269).

8. Elsewhere in Genesis the meaning in this form (Hebrew *Piel* conjugation)
can be *joking* (19:14) or caressing in an intimate, sexual way (26:8; cf.
Exod. 32:6; 1 Cor. 10:7).

Sarah's reaction is to call for Abraham to *drive out* both Hagar and Ishmael (v. 10). The verb is quite harsh. Elsewhere it refers to the banishment of Adam from Eden (3:24) and of Cain from the land (4:14). Moreover, Sarah does not name either Hagar or Ismael, but refers instead to their inferior social status as *the slave woman and her son*. She wants there to be no doubt that her son is the only heir of Abraham's fortune. Of course, God had already made Isaac the sole heir of his covenant with Abraham (17:19). Sarah, though, had her focus on Abraham's wealth.

11–13. Sarah's demand was *very distressing to Abraham because of his son* (v. 11). Note that although Sarah originally gave Hagar to Abraham so that she could have a son for Sarah (16:2), the only acknowledged family ties of Ishmael are to Hagar and Abraham. Given Abraham's distress, it is clear that he considered Ishmael to be his son and may well have left him part of his property as an inheritance. The Code of Hammurabi indicates that in the Ancient Near East the sons of slaves could at times receive an inheritance.[9]

Immediately the narrative switches to God's instructions on this matter. Since Abraham would send Hagar and Ishmael away the next morning, this may have been another instance of God speaking to Abraham at night. Except for *Sarah*, God also does not use names, speaking only about *the boy* and *your slave* (v. 12). God affirms that Sarah is correct in one sense: Abraham's offspring will be reckoned through Isaac. Nevertheless, because Ishmael is Abraham's son, God assures the patriarch that he has not abandoned his promise that Ishmael will also grow into a great nation (v. 13; cf. 17:20). Thus, Abraham can follow the divine directive without concern that he is sending Ishmael to his destruction in the desert.

14–16. Abraham gave Hagar and Ishmael provisions, and she ended up wandering in the area around *Beersheba* in the extreme south of the Promised Land (v. 14). This is apparently the area where Abraham was, as the next story (21:22–34) takes place there, and the use of the name here anticipates the naming of that place (21:31).

9. *ANET* 173.

When their food and water were gone, Hagar apparently gave up hope. Seeking a measure of comfort for her son under a tree, she went *about a bowshot away* (v. 16). Her words are interesting; she did not want to see the boy's death, yet one can see the distance of a bowshot. Perhaps she was still so moved by maternal attachment that she could not separate completely.

17–19. Despite Hagar's weeping, it was the lad's crying that moved the *angel of God* to call to Hagar (v. 17). This is the second time Hagar encountered God in this form (cf. 16:7–12). Here God tells her to resume her vocation as the boy's mother, since God intends to make him a great nation (v. 18). Apparently Abraham had not shared this divine assurance with Hagar. The opening of Hagar's eyes to see the well (perhaps the same well mentioned at vv. 25, 30) showed the means of preserving Ishmael's life. There is an interesting parallel in the next chapter: God would spare Isaac's life by allowing Abraham to see that he had provided a ram caught in a thicket for a sacrifice in Isaac's place (22:13–14).

20–21. The rest of Ishmael's life is now quickly summarized. He will largely disappear from Genesis, except for a brief appearance to help Isaac bury Abraham's body at Machpelah (25:9) and the listing of his descendants (25:12–18). God's love and commitment to Abraham is signalled by the statement *God was with the boy* (v. 20). As this story began with Isaac growing out of infancy (v. 8), it ends with Ishmael's growing into manhood. His skill with a bow would serve him well in hunting game in the *Wilderness of Paran* (v. 21). This area on the extreme south of Canaan was north of the Sinai Wilderness and probably included the site of Kadesh Barnea (cf. 16:11–14). Since Ishmael no longer had a father to arrange a marriage for him, Hagar took on this responsibility and drew on her roots in Egypt to secure her son a bride.

Meaning

In all of this readers are shown the hand of God in providing for both of Abraham's sons. While Isaac may have been the child to whom God's promise was attached, the goal of that promise was to be a blessing to all nations, including the nation that would come from Ishmael.

D. Abraham's covenant with Abimelech (21:22-34)

Context

c.2063 BC

Abraham's last interaction with Abimelech involves his first claim to any part of the Promised Land – a well at Beersheba. Though this may appear to casual readers merely to be a connecting story, it is more important than that because of this well. Moreover, the importance of this account is signalled by its careful crafting that plays on the number seven. The names *Abraham* and *Abimelech* each occur seven times. Abraham presents Abimelech with seven ewe lambs. The Hebrew word for *swear an oath* contains the same letters as the number *seven*. Moreover, the place name *Beersheba* contains an ambiguity, since it could be construed as meaning either *well of the seven* or *well of the oath*.

Comment

22–23. *About that time* (v. 22) probably places this incident near in time to Ishmael's expulsion. *Phicol* is mentioned here and in verse 32. However, a person by that name also appears almost ninety years later accompanying an Abimelech to meet Isaac. It is likely that Phicol was a family name. At various times in antiquity, papponymy – naming one's son after one's father – was common.

Abimelech has a rather long opening address to Abraham, beginning with his contention, borne out of experience (cf. 20:7), that God is with the patriarch. The reason for the king's request that Abraham swear an oath not to deal falsely but to show kindness also appears to be rooted in his previous experience of Abraham's deception. As a reminder of the precarious existence of a non-native of this part of the land, Abimelech notes that Abraham is a *resident alien* (v. 23) in the land despite having God with him. Abimelech has the commander of his army present to reinforce this point.

24–26. Abraham's reply is short and to the point – *I swear* (v. 24) – but then is followed by his complaint about how Abimelech's men have treated him (v. 25). It would seem that Abraham's earlier fear of the men of Gerar (see 20:11) had some basis in fact: to seize one's source of water in an arid land threatened both life and livelihood. Since Abimelech had given Abraham permission to live in the land (20:15), the use of the land's water would have been assumed. Just as he pleaded ignorance in the case of taking Sarah (20:4–5), Abimelech pleads ignorance here, and he must have been put on the defensive when confronted with his men's action. He attempts to deflect the accusation by trying to place the onus of the problem on Abraham for not reporting it (v. 26).

27–32. Now that the two men had made reciprocal declarations, Abraham sealed their relationship with *flocks and herds*, returning to the king the types of animals he had given to Abraham (v. 27; cf. 20:14). Abraham's next action, however, is perplexing: he *separated seven ewe lambs from the flock* (v. 28). When asked about the ewes (v. 29), Abraham placed a condition on Abimelech's acceptance of these seven valuable animals (v. 30); their value was that they were young and would provide milk and offspring for longer than mature ewes. Abraham deftly manoeuvred the king into acknowledging that the well was not a pre-existing one, but one that Abraham had dug. The patriarch was not seizing a water resource from others, but had made one of his own.

We are now told the origin of the name of this place (v. 31). *Beersheba* could mean *well* (Hebrew *bĕ'ēr*) of the *seven* (Hebrew *šeba'*) or of the *oath* (Hebrew *šĕbû'â*), and is a play on words that reminds readers of both the seven ewes and the oath that formed the covenant between the two men.

The covenant discussion ended when Abimelech and Phicol returned *to the land of the Philistines* (v. 32), suggesting that Beersheba was heretofore beyond the recognized territory controlled by the king of Gerar. Apparently the seizure of the well and the presence of the commander of the king of Gerar's army was an attempt to extend Philistine sovereignty to the south-east. Now, apparently due to the covenant, it was to be considered part of Abimelech's territory in which Abraham would dwell as an alien.

33–34. Abraham planted a *tamarisk tree* (v. 33). The tamarisk is a family of both deciduous trees and evergreen trees (genus *tamarix*) that can grow in arid areas along watercourses. At maturity a tamarisk tree can be up to 30 ft (10 m) high and provide a good amount of shade. This is the only time Abraham is said to have planted a tree, and it most likely was a way of declaring his claim to the well and the surrounding land at Beersheba.

His act of planting also appears to be connected somehow with his worship of Yahweh, who here is called *the Everlasting God*, a name that appears in this form nowhere else in the Bible.[10] Perhaps in using this title for the Lord, Abraham is expressing his faith that God who is everlasting will always be present to keep his covenant with the patriarch and his descendants, especially the promise of the land of Canaan. Having claimed a well and planted a tree, Abraham continued to live in this area for some time (v. 34).

Meaning
Tangible evidence of God's promises to Abraham comes to him in this section of Genesis. Immediately after having been told that a son would be born to him and Sarah in a year's time (cf. 18:1–15), that statement seemed to be endangered when Abimelech took Sarah as his own – prompted at least in part by Abraham's own dissembling statement about his relationship to her. Yet God's power was greater than that of the Philistine king. Not only did the Lord procure Sarah's speedy return to Abraham, but he also impressed on Gerar's king the importance of Abraham: although he behaved in a less-than-honourable fashion, Abraham was never-theless a prophet of God. God's people are not without their faults that can even be apparent to those who do not believe. Neverthe-less, through faith they are God's beloved people, and God's commitment to the promises he has made them is absolute.

Isaac's birth, then, took place as God had predicted, and Abraham demonstrated his faith in God and his gratitude for the Almighty's favour by following the instructions he was given: the boy was named Isaac, and he was circumcised, bringing another generation under the covenant that would provide a blessing to all nations. Sarah's laughter was now a sign of her joy (21:6) instead of

10. Hebrew *'ēl 'ôlām*. Isaiah once uses the related name *'ĕlōhê 'ôlām* ('Everlasting God') in connection with describing God as the Creator (Isa. 40:28).

scepticism (18:13). In this way Genesis emphasizes that, although believers sometimes find it challenging to trust and receive comfort from God's pledges, God's promises remain sure and are always fulfilled at the proper time.

However, with Isaac's presence in the household, Abraham now had two sons and understandably would have been attached to each. This was not so with Sarah, however. Her offence at Ishmael's behaviour when Isaac was weaned led to a forced and permanent breach between Abraham and his older son, a breach that distressed father Abraham (21:11). But God nevertheless used this incident to emphasize the importance of Isaac not only in the immediate family of the patriarch, but also as the bearer of his promise that stretched back to Eve that he would redeem the world (3:15). Though Ishmael would be distanced from his father, God was not without compassion, and Ishmael would also become a great nation.

Finally, the narrative returns to include Abimelech once again. This time the Philistines appeared to be attempting to extend the reach of their city-state to include territory outside the immediate environs of Gerar. Since Abraham had been given permission to live in their midst, Abimelech's demand for an oath of kindness to him may have been designed to achieve recognition of his rule as far as Beersheba. Yet this also backfired, since Abimelech was placed into a position of having to acknowledge Abraham as possessor of the well at Beersheba, thereby providing the first permanent possession in the land for Israel's patriarchs. Thus, it is significant that at Beersheba Abraham worshipped the Lord and called on him as God Everlasting, an acknowledgment not only of God's eternal nature but also of the enduring character of his promises which Abraham had now begun to experience first-hand.

12. THE FAMILY OF TERAH: THE PROMISE TO ABRAHAM CONTINUED IN ISAAC (22:1 – 24:67)

The previous narratives in Genesis demonstrated the first steps in the fulfilment of God's promises to Abraham as he both received a son and laid claim to a tiny portion of the Promised Land – a well at Beersheba. In this section the narrative advances by focusing on Isaac as the bearer of the promise in the next generation. It begins with a test of Abraham's faith: will he trust that God can keep his promise to reckon Abraham's descendants through Isaac even if Isaac is slaughtered as a sacrifice (22:1–19)? Abraham passes the test and even during this trial shows his confidence that should Isaac die, God would be able to make Abraham a great nation through this son of Sarah.

The short section on news about Nahor's family (22:20–24) sets the stage for Abraham's successful attempt to find a wife for Isaac so that another generation can pass on the promises of God. But before the story moves on to Isaac's marriage, the account of Sarah's death and burial intervenes (23:1–20). This once again focuses on two important promises of God. With Sarah's death, Abraham must obtain a place for her body's interment. He successfully negotiates the purchase of a cave at Machpelah in Hebron as a family burial site, marking his possession of a second portion of the land that God had promised to him. But more importantly, with the death of Sarah the importance of Isaac is heightened. God had intended all along that Abraham's descendants who would carry the promise forward would be the product of his marriage to Sarah. With Sarah's death, that can now only be Isaac.

Abraham's careful instructions to his servant concerning obtaining a wife for Isaac show how seriously he is focused on God's pledge being continued through Isaac (24:1–67). The culmination of this is the first narrative about the beginning of a marriage since Adam was given Eve (cf. 2:21–24). One of the most poignant and tender reflections on important aspects of what Genesis means when it speaks of husband and wife becoming *one flesh* (2:24) is found here: Isaac's marriage to Rebekah brings him love and comfort (24:67).

A. The sacrifice of Isaac (22:1–19)

Context

C.2045 BC

One of the most important stories in the Old Testament, this account is traditionally called 'The Sacrifice of Isaac' by Christians and 'The Binding of Isaac' by Jews. Abraham's life of faith comes to a climax here. He expresses his confidence in God's providence (22:8, 14) and he receives God's final promise to him (22:16–18).

Comment

1–2. *After these things* provides only a general indication of when this incident took place (v. 1). Considering that Isaac was old enough to question Abraham about the sacrifice and could climb the mountain, there must have been at least a decade between the end of chapter 21 and the beginning of this chapter, and it is likely that Isaac was a teenager at this time, since he was able to carry the wood for the sacrifice (see v. 6).

God's call for Abraham to sacrifice involves three details. First is the sacrifice itself: Isaac. He is described in a threefold way: *your son, your only son whom you love, Isaac* (v. 2). The first part emphasizes God's recognition of Isaac as the son whom he had given to Abraham. The second not only notes the absence of Ishmael (cf. 21:1–21), making Isaac the *only* son, but also remarks on Abraham's attachment to Isaac. This is the first use of the word *love* in the Scriptures. However, love of parents for their children will become an important element in the rest of the patriarchal stories (25:28; 37:3–4; 44:20). The third designation using the name *Isaac* is a reminder of the joy at the birth of this son (21:6).

Second, God specifies *the land of Moriah* as the place for the sacrifice. The place name *Moriah* occurs only one other time in the Old Testament: at 2 Chronicles 3:1 Mount Moriah is identified as the site of the temple in Jerusalem. Some have doubted whether this Moriah is the same, especially in light of the three days mentioned in verse 4. It is said that a three-day journey from Beersheba would have placed Abraham well beyond Jerusalem.[1] However, this is a misunderstanding of the phrase *the third day* in verse 4. It does not denote a three-day journey. Instead, the first day is the first day of the narrative – the day when God commanded the sacrifice; the second day marked the beginning of the journey (v. 3); and the third day was the day of arrival at the mountain and the sacrifice on it. Therefore, the journey occupied only parts of two days, and we ought not doubt that Mount Moriah in Chronicles is the mountain in the region of Moriah where Abraham sacrificed to God.

Third, Isaac was to be a *burnt offering*. Such sacrifices involved killing and dismembering the offering and burning it on an altar. This would have been shocking to the original readers of Genesis, since the law of Moses strictly forbade human sacrifice (Lev. 18:21; 20:2–5), though at times it was practised among non-Israelites and Israelites who adopted pagan practices (2 Kgs 3:27; 17:17). While biblical law required that all firstborn sons be dedicated to Yahweh, the sons themselves were not to be sacrificed. Instead, animals would be offered in their place (Exod. 13:11–16; 22:29; 34:20).

3. Abraham's preparations take place on the next morning. His obedience to God's command is immediate and absolute. Both the

---

1. See the discussion in Mathews (2005: 290–291).

sacrifice and the wood are taken along. However, so are two of
Abraham's slaves. The reason for their inclusion is to have people
to look after the donkey while Abraham and Isaac go up the mountain to sacrifice (see v. 5).

4–6. Abraham's arrival at Moriah prompts his instructions to his
servants. His words *we will come back to you* (v. 5) express his confidence that even after Isaac has been sacrificed, God can raise him
from the dead in order to keep his promise that his offspring will be
reckoned through Isaac (Heb. 11:17–19; cf. Gen. 21:12). Abraham
now makes a division of labour, with Isaac carrying the wood and
he the knife and the fire (perhaps burning coals; v. 6).

7–8. The brief conversation between Isaac and Abraham is
related skilfully. Isaac asks a question with six words (in Hebrew),
and Abraham answers with six words. The conversation begins with
Isaac's *my father* (v. 7) and ends with Abraham's *my son* (v. 8).
Abraham's reply, though vague from Isaac's point of view, is also
a statement of faith: that God will make the necessary provisions
for the burnt offering. *God will provide* is literally 'God will see for
himself'.

9–10. The account of Abraham's obedience on the mountain is
told in quick, broad strokes. This was the fifth altar Abraham had
built in Canaan and it would be the last (cf. 12:7–8; 13:18). That
Abraham bound Isaac marks this as an unusual sacrifice. Nowhere
else in the Bible is binding mentioned with such offerings, and it
appears that Isaac cooperated, thereby also demonstrating his trust
in God's promises. Abraham's *knife* is mentioned a second time
(v. 10; cf. v. 6). The Hebrew word is a specific term for an instrument
used to cut a body into pieces (Judg. 19:29), and may also form a
play on words with the next verse's mention of an *angel*, since the
two Hebrew words are similar in pronunciation.

11–14. The angel's double call to Abraham signals the urgency to
stop the patriarch before he killed his son (v. 11). The angel uses the
language of acquiring knowledge: *now I know you fear God* (v. 12). Yet
the angel also reveals that he is God: *since you have not withheld your only
son from me* (i.e. from God who commanded the sacrifice, cf. vv. 1–2).
While it may seem strange that the all-knowing God learned something about Abraham, in this case we should understand God as
adopting the position of the senior partner in a covenant, such as a

mighty king speaking to his vassal.[2] His language is not simply informative; that is, it is not simply saying what God has learned. Rather, this is evaluative and performative language, stating a conclusion about Abraham's actions and in effect declaring that the patriarch's actions demonstrate that God is justified in bestowing his promise on Abraham and his descendants (cf. vv. 16–18).

Abraham's noticing the ram fulfils his earlier statement that God would provide the sacrifice (see v. 8). While most English versions read *a ram* (v. 13), some Hebrew manuscripts read 'another ram', which would perhaps be a way of stating that this ram was a substitute for Isaac.[3] However, *a ram* is most likely the correct reading, since the ram's being a substitute for Isaac is clearly stated later in the verse.

Abraham's name for the place *The Lord Will Provide* (literally, 'The Lord Will See', v. 14; cf. v. 8) led in the author's day to the saying *It will be provided* [literally, 'it/he will be seen'] *on the Lord's mountain*. This statement highlights God's choice of his own holy mountain, a choice that will later become important for the determination of the location of the temple in Jerusalem (Pss 2:6; 78:68; Isa. 56:7; 57:13; 65:25; 66:20; Ezek. 20:40; Joel 3:17).

15–18. The text is careful to note that God called to Abraham a second time – that is, after he had offered the ram as a sacrifice (v. 15). God's words here are the only divine oath directly recorded in Genesis.[4] In the oath God swears by himself, since there is no higher authority by which to take an oath (Heb. 6:13). The basis for God's oath is stated both at the beginning (*because you have . . . not withheld your only son*, v. 16) and at the end (*because you have obeyed my command*, v. 18).

The oath itself promises three things. The first is that Abraham will be blessed with many offspring, repeating the comparison to

---

2. Chisholm (2007: 15).

3. The difference in Hebrew is only one letter. There is little evidence to support the contention that instead of 'another ram caught in the thicket' the meaning is 'a ram just then caught in the thicket' (e.g. Wenham [1994: 99]).

4. This oath will be referenced again at 24:7; 26:3; 50:24.

the stars in the sky (v. 17; cf. 15:5) and adding for the first time a
comparison to the sand on the seashore. Second, the promise shifts
to a particular offspring of Abraham. Like the English word *offspring*,
the Hebrew word (literally 'seed') can either be a collective referring
to many or a particular referring to only one. To signal the shift to
a particular offspring in Hebrew the verb *possess* is singular, as is the
following pronoun in *his enemies* (not 'their enemies' as in many
English versions).[5] This offspring of Abraham will take possession
of the *gates of his enemies*. This promise is later expanded by Jesus,
Abraham's great offspring. He spoke of the victory his church
will have over the gates of Hades (Matt. 16:18).[6] Finally, the last
promise continues the focus on a particular offspring though whom
all nations will consider themselves blessed (v. 18).[7] Thus, the last
two of these three promises are specifically messianic in nature and
find their fulfilment in Christ.

19. The account ends with Abraham's return to Beersheba where
Abraham would continue to dwell, although a number of years later
he would be living again near Hebron (see 23:2, 19).

Meaning
The account of the great test of Abraham's faith is filled with
tension as the sacrificial knife is raised over his heir. Abraham was
completely committed to obeying God's command and would have
offered his son not only because he was loyal to the God who had
called him from Haran, but also because he believed that God was
the all-powerful creator who could raise the dead to life. The
patriarch knew that the messianic promise to bless all nations
hinged upon this God who could conquer death. In the New Testament the writer to the Hebrews expounds on Abraham's faith in the
resurrection, noting that figuratively speaking Abraham did receive
Isaac back from death (Heb. 11:17–19). As Abraham and Isaac

5. Collins (1997); Alexander (1997); Collins (2003).

6. Steinmann (2017a).

7. Many English versions use a passive construction: 'will be blessed'.
   However, the Hebrew verb is reflexive-estimative: 'consider themselves
   blessed'. See 12:3; 18:18; and Lee (2012).

came down from the mountain they had God's promises ringing in their ears: their great offspring, the promised Saviour, would be victorious, taking possession of the gates of his enemies, and through him all nations would find blessing (22:17–18).

B. News of Nahor's family (22:20–24)

Context

C.2030 BC

This brief section reports news Abraham received of his brother's family. It would appear that Abraham had had little contact with them since leaving Haran, and this news would later prompt him to send his servant back to Haran to find a wife for Isaac (24:1–67). The most important persons in this genealogical note are Bethuel and his daughter Rebekah, who would become Isaac's wife.

Comment

20. The phrase *now after these things* places this incident sometime after the sacrifice of Isaac (22:1–19) and before Sarah's death (23:1–2). The phrase *Milcah also has borne* makes a comparison to Sarah who had borne Isaac. Does this indicate that Abraham had sent word about Isaac to his brother and was now receiving news of Nahor's children?

21–23. *Uz* (v. 21), the firstborn, shares his name with a descendant of Aram (10:23) and a descendant of Edom (36:28). It is also the name of the place where Job dwelt (Job 1:1). *Buz* shares his name with a son of Gad (1 Chr. 5:14). At Jeremiah 25:23 Buz is a place in the mountainous region of northern Arabia associated with Dedan and Tema. Apparently Buz was also the home of Job's interlocutor Elihu (Job 32:2). The land of Bazu, perhaps a variation of Buz, was conquered by the Assyrian king Essarhaddon in 676 BC.[8] *Kemuel* shares his name with an Ephraimite (Num. 34:24) and a Levite (1 Chr. 27:17). His son *Aram* is not the same as the ancestor of the Aramaeans (cf. 10:22). *Kesed* (v. 22) is phonetically related to

---

8. *ABD* 1.794.

the Chaldeans. Perhaps he was their progenitor. The Chaldeans, who were considered Arameans, entered southern Mesopotamia from the north in the early second millennium. *Hazo* is otherwise unknown, though Essarhaddon also conquered the region of Hazu in Arabia in 676 BC. *Pildash* and *Jidlaph* are mentioned only here. *Bethuel* was the father of Rebekah and Laban and is frequently mentioned in Genesis in narratives involving Isaac (24:15, 24, 47, 50; 25:20; 28:2, 5). At 25:20 he is called an Aramean since his home was in Paddan-aram.

The note that *Bethuel fathered Rebekah* (v. 23) is set off in the Hebrew text as a disjunctive clause. This makes it likely that the author added this for readers in anticipation of Isaac's marriage and that it was not part of the original report to Abraham. Note that verse 20 mentions sons, not daughters. This would mean that Abraham did not know of Rebekah before sending his servant to Aram-Naharaim (24:1–67).

24. *Reumah* is introduced to readers for the first time (cf. 11:29). She was a *concubine*, that is, a second-level wife who was acquired without the payment of a bride price, although a concubine may have been originally obtained as a slave. Concubines had fewer legal privileges than ordinary wives, though later the law of Moses would guarantee them certain rights (Exod. 21:7–11). Reumah's sons are later associated with sites in Aram, Lebanon and Syria.[9]

Meaning
With Isaac alive, the narrative turns briefly to news of Nahor's family in anticipation of the way that God will continue Abraham's family line. But before Abraham takes any action to find a wife for his son the storyline turns in a different direction. Sarah dies, and Abraham must obtain a place to bury her. His skill in negotiating allows him to buy a sizeable plot of ground that will serve as the patriarchs' foothold in the Promised Land, the continuing foretaste of God's promise that will be repeated to Isaac and Jacob (see 26:3; 35:12).

9. *ABD* 5.694.

C. Sarah's death and burial (23:1–20)

Context

2029 BC

The account of Sarah's death and burial is important for more than being the notice of the end of life of a woman who had been promised that she would bear Abraham's heir. This story tells of Abraham's first and only purchase of a parcel in the Promised Land, marking only his second acknowledged allotment of property in the land pledged by God to become the land of his descendants (cf. 21:22–34). The importance of Abraham's trust in God's promise to give his descendants the land of Canaan is highlighted in several ways. First, Abraham does not return to his ancestral homeland at Haran to bury Sarah, but will insist on buying land in Hebron no matter what the price. Second, the acquisition of this parcel and its connection to God's promise makes it an important reference point in the rest of Genesis (25:9–10; 49:29–32; 50:24–25). Third, the land of Canaan is mentioned twice, once at the beginning of this narrative (v. 2) and once at the end (v. 19). In both cases there was no need to specify the land of Canaan, since it was well known that Hebron was in Canaan. Instead, the inclusion of Canaan serves to stress Abraham's commitment to the land that God had promised him.

Comment

1–2. The mention of Sarah's lifespan of 127 years is unique among Israel's matriarchs; no such information is given for any other wife of a patriarch in Genesis. In fact, of the matriarchs, only the deaths of Sarah and Rachel are mentioned (see 35:19; 48:7), although the burial place of Rebekah and Leah is noted (49:31).

By this time Abraham had returned to Hebron (cf. 13:18). We are told that Hebron was the newer name of this city, which here is called Kiriath-arba. With the exception of Nehemiah 11:25, whenever the name Kiriath-arba is mentioned in the Old Testament it is always identified as Hebron (Gen. 35:27; Josh. 14:15; 15:13, 54; 20:7; 21:11; Judg. 1:10). Kiriath-arba appears to mean 'city of four', although Joshua 15:13–14 treats Arba as the name of a person connected with this place, in which case Kiriath-arba would mean 'city of Arba'. Some commentators seek to explain the name of the city as signifying one city that was a consolidation of four.[10] These four supposed settlements have even been suggested to have been named Aner, Eshcol, Mamre and Hebron (cf. Gen 14:13, 24).[11] This, however, is unlikely since the place called Mamre is identified as Hebron at 23:19. Moreover, Eshcol and Mamre appear to have been persons whose names were later given to places in or near Kiriath-arba where they lived (on Eshcol, see Num. 13:23–24; 32:9; Deut. 1:24). However, there is no person named Hebron in Genesis, and no place named Aner near Hebron. (There was a city named Aner in the territory of Manasseh west of the Jordan River: see 1 Chr. 6:70.)

Abraham's *mourning* and *weeping* (v. 2) was part of the customary ritual for grieving over a loved one. In the Ancient Near East this grieving was expected to be done publicly. As the first part of verse 3 makes clear, Abraham's mourning was public, conducted near the city gate (cf. vv. 10, 18).

3–6. After finishing his grieving, Abraham addressed the inhabitants of Hebron, who are repeatedly identified as *Hittites* in most English translations (vv. 3, 5, 7, 10, 16, 18, 20; cf. 49:32). However, these are not the better-known Anatolian Hittites whose kingdom was in what is now eastern Turkey and who later occupied part of Syria (see Josh. 1:4; Judg. 1:26; 2 Sam. 24:6; 1 Kgs 10:29; 11:1; 2 Kgs 7:6; 2 Chr. 1:17). The Hebrew text calls them 'sons of Heth', making them Canaanites (see 10:15).[12] Perhaps it would be better to call them *Hethites*.[13] In fact, as expected of descendants of Canaan, every Hittite personal name in the Old Testament is a Semitic name: Ephron (vv. 8, 10, 13–14, 16), Zohar (v. 8), Judith,

10. Hamilton (1995: 126).

11. Mathews (2005: 315).

12. Wood (2011). While some would argue that this chapter is replete with customs stemming from the Anatolian Hittites, Tucker (1966) has demonstrated that those same features can be found in (Semitic) Neo-Babylonian documents of sale.

13. See, for instance, CSB which consistently uses *Hethites* throughout this chapter.

Beeri, Basemath, Elon (26:34), Adah (36:2), Ahimelech (1 Sam. 26:6) and Uriah (2 Sam. 11).

Abraham began his request of the Hethites by noting that he was a resident alien among them. This implied that he owned no land in this area and was a prelude to his request. His words *Give me burial property among you* (v. 4, CSB) were not a request or demand that they gift him property, but an opening offer to obtain a tract of land as a permanent possession, an offer to purchase. The language of negotiation initiated by Abraham and continued by the Hethites appears obtuse and oblique to the modern Western reader, but it was the polite and public language of barter in the Ancient Near East.

The Hethites' reply is polite and respectful. They call Abraham *my lord* and *a mighty prince* (v. 6).[14] They recognize his status as a wealthy man of some influence, and they show respect for him and his dead wife in their courteous reply. Yet they also deftly deflect his offer to purchase land and become a permanent inhabitant of the area by offering Abraham the use of their finest burial plot without selling him any property. They even allow Abraham to choose which place by stating, *none of us will withhold from you his burial place.*

7–9. Abraham, who had been sitting during the Hethites' reply, now again stood and then bowed in a show of respect for them. Here the Hethites are called *the people of the land* (v. 7), a description which will be used twice more (vv. 12, 13). This appears to place them in distinction to Abraham, the resident alien. Elsewhere in the Pentateuch this phrase signifies permanent landed inhabitants (42:6; Exod. 5:5; Lev. 4:27; 20:2, 4; Num. 14:9).

Abraham's appeal is for the Hethites to engage one particular man in negotiations for a burial place (v. 8). This indirect appeal to Ephron was part of the polite and diplomatic barter. That Abraham wanted to engage with a particular man and purchase a particular cave shows that he had this location in mind from the beginning.

---

14. Literally 'a prince of God'. At times Hebrew uses 'God' as a way of describing someone or something that is surpassingly great. See 'a very great panic' ('a panic of God'; 1 Sam. 14:15); 'like mighty mountains' ('like mountains of God'; Ps. 36:6); 'a very great city' ('a great city to God'; Jon. 3:3).

The place name *Machpelah* (vv. 9, 17, 19) may mean 'double' (the LXX translates it this way). Abraham asks only for the cave, but offers the full price for it, now pressing his case for not simply a resting place for Sarah's body but a tomb for his family.

10–11. Ephron now takes up the negotiation with Abraham with a very polite *my lord* (v. 10). The mention of the people who came to the city gate demonstrates that this is an offer made before witnesses. He offers gratis not simply the cave but also the field in which it is located. Ephron's magnanimity is designed for public display of his gift, a gift that certainly would place Abraham in his debt. Therefore, if Abraham accepted, he would be permanently obligated to the Hethites. Ephron's offer was perhaps designed to make Abraham drop his pursuit of land ownership – a continuation of the Hethites' first offer that deflected Abraham's appeal for property (see v. 6). Ephron also states, *Bury your dead* (v. 11), thereby ensuring that Abraham is not using Sarah's death as a way of obtaining property for other purposes and simply using burial as pretence.

12–13. Abraham's response is to offer to purchase the field in addition to the previous offer to buy the cave. In response to Ephron's challenge, he also reiterates his intention to use the tract as a burial place.

14–16. Ephron's reply is to offer the field and cave for 400 shekels of silver. His statement *What is that between you and me?* (v. 15) is intended once again to entice Abraham to accept the property without payment. Although we cannot be certain, Ephron's stated price appears to place a very high value on this field (200 shekels would be about 10 lb or 4.5 kg of silver). David paid only 50 shekels to purchase the temple site from Araunah (2 Sam. 24:24). Omri paid two talents (6,000 shekels) for the large hill of Samaria, a mound spacious enough to situate an entire city (1 Kgs 16:24). Jeremiah paid 17 shekels for a field in Anathoth (Jer. 32:9). It therefore appears that Ephron is either vastly overpricing the field or offering a very expensive field at market rate. Either way, he must have done this in order again to discourage Abraham from making the purchase.

Abraham, however, does not blanch at the price. In a sense he calls Ephron's bluff and agrees without further haggling, weighing out the silver according to the agreement made *in the hearing of the Hethites* (v. 16). This phrase emphasizes that Ephron was obligated to take the sum that Abraham offered, since there were witnesses to the price he himself had requested.

17–18. The description of the land is very precise, noting the location of the plot of ground – *at Machpelah near Mamre* (v. 17) – as well as the cave and all the trees within the field. We are told that the field was now recognized as Abraham's *in the sight of all the Hethites who came to the gate*; that is, all the prominent citizens of Hebron were now obliged to acknowledge Abraham as a fully fledged property owner.

19–20. The next action noted is that Abraham buried Sarah in the property he purchased, and the last statement in the chapter affirms that the field and cave came to Abraham from the Hethites as a property to be used for burials. This confirms two things. First, it verifies that Abraham was not using Sarah's death as a pretence to buy the land for other purposes. Second, the mention of *Hebron in the land of Canaan* (v. 19) demonstrates Abraham's commitment of himself and his descendants to the land God had promised them. The burial of three generations of Abraham's family in the cave (Abraham and Sarah, Isaac and Rebekah, Jacob and Leah; 49:29–32; 50:13) shows that that commitment was an abiding feature of the patriarchs' faith.

Meaning

Abraham 'by faith . . . stayed as a foreigner in the land of promise, living in tents as did Isaac and Jacob, coheirs of the same promise' (Heb. 11:9, CSB). This led him to obtain a burial place for Sarah in Canaan since she also believed 'when she was unable to have children . . . even though she was past the age, since she considered that the one who had promised was faithful' (Heb. 11:11, CSB). Abraham's patient but persistent negotiations with Ephron the Hethite demonstrate his firm grasp of God's promise and his determination to live and die in the Promised Land.

D. Isaac marries Rebekah (24:1–67)

Context

2026 BC

The account of the acquisition of a wife for Isaac is the longest single narrative in Genesis. Here Abraham provides for his son, furthers the line bearing the messianic promise and conducts his last major action in Genesis. This story also introduces readers to two very important people in the life of Abraham's grandson Jacob: his mother Rebekah and his uncle Laban. This story is the first of three narratives in the Pentateuch where a woman meets a man at a well and it leads to marriage. The other two are Genesis 29:1–14 (Jacob meets Rachel) and Exodus 2:15–21 (Moses meets Zipporah).

This narrative divides easily into five scenes: Abraham commissioning a servant to find a wife for Isaac, the servant's encounter with Rebekah, the servant's negotiation with Laban to arrange Rebekah's marriage to Isaac, Rebekah's decisive commitment to go to Canaan for the marriage, and the marriage of Isaac and Rebekah.

Comment

i. Abraham commissions his servant (24:1–9)

1. Abraham is described as *old, getting on in years*, a description that occurs elsewhere only of Joshua (Josh. 13:1; 23:1) and David (1 Kgs 1:1) at the very ends of their lives. We are also told that *the Lord had blessed him in everything*. This points back to the fulfilment of God's promises to Abraham in granting him Isaac, through whom Abraham would grow into a great nation and through whom the line leading to the Messiah would pass. It also summarizes Abraham's acquiring land in Canaan at Beersheba (21:22–34) and later at Hebron (23:1–20) as incipient signs of the pledge to give the land to Abraham's descendants. At the same time, by pointing to the fact that God had fulfilled his promise to bless Abraham, the narrative prepares the reader to move forward in the continuing story by leaving Abraham behind and continuing on to Isaac.

2–4. The last-recorded words of Abraham begin with these verses. The importance of his concern for Isaac to be married is mirrored in his choice of someone to obtain the wife for his son. He chose his most trusted slave, the *senior servant of his household who managed all that he owned* (v. 2). The servant was to place his hand under Abraham's *thigh*, which is most certainly a euphemism for genitalia[15] (cf. 46:26 and Exod. 1:5, where Jacob's descendants are

---

15. For a parallel Mesopotamian custom, see Malul (1987).

said to have come out of his thigh; and Judg. 8:30, where Gideon's sons are characterized by the same phrase). The oath Abraham required of his servant was sworn by *Yahweh, God of heaven and God of earth* (v. 3). Although this title for God is unique in the Bible, it appears to be a variation of the divine description used in Melchizedek's blessing (14:19–20) and in Abraham's oath as he described it to the king of Sodom (14:22).

Abraham's insistence that his son not marry a Canaanite woman will find its later expression in the laws given by Moses for all Israel (Exod. 34:16; Num. 25; Deut. 7:3). This may also have been a factor in Rebekah's problems with Esau's wives who were taken from Canaanite Hethites (see 26:34–35; 27:46).[16] To that end, Abraham's instructions sent the servant to *my land and my family* to find a wife. Therefore, the servant had to travel back to Haran, where Abraham had been living when God first called him (12:4).

5–9. The servant does not object to finding a wife for Isaac or even doubt that he can find an acceptable bride. However, he is concerned that the woman will not wish to accompany him back to Canaan (v. 5). In order to be able to resolve such a situation he asks whether it is permissible for Isaac to return to Haran. This shows the reader the knowledge possessed by this senior servant who had been with Abraham for a long time. He knew of Abraham's commitment to the land of Canaan and had observed his actions to establish himself there, such as his acquiring the rights to Beersheba (21:22–34) and ownership of the cave at Machpelah (23:1–20). Perhaps he also knew of God's promise of the land to Abraham. So, instead of presuming that he could arrange the marriage under any terms that obtained a wife from Haran for Isaac, the servant enquired as to whether Isaac could be brought to Haran if necessary.

Abraham's reply not only forbids Isaac to return to Haran (v. 6), but also explains why he is forbidden: because of God's promise of the land to Abraham's offspring (v. 7). The patriarch also affirms

---

16. Note that at 27:46 these women are called *daughters of Heth* (i.e. Hethite women) in the Hebrew text. Heth was a descendant of Canaan (10:15).

that God will be with the servant on his mission: *he will send his angel* before the servant so that he will be successful in taking a bride for Isaac (cf. vv. 27, 40). Elsewhere in Genesis, Yahweh's angel is identified as Yahweh himself (see 16:7–14; 21:17–18; 22:11–18; 31:11–13; 48:15–16). Yet, if the servant has any doubts as to whether he will be successful, Abraham gives the servant a release from his oath if the woman refuses to come to Canaan, as long as Isaac does not leave Canaan to be married (v. 8).

After having had his doubts addressed, the servant takes the oath as Abraham instructed (v. 9). Here the servant is characterized as Abraham's slave. Later the servant will identify Isaac as his master (v. 65), demonstrating that Isaac is Abraham's full heir and also signalling to the reader that the central figure of the narrative is shifting from Abraham to Isaac.

ii. The servant meets Rebekah (24:10–27)

10–11. The servant's trip is summarized briefly, but with an eye to items important for the rest of the story. The *ten camels* (v. 10) will be important in allowing the servant to observe Rebekah as she waters them. The mention of his taking all kinds of Abraham's choice goods must include the ring and bracelets given to Rebekah (v. 22) as well as the gifts given to her, Laban and her mother (v. 53). The goal of his trip is stated by region – *Aram-Naharaim* – and city – *the city of Nahor* (v. 11). Aram-Naharaim is the same region called Paddan-aram elsewhere (25:20; 28:2, 5–7; 31:18; 33:18; 35:9, 26; 46:15). The city is most certainly Haran (cf. 11:31–32), not a city named Nahor.[17]

The connection of evening and women drawing water anticipates the next verses. It was common for women, especially unmarried girls, to be given the task of drawing water for the family and their animals (29:9–10; Exod. 2:16; 1 Sam. 9:11).

12–14. The servant's prayer to the *Lord, God of my master Abraham* shows that he believed Abraham's promise that God's angel would lead him to the right place and that he, as a circumcised member of

---

17. As discussed by Wenham (1994: 143), Hamilton (1995: 144–145) and Mathews (2005: 332).

Abraham's household (17:27), shared the patriarch's faith. The prayer itself begins with the servant describing his situation: he is at the place where *daughters of the men of the city* (v. 13) will be gathering, an ideal setting for finding a bride for Isaac. He then devises a way to discern which woman has already been chosen by God for Isaac: she will not only offer him water, but also offer to water the camels. This would be a significant chore, since it would involve several trips to the well to haul water back for the beasts. Finally, the servant prays that by this sign he will know that God has shown kindness to *my master* (v. 14). The kindness, of course, would benefit the servant in that he would be able to fulfil his mission and be released from his oath. However, the servant had no promise from God equal to the promise God had spoken directly to Abraham. By calling on this promise, the servant was invoking God's irrevocable promise to bless Abraham with many descendants through Isaac (17:19; 22:15–18).

15–17. God knows our prayers before we pray them (Isa. 65:24). So before Abraham's servant finished speaking, Rebekah arrived at the well with *a water jar on her shoulder* (v. 15), making her a potential answer to the servant's prayer. Rebekah is identified by her genealogy which is traced through her father to her grandmother Milcah. It appears that the matriarchal line is given prominence in this narrative (cf. vv. 24, 28, 53, 55), so Nahor is mentioned as Milcah's husband and then as Abraham's brother. Thus, Rebekah was Abraham's great-niece and Isaac's first cousin once removed.

The description of Rebekah as a *girl* (v. 16) denotes her as a young woman. In characterizing her as very beautiful, the author places her in company with other wives of the patriarchs: Sarah (12:11, 14) and Rachel (29:17).[18] She is also said to be a virgin, which is further defined as not having had sexual relations with a man (cf. Judg. 21:12). It appears that the Hebrew word does not always denote a virgin but a woman of childbearing age who has not been

---

18. See other biblical women who were said to be beautiful: Abigail, David's wife (1 Sam. 25:3); Bathsheba (2 Sam. 11:2); David's daughter Tamar (2 Sam. 13:1); Absalom's daughter Tamar (2 Sam. 14:27); Abishag the Shunammite (1 Kgs 1:3); Esther (Esth. 2:2–3, 7).

married.[19] Apparently noting her beauty, the servant decided to apply the test set forth in his prayer to see whether she was the one chosen by God for Isaac, and *ran to her* with his request for water (v. 17).

18–23. Rebekah's immediate reply was not a fulfilment of the sign that the servant had devised. Granting a stranger a drink was expected hospitality. However, her voluntary offer to water the camels *until they have had enough to drink* (v. 19) went well beyond simple helpfulness. The text is careful to note that Rebekah *drew water for all his camels* (v. 20), and that the servant *silently observed her to see whether or not the Lord had made his journey a success* (v. 21). Considering that she had to go down to the spring and carry the water back up (see v. 16), she was exerting a lot of effort to show kindness to this stranger. Her diligence in finishing the task would be observed and lead to the conclusion that God had answered the servant's prayer.

When she had completed her task the servant presented her with gifts for her industriousness. The ring was a half-shekel of gold, or about 0.4 oz/11 g, which is a fairly large amount of gold for a woman's ring. He also gave her two 10-shekel (4 oz/113 g) gold bracelets. This was a very handsome reward for a simple task, and may have hinted at the servant's intention of obtaining her as a bride for his master. However, Rebekah seems to have been unaware of this. The servant's questioning of her did not hint at a possible marriage, either. Instead, he enquired about her parents and whether they might provide him with lodging for the night.

24–25. Rebekah identifies herself almost identically to the way that the narrative introduced her (v. 24; cf. v. 15): by naming her father, grandmother and grandfather. In answering his second question she once again shows concern for the servant's camels – *we have plenty of straw and feed* (v. 25) – before noting that her family have a place for him to spend the night. The focus on the camels was further confirmation that Abraham's servant had found the right bride for Isaac.

---

19. Wenham (1972). Note especially Joel 1:8, where the virgin (Hebrew *betulah*) mourns 'the husband of her youth'.

26–27. For the second time in this story the servant worships. Instead of a prayer of petition to God, he now utters praise and thanksgiving. It is noteworthy that only after Rebekah's offer of lodging did the man acknowledge that God had demonstrated his kindness. His opening words, *May the Lord God of my master Abraham be blessed* (v. 27), follow a common formula for praising Yahweh as the God worshipped by some person or persons.[20] His praise places his master first – for God's favour towards Abraham, the recipient of God's special promises – and then himself second – for Yahweh's kindness in leading him to Abraham's relatives (cf. v. 7).

iii. The servant obtains Rebekah as a wife for Isaac (24:28–54a)

28–30. Rebekah wasted no time in leaving Abraham's servant at the spring and reporting her encounter with him to *her mother's household* (v. 28) – another indication of the importance of the matriarchal line in this family. In addition, we are introduced to Laban through a parenthetical comment linking him to Rebekah and noting his motivation for going to the spring to see the man (vv. 29–30). Rebekah's new possessions and report of the man's words were the basis for Laban's next actions: the ring and bracelets signalled wealth, and the man's words sought lodging. Laban hurried out to the spring to find his great-uncle's servant.

31–33. Laban's greeting characterized Abraham's servant as *blessed by Yahweh* (v. 31), a judgment based on the man's apparent riches. Laban concluded from the expensive gifts given to Rebekah that Yahweh had blessed this man. Laban's actions also demonstrated that he was eager to obtain some of the riches this man had. His invitation to the servant to come for lodging was phrased as almost placing Abraham's servant under obligation to accept hospitality, since everything had been prepared. The cordiality shown was thorough: the camels were unloaded and were given food and straw for bedding; and not only were the feet of Abraham's servant washed, but also the feet of the men who had accompanied him. Then he also was fed.

---

20. See 9:26; 1 Sam. 25:32; 1 Kgs 1:48; 8:15; 1 Chr. 16:36; 2 Chr. 2:12; 6:4; Ezra 7:27; Pss 41:13; 106:48.

However, the servant was not at Laban's table to eat, but to find a bride for Isaac. To refuse to eat first would have almost been an insult to one's host, and here it signalled that the servant wanted to make his intentions clear so that no wrong impressions were given. Laban, perhaps anxious to receive some valuables like those given to his sister, showed no sign of being offended. Instead, he asked the servant to speak his mind.

34–36. After identifying himself as Abraham's servant, the servant started his speech with a preface which was designed to convince Laban that *the Lord has greatly blessed my master* (v. 35). He began with the wealth that Abraham had accumulated – a feature of God's blessing that obviously had got Laban's attention. Wealth was not measured in money, which had not yet been invented, but in possessions: animals, precious metals and slaves. The servant then mentioned another blessing that could only have come from God: Sarah's bearing a son *in her old age* (v. 36). This not only moved the conversation to Isaac, but also implied that Isaac was still young enough to marry his uncle's granddaughter. Then, as a way of returning to Abraham's wealth, he noted that Isaac was the sole heir of Abraham's possessions. Interestingly, the servant avoided an extended discussion of other blessings promised to Abraham: possession of the land of Canaan and the messianic promise that all peoples would be blessed through him and his offspring. Perhaps he judged that these would be of little interest to Laban in the negotiations to obtain Rebekah's hand in marriage for Isaac.

37–41. Next, the servant moved on to describe his conversation with Abraham concerning the oath he had sworn. As might be expected, the servant did not give an exact word-for-word recounting of his exchange with the patriarch, but instead presented a descriptive paraphrase. For instance, he did not state by whom he swore the oath (v. 37; cf. v. 3). Instead, he concentrated on Abraham's instructions to get a wife from his own family instead of from the Canaanites (v. 38).

He then noted that he raised the concern that he might not be able to obtain a bride for Isaac in that way (v. 39). He repeated Abraham's promise that Yahweh's angel would accompany the servant and added that the angel would make his journey a success

(v. 40). However, he omitted Abraham's promise to release the servant from the oath if the woman would not come to Canaan (cf. v. 8). By not broaching this possibility, he was avoiding suggesting the question whether Isaac would leave Canaan to be married in Haran. By not raising that scenario he was not giving the materialistic Laban hope that Isaac might come and bring his wealth to Paddan-aram to add to the family assets there. Instead, he emphasized that there were two ways for him to be released from the oath: either he was successful and obtained a wife, or he found a woman, but the family was not willing to agree to the marriage (vv. 40–41).

42–48. Skipping any description of his travels from Canaan, the servant then related his prayer at the spring that day. It is an accurate paraphrase of his prayer (cf. vv. 12–14). However, when he quotes the young woman's words *Drink and I'll water your camels also* (v. 44; cf. v. 14), this is nearly identical to the words in his prayer when he asked for a sign.[21] There are a number of changes from the previous account of these events that are due to the servant summarizing and explaining the events:

1. Rebekah's two statements are combined into one: *Drink, and I'll also water your camels* (v. 46; cf. vv. 18–19). This served to summarize quickly his initial encounter with Rebekah.

2. In the narrative the servant gave Rebekah the ring and bracelets before asking who she was (vv. 22–23). In his recounting he reversed this order (v. 47). This clarified that these gifts were more than simply a gratuity for Rebekah's service; they were the opening of negotiations with her family to obtain her as Isaac's wife.

3. In retelling the events, the servant omitted his request for lodging (cf. v. 23). There was no need to include this, since he had already received Laban's hospitality

---

21. The only difference is the verb for 'water': *'ašqeh* (v. 14) versus 'draw water': *'eš'āb* (v. 44). The difference may be due to his speaking to family members who have been living in Aram and speaking Aramaic (see 31:47). The verbal root *šqh* ('water, give a drink') does not occur in Aramaic, but the root *š'b* ('draw water') does. For the Aramaic flavour of this chapter, see Rendsburg (2002: 24–35).

4. In the narrative, in his prayer of thanksgiving he spoke of Yahweh's kindness to Abraham and Yahweh's leading him to his master's relatives (v. 27). In the recounting he did not repeat the prayer, but instead stated that he praised God for guiding him to find a bride for Isaac (v. 48). This served to end his recitation of events with the purpose of his trip to Haran and as an indirect way to propose marriage on Abraham's behalf. He is, in effect, negotiating the marriage agreement to be made between Abraham and Laban for Rebekah to marry Isaac.

49. The servant's final statement is also indirect: it is a request for a decision on the marriage proposal by asking Laban to *show kindness and faithfulness* to Abraham.

50–51. For the first and last time Bethuel, Rebekah's father, is a participant in a narrative in Genesis. He and Laban accept the testimony of the servant and agree to his offer of marriage. However, it appears that Laban, Rebekah's brother, and not Bethuel, her father, took the lead in these negotiations, much as Simeon and Levi would later do for their sister Dinah (see 34:8–17). Both men recognized that Yahweh had made the choice of Rebekah as bride for Isaac since he exactly fulfilled the sign requested by Abraham's servant in his prayer. Curiously, they never enquire as to the name of Abraham's son, and the servant never offers it to them. They simply call him *your master's son* (v. 51).

52–54a. The servant's first reaction is to worship Yahweh, who had enabled him to fulfil his duties according to the vow he took. Then he presented engagement gifts to Rebekah – not only jewellery but also finery for the bride. To pay the customary bride price he gave gifts to the family – here specifically Laban and Rebekah's mother. Later, the law of Moses placed a limit on the bride price in Israel of 50 silver shekels, about 20 oz or 567 g. That would have been a substantial sum, although we cannot know whether the servant paid more than this. Only after the agreement was consummated did the servant eat and accept lodging (v. 54a; cf. v. 33).

iv. Rebekah's departure (24:54b–61)

54b–58. Abraham's servant was anxious to leave, but apparently the family wanted some time with Rebekah before they sent her away to live in a distant land. They proposed keeping her *about ten* *days* (v. 55).[22] The servant, however, appealed to Yahweh's action in leading him to a bride for Isaac as a reason why he should depart that day to his *master* (v. 56; cf. v. 54). When he returned, this master would be Isaac (see v. 65).

It appears that the servant and Rebekah's family were at a stalemate. One desired to keep Rebekah for some time, while the other offered a convincing reason why she ought to leave immediately. So they allowed Rebekah to decide. Her answer is brief and decisive: *I will go* (v. 58).

59–61. The description of the departure starts and ends with an explanation of who left (vv. 59, 61). Rebekah was allowed to take Deborah, the slave who had nursed her (v. 59: cf. 35:8), and other slaves (v. 61). In the centre is the blessing that Rebekah's family placed on her. This blessing appears to be a variation of God's blessing on Abraham at 22:17. Like that blessing, it bestows two distinct benefits: many offspring and possession of the gates of their enemies. By these words they acknowledge that Rebekah is the chosen instrument of God to further the promise made to Abraham.

It is not stated how they knew the words God had spoken to Abraham. However, it may be that verses 34–35 present only a summary of the servant's description of Yahweh's blessing on Abraham and that he had also described God's words of blessing given to the patriarch. Thus, Laban and his mother learned of God's words of blessing and used them to confirm their statement that this marriage arrangement was Yahweh's doing (cf. v. 50).

v. Isaac marries Rebekah (24:62–67)

62–66. Immediately the narrative skips to Isaac in Canaan. We are told that he *had come from Beer-lahai-roi* (cf. 16:14), where he had

---

22. The Hebrew is unusual: 'days or ten'. Some have argued this means a longer period and that they are requesting 'a year or so' (see Wenham [1994: 150]). This seems improbable, however, since Abraham's servant understands the request as also delaying his departure (v. 56). It is doubtful that he understood them to be requesting that he stay with them for a greatly extended period of time.

made his home in the Negev. We are not told the reason why he had
come to Hebron. The timing, however, was propitious. What Isaac
was doing in the field in the evening is not certain, since the Hebrew
verb is used only here. Some versions say he was *walking in the field*
(v. 63; CSB, NRSV, TNK; cf. v. 65), while others read *meditating/praying
in the field* (LXX, ESV, GW, NIV). It was there that he saw the camels,
and Rebekah in turn saw him and dismounted her camel. Rebekah's
question about the identity of the man assumes that they were near
their destination and that Abraham's servant would know the locals.
For the first time the servant calls Isaac *my master* (v. 65), acknowledging that he is the sole heir (cf. v. 36) and is now replacing
Abraham. Rebekah covered her face with a veil. Elsewhere the Old
Testament indicates that it was proper decorum for a betrothed
woman to wear a veil in the presence of her fiancé (Song 4:1, 3; 6:7).

Upon his arrival the servant *told Isaac everything he had done* (v. 66).
Once again the servant is treating Isaac as his master. Isaac has
supplanted Abraham as the messianic promise-bearer.

67. Just as Isaac has succeeded his father Abraham, Rebekah
now succeeds Sarah. In *his mother's tent* Rebekah became his wife.
For the first time the Bible mentions the love between a man and
his wife. This love enabled Isaac to find comfort after the loss of
the other significant woman in his life: his mother.

Meaning

This part of the Abraham cycle brings God's promises to him to a
climax while simultaneously transitioning to Isaac as the new bearer
of God's pledges. These pledges not only guarantee to make him
into a great nation and give his descendants the land of Canaan, but
most importantly they assure him that all nations will be blessed
through him. Yahweh has made it clear that these promises will pass
through Isaac. This high point in the telling of Abraham's story
focuses Abraham's attention – and thus also readers' attention –
on Isaac.

However, the promise cannot be fulfilled without Isaac also
having a son. So sometime after Sarah's death, Abraham sends his
servant to Haran to obtain a wife for Isaac from among his relatives.
In this longest chapter in Genesis, the tension once again builds:
will the servant be successful in his mission? In this instance God

grants success and reveals his will by answering the prayer of
Abraham's servant, a sign that is also recognized by Rebekah and
her family. In the end the promise moves on from Abraham to
Isaac, and the matriarch Sarah is succeeded by a new wife who will
become the mother of the next heir of the promise.

13. THE FAMILY OF TERAH: THE END OF ABRAHAM'S LIFE (25:1–11)

Context

These last verses of the Abraham cycle serve to quickly summarize the rest of his life and his burial. They are brief, since with the marriage of Isaac and Rebekah the focus of the narrative has shifted to them and away from Abraham. As is typical in Genesis, there is a genealogy of Abraham's other sons by his wife Keturah. However, since these descendants are not germane to the main storyline, this is all we are told about them. Another indication that Abraham is no longer at the centre of the narrative is that his death is related before the birth of Jacob and Esau, even though they were born fifteen years before he died (cf. 21:5; 25:7, 26).

Comment

A. Abraham's other sons (25:1–6)

2029–1991 BC

1–2. It is impossible to tell whether Abraham took *Keturah* as a wife before or after Sarah's death. Some versions read *Abraham had* *taken another wife* (v. 1; CSB, NET, NIV), implying that he might have married before Sarah's death, while others read *Abraham took another wife*, implying that he married after Sarah's death (ESV, GW, NRSV, TNK). The name *Keturah* is related to the Hebrew word for 'incense', and several of the names of her sons appear to be associated with the spice trade from Arabia (Isa. 60:6; Ezek. 27:22).

Zimran (v. 2) is also mentioned at 1 Chronicles 1:32, as are *Jokshan* and *Medan*. *Midian* is the father of the Midianites who appear later as traders at Genesis 37:28, 36. There they are associated with the Ishmaelites, who were descended from Midian's half-brother Ishmael, the son of Abraham's wife Hagar. It appears that they melded with the descendants of Ishmael and were considered Ishmaelites, as indicated also by their identification as Ishmaelites at Judges 8:24. Moses' wife Zipporah was a Midianite (Exod. 2:15–22). Traditionally their home was in north-west Arabia along the eastern shore of the Gulf of Aqaba. *Ishbak* and *Shuah* are mentioned again at 1 Chronicles 1:32. Job's friend Bildad was a descendant of Shuah (Job 2:11).

3. The sons of Jokshan, *Sheba* and *Dedan*, bear the same names as the sons of Raamah at Genesis 10:7. We cannot be certain which pair were the Arabian traders mentioned at 1 Kings 10:1–13; Psalm 72:10, 15; Isaiah 60:6; Ezekiel 27:15. However, the mention of Midian's son *Ephah* along with Sheba and Dedan at Isaiah 60:6 favours these sons of Abraham as the Arabians. Another Sheba, a descendant of Shem, had a father named Joktan, a name that sounds similar to Jokshan but has no relationship to it (see 10:26, 28–29). Dedan's descendants are listed as three ethnic groups: *Asshurites, Letushites* and *Leummites*.

4. The sons of Midian are rather obscure. Only *Ephah* is mentioned again (Isa. 60:6).

5–6. Abraham distributed his wealth before his death. This was not unusual in the ancient world, and is assumed in passages such as Deuteronomy 21:15–17 and Luke 15:12. Until his death the father would continue to enjoy the benefits of his wealth that was now managed by his sons. Abraham's inheritance went solely to Isaac as the only son of his wife Sarah. However, he still provided for the sons of his *concubines* (v. 6), which must be a reference to the sons of Hagar and Keturah. Concubines were second-level wives, usually wives who were obtained without having to pay a bride price. Their children did not expect to inherit from their father. Nevertheless, Abraham gave them gifts before sending them away to the east. Since Isaac was the heir of God's promises, including the promise of the land of Canaan, the sons of the concubines were sent eastwards. The *land of the East* was a term for the land on the eastern fringes of Canaan and beyond into the Arabian Desert. The peoples living there, including the Moabites, Ammonites and Edomites, were often collectively called 'sons of the east' in Hebrew (Gen. 29:1; Judg. 6:3, 33; 7:12; 8:10; 1 Kgs 4:30; Job 1:3; Isa. 11:14; Jer. 49:28; Ezek. 25:4, 10).

B. Abraham's death (25:7–11)

1991 BC

7–8. The notice of Abraham's lifespan and death is the longest in Genesis, underscoring his importance as the founding patriarch of Israel. The only other notices of similar length to this are for Isaac (35:28–29) and Jacob (49:33). Abraham's age of *175 years* (v. 7) means that he had lived a century since first coming to Canaan (cf. 12:4). The description of Abraham's death is replete with stereotypical phrases: *he took his last breath* (v. 8; cf. 25:17 [Ishmael]; 35:29 [Isaac]; 49:33 [Jacob]); *good old age* (Judg. 8:32 [Gideon]; 1 Chr. 29:28 [David]; cf. Gen. 15:15); *old and contented* (35:29 [Isaac]; 1 Chr. 23:1 [David]; 2 Chr. 24:15 [Jehoiada]; Job 42:17 [Job]); and *gathered to his people* (25:17 [Ishmael]; 35:29 [Isaac]; 49:29, 33 [Jacob]; Num. 20:24 [Aaron]; Deut. 32:50 [Moses]).[1] The last phrase implies that the deceased has joined his ancestors and is a hint of reunion with those who had previously died with faith and were now in God's presence (see Rev. 7:9–17).

9–10. The only passage that places Isaac and Ishmael together as adults is verse 9 at the burial of their father. The rest of these two verses is a rather complete description of the burial site that Abraham obtained for Sarah's interment (cf. 23:1–20). This careful

---

1. Judg. 2:10; 2 Kgs 22:20; and 2 Chr. 34:28 use a related phrase: 'gathered to . . . ancestors'.

summary underscores the importance of this possession in the land of promise that will serve as the burial spot for Israel's three patriarchs and their wives.

11. It appears that even before Abraham's death, Isaac had chosen to live in the southernmost part of Canaan at Beer-lahai-roi, where Hagar had once seen God (see 16:13–14; 24:62). God had stated unequivocally that Isaac would be the recipient of divine blessing as the heir of the promises he had made to Abraham (17:19). That blessing, however, was not something Abraham could bestow as part of the inheritance (cf. v. 5), since it was God's alone to impart upon someone. The mention of this blessing concludes a major section of Genesis (12:1 – 25:11) with a hint of what is to come in the next major section (25:19 – 35:29).

Meaning

While these eleven verses at the beginning of Genesis 25 may seem to be a quick summary of Abraham's life after Sarah's death, they are more than that. They serve to emphasize that even as Abraham is passing out of the chronicles of the patriarchs in favour of his son Isaac, he has left a major mark on the overall narrative arc of the entire book. He has now had many sons in addition to the son God had promised. Yet the promised son is the inheritor of his wealth and the recipient of the promises repeatedly spoken to him by God. At Abraham's death the blessings God had bestowed on him during his life are summarized by his nearly 100 years of residence in Canaan, his good old age, and his being gathered to the ancestors who died in faith before him.

14. THE FAMILY OF ISHMAEL (25:12–18)

Context

These seven verses compose one of the ten major sections whose beginnings are marked by the phrase *these are the family records of . . .*[1] As is customary in Genesis, the narrative first discusses the lines of minor figures before moving on to longer sections for the major characters in the overall storyline. Therefore, Ishmael's descendants are discussed before returning to the main narrative concerning Isaac and his sons (25:19 – 35:29).

Comment

12. Ishmael is identified not only as Abraham's son but also by his relationship to his mother, who is called both *the Egyptian* and *Sarah's maidservant*, before noting that she bore him to Abraham. In this way not only are the narratives involving Ishmael's birth and his

---

1. See 'The *tôlĕdôt* formula and the sources used in composing Genesis' in the Introduction.

expulsion referenced (16:1–16; 21:8–21), but also the reason for placing this discussion of his sons before the main account concerning Isaac and his sons is clarified: he is not the son favoured by God's promise to Abraham. Nevertheless, like Isaac, he was *the son of Abraham* (cf. v. 19), thereby connecting him to the blessing promised to his father (17:20) and to his father's faith.

13–16. The phrase these are *the/their names* occurs three times in these four verses concerning Ishmael's sons. This emphasizes that the narrative is not focused on any events in the lives of Ishmael and his sons, but is simply concerned about telling readers in summary fashion who they were.

Nebaioth (v. 13) is identified as the firstborn son of Ishmael. Genesis 28:9 identifies Esau's wife Mahalath as his sister, whereas 36:3 notes that another sister, Basemath, was another wife of Esau. Since these two women are said to be sisters only of Nebaioth, it is implied that Ishmael eventually married additional wives (cf. 21:21). Nebaioth is also mentioned at 1 Chronicles 1:29 and Isaiah 60:7.

Kedar apparently was the ancestor of an Arab tribe that was known by his name and that occupied northern Arabia. In the Old Testament Kedar is the most frequently mentioned of the Arab tribes (1 Chr. 1:29; Ps. 120:5; Song 1:5; Isa. 21:16; 42:11; 60:7; Jer. 2:10; 49:28; Ezek. 27:21).

Abdeel and *Mibsam* are mentioned again at 1 Chronicles 1:29. The eighth-century BC annals of the Assyrian king Tiglath-Pileser III mention a tribe called Idibail, possibly the descendants of Abdeel, living in the northern Sinai Peninsula.[2]

Mishma (v. 14) is mentioned again at 1 Chronicles 1:30. Jebel Misma, about 160 miles east of Tema in the Arabian Desert, may have been their main settlement.[3]

Dumah is mentioned at Joshua 15:52; 1 Chronicles 1:30; and Isaiah 21:11. His tribe may have been associated with Adumatu, the stronghold of the Arabs which the Assyrian king Sennacherib conquered.[4]

---

2. *ANET* 297–301.

3. Winnett (1970: 194).

4. *ANET* 291.

Massa is mentioned at 1 Chronicles 1:30. The annals of Tiglath-Pileser III mention a place named Mas'a or Mas'ai in conjunction with Tema in northern Arabia.[5]

Hadad (v. 15) is mentioned again at 1 Chronicles 1:30. He is not associated with the Edomite kings who also bore this name (36:35–36; 1 Kgs 11:14–25; 1 Chr. 1:46–51).

Tema is mentioned at Job 6:19; Isaiah 21:14; and Jeremiah 25:23. His tribe settled at the important north-west Arabian oasis called Tema (modern Tayma') where caravan routes converged.

Jetur and *Naphish* are mentioned at 1 Chronicles 1:31. Their descendants were among the peoples living east of the Jordan River whose territory was conquered under Moses' leadership and given to Reuben, Gad and half of the tribe of Manasseh (1 Chr. 5:19). Jetur may have given his name to the later Roman province of Ituraea that was ruled by Philip, son of Herod the Great (Luke 3:1).

Kedemah is mentioned at 1 Chronicles 1:31. Nothing else is known about him.

Ishmael's sons gave their names to *settlements and encampments* (v. 16), and the Ishmaelites were divided into twelve clans, each from one of his sons.

17–18. The summary of Ishmael's life is similar to that of his father Abraham (see vv. 7–8). He is the only person outside of the patriarchal line of promise or of Israel who is said to have been *gathered to his people* (v. 17; cf. v. 8; 35:29 [Isaac]; 49:29, 33 [Jacob]; Num. 20:24 [Aaron]; Deut. 32:50 [Moses]). This most likely indicates that this circumcised son of Abraham (17:23) also was a believer in Yahweh (who had twice spoken to his mother Hagar, 16:7–14; 21:17–18).

The settlements of Ishmael's descendants are said to be *from Havilah to Shur as you go towards Asshur* (v. 18). Havilah appears to be a location in Arabia (2:11; 1 Sam. 15:7) and Shur is the name of the wilderness in the north-western Sinai Peninsula near Egypt (Gen. 16:7; 20:1; Exod. 15:22; 1 Sam. 15:7; 27:8). Asshur is Assyria, and this helps locate Shur in the Sinai since it is on the way north to Mesopotamia as one is travelling from Egypt.

---

5. *ANET* 283–284.

Finally, it is said that Ishmael lived *near his relatives* or *in opposition to his relatives*. The Hebrew phrase is ambiguous. However, this phrasing is repeated from 16:12 where Yahweh had stated that the Ishmaelites would settle in the northern Sinai Peninsula, south of their Israelite kinsmen who lived in Canaan.

Meaning

Although Ishmael was not the son God had promised to Abraham, God nevertheless promised to bless him, make his descendants numerous, have twelve tribal leaders come from him and make him into a great nation (16:10; 17:12). This demonstrates that Yahweh is not only the God of Abraham, Isaac and Jacob, but also the God who wishes to bless all nations, even those who do not come from the line of the messianic promise. As both a circumcised child of Abraham and as a people who would be blessed through Abraham's great descendant Jesus (12:3; 18:18; 22:18), Ishmael would die and be gathered to his people (v. 17), benefiting from the promise given to his father just as all who die with faith in God's promises benefit from God's grace revealed to Abraham.

15. THE FAMILY OF ISAAC: ISAAC AS THE BEARER OF THE PROMISE (25:19 – 26:35)

Context

The first part of this large section of Genesis (i.e. 25:19 – 35:29) that is labelled *the family history* [or 'records'] *of Isaac* (25:19) concentrates on events in Isaac's life, with only one short narrative not having Isaac or Rebekah as a participant: Esau's selling his birthright to Isaac (25:27–34). Among the patriarchs Isaac is a transitional character between Abraham and Jacob. Abraham occupies a large part of the narrative in Genesis, and the stories concerning Jacob are second in length only to the narrative about Abraham. In contrast, after 28:8 Isaac hardly appears in the storyline. The only major exception is the report of his death (35:27–29). Even though Isaac plays a role in the storyline after 26:35, the focus shifts to Jacob and his actions. So what is Isaac's transitional role? He links the past – Abraham – to the future – Jacob. In Genesis 25 – 26 Isaac obtains sons to perpetuate the line of Abraham (25:19–26), receives the divine promises given to his father (26:1–5) and in many ways repeats the experiences of his father with the Philistines at Gerar (26:6–33). At the same time, he plays a pivotal role in the passing on of God's promises to Jacob. By his favouring Esau over Jacob he increases the rivalry between the two boys who first contested with each other in Rebekah's womb (25:22–23). This naturally leads to the next part of Isaac's family history: Jacob receiving the promise and struggling to build a family that will become the nation who will inherit the Promised Land (27:1 – 35:29).

Comment
A. The birth of Esau and Jacob (25:19–26)

2026–2006 BC

19. This opening verse follows the standard form *these are the family records of*. . . However, the added sentence at the end – *Abraham fathered Isaac* – is unique. It likely serves to underscore the family line: Abraham – Isaac – Esau and Jacob. In this way it builds anticipation as to how the promise will pass down from Abraham to Jacob.

20–21. The mention of Isaac's marriage to Rebekah repeats her lineage and recapitulates the narrative of chapter 24. The only new information here is Isaac's age of forty when he got married, the location of Rebekah's homeland – Paddan-aram (cf. 28:2, 5–7; 31:18; 33:18; 35:9, 26; 46:15) – and Rebekah's barrenness, which repeats his father's struggle to have an heir. Isaac's concern over the years of waiting for a son is summarized simply in the words that he *prayed to the Lord on behalf of his wife* (v. 21). The Hebrew word translated *prayed* here is commonly used for intercessory prayer (e.g. Exod. 8:8–9, 28–30; 9:28; 10:17–18). God's response was that he answered and Rebekah conceived.

22–23. Rebekah's pregnancy is revealed to be the result of a multiple conception when the boys *struggled with each other* (v. 22). The verb indicates both an intense clash (Judg. 9:53; Isa. 36:6) and reciprocating hostility. The violence within her prompted her question concerning her state, an almost inarticulate question in the Hebrew.[1] It amounted to saying, 'Why am I enduring this?' Her perplexity over the situation prompted her to *enquire of Yahweh*

---

1. The Hebrew is literally 'Why this I?'

(v. 22). This phrase is often used in the Old Testament of enquiring of a prophet (Exod. 18:15; 1 Sam. 9:9; 1 Kgs 22:8). The details are not given, but she probably consulted Yahweh through her husband who, along with Abraham and Jacob, is called a prophet in Psalm 105:15 (= 1 Chr. 16:22).

Yahweh's words to her are not simply that she is to have twins but that *two nations . . . two peoples* are in her womb. These two nations will separate from one another and one will be stronger. In the last line of the oracle the stronger one is revealed to be the younger son whom the elder will serve. The subsequent historical domination of Edom by Israel was the fulfilment of this prophecy (e.g. 1 Sam. 14:47; 2 Sam. 8:12–14). But more importantly, God's choice of Jacob over Esau reflects that his favour is graciously given, not earned by works or deserved by position (i.e. firstborn), as Paul emphasizes at Romans 9:10–13.

24–26. The narrative quickly skips to the birth and affirms that the prophecy was accurate: she had twins. The firstborn is described as *completely reddish like a coat of hair* (v. 25). The word for 'red' in Hebrew gives Esau his other name: Edom. Interestingly, the other person in the Old Testament described as 'reddish' is David (1 Sam. 16:12; 17:42). Esau's covering of *hair* is a play on words with his eventual home, the mountains of *Seir* (36:8–9). The origin and meaning of the name *Esau* is a mystery.

Jacob's birth is highlighted by the notable observation that he was *grasping Esau's heel with his hand* (v. 26), an incident remembered later by the prophet Hosea: 'in the womb he grasped his brother's heel' (Hos. 12:3, csb). This led to his being named *Jacob*, which contains the same consonants as the Hebrew word for 'heel'. It is generally agreed that this name, which is known to have been common elsewhere in the Ancient Near East, means 'may he [i.e. God] protect'.[2] However, it also could be understood to mean 'he grabs the heel' or 'deceiver'. All three would be important aspects of Jacob's life.

We are told that Isaac was sixty years old when the twins were born. Thus, his prayers for Rebekah must have occupied the better

---

2. Wenham (1994: 176); Hamilton (1995: 178–179); Mathews (2005: 391).

part of the first twenty years of his marriage (cf. v. 20). While the struggles of Abraham and Sarah to have a child are chronicled in great detail in Genesis, the long wait of Isaac and Rebekah for a son is barely visible to readers.

B. Esau sells his birthright (25:27–34)

c.1976 BC

27–28. The narrative jumps immediately to Esau and Jacob as men. Esau's description as *an expert hunter, an outdoorsman* (v. 27, CSB) marks him as a man of action. Jacob, in contrast, *was a quiet man who lived in tents*, much more in keeping with the lifestyle of his grandfather Abraham and his father Isaac, both of whom were shepherds rather than hunters. The characterization of Jacob as *quiet* is challenging. The Hebrew word often denotes someone of high moral character (cf. 6:9; Job 1:1, 8; 2:3). That is clearly not the meaning here, since it stands in contrast to Esau as a hunter. Instead, it appears to mark Jacob as more thoughtful in contrast to his brother as a man of action.

The affection of the parents is split between the sons. Isaac's reason for his favouring Esau is given: *because he had a taste for wild game* (v. 28). However, Rebekah's reason for favouring Jacob is not stated. Perhaps this is to emphasize that Isaac was drawn to Esau's actions whereas Rebekah was drawn to Jacob's person.

29–30. The difference between the twins is extended into a story from their interaction one day. Jacob's having food is in contrast to Esau's being exhausted. One has what the other lacks. Esau immediately requests Jacob's food, which he calls *the red stuff, this red stuff* (v. 30), his repetition showing the urgency in his plea. This second mention of the colour red in connection with Esau (cf. v. 25) leads to an editorial note that this is how Esau got the name Edom (i.e. Red).

31–34. As urgent as Esau's request was, it was matched by the brusque and calculating reply of Jacob: *First sell me your birthright* (v. 31). Esau, exaggerating his exhaustion, claimed that a birthright meant nothing because he was on the verge of death. But Jacob was insistent and knew that Esau's hyperbole might well betray an unwillingness to keep his side of the bargain. He demanded an oath, and Esau complied. Jacob provided both bread and lentil stew, hardly a proper payment for the birthright. Yet Esau was willing, and the narrative stops a second time for an editorial observation: *Esau despised his birthright* (v. 34). The writer to the Hebrews calls Esau's attitude 'worldly' or 'irreverent' (Heb. 12:16), implying that Jacob was focused on matters that went beyond simple temporal concerns for food and drink. In these four verses the word *birthright* occurs four times. Not only is it a theme for the struggle between the two brothers, but it also forms an anagram in Hebrew with the word *blessing*. The next time the twins enter Genesis' narrative they will be seeking Isaac's blessing (27:1–40). The blessing will acknowledge the principal heir and seal the birthright of divine promises given to Isaac's father Abraham (28:3–4).

Meaning

This section begins with a short account of Isaac and Rebekah's struggle to have children and culminates in a double birth that reveals God's plan for the future of this family and the transmission of the messianic promise. It then skips over the childhood of the twins to a time when they were adults. The incident involving Esau selling his birthright to Jacob demonstrates why God from the beginning was correct in choosing Jacob as the heir of the promise. The parents each favoured a child based on their personalities: Esau the game hunter appealed to Isaac while Jacob the quiet homebody appealed to Rebekah. However, a completely different reason was behind God's choice: Esau did not value the divine gift of the promise and was willing to sell it for a quick meal, even though he had just returned from the hunt with meat that only needed to be prepared to eat. Jacob, on the other hand, was focused on more weighty matters with eternal consequences. His rather mercenary tactics in gaining the patriarchal birthright portray him in a somewhat unfavourable light. He was not perfect. Yet God works through imperfect humans to accomplish his purposes. He looks for faith in the heart which is credited to unrighteous humans as righteousness (15:6). Jacob's method is not commended here, but his faith is nevertheless evident.

C. Yahweh's promise to Isaac (26:1–6)

Context

c.1970 BC

This chapter contains the only accounts from Isaac's life in which he – not his father or mother and not one his sons – is the central character (26:1–33). Nevertheless, the chapter is designed to portray Isaac as a true son of his father by relating incidents from his life that are parallel to episodes from Abraham's life, as shown in Table 11.[3]

Table 11 Parallels between Isaac's and Abraham's lives

Isaac's life	Abraham's life		
26:1	12:10		Famine in Canaan
26:1–11	12:10–20	20:1–18	Claim that wife is sister
26:12–22	13:2–10		Wealth leads to quarrels
26:15–21		21:25	Disputes about wells
26:23	13:11–12		Separation in order to end the quarrels
26:24	13:14–17		God's promises concerning descendants
26:25	13:18		The patriarch builds an altar
26:26		21:22	Abimelech and Phicol
26:28		21:22	'Yahweh is with you'
26:28		21:23	An oath proposed
26:29	14:19–20		Patriarch blessed by foreign king
26:30–31		21:24–31	Agreement made with the Philistines
26:32–33		21:31	Naming of Beersheba

Comment

1. The reference to *another famine in the land* invites readers to compare this part of Isaac's life with Abraham's. We are told that *Isaac went to Abimelech*, which contrasts with the account of

---

3. Wenham (1994: 187).

Abraham's action at 20:1 which simply says that Abraham lived as a resident alien at Gerar. Abimelech is identified as *king of the Philistines at Gerar*. The Abimelech in Abraham's day was simply called *king of Gerar* (20:2). This Abimelech cannot be the same as the one who interacted with Abraham about a century earlier. The name *Abimelech*, which means 'My Father is King', was probably a throne name or a popular name in this dynasty.[4]

2–5. The only persons in Genesis to whom it is said that *Yahweh/ God appeared* (v. 2) are Abraham, Isaac and Jacob (12:7; 17:1; 18:1; 26:24; 35:9). In each case God offers one of the patriarchs his blessing. Here Yahweh prefaces his blessing with an instruction that serves as a condition for receiving the blessing: Isaac must not go to Egypt to escape the famine as Abraham did (see 12:10). Isaac's presence is to be a sign of his trust in God's promise to give *these lands* to him and his descendants, even though he will be in the land as *an alien* (v. 3). The plural *these lands* (vv. 3, 4) is unique, occurring only here among the patriarchal promises. It emphasizes that Isaac's descendants will receive not only the lands of the Canaanites but also the land now occupied by the Philistines among whom he is living. God's response to Isaac's obedience is the promise *I will be with you and bless you*. This is the first time that God's promise to be with someone is recorded in Scripture. Later, God will repeat it to Jacob (28:15; 31:3; 46:4). God's promise to bless Isaac ties this promise to the original promise made to Abraham when God called him from Haran (12:2). Moreover, God himself now confirms to Isaac that he is the heir of the promises first sworn on oath to Abraham (v. 3; see 17:19).

God's confirmation of the promise to Abraham is laid out in more detail in verse 4. Isaac's offspring will be numerous like the stars (cf. 15:5; 22:17). His descendants will possess the land (cf. 12:7; 13:15; 15:18; 17:8). All nations will consider themselves blessed through Isaac's offspring (cf. 22:18). This is followed by verse 5,

---

4. For parallels, see the repeated names Amenhotep and Thutmose in Egypt's eighteenth dynasty, or the repeated name George among the British kings of the House of Hanover in the eighteenth and nineteenth centuries.

which points out that Abraham received God's promise through his faithfulness.

6. Isaac's obedience is pointed out succinctly: he stayed Gerar. That is, he did not go to Egypt.

D. Isaac among the Philistines (26:7–33)

Context

c.1970 BC

This section contains the third so-called wife/sister account in Genesis (cf. 12:10–20; 20:1–18). Critical scholars often contend that these three stories stem from a single event that gave rise to them as oral or literary variants handed down in different streams of tradition. Nevertheless, an increasing number of scholars hold that these are not three variants of the same tale but three unique episodes that share some similar details. There are good reasons to believe that these narratives come from three different incidents. For instance, the second account presumes knowledge of the first one, giving the impression that Abraham twice claimed that Sarah was his sister (see comments at 20:1–18). In the case of this account of Isaac repeating his father's deceptive ways, there are several indications that the author presupposes the previous two episodes and presents this one as independent of the other two. For instance, this account is the only one that reports men asking about the wife's relationship to her husband (v. 7). This also is the only time that the woman is not taken into the king's harem (v. 8; cf. 12:15; 20:2). It is also the only account where the king learns of the patriarch's duplicity through observation rather than through indirect or direct revelation from God (v. 8; cf. 12:17–19; 20:3–7). At the same time there are indications that the author assumes readers' knowledge of the previous two incidents in Abraham's life:[5] Abimelech's annoyance and fear for the lives of his people because of Isaac's deception (vv. 10–11) makes the most sense if the Philistines had previous experience of the duplicity practised by his father (cf. 20:3). The setting of this story also alludes to Abraham's first use of this ruse

---

5. Kidner (1967: 163).

in Egypt (v. 1). Finally, it should be noted that the brevity of this narrative compared to the other two also indicates that the author assumed his audience had already read those narratives.[6]

While Abraham was the first in this family to practise deception, this incident from Isaac's life begins to show that trickery is on its way to becoming a family trait. Later, Rebekah and Jacob will dupe Isaac into giving his blessing to his younger son (27:1–40). Jacob's uncle Laban will hoodwink him (29:13–30). Jacob will be tricked by his sons into believing that Joseph has been killed by a wild animal (37:31–35). Simeon and Levi will deal deceitfully with the men of Shechem (34:1–31). Judah's daughter-in-law will trap him into impregnating her (38:1–30). These repeated acts of deception serve as a warning to parents about the bad examples they can be to their children who learn behaviours by observing them. But more importantly, this pattern of behaviour demonstrates that Genesis is not engaged in presenting the patriarchal families as ideal clans who merited God's favour. On the contrary, God's favour is given *despite* the dreadful misbehaviour of these people in order to teach that God's grace is freely given to sinners.

Comment
i. Isaac deceives Abimelech (26:7–11)

7. When the men of Gerar enquired about Rebekah, Isaac claimed that she was his sister. There is no indication that Rebekah was complicit in this deception. We are told of Isaac's motive for lying: he did not trust the Philistines to respect his life or, therefore, his marriage because of Rebekah's beauty. This mirrors Abraham's earlier words to Sarah (12:11–12). While not excusing Isaac's behaviour, the balance of the narrative concerning him and the Philistines indicates that his assumption that the Philistines could regularly behave corruptly is not without foundation. Abimelech's subsequent order about Isaac and Rebekah is a tacit admission that this was a real possibility (v. 11). The Philistines' envy, maliciousness vandalism and contentiousness are evident elsewhere in this chapter (vv. 14–16, 18, 20–21).

---

6. Wenham (1994: 190).

8. Isaac's reply must have been reported to Abimelech, since it is he who was surprised to see *Isaac caressing his wife Rebekah*. The verb *caressing* forms a play on words with Isaac's name, which comes from the same root.[7]

9-10. Abimelech's outrage is palpable in his conversation with Isaac. Isaac's only response is that he thought that he *might die on account of her* (v. 9). Isaac's words are careful in that he does not directly state that he would be killed (cf. v. 7), which would have amounted to an accusation of murderous intent on the part of the men of Gerar. Abimelech's concern, however, is that someone might have slept with Rebekah and *brought guilt on us*. Abimelech's words show his fear that his people might have been judged guilty and therefore have fallen under divine wrath. This reveals his knowledge of the earlier threat of Yahweh to his predecessor (20:3). This also creates irony within this chapter of Genesis: Isaac was to be God's instrument to bring blessing to all nations (v. 4), but here he almost brought a curse on the Philistines.

11. Abimelech's fear of God is evident in his warning to his subjects. With the discovery of Isaac's dissembling, the Philistines had another motive for harming either Isaac or Rebekah. This statement introduces more irony into this chapter, since it shows that Abimelech believed more firmly that God was with Isaac than Isaac himself believed (cf. v. 3).

ii. Conflict over wells (26:12–22)

12-14. Isaac is the only one of Israel's patriarchs to be depicted as cultivating grain. His harvest of a hundred times what he had sown was most likely the maximum one could expect in Palestine (cf. Matt. 13:8). Considering that this harvest came during a famine

---

7. This is a common verb in Genesis, occurring ten times there out of a total of twelve times in the entire Old Testament. Its basic meaning is 'laugh' (17:17; 18:12–13, 15; 21:6). However, it can also be used in a causative conjugation (*Piel*) to mean 'amuse', in the senses of jesting (19:14), mocking (21:9), acts of a sexual nature (26:8; 39:14, 17; Exod. 32:6; cf. 1 Cor. 10:7–8) or performance (Judg. 16:25).

(cf. v. 1) – probably due to drought – Isaac was enjoying extremely great benefit from God's blessing. So, as he had promised, *the Lord blessed* Isaac (v. 12), which led to Isaac's very great wealth that is enumerated as flocks, herds and slaves. While Isaac had been worried about the Philistines' envy concerning his wife Rebekah (v. 7), the Philistines' jealousy actually came in response to God's blessing of wealth.

15–16. The Philistines' vandalism of the wells Abraham had dug negated the agreement made between the earlier Abimelech and Abraham (21:21–34). Perhaps because Abraham was a resident alien the Philistines felt no obligation to honour the treaty beyond Abraham's lifetime, not recognizing a right of inheritance in this case. Later Israelite law would prohibit differing treatment for natives and resident aliens (Exod. 12:49; Num. 9:14; 15:16). In this case the current Abimelech seems to have supported the actions of his subjects, urging Isaac to leave his realm altogether.

17–18. Isaac, however, did not go very far from Gerar, but set up his tents in the valley that was named after the city. His motive for this may have been to make new use of the wells his father had dug. By using the names Abraham had used for these wells, Isaac was asserting his ownership of them.

19–21. Isaac's servants also dug a new well, and this one turned out to be an artesian well, a constant source of flowing water. Thus, this well was very valuable and also indicated God's continued blessing on Isaac. The Philistine herdsmen, however, made this water a point of contention with Isaac's servants, so Isaac asserted his claim to it by calling it *Esek* (v. 20), 'Argument'. The next well also proved to be an occasion for quarrels over water resources, so Isaac called it *Sitnah* (v. 21), 'Hostility'.

22. Isaac finally decided to move from the Gerar Valley, this time far enough away that the Philistines did not try to commandeer his well. The name Isaac gave to this well, *Rehoboth*, 'Open Spaces', is explained by his words. Yahweh's blessing was that he had made space for Isaac's household, and Isaac anticipated further blessing in that they would be *fruitful in the land*. This expectation combines two promises given to Abraham: the land and fruitfulness (see 17:6). Isaac would later pass the blessing of fruitfulness to Jacob (28:3).

iii. Yahweh blesses Isaac at Beersheba (26:23–25)

23. Isaac's return to Beersheba probably signals that the drought that took him to Gerar had ended (cf. v. 1).

24. Yahweh's appearance on the night following Isaac's arrival at Beersheba is significant. This was a place where Abraham had worshipped (21:33), and Yahweh identified himself as *the God of your father Abraham*. Three aspects of God's previous promise to Isaac are repeated: God will be with Isaac, will bless him and will give him many offspring. No mention, however, is made of giving this land to Isaac's descendants (cf. vv. 3–4), since the land at Beersheba had already been acknowledged as Abraham's (21:27–32). As Yahweh clearly states, these promises came to Isaac because of *my servant Abraham*.

25. Four actions of Isaac demonstrate his trust in God's promise. First, he built an altar, following the example of Abraham (12:7, 8; 13:18; 22:9) and setting a precedent for his own son Jacob (33:20; 35:7). Second, he *called on the name of Yahweh*, worship that also followed Abraham's example (12:8; 13:4; 21:33). Third, he *pitched his tent there*, making this his residence. Finally, he once again had his servants dig a well, the fourth well he had dug since leaving Gerar.

iv. Isaac's covenant with Abimelech (26:26–33)

26–27. Abimelech now came to Isaac at Beersheba, leading a party of three. *Ahuzzath* is called his *advisor*. In Hebrew the name Ahuzzath appears to be similar to the name Ahaz. However, it has the same form as the name for a later Philistine from Gath, Goliath. *Phicol* was also the name of the commander who had accompanied the earlier Abimelech when he came to Beersheba to meet Abraham (21:22, 32). It is likely that Phicol was a family name. At various times in antiquity, papponymy – naming one's son after one's father – was common.

Isaac, however, was less than happy to see them. He characterized their attitude to him as hatred – after all, Abimelech had spoken sharply to him, and the Gerarites had vandalized some of his wells and contested others (vv. 9–10, 15, 18, 20, 21).

28–29. The three Philistines are depicted as speaking together to Isaac, and their words always reference themselves in the first person plural (*we, us*). They have observed that Yahweh is with

Isaac – his hundredfold crop and large flocks and herds (vv. 12, 14) that sparked their jealousy. Now they have come to Isaac to seek a peaceful coexistence with this powerful man who lives in the vicinity of their territory. Their proposal is to formalize this relationship in an oath that leads to a covenant.

The content of the agreement is to be that *you will not harm us, just as we have not harmed you* (v. 29). They then dissemble about their treatment of Isaac, claiming that they have done only good to him. Moreover, they reply to Isaac's accusation that they expelled him by claiming that they sent him away peaceably. This, of course, is diplomatic language intended to cover over their differences in the past in order to pave the way for an amicable future. They want to be favoured by one who is *now blessed by Yahweh*.

30–31. Isaac apparently accepted their proffer, since a feast was customary when entering into a covenant (31:46, 54; Exod. 24:11). The next morning the covenant was sealed with an oath, and we are told that the Philistines were sent away and that they left in peace, that is, with a harmonious relationship with Isaac.

32–33. The news of Isaac's servants finding water *on that same day* (v. 32) was timely, since he now had a treaty with Gerar and could count on them not contesting this new well. Isaac's name for the well, *Shibah*, means 'seven' (v. 33). Perhaps this is a reference to Abraham's previous treaty with the king of Gerar when seven ewes were exchanged (21:28). However, it may well have been the seventh well Isaac used in southern Canaan. He had dug the wells Esek (vv. 19–20), Sitnah (v. 21) and Rehoboth (v. 22), as well as a well when he returned to Beersheba. In addition, he had reopened wells – perhaps two – that Abraham had previously dug (v. 18). That would make Shibah the seventh well. This second naming of the well of Beersheba (cf. 21:31) made the name of the city associated with it permanent, and it was still called that when Genesis was written.

E. Esau's Hethite wives (26:34–35)

Context
1966 BC
This short section serves to round out the treatment of Isaac's life that began at 25:19. Esau's marriages led to bitterness for the

patriarch and his wife. At the same time this section connects forward to the treatment of Jacob's life that will run from 27:1 to 35:29 (see 27:46).

Comment

34. Esau's age at marriage, forty years, matches that of Isaac (cf. 25:20) and means that Isaac was 100 years old at this point (cf. 25:26). Esau's marriages appear to have been a result of his own initiative and not that of his parents as was common. Both of his wives were daughters of Hethites, the Canaanite descendants of Heth (see 10:15). The name *Judith* means 'praised' and is the feminine equivalent of Judah. Her father's name *Beeri* means 'my well'. Esau's second wife's name, *Basemath*, means 'balsam tree'. Her father's name *Elon* means 'large tree'.

35. We are not told how these wives embittered the lives of Isaac and Rebekah. The Hebrew says that they were *bitterness of life* to the patriarchal couple. Perhaps they were concerned about Esau's adopting Canaanite religious practices and so were bitter about what they perceived as the wives' bad influence on Esau. Indeed, Esau had despised his birthright, including the promises of Yahweh (25:34), so it is not surprising that he was indifferent to maintaining the family's faith in Abraham's God.

Meaning

Isaac's experiences in Canaan depict him as a true heir of his father. Like Abraham's wife Sarah, his wife is barren for years before bearing children. The children are the subject of the question as to which will receive the promise given to Abraham, and their struggle in the womb and Esau's selling of his birthright contrast these two sons much as Ishmael was contrasted with Isaac. God's twice-repeated promises to Isaac (26:2-5, 24-25) recall his reiterated promises to Abraham. Isaac's deception in Gerar and covenant with Abimelech recall similar incidents in the life of Abraham. The bitterness Isaac's older son brings to him and Rebekah in some ways mirrors the bitterness introduced into Abraham and Sarah's relationship due to Ishmael.

What does all of this tell readers? First, it reminds them that God is faithful, even relentless, in fulfilling his promises. His commitment to his pledges does not waver. Moreover, this is all the more the case for these promises, because they were not simply for the patriarchs and their descendants; through the messianic promise they were for all nations (26:4).

Second, it shows us that to accomplish his goals God works through everyday events, even seemingly mundane acts such as the digging of wells (26:18–22). Isaac acknowledged as much when he stated that Yahweh had made room for his household in the Gerar Valley (26:22).

Third, it demonstrates that even the sins of God's people cannot cancel out his dedication to show his grace and favour to all humanity. In fact, even those who are not among God's people can at times recognize his blessing and seek to obtain it for themselves, as Abimelech, Ahuzzath and Phicol did (26:26–31).

Finally, these accounts of Isaac in Canaan demonstrate that parentage alone is not enough to ensure anyone of a right appreciation for God's love and favour. Esau had the same examples of faith exhibited by his parents as did Jacob. Yet Esau despised the promises and married into pagan families, bringing bitterness into the life of Isaac and Rebekah. God desires faith in the heart, a willingness to sincerely repent and a reliance on his work and gifts rather than on one's own accomplishments (Ps. 51:17).

16. THE FAMILY OF ISAAC: JACOB STRIVES TO RECEIVE THE PROMISE (27:1 – 28:22)

Jacob had his eyes constantly focused on the great family heritage of God's promise (see 25:29–34). This section of Genesis is the first to record one patriarch passing on this heritage to the next generation, something that Jacob himself will do later when he is near death (49:1–27). There are three narratives here that are tied together by the theme of God's blessing: Isaac's blessing when Jacob deceived him, Isaac's second blessing of Jacob, and God's blessing of Jacob at Bethel. Interspersed are depictions of Esau: begging for a blessing from his father, scheming to kill his brother and marrying Ishmael's daughter in order to please his father. After this, Isaac, Rebekah and Esau disappear from the storyline. Rebekah will lose her more beloved son, and will not be part of any narrative in the rest of Genesis.[1] Esau will reappear in the narrative at 33:1–16 when Jacob returns from Paddan-aram, and at Isaac's burial (35:29). Isaac will have only a small role to play again when Genesis

---

1. She will be mentioned in minor ways at 28:5; 35:8; 49:31.

mentions his death and burial (35:28–29). Instead, the focus is now clearly on Jacob as the recipient of God's promise. The actions of Isaac and Rebekah drive these narratives, yet their focus is on God's blessings for Jacob.

A. Jacob deceives Isaac in order to receive the blessing (27:1–46)

Context

1930 BC

The events in this chapter and the next took place in a single year. The date can be determined by working backwards from the date of Israel's exodus from Egypt (1446 BC) using chronological data supplied in Genesis and Exodus.[2]

Comment

i. Isaac sends Esau to hunt game (27:1–4)

1. Isaac would have been 136 years old at this time. His failing eyesight was associated with old age (cf. 48:10; 1 Sam. 3:2; 1 Kgs 14:4). Isaac was obviously concerned that he would not live much longer, though he would live forty-four more years (cf. 35:28). Yet his signs of physical weakness prompted his summoning of *his older son Esau*. Though not used to describe Esau elsewhere, this characterization of Esau will be used twice more in this chapter (vv. 15, 42) as a way of emphasizing the stolen blessing that Esau considered to be rightfully his.

2–4. Isaac clearly was anticipating the end of his life, saying he did not know when he would die. His desire was to taste once again some of the game Esau was known for hunting (25:27–28) and to bless Esau. Isaac's desires ran counter both to the prophecy given to Rebekah (25:23) and to the bitterness that Esau had brought into his life (26:35). Clearly, Isaac's appetite overruled his better judgment as he intended to act counter to God's revealed will.

---

2. See Steinmann (2011: 74).

ii. Rebekah sends Jacob to Isaac (27:5–17)

5–10. Rebekah's eavesdropping on Isaac speaking to *his* son (v. 5) was an activity she practised just as her mother-in-law had (18:10). She continued to be a woman of initiative (cf. 24:18–21) and used Esau's absence while he hunted to recruit Jacob, *her son* (v. 6), to execute her plan to get him Isaac's blessing. Rebekah carefully framed her words. She refers to Isaac as *your father* (vv. 6, 9, 10) and to Esau as *your brother* (v. 6). This not only was intended to incite Jacob concerning his rivalry with Esau, but also served to distance her from the actual act of deception. She began by relating Isaac's words to Esau, but with one important addition: that Isaac would bless Esau *in Yahweh's presence* (v. 7). Thus, she was stating that Isaac would be acting as a prophet and would give the great family blessing of Abraham to Esau. That may have been Isaac's intent – though he did not say it was. Nevertheless, it betrays a misunderstanding of the role of the prophet, who does not determine God's will but simply communicates it. This misunderstanding would later be displayed by the pagan king Balak (Num. 23:11–12, 25–26; 24:10–13).

Rebekah's instructions to Isaac appear almost to have been an order to him when she addressed him as *my son* (v. 8). While she would not use wild game to prepare the meal for Isaac, she would make *a delicious meal for your father, the kind he loves* (v. 9). The word for *delicious food* occurs repeatedly in this chapter (vv. 4, 7, 9, 14, 17, 31), but most often in this section where Rebekah prepares food for Isaac, knowing well that this is Isaac's weakness. Outside of this chapter this word is found only at Proverbs 23:3, 6, where such food is labelled as deceptive, as it certainly was for Isaac.

11–13. Jacob's objection to his mother's scheme is based on their very different appearance. Esau previously was characterized as *hairy* (v. 11; cf. 25:25), but this is the only time that Jacob is called *smooth*. Jacob's real concern, however, is that if the deception is discovered, he will bring a curse on himself instead of the blessing. To mollify him Rebekah apparently offered to let Isaac transfer the curse to her, if such a thing could be done.

14–17. The execution of Rebekah's plan went beyond preparing food. She left nothing to chance, dressing Jacob in Esau's best clothes and placing goat skins on his hands and neck, and even providing bread as a sop for the food. The initiative is depicted as entirely Rebekah's. The only action attributed to Isaac is the fetching of the goats.

iii. Jacob deceives Isaac and receives a blessing (27:18–29)

18–19. When Jacob came to Isaac, the patriarch began by asking which son was before him, re-emphasizing for the reader Isaac's blindness. Jacob was too loquacious at this point. He used the Hebrew emphatic construction to say *I am Esau* (v. 19), perhaps betraying his anxiety as he lied to his father. He then prattled on by adding that he was the firstborn (as if Isaac needed reminding), talking of having fulfilled Isaac's instructions and imploring Isaac to eat so that he could receive the blessing. Jacob's insecurity is highlighted by the fact that the Hebrew words for *firstborn* and *bless* contain the same three consonants though in different order.

20. If Jacob's lie to his father was not a grave enough sin, when Isaac enquired as to how he was able to find the game so quickly, Jacob blasphemed by invoking God's name to justify his speedy return with the food already prepared.

21–23. Isaac, however, was still unconvinced that Esau was before him. Rebekah's preparations worked, yet Isaac continued to have his doubts about his son's identity. His pronouncement that the voice did not match the hands gave him more reason to test Jacob. Yet the narration at this point says that Jacob's hands were hairy like Esau's so that is why Isaac blessed him.[3] The hair apparently was the deciding factor, with Isaac choosing his sense of touch over his hearing.

24–25. Isaac's third test was to again hear Jacob's voice, but this time Jacob, now circumspect about talking too much, replied with only one word of two syllables in Hebrew: *I* [am].[4] With that, Isaac ate, and Jacob even added wine to the meal.

26–27a. Despite tasting the food that Rebekah had prepared to Isaac's liking, he had one last test to ensure that he was blessing

---

3. Ska (1992: 518–521).

4. Earlier in identifying himself as Esau, Jacob had used the longer, three-syllable Hebrew word for *I* (v. 19).

Esau. He asked to exchange kisses with his son and used this to smell his clothes. However, since the clothes were Esau's (cf. v. 15), Isaac was fooled.

27b–29. Isaac's blessing is in three parts: a description of his son (v. 27b), a blessing for agricultural prosperity (v. 28) and a blessing concerning his relationships with others (v. 29).

The description is most fitting for Esau, but ironically applies to Jacob, since God has promised him the blessing all along. The agricultural blessing involves sky and land, referencing all of creation. *Grain and new wine* (v. 28) are often mentioned together as products of the land of Canaan (Deut. 7:13; 28:51; 33:28; 2 Kgs 18:32; Hos. 7:14; Joel 1:10).

The final blessing mirrors and expands upon the prophecy given to Rebekah before the birth of Esau and Jacob (25:23). Instead of the older serving the younger, Isaac's blessing says *may peoples serve you* (v. 29).The mention of Jacob's *brothers* and *mother's sons* is not simply poetic hyperbole: the Hebrew word *brothers* can also be used more widely to refer to male relatives (e.g. 31:46), and the word *sons* can be used in a broader sense to denote descendants in later generations (see, for example, the phrase 'sons of Israel' which throughout most of the Old Testament denotes 'Israelites').

Isaac's final statement concerning those who curse or bless bequeathed to Jacob the promises of God first given to Abraham (12:3). However, it has its closest parallel in Balaam's later blessing on Israel at Numbers 24:9 which uses the same four Hebrew words but places those who bless before those who curse.

iv. Esau discovers Jacob's deception and begs for Isaac's blessing (27:30–40)

30–31. Apparently Esau just missed Jacob leaving Isaac's presence when he arrived with his game. Ironically, the same verb is used of Jacob going out from Isaac that was used of Esau coming out of the womb before Jacob (25:25). Esau may have been the first to be born, but Jacob was ahead of Esau when it came to receiving the firstborn's blessing. Once Esau prepared the food, his presentation to Isaac specifically connected the food he brought with his father's blessing in words that are nearly identical to those used earlier by Jacob (v. 19).

32–33. Isaac's alarm is palpable in his question *Who are you?* (v. 32). Esau's answer is emphatic, perhaps expressing his bewilderment at his father's question: *I am your son – your firstborn – Esau.* Isaac's alarm became violent trembling, and his questions conveyed to Esau what had happened. They were not designed for Esau to answer, but were rhetorical, thereby expressing his outrage. Most importantly, he asserted that the blessing would not be revoked. After all, Isaac had invoked Yahweh in pronouncing his blessing on Jacob (see vv. 27–28), and one could not annul any words that called on God.

34–35. Esau's reaction was a cry of anguish which is described as *loud and bitter* (v. 34), and he begged for a blessing. Isaac's response was that Jacob had committed fraud and had taken the blessing intended for Esau. If that was so, then Isaac was also admitting his own sinful desire to give to Esau the blessing God intended for Jacob (cf. 27:29 with 25:23).

36. Esau's statement about Jacob contains two wordplays: the name *Jacob* is from the same root as *he cheated me*, and the word for *my birthright* is an anagram of *my blessing*. He then enquired whether Isaac had saved some blessing for him, thinking that he may have held something back, perhaps intended as a blessing for Jacob.

37. Isaac, however, spelled out for Esau what he had given to Jacob, though in reverse order, placing the promise of dominance over others (cf. v. 29) before blessings from the earth (cf. v. 28).

38. The pathos in Esau's pleading for his own blessing is evident as he practically accuses his father of not holding a blessing in reserve while begging for his own.

39–40. Isaac's reply amounts to an anti-blessing. He reverses the order of the earth's bounty – *richness of the land* and *dew of the sky* (v. 39; cf. v 28) – since these will not be Esau's inheritance. Instead, he will have to make a living by the sword – plundering others rather than reaping bountiful crops. Yet there is one ray of hope for Esau: even though he will serve his brother, there will come a time when Esau *will break his yoke* (v. 40). While Jacob's descendants in David's dynasty would dominate Edom, in the days of Judah's King Jehoram the Edomites would successfully rebel (2 Kgs 8:20–22; 2 Chr. 21:8–10).

v. The result of Jacob's deceit (27:41–46)

41. Though Jacob and Esau had a history of sibling rivalry, Esau's murderous grudge is specifically linked to Jacob's having received Isaac's blessing. His scheme was to wait until after Isaac's death. Perhaps Esau, like Jacob, was wary of doing something to bring his father's curse upon himself (cf. v. 12).

42–45. We are not told how Esau's fratricidal thoughts were expressed, but it appears that he made his plans known, and they were told to Rebekah. Her instructions to Jacob were for him to seek refuge in Haran with her brother Laban, and they included the thought that he would not have to stay there long – *only a few days* (v. 44) – before Esau lost his rage and she could summon Jacob to return. Her words in retrospect will seem ironic, since Jacob's few days with Laban will turn into twenty years (31:38, 41). Her rhetorical question *Why should I lose you both in one day?* also drips with irony. She was afraid of losing Jacob to murder and Esau to execution for murder. However, she would lose her beloved son Jacob permanently, since it appears that she never summoned him and never saw him again.

46. Being the consummate schemer, Rebekah knew that she could not simply send Jacob away without arousing suspicion about her role in the affair of the stolen blessing. So she cleverly came up with a way to make Isaac think he was sending Jacob to Paddan-aram. The Hethite wives of Esau had embittered Isaac's life just as much as Rebekah's (cf. 26:34–35), so she used the possibility of Jacob marrying one of these Canaanite women to nudge Isaac so that he would command Jacob to find a wife elsewhere.

Meaning

The behaviour of all four persons in this chapter is questionable. Isaac sought to give God's blessing to Esau despite God's explicit revelation that the older would serve the younger (25:23). Esau plotted to murder his brother whom God favoured through Isaac's blessing, a near replay of Cain and Abel. Rebekah used her position as wife to devise a scheme to deceive her husband and her position as mother to goad her son into hoodwinking his father. Jacob not only deceived his father but also blatantly lied to him (27:19). This lends an ironic hue to the entire chapter. God wanted Jacob to receive the greater blessing, and, indeed, he received it. This happened despite Isaac's suspicion that led him to question whether Esau was actually the son who had come to him with food. Yet none of that excuses the behaviour of Rebekah or Jacob. God did not ask for their aid in conveying the blessing to Jacob, and their taking the initiative in an attempt to carry out God's plan involved fraud – something that is contrary to God's holy nature. As a result Rebekah lost her favourite son and may have been estranged from her elder son as well. In all this, however, God's will was advanced. No human act – not even the most evil of acts – could thwart God's gracious will to bless all peoples through the patriarchal line. He did not abandon his gracious promise but used even the misguided acts of Isaac and the members of his family to further his plan for the salvation of the world.

B. Jacob leaves for Paddan-aram (28:1–9)

Context

1930 BC

The rivalry between Jacob and Esau continues even after Jacob's departure as Esau, learning of his father's instructions to Jacob not to marry a Canaanite wife, marries into the family of Ishmael. However, the real blessing remains with God's chosen servant Jacob, whom Isaac sends to Paddan-aram with the blessing first given to Abraham.

Comment

1–2. Isaac responded to Rebekah's concern about having another Canaanite daughter-in-law by summoning Jacob for blessing and instruction on marriage. That Jacob was forbidden marriage to any Canaanite woman testifies to Esau's having done just that: the Hethite women he married were Canaanites, descendants of Heth, Canaan's second son (10:15; 1 Chr. 1:13). Then Isaac was more specific, directing Isaac to marry within the larger family of Rebekah by taking one of Laban's daughters as a wife. Marriage to a cousin who was a child of the opposite-sex sibling of one's own parent was not uncommon in ancient societies and minimized the chance of passing on genetic diseases. Thus, it stood midway between marrying too closely inside one's own family and marrying outside the family.

3–4. Isaac blessed Jacob in the name of *God Almighty* (Hebrew *'ēl šadday*, v. 3). This name of God, first revealed to Abraham (17:1), is most often used in association with Jacob (35:11; 43:14; 48:3). The blessing is described as *the blessing of Abraham* and it largely repeats blessings given by God to Isaac's father (12:2–3, 7; 13:15, 17; 15:7–8, 18; 17:1, 6, 8, 16, 20; 22:17; 24:7) and passed on to Isaac (26:3–4, 24). The last part of the blessing is the most important: the promise of the land. Jacob will spend twenty years away from the land in Paddan-aram, but God's promise will bring him back to this land. He will end his life in Egypt, but even there he will cling to the promise of the land of Canaan (49:29–32).

5. This verse not only summarizes Isaac's action but also clearly delineates his instructions in detail. It contains the geographic goal: Paddan-aram; the familial goal: Laban son of Bethuel; the identity of the other branch of the family: Aramean; the side of the family: Rebekah's side; and Rebekah's role in the family as mother of two sons.

6–7. The focus now turns to Esau's observations. He observed a further patriarchal blessing for Jacob connected with marrying a cousin. This is made more emphatic by the inclusion of the direct quotation of Isaac's words *Do not marry a Canaanite woman* (v. 6). Furthermore, Esau observed that Jacob obeyed his father's instructions.

8–9. Still seeking a blessing from Isaac (cf. 27:34, 36), Esau imitates his father's instructions by marrying into the family of Abraham in a different way: by going to Ishmael (that is, Ishmael's clan, since Ishmael had died some thirteen years earlier; see 25:17). His wife is identified as *Mahalath*, a sister of Ishmael's firstborn son *Nebaioth* (25:13). The names of Esau's wives are confusing, since Mahalath is called *Basemath* at 36:3, and one of Esau's Hethite wives is called *Basemath* at 26:34 but *Adah* at 36:2. Perhaps *Basemath*, meaning 'balsamic' or 'fragrant', was a nickname.

C. Yahweh's promise to Jacob at Bethel (28:10–22)

1930 BC

God's first appearance to Jacob takes him by surprise. He was not seeking God's presence, but God was seeking Jacob to grant him a

threefold blessing as he left the Promised Land. In response to
God's pledge to him, Jacob vows to honour him. Here we see Jacob
motivated not by any of God's demands but by God's grace.

10–11. The mention of the beginning and end points of Jacob's
journey (Beersheba and Haran, v. 10) emphasizes Jacob's separation
from his family and from the land of God's promise. Since the
name of this place where Jacob stopped for the night plays an
important part in Jacob's coming to realize the depth of God's
commitment to him, the narrative is careful at this point not to
reveal it, though it has been mentioned previously (12:8; 13:3). In
this way the story emphasizes Jacob's unfamiliarity with the place as
well as his inexperience with God's ways. The stone that Jacob
placed at his head is often depicted as his pillow, though the
narrative does not say that.

12. The description of Jacob's dream reveals some kind of portal
for God's angels on their journeys to and from heaven. Scholars are
divided as to what exactly Jacob saw. Traditionally, based on the
Septuagint, it is called a ladder, though many modern versions call
it a stairway.[5] Other suggestions include a hill (perhaps the hill
where the high place at Bethel was located), a portal or a ramp.[6]

13–15. God, as the earth's sovereign, was standing at the top of
the angel's ascent.[7] Here God identified himself as Yahweh who
had taken Abraham and Isaac as his own. Now he was passing on
the promise of the land he had given to them (12:7; 13:15, 17; 15:18;
17:8; 26:4), confirming the words of Isaac (28:4). God's second
promise concerned Jacob's offspring, not only pledging that they
would be numerous and live in the land in all four directions from
this place, but also restating the messianic promise – that all peoples
would be blessed though Jacob's offspring (12:3; 18:18; 22:18; 26:4).
Though Isaac had given Jacob many items in his blessing (see

---

5. CSB, GW, NET, NRSV.

6. Griffiths (1965); Hoffner (1967); Houtman (1977); Millard (1966); Oblath
(2001).

7. Some understand the text to say that God was standing over (i.e. beside)
Jacob (CSB, NRSV). That, however, is less probable given the wording in
the Hebrew text.

27:27–29), it was God alone who pronounced Jacob blessed in order to be a blessing to all peoples. The third promise of God was to be with Jacob and to watch over him in all his journeys, eventually bringing him back to this land of the promise.

16–17. Jacob's awestruck response to the dream begins with acknowledgment of his lack of acquaintance with Yahweh's presence. His fear increased as he realized that he was in the house of the holy God of all the earth and at the gateway to heaven. It is interesting to contemplate the contrast between this gateway to heaven which God revealed and the tower at Babel where human beings tried to reach heaven (11:1–9). Human effort to reach God in heaven brought only judgment, while God's gracious revelation of himself at the top of heaven's gateway brought blessing.

18–19. Jacob's act of setting up the stone and consecrating it with oil was an act of worship similar to Abraham and Isaac's building altars in places where God appeared to them (12:7; 26:24–25). Later, at God's command, Jacob would build an altar here (35:1, 3, 7). Jacob's practice would consistently be to set up stone markers at places where God appeared to him (35:14). He would also use stone markers to mark other important places, such as where he made an agreement with Laban (31:45) and at Rachel's tomb (35:20). Jacob's naming of the place *Bethel*, meaning *house of God* (v. 19), finally reveals his location to the reader. The nearby city had previously been called *Luz*, which is sometimes noted elsewhere when Bethel is mentioned (35:6; Judg. 1:23). At times it appears that a distinction is made between the exact place where Jacob slept at the southern base of a hill, called *Bethel*, and the nearby hilltop city, called *Luz* (Josh. 16:2; 18:13).

20–22. In response to God's three promises, Jacob makes a threefold vow. Like vows elsewhere in the Bible, there is a condition that states what God will do, followed by a pledge to do something in return (Judg. 11:30; 1 Sam. 1:11). Such vows were made not to coerce God into granting something but to state how the person making the vow would demonstrate gratitude to God if he graciously provided a particular favour. Jacob's three pledges are conditioned on God's keeping his promise to watch over Jacob and bring him back to the Promised Land. Jacob's first pledge is to worship Yahweh. His second is to make this place God's house, a pledge fulfilled when he built an altar at Bethel (35:7). His third pledge is to give God a tenth of his wealth. This is the second mention of tithing (see 14:20).

Meaning

Even after Jacob received his orders to marry one of Laban's daughters, Esau was jealous of his brother and sought to curry favour with his father by marrying into a different branch of Abraham's family. Meanwhile, Jacob was journeying to Haran and came to know the God whose blessing he had so coveted because of his continued struggle with his twin brother. Now in a dream he learned of God's grace and began to appreciate God's choice of him without the necessity of having his rivalry with his brother motivating his desire for blessing.

The narratives of chapters 27 and 28 together emphasize that God's people sometimes seek the right things but, in their sinful desires, often try to obtain them in the wrong way. While God wants us to desire his blessings, and Jesus taught his followers to pray for both the blessings of his kingdom and the blessings that fulfil our material needs (Matt. 6:9–13; Luke 11:2–4), he also wants us to shun any underhanded and deceitful ways of obtaining them (Eph. 4:20–24). When Jacob did receive his blessing directly from God, it involved no effort on his part; he did not even realize he was in God's house and at the gateway to heaven. This reminds us that even when God blesses our efforts, we are still completely dependent on him to bless them with his rewards. Like Jacob, God's people learn from his freely given and completely undeserved love, and they willingly respond by pledging him their loyalty, worship and material blessings.

17. THE FAMILY OF ISAAC: JACOB IS BLESSED BY GOD (29:1 – 30:43)

These two chapters cover the twenty years of Jacob's life spent in Haran. Three themes are intertwined here. One is Laban's taking advantage of Jacob: he deceives him into marrying Leah, and makes him work another seven years for Rachel. Jacob, it appears, meets poetic justice: the one who deceived his father is in turn deceived by his uncle. A second theme developed here is rivalry between Jacob's two wives. While Jacob has finally escaped his sibling rivalry with Esau, he now experiences sibling rivalry as an outsider to the two competitors, his wives. The third theme, however, is the most important: no matter what circumstances Jacob encounters, he prospers because Yahweh is with him and is blessing him. This blessing comes not only in the form of God providing children (29:31; 30:22) but also in the form of Jacob's own cleverness in breeding sheep (30:37–43). Thus, the account of Jacob's years in Laban's household build on themes already introduced in previous narratives: cunning and deception as a character flaw in several generations of Abraham's family (12:10–19; 20:1–18; 26:7–11; 27:1–10), family rivalry (16:1–16; 21:8–13; 25:22–23, 27–34) and God's blessing in his commitment to his promise to Abraham (12:1–3; 22:16–18; 26:2–5; 28:13–15).

A. Jacob meets Rachel (29:1–14)

Context

1930 BC

Jacob's meeting his future bride Rachel at a well far from home parallels two other Pentateuchal stories of meetings at wells that led to marriage. Earlier, Abraham's servant met Rebekah at a well outside town – perhaps this same well. Later, Moses would meet Zipporah at a well in Midian (Exod. 2:15–22).

Comment

1. After Jacob left Bethel, no other stops along the way to his destination are mentioned. We are simply told that Jacob went to the *land of the peoples of the east*. While Haran is mostly north of Palestine, it is east of the Euphrates. The eastern peoples included the Arameans as well as various descendants of Abraham (cf. 25:1–6, 12–18).

2–3. Readers are not yet told of Jacob's location, just that he saw a well and three flocks of sheep beside it. The large stone over the well apparently ensured that no one person could take the water for him- or herself, since it is implied that it took several men to move it. When all the local flocks were watered, they moved it back again to serve as the well's silent guardian.

4–6. Jacob's conversation with the men at the well first asks about their home – perhaps Jacob did not know how close to Haran he was. Upon discovering that Haran was nearby, his next questions were intended to learn about Laban. While news of Laban's family – that he had daughters – had apparently reached Isaac (28:2), there may have been no word from Laban for a long time. The shepherds not only told Isaac that Laban was well, but also tried to divert his attention from them to Rachel, whose flock was arriving.

7–8. Jacob's next words appear abrupt and presumptuous. Broad daylight is not the time to gather the sheep; it is the time to graze them. So he tells them to water them and leave. It may be that Jacob wanted to introduce himself to someone from Laban's household without onlookers. However, the men note that they cannot water the sheep until all the local flocks gather – perhaps a way of ensuring that the water was shared equitably.

9–10. Rachel's arrival seems to have brought the conversation to a halt. Rachel is introduced as a shepherdess of her father's sheep, a clue that she was young and unmarried (cf. Exod. 2:16). Jacob's eagerness to meet Laban is shown by his feat of strength in moving the stone by himself as well as by his watering the sheep for Rachel. Either Jacob broke local protocol in moving the stone or Rachel's was the last of the flocks to arrive. Either way, the men did not dare protest to a man who displayed such impressive strength.

11–12. There is no hint yet of Jacob's attraction to Rachel. His kissing her and weeping is a sign of greeting among long-separated relatives. While a man kissing a woman is not commonly mentioned in the Bible, there are a few occasions when a kiss is exchanged between male and female relatives as a greeting or farewell (31:55; 1 Kgs 19:20).[1] Jacob's action, however, appears to be in the wrong order: he kisses and weeps before identifying himself as a relative of her father on his mother's side of the family. Yet Rachel appears to have taken no offence as she ran off to inform Laban.

13–14. Laban apparently also was anxious to meet Jacob, as his embrace and kiss suggest. Considering his previous encounter with someone from Abraham's family and the wealth it displayed (24:29–30), Laban may have been motivated by what material blessings he could obtain through Jacob, so that he was not simply acknowledging family connections. Certainly his later actions betray his interest in using Jacob to help him amass wealth. Jacob told Laban *all that had happened* (v. 13), meaning he shared news of the family in Canaan and perhaps also his father's instructions to marry one of Laban's daughters. Whatever it was that Jacob shared, it convinced Laban that Jacob was a blood relative. So we are told that Jacob

---

1. This is different from a romantic kiss on the mouth; see Song 1:2. Prov. 7:13 probably also refers to a romantic kiss (cf. Prov. 7:16–18). Also note the honeyed lips and smooth palate of the woman at Prov. 5:3.

stayed one month with Laban. The Hebrew phrase is *a month of days* (v. 14), reminiscent of the 'few days' that Rebekah had in mind when she sent Jacob to Laban. However, as the story unfolds, the month will turn into two decades.

B. Jacob deceived by Laban (29:15–30)

Context

1923 BC

Jacob was sent to Laban for the purpose of marrying one of his daughters (28:2). Little did he know at the time that he would end up marrying both of them! While Jacob is deceived by Laban, the greatest of Laban's indiscretions may actually lie in his cynical use of his daughters in his scheme to defraud Jacob, something they themselves will eventually admit (31:15). Interestingly, this narrative shares a number of features with that of another father using his daughters to serve his own ends: Saul and his promise of one of his daughters to David (see Table 12).

Table 12 Similarities between the Laban–Jacob and Saul–David narratives

	Laban gives Jacob wives (Gen. 29)	Saul gives David a wife (1 Sam. 18)
Non-monetary bride price	7 years' service	100 Philistine foreskins
Misused daughters	Leah and Rachel	Merab and Michal
Double payment	14 years' service	200 Philistine foreskins

One major difference, of course, is that Jacob married both sisters, whereas David married only one. However, due to the law later given through Moses, a man was forbidden from simultaneously being married to sisters (Lev. 18:18). So, while it was possible for Jacob to marry Rachel while being married to Leah, David would not have that option with Merab and Michal. In fact, the law in Leviticus may be understood in the light of the strife in Jacob's family arising from rival wives who were also rival siblings.

Comment

15. Laban's offer to pay Jacob for his work appears to be magnanimous. Jacob is not a simple hired hand, he is a relative. However, the dilemma is setting Jacob's wages, and Laban places the burden of determining a fair wage on Jacob. The words *work* (sometimes translated 'serve') and *wages* will be key terms in the following narratives (29:15, 18, 20, 25, 27, 30; 30:26, 28, 29, 32, 33; 31:6, 7, 8, 41) and bitter reminders of Laban's exploitation of both Jacob and his daughters (31:6–7, 14–15, 41).

16–17. Before the narration can move on, some information is needed so that the reader can understand Jacob's proposal. Laban had two daughters, distinguished as *the older* and *the younger* (v. 16) – a detail that will be important later (see v. 26). *Leah* probably means 'cow', whereas *Rachel* means 'ewe'. The two sisters are also distinguished by their appearance. There is debate about what is meant by Leah having *tender eyes* (v. 17, CSB), but since she is contrasted to Rachel who was *shapely and beautiful*, it probably means that she did not have any sparkle in her eyes to make her attractive to Jacob. Rachel would later pass on her good looks to Joseph, who is the only other person in Scripture described as having both a beautiful/handsome form and a beautiful/handsome appearance (39:6).[2]

18–20. Jacob's specifying his work and wages is quite precise in its term (seven years) and Laban's payment, *your younger daughter Rachel* (v. 18). Laban appears to accept Jacob's generous proposal. Indeed, during this era a labourer's wages varied between one-half to one shekel per month.[3] So Jacob was offering labour worth between 42 and 84 shekels. Since the Mosaic law appears to set the maximum bride price at 50 shekels (Deut. 22:29), Jacob's offer was more than generous. The seven years pass as quickly for the reader as they did for Jacob, to whom *they seemed like only a few days* because of his love for Rachel (v. 20). Of course, this echoes Rebekah's words that Jacob was to stay a few days with Laban (27:44).

21–24. At the end of his required service, Jacob's demand to be married to Rachel is rather brusque, but Laban appears not to have

---

2. Esther is described with similar, but not identical, terms (Esth. 2:7).

3. Driver and Miles (1952: 1.470–471).

taken any offence. That Jacob called Rachel *my wife* reveals that accepting a marriage contract was tantamount to marriage even before the couple cohabited, and the Mosaic law makes a similar assumption (Deut. 22:23–24), as does the New Testament (Matt. 1:18–20). As the bride's father, Laban gave the customary wedding feast, inviting his community. At this point only is the reader introduced to Laban's deception: he gave Leah instead of Rachel to Jacob, and the marriage was consummated. Modern readers may ask how such a deception could be successful, while the text assumes that the ancient readers would have no trouble understanding. One factor may have been that brides were traditionally veiled (24:65; Song 4:1, 3; 6:7). Another factor may be that Jacob could have been more than a little inebriated from the wine customarily served at wedding celebrations (cf. John 2:1–10). Interestingly, it is after reporting the consummation of the marriage that the author notes that Laban provided for Leah by giving her a slave girl, Zilpah. This introduces a woman who would later bear other children to Jacob (30:9–13). While this note may seem out of place, it actually serves two purposes. First, it shows Laban keeping all the expected wedding customs, including the giving of a present to one's newly married daughter (cf. Josh. 15:19; Judg. 1:15; 1 Kgs 9:16). Second, it delays the reporting of Jacob's discovery of Laban's deception, thereby heightening the suspense for the reader.

25–27. Jacob's surprise at having married Leah is conveyed by three short words in Hebrew. In contrast, his outrage towards Laban is expressed in three accusatory questions. He clearly claimed that he had worked for Rachel, as he had carefully specified (cf. v. 18). In a classic case of deflection, Laban did not even bother to answer Jacob's first two questions and only offered a lame excuse in response to the third one. To say that he could not give Rachel because it was against local custom *to give the younger before the firstborn* (v. 26) was disingenuous in the extreme, considering that Laban had had seven years to clarify this with Jacob or to find a husband for Leah. Nevertheless, the irony of Jacob the deceiver being deceived appears to be poetic justice. After all, Jacob the younger son of Isaac put himself in the place of the firstborn Esau in order to steal his brother's blessing. Laban, however, appeared to admit that he owed Rachel to Jacob by quickly offering to give her to Jacob immediately after the end of the week's wedding feast. Neverthe-less, he also extracted from Jacob the obligation of seven more years of labour.

28–30. Jacob, perhaps, felt that he was in no position to protest further, especially given Laban's attempt to mollify him with the promise of Rachel as his wife in only a few days. We are simply told that Jacob and Laban abided by this new agreement. A few details round out the story. Rachel was also given a slave, Bilhah, who would become mother of two sons for Jacob (30:3–8). After Jacob had consummated the marital relationship with Rachel, we are told that *indeed, he loved Rachel more than Leah*. Experiencing marriage with both women did not change his initial attraction to Rachel over Leah. This observation prepares readers for the strife and competition in bearing children between Leah and Rachel.

Meaning

The deceived deceiver (Jacob) is only one of several important themes introduced in this first part of the story of Jacob in Laban's household. It explains, however, why in the ensuing narratives Jacob is constantly suspicious of Laban. For the reader, Laban's duplicity comes as a new insight into his character that will eventually lead to him being the deceived deceiver (31:33–35). Laban's fraud coupled with Jacob's favouring one wife over the other introduces another theme that will be developed in the next account concerning the births of Jacob's sons and daughter. However, this account of Jacob's marriages prepares for the work of God (who is not mentioned at all in 29:1–30). Despite the wrong that was done to Jacob – indeed, *through* the wrong that was done to him – God will bring forth a large and prosperous family.

C. The births of Jacob's sons (29:31 – 30:24)

Context

1922–c.1915 BC

The story of the births of Jacob's children is marked with pathos (Leah's constant longing for Jacob's love, 29:32, 33, 34; 30:20), envy, desperation and even superstition. Yet even through this human story, God is at work providing for the promise of a great nation

that was given to Abraham (12:2). In order to emphasize that God
provided children through Jacob's wives, this account divides into
four sections, highlighting God's work in the first and fourth
sections, and the women's actions in the second and third (see
Table 13).

Table 13 Four sections in the account of the births of Jacob's children

29:31–35	*God saw* ... (29:31)	children for Leah
30:1–8	*Rachel saw* ... (30:1)	children for Rachel (borne by Bilhah)
30:9–21	*Leah saw* ... (30:10)	children for Leah (borne by Zilpah and by Leah)
30:22–24	*God remembered* ... (30:22)	a child for Rachel

Moreover, the entire account is framed by God's solution to the
plights of Leah and Rachel: he opens their wombs (29:31; 30:22).
The striking feature of this part of Genesis is Jacob's passivity. He
speaks only one sentence (30:3), names none of his children, and
even accepts his wives' determination as to with whom he should
have sex (30:3, 9, 16). Thus, the patriarch received the fulfilment of
God's promise even when he was not actively pursuing it.

Comment
31–35. The background information for the births of Jacob's
children is given as God's action: he saw Leah's plight and *opened her
womb* (v. 31). This phrase occurs in the Bible only in regard to Jacob's
wives, thereby emphasizing that the rise of the nation of Israel was
God's doing. Leah names her first son *Reuben*, meaning 'behold a
son'. However, the name is also a play on her words *the Lord has seen
my affliction* (v. 32). Her assertion that this birth would bring her
Jacob's love apparently was wrong (cf. vv. 33, 34; 30:20). Leah
named her second son *Simeon,* meaning *heard*, on the conviction that
God had heard about her being unloved. Her third son was named
Levi, a play on the word *attached* (v. 34), since she hoped that after
three sons Jacob would become committed to her. With the naming
of her fourth son, *Judah,* a name derived from the Hebrew word for
praise, Leah focused on her relationship with Yahweh alone.

30:1–4. Rachel's envy of her sister's fertility led her to make a preposterous demand of her husband. Jacob's angry reply is understandable, since he acknowledged that God was ultimately responsible for the blessing of children (Ps. 127:3). Rachel then proposed that her slave Bilhah bear children in her place. The Hebrew idiom here is *she will bear upon my knees.* This is adoption language and later would be used of Joseph's adopting Machir's children (50:23). Rachel's words *that through her I too can build a family* (v. 3) are reminiscent of Sarah's words about Hagar (16:2). After a brief flash of anger, Jacob now became compliant with his wife's demand, and received Bilhah as his third wife.

5–8. Bilhah's role is no more than that of a surrogate, and her only action is to conceive and bear a son. Rachel claims the right to name the son. Her claim of vindication by the action of God who heard her leads to the name *Dan,* which is derived from the same root as 'vindicate' in Hebrew. The second son of Bilhah also is occasion for Rachel's words and naming. She claimed that she had *mighty wrestling* or *wrestling of God* (v. 8; the Hebrew could mean either) as she wrestled with her sister. Thus, the name of the child was *Naphtali,* which is a play on words with the Hebrew verb that means 'wrestle'.

9–13. If Bilhah was given to Jacob about the time of the birth of Judah (29:35), then Leah's observation that she had stopped bearing children and her giving of Zilpah to Jacob must have happened about a year after Judah's birth. In this case, no words of Leah are recorded, but once again Jacob complies and receives a fourth wife whose role is depicted, like Bilhah, as no more than that of a surrogate. The name of the resulting child, *Gad,* means *good fortune* in keeping with Leah's words. Leah named the second son of Zilpah *Asher,* a play on words with the Hebrew word for *happy* or *blessed.*

14–16. The scene now shifts to Reuben's action during the wheat harvest in late spring. He would have still been a young boy at this time, and his bringing of mandrakes to Leah probably was a gift of the fragrant flowers or perhaps the fruit of this plant (Song 7:13). Mandrakes were thought to be an aphrodisiac and a stimulant for female fertility. In fact, the Hebrew word for 'mandrake' is related to one of the Hebrew words for 'love'.

Rachel's polite request for the mandrakes appears to accept the superstitious belief in the power of mandrakes. Leah, however, rebukes her sister. She also, it appears, was not above envy (cf. v. 1). In this case she accused Rachel of stealing her husband's affections. Perhaps when Leah ceased bearing children, Jacob favoured sharing Rachel's bed and was thereby neglecting Leah. Thus, Leah expressed her outrage at her sister also coveting the fertility-inducing mandrakes. Rachel seems to have understood Leah's desire for Jacob's love, and she used it to strike a bargain: one night with Jacob for the mandrakes. The exchange gave neither woman what each desired. Leah would never obtain the level of intimacy with Jacob that she wanted, and the mandrakes did not make Rachel fertile.

17–18. Once again Jacob is depicted as compliant with his wives' will. Leah was able to hire Jacob for the night, and he submitted to simply being part of a transaction between the two sisters. Leah's fifth son was a result of God's action, not induced by mandrakes. He *listened to Leah* (v. 17), implying that Leah was praying for another child. Leah's naming of *Issachar* is a pun on the words for *hire* and *wages*. She *hired* Jacob (v. 16), and she said, *God has given me my wages* (v. 18). Ironically, she viewed God's reward as being prompted by her having given Zilpah as a wife to Jacob, which she may have seen as a selfless act.

19–21. Leah's resumed fertility must have given Jacob reason to divide his affections more evenly between Leah and Rachel, since Leah bore two more children. She makes two statements at the birth of her sixth son. One is that God has given her a good gift, while the other is an explanation of that gift: her husband will honour her. The boy's name, *Zebulun*, is a pun on the second statement, containing the same consonants as the Hebrew word for *honour*.[4] We are told that *later she bore a daughter* (v. 21). This statement most likely

---

4. The first statement uses the word *gift* (Hebrew *zebed*), which shares two consonants with the name *Zebulun*. However, the second statement uses the word *honour me* (Hebrew *yizbělēnî*), which shares four consonants with the name *Zebulun*. Thus, it appears that the first statement is an anticipatory pun for the actual pun on the name.

places Dinah's birth after the birth of Joseph.[5] The name *Dinah* is the feminine equivalent of *Dan* (i.e. *vindicated*; cf. v. 6), but unlike the naming of sons, no statement is given to explain the choice of this name. While Rachel may have remained the wife favoured by Jacob, Leah appears favoured by God with the ideal number of children: seven.

22–24. The account of Jacob's children comes to a climax when *God remembered Rachel* (v. 22). As he did for Leah years earlier, God *opened her womb* (v. 22; cf. 29:31). Just as Leah spoke two statements at the birth of Zebulun, so Rachel spoke twice at Joseph's birth. First she noted that God had removed her disgrace, and then she uttered a wish that God would add another son. The name *Joseph* means *may he add*.[6]

D. Yahweh blesses Jacob: his flocks increase (30:25–43)

Context

1915–1910 BC

This account of Jacob's obtaining riches and building a flock covers his last six years in Paddan-aram (cf. 31:41). While Jacob may have manipulated the mating of the sheep and goats (30:37–42), it was God who blessed the patriarch with large flocks (31:7–9).

Comment

25–26. With Joseph's birth, Jacob's seven years of service for Rachel must have ended.[7] Jacob was ready to go back to Canaan,

---

5. See Steinmann (2011: 76–78).

6. As with the naming of Zebulun, there is an anticipatory pun on Joseph's name. *Taken away* (Hebrew *'āsap*) is the anticipatory pun, sharing two consonants with the name *Joseph*. But the word *may he add* (Hebrew *yōsēp*) is identical in pronunciation to the name *Joseph*.

7. This is required by 31:41, which says that Jacob served fourteen years for Laban's daughters and six years to build his own flock. Since Jacob's service for the flocks did not begin until *after* the birth of Joseph, Joseph must have been born shortly before the end of Jacob's seven years of service for Rachel.

and requested Laban's release. Jacob claimed only his wives and children as his: he abided by his agreement with Laban despite Laban's deceit. His evidence that he had fulfilled the terms of their arrangement was Laban's own knowledge of Jacob's hard work.

27–28. Laban, however, did not want Jacob to leave. His words acknowledge that he had no hold over Jacob at this point, as he begins his appeal with *If I have found favour in your eyes* (v. 27). This phrase was normally used in polite speech to a superior (18:3; 30:27; 33:10; Exod. 33:13, 16; 34:9; Num. 11:15; Judg. 6:17; Ruth 2:10; 1 Sam. 27:5; 2 Sam. 14:22). He then claims to have learned by some type of divination that Yahweh had blessed him because of Jacob. Elsewhere in the Old Testament divination – using occult methods to learn of God's will – is condemned (Lev. 19:26; Deut. 18:10; 2 Kgs 17:17; 21:6; 2 Chr. 33:6). Next Laban once again invites Jacob to name his wages (see 29:15). It appears that Laban was unconcerned about giving Jacob the privilege of setting the terms of their agreement because Laban never exhibited any commitment to keeping his obligations (cf. 29:23–26; 31:6–7).

29–34. Jacob's reply begins with his account of his work for Laban. This is the first mention of the kind of work he did: tending Laban's animals. Laban's increased wealth because of Jacob's work was noticeable over the fourteen years he had served for his two wives. From that alone he could state *Yahweh has blessed you because of me* (v. 30). Divination was not needed to see the growth in Laban's wealth, and only faith could know its source. But Jacob's real concern was that he needed to do something for his own household. His words emphasize that he needed to benefit materially from his own work.

When Laban again asks Jacob what his wages should be, Jacob asks for nothing – that is, Laban will not have to give Jacob any silver or other currency. Instead, Jacob will settle for all of the variegated goats and dark sheep among Laban's flock. Since sheep were normally all white and goats normally all dark (brown or black), Jacob was offering to receive a distinct minority of the future offspring of the flocks. Variegated goats – streaked, spotted or speckled – or dark sheep were a small minority of the animals. Jacob proposed to begin his own flock with Laban's few irregular animals.

His rationale was that this would be a simple way of checking whether he had taken any animals out of Laban's flock that he would also be tending. Laban's ready agreement was deceptive, because he did not plan on giving Jacob any animals.

35–36. Laban did not wait for Jacob to remove the agreed animals from the flock. Instead, he himself removed them and gave them to his sons. He then separated his sons' flocks from Jacob so that there could be no way for Jacob to claim those animals. In this way Laban thought to limit Jacob's gain when the animals mated, since all-dark goats and all-white sheep would produce few animals for Jacob. In effect, Laban thought he could practise selective breeding by leaving Jacob with a gene pool of animals with the dominant trait that would produce very few variegated goats or dark sheep.[8] In addition, Laban was already cheating Jacob by reducing the flock before Jacob could separate the agreed-upon animals into his own starter flock.

37–40. Jacob, however, had a plan, making use of branches from three different trees placed into the drinking water of the animals. One of the names of the trees – the poplar – forms a pun in Hebrew with Laban's name, giving this account of Jacob's technique an ironic twist. Jacob's efforts produced variegated animals. It has been commonly thought that Jacob's procedure was simply superstition or a folk custom that was not actually responsible for the fur colour of the sheep.[9] However, it has been recently proposed that Jacob's use of the branches actually has an explanation in epigenetics – heritable changes in gene expression without a change in an organism's DNA.[10] It is now known that prenatal nutrition can affect gene expression. Jacob's stripping the bark from the branches may have exposed some nutrient that was then in the drinking water of the pregnant animals, thereby changing the colour of the coats of the young that they bore. Jacob also separated the

---

8. Although the ancients had no knowledge of molecular genetics, they did understand selective breeding of animals in order to enhance or suppress various traits.

9. Hamilton (1995: 284); Mathews (2005: 591).

10. Backon (2008).

flocks (v. 40) so that his animals did not mate with Laban's, thereby limiting the number of fully dark animals that would be born in his own flock.

41–43. In addition, Jacob practised selective breeding. He specifically bred the more vigorous animals to be variegated, but allowed the more feeble animals to produce solid-coloured young. While his flock remained healthy and vital, Laban's became less fit. Finally, we are told that Jacob's success with the flocks made him so wealthy that he could afford slaves and pack animals.

Meaning

Jacob arrived in Paddan-aram with few possessions and no way to pay the bride price in order to marry into Laban's family. Moreover, his uncle was deceitful and materialistic, seeking to take advantage of Jacob at every opportunity. Laban even used his daughters to get the most work out of Jacob. Then, when he had no more hold over Jacob, he sought to cheat the patriarch in his wages.

Jacob's life was also beset with strife in his own household as Leah and Rachel vied for his attention, approval and affection. Rachel confronted him with an unreasonable demand (30:1), and Leah purchased his affections with her son's mandrakes (30:16). In addition, heartache would also be the lot of his wives – a consequence of Laban's deceptive acts. Through her fertility, Leah would continually look for her husband's esteem, but never seem to get what she wished. Rachel would be unable to bear a child for seven years, envying her sister who bore six sons during that period.

Despite the difficulties of these twenty years, God continued to give blessings to Abraham's grandchild: his family grew to twelve children, and eventually a thirteenth child (Benjamin) would be added (see 35:16–18). He eventually was able to gain wealth to support that family. All of this was God's work. Jacob may have determined the colour of the fur of his animals through the obscure use of branches in the watering troughs and selective breeding, but even he knew that all of this would have yielded no gain without God's blessing (31:4–8). But the Lord's blessings did not stop there: the eleven sons of Jacob were the first sign of the great nation promised to Abraham. At this point, eleven of the twelve tribes of Israel were named, and contained within them was the promise of the Messiah.

Additional note on the chronology of the births of Jacob's children

It may at first seem difficult to fit the births of Jacob's twelve children into the seven years between his marriages to Leah and Rachel in 1923 BC and the birth of Joseph in 1916 BC.[11] However, Genesis clearly indicates that the eleven sons were born in the seven years when Jacob worked for Laban in payment of his bride price for Rachel (31:41) (see Table 14 on p. 292). Leah bore six sons during this time. Reuben, therefore, had to be born in 1922 BC (29:32). Simeon followed in 1921. The next year Levi was born (29:34), and Judah one year later in 1919 (29:35).

Jacob's concubines also bore four sons. Most likely Bilhah was given to Jacob when Leah was pregnant with Judah so that her first son Dan was born about 1919 (30:1–6). Sometime later Bilhah bore Naphtali – probably in 1918 or 1917 (30:7–8).

Some months after bearing Judah, Leah noticed that she had not become pregnant again. This probably was during the first half of 1918. In her competition with Rachel, she gave Zilpah to Jacob, and Zilpah bore Gad, probably early the next year. Zilpah's second son was probably born in early 1916 (30:12–13), because he had to have been born before Joseph, who was the youngest of the eleven sons of Jacob born in Paddan-aram.

Leah also bore two more sons before Joseph's birth in 1916. Therefore the births of Issachar and Zebulun must have occurred early in 1917 and early in 1916 (30:14–20). Most likely, Dinah, who according to 30:21 was born 'later', was born in 1915. This is confirmed by the narrative about her at 34:1–31. At that time, as Jacob lived near Shechem in 1902, Dinah would have been about thirteen years old – she had reached puberty and the minimum

---

11. For the evidence and reasoning leading to these dates, see Steinmann (2011: 35–76).

marriageable age. A year later Rachel died in childbirth, bearing
Benjamin near Bethlehem (35:16–20).

Table 14 The births of Jacob's children

Year	Leah	Rachel	Bilhah	Zilpah
1922	Reuben			
1921	Simeon			
1920	Levi			
1919	Judah		Dan	
1918			Naphtali	
1917	Issachar			Gad
1916	Zebulun	Joseph		Asher
1915	Dinah			
1901		Benjamin		

18. THE FAMILY OF ISAAC: JACOB RETURNS TO THE PROMISED LAND (31:1 – 33:20)

The accounts in these three chapters revolve around Jacob's three struggles that he engages with as he returns to the land of Canaan. He will be pursued by Laban, whose manipulative and exploitative ways kept him in Haran for twenty years. His escape from Laban is aided by God, who warns Laban concerning his treatment of Jacob (31:24) and shows his blessing on Jacob's return by sending his angels (32:1–2). Jacob also will have to face his brother Esau, whose murderous intentions had led to his being sent to Haran. Although Jacob anticipates trouble with his brother, Esau's greeting is cordial and even poignant (33:4). Between these two encounters Jacob will spend a night wrestling with a stranger whom he will come to realize is God (32:30). God will pronounce Jacob victorious in his struggles (32:28).

Jacob's arrival in Canaan marks his claim on the land first promised to Abraham and passed on to him by Isaac's blessing (see 27:28). That claim, however, can only be realized by God's blessing. Therefore, God's warning to Laban and his granting Jacob the name *Israel* are key to these narratives concerning Jacob's arrival in the

Promised Land. Jacob acknowledged that God's blessings accompanied him back to Canaan (33:5, 10–11). His purchase of land near Shechem presses his claim on the land which he connects with God, the God of Israel (33:20).

A. Jacob leaves Paddan-aram (31:1–21)

Context
April or May 1910 BC
Jacob's departure took place at the time of sheep shearing – late April or early May (31:19). While Jacob had observed that he had fallen out of favour with Laban (31:2), it was not his decision to leave; it was God's prompting and promise to be with him that precipitated Jacob's sudden parting from Laban (31:3).

Comment
1–3. Jacob somehow heard about the accusations made against him by Laban's sons. Their complaints were surely unjust, considering that Jacob had been underpaid for the fourteen years of service he had given to Laban (cf. 30:30) and Laban's cheating on their agreement during the last six years (30:35–36; 31:7, 41). Nevertheless, these accusations caused Jacob to pay closer attention to Laban's attitude towards him and learn that his avaricious father-in-law was no longer looking at him favourably. God knew Jacob's predicament and instructed him to return to Canaan. Interestingly, this call to return came with the same promise of God to be with Jacob as was given him as he left Canaan, and recalls God's previous appearance to him (28:15).
4–9. Jacob, however, did not trust Laban. So in order to speak to his wives in private, he summoned them to the flocks in the field away from town (v. 4). His conversation with Leah and Rachel is long by biblical standards and serves to demonstrate to readers the reasons for Jacob's departure: Laban's attitude and duplicity, the disenchantment of his wives with their father, and – most importantly – God's instructions and promises. Jacob's opening words to his wives contrast Laban's actions with God's:

Laban's attitude has changed	but God is with Jacob (v. 5)
Laban cheated Jacob despite his honest work	but God did not allow Jacob to be harmed (vv. 6–7)
Laban's changing designation of Jacob's portion	God gave the herds to Jacob (vv. 8–9)

Throughout this speech Jacob never refers to Laban by name, but always calls him *your father* (vv. 5, 6, 7, 9). This contrasts with God whom he calls *the God of my father* (v. 5). In this way he sought to persuade Rachel and Leah that his father – and, more importantly, his father's God – was more welcoming to them than their father.

In addition, Jacob made a claim about Laban's cheating – a Hebrew word that also carries the connotation of deception (Job 13:9; Isa. 30:10). In this case the deception was Laban's constant changing of the terms of Jacob's wages. Jacob was supposed to receive all the variegated sheep (30:32), but Laban made it more specific: spotted sheep and then streaked sheep (v. 8). Jacob's statement that his wages were changed *ten times* (v. 7) is probably hyperbole and uses a round number to make his point (see also v. 41).

10–13. To press his case further Jacob also related what apparently was a recent dream.[1] In his account of the dream Jacob identified the speaker as *the angel of God* (v. 11). The angel assured Jacob that he knew Laban's ways and was in control of the breeding

---

1. Awassi sheep – the species found throughout the Near East – breed as early as April (A. Q. Talafha and M. M. Ababneh, 'Awassi Sheep Reproduction and Milk Production: A Review', *Tropical Animal Health and Production* (2011) 43: 1319, <https://doi.org/10.1007/s11250-011-9858-5>, accessed 12 January 2018). The domestic goat (*capra hircus*) breeds from late summer through to early winter (Adam Mileski, '*Capra hircus*: Domestic Goat', Animal Diversity Web, accessed 12 January 2018, <http://animaldiversity.org/accounts/Capra_hircus/>). Depending on what he meant by *when the flocks were mating* (v. 10), this would indicate that Jacob's dream took place either in early winter, about November, if he saw goats mating, or in early April.

so that only steaked, spotted and speckled rams mated with the ewes and female goats. The angel then identified himself as *the God of Bethel* (v. 13) to whom Jacob had made a vow (see 28:22). It was now time to return to the land and, by implication, for Jacob to keep his vow to tithe when he returned to Canaan.

14–16. Rachel and Leah did not need to be convinced of the need to leave for Canaan. They recognized that there was no benefit for them in staying in their father's household. He had treated them like commodities to be sold (v. 15). Moreover, he had spent the purchase price he got for them. It was expected that when a father received a bride price he would keep it in reserve to support his daughters and their children in the event that they lost their husbands. However, Laban had not done this. Instead, they recognized that God had extracted this wealth from their greedy father and given it to them.

17–18. Jacob put his wives and children on camels to facilitate their rapid departure. He, however, stayed on foot, bringing his possessions and driving his herds ahead of him. This picture of Jacob, therefore, serves as a contrast to Laban. Whereas Laban valued his prosperity more than his daughters, Jacob put the welfare of his wives and children above his own.

19–21. Two furtive acts took place when Jacob left Haran. First, we are told that when Laban had gone to shear his sheep, an activity that normally took place in an outlying location and required considerable manpower (38:12–13; 1 Sam. 25:2; 2 Sam. 13:23), Rachel stole *her father's teraphim*. These are later referred to as Laban's gods (vv. 30, 32). Often these are identified as household gods. Based on fifteenth-century BC documents from the ancient city of Nuzi in upper Mesopotamia, it is often supposed that Rachel took these images because possession of them identified the legal heir of the family estate.[2] However, it is not certain that that is what the Nuzi documents indicate.[3] Moreover, it is hard to see how Rachel or one of her sons could have pressed a claim upon Laban's estate from faraway Canaan. Others view Rachel's theft as an act designed to use

---

2. See the discussions in Greenberg (1962) and van der Toorn (1990).

3. Mathews (2005: 518–519).

these gods as protection on the journey, since 35:2–4 indicates that some members of Jacob's family had such gods in their possession as objects of worship.[4] It is also possible, however, that the teraphim were cast from some precious metal and that Rachel simply took them for their value as currency (cf. Judg. 17:3–5). The context would suggest this, since she and her sister felt that Laban had wasted the value of Jacob's labour that was paid for them (v. 16).[5]

The second furtive act was Jacob's leaving without notifying Laban, crossing the Euphrates River southwards and heading for Gilead east of the Sea of Galilee. This deception was most likely viewed as disregarding proper etiquette, as implied later by Laban (vv. 27–28). Laban is called *Laban the Aramean* (vv. 20, 24), thereby emphasizing that his homeland was different from Jacob's.

Meaning

Jacob's departure from Laban's household was originally to have taken place at a time when his mother summoned him home to Canaan (27:45). That summons never came. Instead, Jacob left when God called him to return to the Promised Land. This was the first step in God bringing Jacob safely back to what he had characterized as *my father's family* (28:21). There were two more hurdles to clear before that would be accomplished: he would have to survive Laban's pursuit of him, and he would have to meet Esau. In what follows we will see that God provided Jacob with safe passage back to Canaan both by speaking to Laban in a dream (31:29) and by providing Esau with plenty, so that he no longer resented Jacob's having stolen the blessing from Isaac (33:9).

B. Jacob and Laban part ways (31:22–55 [MT 31:22 – 32:1])

Context

1910 BC

Although Laban came in pursuit of Jacob, it is difficult to understand what he hoped to accomplish. Jacob had rightly taken his

---

4. Wenham (1994: 274); Hamilton (1995: 295).

5. Mathews (2005: 520).

wives and the animals in his flock. While his abrupt and un-
announced departure may have been a breach of etiquette, it was
hardly a crime. Despite Laban's accusations (vv. 26–30), the only
substantive charge he could make against Jacob was that his
gods had been stolen. Even that, however, was speculation, since
no-one had witnessed the theft, and all Laban could state with any
certainty was that the teraphim were missing. While the reader knows
that Rachel had taken the teraphim, no-one else was aware of that
fact. This lends tension to the first part of the interaction between
Jacob and Laban (vv. 25–35). The second part of their interaction
(vv. 36–55) revolves around Laban's inability to acknowledge that he
no longer had a claim on Jacob's wives, sons and flocks.

Comment
i. Laban pursues Jacob (31:22–35)
22–23. Word did not reach Laban until the third day of Jacob's
flight from Haran. We are also told that Laban took his kinsmen
with him and pursued Jacob for seven days. Many commentators
assume that seven days is an idiom and not to be taken literally.[6] It
would hardly have been possible for Jacob and his party, including
his flocks, to cover the distance from Haran to the hill country of
Gilead – some 350 miles (560 km) – in ten days. However, there is
no indication in the text that Laban left *immediately* upon hearing
that Jacob had fled. Sheep shearing was a labour-intensive task that
involved hiring large numbers of labourers. It would have been very
costly for Laban simply to abandon the shearing by dismissing his
labourers before they had finished. So it may be that Laban was
forced to wait some days before beginning his seven-day pursuit of
Jacob.
24. God's promise to protect Jacob now came in the form of a
dream message to Laban. In English versions God's message to
Laban was that he should not say anything to Jacob *either good
or bad*.[7] However, the Hebrew text says *from good to bad*. This

---

6. Wenham (1994: 274); Hamilton (1995: 299); Mathews (2005: 522).

7. CSB, ESV, NIV, NRSV, TNK. This is different from the phrase in Hebrew
good or bad meaning 'anything' (see 24:50).

expression occurs only here and in Laban's recounting of God's words (v. 29). It likely indicated that God was prohibiting Laban from his former deceptive practice of saying something to Jacob which appeared to be good but which he then turned into something disadvantageous to Jacob, thereby justifying Jacob's charge that Laban frequently changed his wages (vv. 7, 41). Certainly Laban did not understand it to mean that he could not say anything – either good or bad – to Jacob, since he said quite a lot (vv. 26–30, 43–44, 48–53).[8]

25–28. Jacob had not reached his ultimate destination when Laban overtook him. The camps were set up in the hill country of Gilead, the region east of the Jordan River between the Yarmuk and Jabbok Rivers that would later become part of the territory of the tribe of Manasseh.

Laban's first words to Jacob are ironic, since *What have you done?* (v. 26) mirrors the words used by Jacob when Laban deceived him and gave him Leah instead of Rachel (29:25). Laban then accused Jacob of forcibly removing his daughters. This, of course, not only is in error, since Rachel and Leah had agreed to leave Haran (vv. 14–16), but it also attempted to subordinate Jacob's role as husband to Laban's role as father.

Laban's further outrage, however, appears to be less than sincere and more for public demonstration. He questions why Jacob would flee without notice, although given his actions over the last twenty years the answer to his question should have been obvious. Laban's description of the supposed grand send-off he would have given Jacob and his family complete with kisses for his daughters and grandchildren surely strikes most readers as if he is trying too hard to press a weak and lost case. Surely a man who was so miserly as to cheat Jacob out of a few speckled and spotted goats and dark sheep (30:25–36) was not about to cheerfully finance an ostentatious farewell.

---

8. The suggestion of Clark (1969: 269) that this expression forbade Laban from pursuing any legal claim against Jacob, even one that was justified, is contradicted by Jacob's words in v. 32 which understand Laban as having a legal right to prosecute just claims.

Finally, Laban accused Jacob of acting foolishly (v. 28). Yet in this incident it appears that Laban is the fool. He was caught unawares by Jacob's departure and was oblivious to his estrangement from his daughters.

29. Laban's next claim – that he had power to do harm to Jacob's family[9] – was more posturing on Laban's part. Laban had no right to punish Jacob for leaving. He had no claim over his daughters, whom he had legally given in marriage to Jacob and for whom Jacob had rendered fourteen years of labour. Neither could he claim the flocks, since Jacob had also received them for six years of labour. Nevertheless, Laban asserts these claims throughout this encounter with Jacob (cf. v. 43). Laban might even have taken violent action to retrieve his daughters and the animals had not – as he himself admitted – God intervened and warned him not to do any such thing.

30. Finally, Laban accused Jacob of returning simply because he was homesick for his family. This allegation demonstrates to the reader Laban's ignorance that has led him to make unfounded statements. While Jacob may have missed his family, he left because of Laban's actions and attitude (vv. 2, 6–8) and at God's command (vv. 3, 13). However, Laban's charge of homesickness on Jacob's part was intended as a lead-in to the most damning indictment of Jacob: that he had stolen Laban's gods. Every other action of Jacob was understandable in the light of Jacob's longing for home, Laban was implying, but the theft of gods was inexplicable. What good would gods foreign to Canaan do for Jacob? After all, Jacob's God, the God of Isaac, had spoken to Laban, and Laban had respected his warning. Why had Jacob not respected Laban's gods?

31–32. Jacob's first reply to Laban addresses his father-in-law's charge that he was foolish to leave Laban's household without advance notice. Jacob was afraid that Laban would do what he claimed to be able to do: great harm to Jacob by taking his wives away from him. In essence, Jacob was turning Laban's accusation back on him. Laban had acted faithlessly before, and Jacob was afraid he would once again renege on his agreements if Jacob

---

9. In the phrase *do you great harm*, the pronoun *you* is plural.

announced his intention to return to Canaan. Laban, he thought, would forcibly remove Leah and Rachel (and perhaps also their children, cf. v. 43), and Jacob would return home with none of the family he had built in Haran. In regard to Laban's final charge of theft, of course, Jacob knew nothing concerning the whereabouts of Laban's gods. The reader knows this, and it serves to build the tension in the narrative. Laban assumed Jacob's guilt, and Jacob knew he was innocent. Leah, Jacob's sons and Jacob's concubines knew nothing about the theft. Only Rachel, the beloved wife, was involved, and Jacob could indeed suffer grievous harm at Laban's hand should she be found to be in possession of the teraphim.

Jacob's denial of Laban's claim is so emphatic that he endangered the wife he loved so much, granting Laban even the right to execute anyone found to have taken the teraphim. He felt so righteous in this instance that he defied Laban to find anything that was his and willingly ceded that Laban could take any such item that he found. The text, however, immediately undercuts Jacob's bold words by reminding readers that Jacob was ignorant of Rachel's larceny.

33. The tension in the story builds as Laban's search starts with Jacob's tent and then proceeds to the tents of three of Jacob's wives – Leah and his two concubines. It appears that, despite the order in which the text mentions the tents belonging to Jacob's wives, Laban first searched the concubines' tents before entering the tent of his elder daughter Leah. Then, leaving Leah's tent, he entered Rachel's. Thus, Laban trusted Jacob the least of all, and he trusted the concubines less than his daughters. Laban's action in searching his daughters' tents last also demonstrates his growing realization that he was mistaken in his assumption that Jacob had taken them against their will (cf. v. 26).

34–35. Before reporting the search of Rachel's tent, the text inserts a parenthetical comment. Rachel, whose tent was searched last, had time to devise a plan to conceal the teraphim from her father. The gods must have been small images, since she was able to put them in her camel's saddlebag and sit on it inside the tent while Laban searched it. Rachel's garment may have concealed the saddlebag, so that he could not detect Rachel's duplicity. Twice we are told that Laban searched Rachel's tent. Between those two statements we find out how Rachel avoided standing out of respect when her father entered the tent thereby exposing the saddlebag to Laban's examination: she claimed she was in the midst of her menstruation. It is impossible to know whether she was telling the truth about this, but to the ancient Israelite reader this would also signal a fitting condemnation of Laban's devotion to these pagan idols even if Rachel was simply deceiving her father about her menstruation. They are portrayed as defiled, since anything upon which a menstruating woman sat was rendered ceremonially unclean under the laws given by Moses (Lev. 15:20). What kind of god allows himself to be desecrated like this? Only a god who is no god, an idol that has no life and no real existence, would allow this to happen (Pss 96:5; 106:28; Isa. 37:19).

ii. Jacob's covenant with Laban (31:36–55 [MT 31:36 – 32:1])

36–37. With Laban's search a failure, we are told that Jacob felt justified in venting his anger and in disputing Laban's actions. He begins with two challenging questions: *What is my crime?* and *What is my sin that you came in hot pursuit of me?* (v. 36). Laban offered no answer, and none was expected, since these were rhetorical questions that assumed that they had already been answered by Laban's search: there was no crime or sin. The next, more specific question and challenge to Laban ramped up the rhetoric: had Laban found anything? Jacob defied him to produce it as evidence to be viewed by witnesses on both sides – *my relatives and yours* (v. 37).

38–41. Having silenced Laban's accusation, Jacob now proceeded to build a case for his own accusations. He notes his diligence in his work for Laban during the last twenty years:

1. Because of his careful oversight the ewes and female goats had not miscarried (v. 38).
2. Jacob had not helped himself to the rams as food (v. 38; one normally ate the rams, not the ewes or female goats, since it was the females who bore the young, and one needed only a few rams to impregnate all the females).
3. Jacob had borne the loss for any animals that were killed by wild animals (v. 39). In the Ancient Near East, shepherds

generally were not held liable for such losses.[10] Jacob claimed, however, that at Laban's insistence he had been required to go beyond what was normally expected of a shepherd.

Moreover, Jacob did all of this in the harsh outdoors of the Syrian wilderness, with its blistering heat of the day and chilling cold of the night (v. 40).

With this evidence of his diligence in his labours, Jacob set out his complaint. He had worked for specific wages over these twenty years, and he laid them out in detail: fourteen years for two daughters and six for the flocks (v. 41). Then came Jacob's devastating accusation that he had made previously, but only to Rachel and Leah: Laban continually changed his wages (cf. v. 7). The charge of failing to pay a worker the wages due is one of the most damning accusations that can be brought against an employer and is roundly condemned elsewhere in Scripture (Lev. 19:13; Job 7:2; Mal. 3:5; 1 Cor. 9:7–12; 1 Tim. 5:18).

42. Jacob went on to note that while Laban may have tried to cheat on their agreement, God had set things aright despite Laban's actions. All along God had observed Jacob's conscientious labour and had provided wages that Laban would not (cf. v. 9). Jacob's titles for God are important here. He calls him *the God of my father, the God of Abraham, the Fear of Isaac.* Laban had accused Jacob of absconding for Canaan because he was homesick for his father's family (v. 30). Jacob, however, returned to Canaan because of his father's God (cf. v. 3). The title *Fear of Isaac* occurs only in this narrative in all of Scripture (cf. v. 53). There have been other proposals as to the proper translation of this phrase.[11] However, *Fear of Isaac* best fits the context. Isaac's God is the God who can implant fear into the hearts of those who seek to harm his people. That is exactly what God did when he spoke to Laban (see vv. 24, 29).

43–44. Laban's reaction to Jacob's accusation is pathetic, and one can almost hear him whining as he asserts his right to his daughters

---

10. See, for example, Code of Hammurabi 266. *ANET* 177. See also Exod. 22:12.

11. Wenham (1994: 278); Hamilton (1995: 308–310); Mathews (2005: 529–530).

and their children as well as the flocks. *Everything you see is mine!*, he protested (v. 43), though he could offer no rightful claim in the face of Jacob's diatribe. Instead, he utters a face-saving rhetorical question of his own: what could he do to benefit his daughters and children? That is, Laban will make a show of being the magnanimous father by urging Jacob to enter into a covenant with him. Note that whenever someone sought to make a covenant or a binding oath with one of the patriarchs, it was invariably an admission of the patriarch's superior rights and claims (cf. 21:22–24; 26:26–31). Because Laban found himself in a weak position, he wanted a covenant in order to protect himself from Jacob, whom God had defended.

45–47. Jacob did not reply to Laban, and the author records no further words of Jacob to Laban throughout the rest of the chapter. Jacob has made his case, and Laban is now in the position of seeking Jacob's cooperation. Jacob's replies to Laban come in the form of action. First he set up a stone, much as he had done at Bethel when he left Canaan for Haran (28:18). That first stone came at a transition point in his life, and this one does also. He is signalling his independence from his father-in-law, just as his independence from his father was confirmed by God's blessing at Bethel (cf. 28:13–15). Then Jacob ordered his relatives to gather stones for a second marker, a mound where they also ate a meal. Meals could be part of making a covenant, a binding agreement between two parties (26:30–31; Exod. 24:11). Both Jacob and Laban named the heap of stones. Laban called it *Jegar-sahadutha* (v. 47), using Aramaic, the language of ancient Syria. This may well be part of the reason why he is called *Laban the Aramean* twice in this chapter but nowhere else (see vv. 20, 24). Jacob, on the other hand, used the language of his people, Hebrew, calling the heap *Galeed*. Both names mean 'mound of witness'. However, the Hebrew name forms a play on words with the name of the region Gilead, where Galeed was located (cf. v. 25). Thus, Jacob's wordplay reinforces his superior position with respect to Laban.

48–50. Laban affirmed the function of the mound of stones as witness to the covenant between himself and Jacob. The editorial comment that the place is known as both Galeed and Mizpah looks both backward to Laban's statement (*witness*, v. 49, referring to

Galeed) and forward (*Mizpah*, meaning 'watchtower') since Laban also called on Yahweh to watch between the two of them (v. 49). Laban's warning to Jacob about mistreating his daughters is ironic and also portrays Laban as virtually clueless as to his own treatment of them (cf. vv. 14–16). He cannot quite bring himself to acknowledge that his daughters are rightfully Jacob's wives (cf. v. 43), yet he calls on Yahweh to watch that Jacob take no other wives.

51–53. Laban next explains the mound as a boundary marker between Jacob and Laban that neither will cross to do the other harm. Laban's final statement affirms his polytheistic beliefs, since it is an oath in the name of multiple gods – the God of Abraham but also the gods of Nahor (v. 53).[12] While some English versions read 'the god of Nahor' (ESV, NET, NIV, NRSV, TNK), Joshua 24:2, 14–15 affirms that Israel's ancestors – including Terah and his sons – worshipped many gods. Therefore, it is best to understand Laban as calling on *the gods of Nahor* (cf. CSB). Jacob, as a monotheist, took his oath to the covenant by *the Fear of his father Isaac*, the description of Yahweh that he had used earlier (see v. 42).

54–55. The sacrifice and communal meal sealed the oaths. Laban's departure the next day is a picture of what he claimed he would have done for his daughters had Jacob made his intentions known before fleeing Haran (cf. vv. 27–28).

Meaning
Laban's pursuit of Jacob increases the tension from the first part of the chapter where Jacob had fled Haran without informing Laban. When Laban's overtaking Jacob and his party is related, the reader is given a greater insight into why Jacob was highly suspicious of Laban: Laban pressed a claim on his daughters although he had married them to Jacob and had received the agreed-upon bride price. Laban even claimed authority over Jacob's children and flocks (31:43)! However, Laban's enforcing those claims was checked by God (31:29). The one rightful claim he had – ownership of the household gods that Rachel had stolen – he was unable to prove to be legitimate. In the end, he was forced to make an agreement with

---

12. The Hebrew verb for *will judge* is plural.

Jacob, a covenant that permanently separated him from Jacob and also, therefore, from his daughters and grandchildren. As the covenant is sealed it is clear that Jacob's God, the *Fear of his father Isaac* (31:53), had delivered Jacob from his rapacious uncle, while the idols worshipped by Laban – the gods of Nahor – were powerless.

C. Jacob returns to Canaan (32:1 – 33:20 [MT 32:2 – 33:20])

Context

1910 BC

With the departure of Laban, the narrative turns its focus on Jacob's return to the Promised Land. In this section Jacob encounters angels (32:1–2), God (32:24–31) and finally Esau (33:1–17). Parallels with Jacob's departure twenty years earlier are evident in this narrative: angels and God appeared to him in his dream at Bethel (28:10–22); when Jacob prays to be rescued from his brother Esau his words echo Yahweh's promises at Bethel (cf. 32:9, 12 with 28:13–15); and God's first steps in fulfilling the promise to make Jacob's descendants numerous (28:14) are emphasized several times (32:10–12; 33:1–2, 5–7).

Jacob's return to Canaan could not be complete without an attempt to reconcile with his twin brother. He had left Canaan to escape Esau's murderous threats (27:41–42), and he was to return when his mother saw that Esau's anger had subsided (27:45). However, Rebekah never summoned him. Instead, Jacob was returning at God's command (31:3). Much of the tension in this section is built upon Jacob's fear of Esau's wrath contrasted with God's promises and blessings bestowed upon Jacob (32:12, 29).

Comment

i. Jacob sends word to Esau of his return (32:1–23 [MT 32:2–24])

1–2. Jacob's encounter with God's angels marked his separation from Laban and his return to the Promised Land, just as his dream of the angels at Bethel denoted his departure from the land and from his family (28:10–22). Moreover, just as he recognized the place where he saw God and his angels as God's house, naming it *Bethel* (28:17, 19), so, too, he recognized this spot as God's camp and named it *Mahanaim*, meaning 'two camps' (v. 2). It would become a

Levitical city in Gad (Josh. 13:26; 21:38) and also the capital of Ishbosheth's short-lived kingdom (2 Sam. 2:8–9). David would find refuge there during Absalom's rebellion (2 Sam. 17:24). The information in these passages locates it a short distance north of the Jabbok River. The word *camp* will be a theme term in this account of Jacob meeting Esau, occurring six times (vv. 2, 7, 8, 10, 21; 33:8).[13] It is not clear why Jacob chose to call this place 'two camps' instead of *God's camp*.[14] However, it ought to be noted that Jacob would soon divide his entourage into two camps (vv. 7, 8, 10).

3–5. The two camps supply two sets of messengers: God's angels and now the messengers that Jacob sent to Esau. (The Hebrew word translated *angel* is the same word for *messenger*.) The messengers are sent to Esau's adopted land, referred to both as *the land of Seir* and *the territory of Edom* (v. 3). *Seir* recalls Esau's hair (Hebrew *śēʿār*, 'hair', and *śāʿîr*, 'hairy'; 25:25; 27:11, 23). *Edom* references Esau's sale of his birthright to Jacob for a serving of red stew (Hebrew *ʾādōm*; 25:30) as well as his red (Hebrew *ʾadmônî*) hair (25:25). Jacob's message appears to reverse the blessing of his father Isaac that he would be master over his relatives (27:29). Jacob used terms that depicted him as subservient to Esau. He calls himself *your servant* (v. 4), a term of self-abasement before an overlord. He calls Esau *my lord* (v. 5). Most importantly, he sent the messengers *to seek your favour*. This is language that is typically reserved for a subordinate who is hoping to obtain acceptance from a superior (Exod. 33:13; 2 Sam. 16:4).

6–8. The messengers returned with news but without a message from Esau. His entourage of four hundred men was impressive – but was it a sign of Esau's favour or of aggression? The men may simply have been an indication of Esau's prosperity, a counterpart to Jacob's many animals and slaves (cf. v. 5). Without any indication of Esau's intent, Jacob, though frightened, was not paralysed with fear. Realizing that he could not mount an active defence against

---

13. *Camp* is used only seven times in all of Genesis (see 50:9: 'procession' [CSB]; 'company' [ESV, NIV, NRSV]).

14. See the discussion in Wenham (1994: 245); Hamilton (1995: 317–318); Mathews (2005: 547–548).

Esau's large party should they attack, he devised a more passive strategy of dividing his people and animals into two camps – just like the name of the place where God's angels met him. This would allow one to survive if the other was attacked.

9–12. Jacob's prayer was clearly prompted by his fear of what Esau might do to him and his family (v. 11). However, it was also a prayer of faith that emphasized God's promises to him and called on Yahweh to honour his pledges.

The opening of the prayer calls on the *God of my father Abraham and God of my father Isaac* (v. 9), mimicking the way Yahweh had identified himself to Jacob twenty years earlier when he had fled Canaan in fear of Esau (28:13). At that time God had promised to give the land to Jacob's offspring. By addressing God this way, Jacob was reminding God of that promise and implying that Yahweh now had a responsibility to protect Jacob's children. Jacob also reminded God of his recent command to return to Canaan, using language that is nearly word-for-word the same as God's (cf. 31:3). Jacob paraphrased God's promise to be with him as *I will cause you to prosper* (v. 9, CSB).

Jacob admitted that he did not deserve God's favour, yet noted that God had already begun to keep his promises: Jacob had left Canaan with only a staff and was now returning as a large family – two camps. Yet in his prayer he openly admits his fear of Esau and his concern for his family. Like all believers, Jacob had both trust in God's promises but also doubts or concerns in the face of trials and dangers.

Finally, Jacob appealed to God's pledge that he would make his offspring *like the sand of the sea, too numerous to be counted* (v. 12). Here Jacob was stating his belief that he was heir to God's promises to Abraham, to whom this promise had been given (see 22:17). Jacob also expressed his understanding of that promise by interpreting it as offspring beyond numbering.

13–16. Apparently still near Mahanaim, *he spent the night there* (v. 13). The time was passed in activity that demonstrated his frantic search for a way to appease his brother and prepare for the worst. He not only set aside a large number of animals as a present for his brother – 550 in all – but he also gave Esau the most valuable: many more female animals than males. The females ensured the growth of even larger herds, since they would bear the young. A comparatively smaller number of males were included, since a single male goat or a ram or bull could impregnate numerous female goats, ewes or cows. The lactating camels and their young were a more exotic gift, but of little use to Esau as a settled inhabitant in the mountains of Seir. They were more valuable to caravanning merchants who might have travelled throughout Mesopotamia or through Canaan to Egypt.

17–18. Jacob's instructions to his servants who would take the animals ahead of him anticipated Esau's reaction. In addition, they also sought to mollify his brother, not only with gifts but also in his attitude, presenting himself as *your servant Jacob* and his brother as *my lord Esau* (v. 18; cf. vv. 4–5).

19–20. Emphasizing to the second and third servants he sent that they were to repeat the same message given to the first servant, Jacob clearly was hoping that three waves of herds as gifts would demonstrate his extreme humility and regret for having stolen Isaac's blessing. Jacob's thought about how to reconcile with Esau is a fourfold play on the word *face* (v. 20): he hoped to *appease* Esau (the Hebrew idiom 'cover his face') by sending a gift *ahead of me* (the Hebrew idiom 'walking to my face') so that Jacob could then *face* Esau (literally 'see his face') so that perhaps Esau might *forgive me* (the Hebrew idiom 'lift my face').

21–23. After sending his servants with the presents, Jacob spent the night in the camp. Yet in the middle of the night, he took his family and sent them across the Jabbok River with the rest of his possessions. This left Jacob alone for his most important encounter with Yahweh.

ii. Jacob wrestles with God (32:24–32 [MT 32:25–33])

24–25. Why Jacob remained alone on the north side of the Jabbok River is not stated. Perhaps he was simply ensuring that no-one was left behind. The text, however, contains an abrupt transition to a wrestling match with a man. The reader is given no other identification of this person, heightening the mystery of what is happening with Jacob. However, there is another multiple play on words that alerts readers to the importance of this encounter from the beginning. It involves three words which have three consonants in common, *b, y, q: Jabbok* (Hebrew *ybbq*, v. 23), *Jacob* (Hebrew *y'qb*, v. 25) and *wrestled* (Hebrew *wy'bq*, v. 25). The struggle between Jacob and the man is not described or explained. Instead the narrative simply skips immediately to the end of the scuffle when the man realized that he could not defeat Jacob and instead struck him on the hollow of his thigh, dislocating Jacob's hip. This reveals the man's extreme power, since the dislocation of a hip joint normally occurs during high-energy impacts.[15] This supplied Jacob with the first hint of the identity of his adversary. By this point the reader, too, must suspect that this is no ordinary man – it is God in his manifestation as the Angel of God (cf. v. 30; 48:15–16; Hos. 12:3–4). That God could not prevail in a wrestling match with Jacob might strike some readers as incomprehensible. However, here God is depicted as assuming human form and, therefore, also imposing upon himself the physical limits of a man until the very end of the struggle.

26–28. Having disabled his opponent, the man demanded that Jacob release his hold, since the new day was dawning. There has been much discussion as to why dawn would necessitate that Jacob let loose the man. It is often suggested that since this man would later be revealed as God, and since no-one can see God and live (Exod. 33:20), Jacob's survival depended on it.[16] Yet Jacob demanded a blessing, acknowledging that his opponent was a superior.[17]

Before proceeding to the blessing, the man enquired about Jacob's name. The point is not that the man was ignorant of Jacob's

---

15. The most common causes of contemporary hip dislocations are vehicle accidents, which are able to supply a large jolt of energy to the hip joint. See Kenneth A. Egol, Kenneth J. Koval and Joseph D. Zuckerman, *Handbook of Fractures*, 5th edn (Philadelphia: Wolters Kluwer Health, 2015), p. 25.
16. Kidner (1967: 180); Wenham (1994: 296); Mathews (2005: 560).
17. Throughout Genesis blessings are offered by someone in a superior position, most often by God, but occasionally by humans such as the priest Melchizedek (14:19), Rebekah's brother (24:60), Isaac blessing Jacob (whom he presumed to be Esau, 27:23) or Jacob blessing his sons (49:28).

identity, but that Jacob had to admit to who he was, and therefore to what he had done to Esau, whom he feared (cf. 27:36). The new name given to Jacob is constructed of two elements: the word *'ēl*, meaning 'God', and the verb root *śārāh*, meaning 'contends'. The explanation for this name is given by the man who had wrestled with Jacob. It was to serve as a reminder that Jacob had struggled with God and with men and had prevailed, thereby implying that this man was God himself (v. 28). While the meaning of the name is often taken to be *he* [i.e. Jacob] *struggled with God*, that is not the case, since in names involving a name of God, God is almost invariably the subject of the verb. Instead, it should be borne in mind that the explanation of a given name in the Bible generally takes the form of a play on the name rather than revealing the precise meaning of the name.[18] There is an irony in the explanation for this name in that the man was not able to overcome Jacob, but Jacob overcame *God and . . . men*.[19] He had prevailed in this wrestling match to receive a blessing, just as he was blessed and overcame the machinations of his uncle Laban.

29. Jacob now reverses the relationship and asks the man his name, though Jacob includes a polite *please*. The man's reply is only a question about why Jacob asked for his name, not an explanation of why he would not tell it to Jacob (contrast Judg. 13:18). Then we are told that he gave Jacob a blessing – presumably in addition to the blessing that came with the new name *Israel*. With that the man disappears from the narrative without any explanation of his departure.

30. Jacob's realization that the man he had encountered that night was God is shown in his naming of the place *Peniel*, meaning 'face of God'. Elsewhere this place is called *Penuel* (v. 31; Judg. 8:8–9, 17; 1 Kgs 12:25), but here the name is presented in a form that sounds more like 'face of God' to make it match more closely

---

18. Wenham (1994: 296).

19. Hamilton (1995: 335, n. 34) suggests that *God and men* is a hendiadys for 'everyone'. He cites 'gods and men' at Judg. 9:9, 13. However, the phrasing here is *with God and with men*, not 'with God and men', making it unlikely that this is a hendiadys.

Jacob's reason for naming it.[20] Jacob's explanation was not simply that he had seen God face-to-face, but, most importantly, that his life had been spared even though he had seen God. The fear of sinful humans to look upon the holy and righteous God is mentioned repeatedly in the Old Testament (Exod. 3:6; Judg. 6:22; 13:22; Isa 6:5). Yet God spared Jacob's life, another sign of his favour towards the patriarch.

31–32. By the time Jacob was on his way it was fully sunrise, and he was left with a limp because of his dislocated hip. The final verse of this chapter contains a rare (for Genesis) editorial comment: the linking of the Israelite tradition of not eating the muscle around the hip socket because of Jacob's injury. It is noted that Israel had kept that tradition *to this day* (v. 32), that is, to the time of the writing of Genesis. This custom is not mentioned elsewhere in the Bible, and was not part of the divine legislation for Israelite dietary practices given through Moses. This final verse also gives a sense of closure to this incident through the arrangement of anatomical features mentioned in it: *thigh muscle . . . hip socket . . . hip socket . . . thigh muscle.*[21]

Meaning

Jacob's mysterious night of wrestling came on the heels of a stressful day. He was clearly worried about his forthcoming encounter with Esau and how to pacify his brother who had previously plotted to kill him (27:41–42), and he took extraordinary measures to court his brother's favour. As he planned for his meeting with his brother, Jacob appeared to be doubleminded concerning his faith in God. He was encouraged by the appearance of God's angels (32:1–2), and this moved him humbly to ask Yahweh to rescue him from Esau (32:9–12). At the same time, he sent gifts to Esau in stages in order to placate him, not entirely certain that God's work alone was enough to protect him from his brother. This struggle to cling on to God's promises instead of relying on his own effort was addressed by God himself in the wrestling match with the

---

20. Wenham (1994: 297).

21. Geller (1982: 40)

mysterious man. As the account of this struggle unfolds, it becomes increasingly clear to readers that this is no ordinary man who has engaged in this scuffle with the patriarch. The readers learn that Jacob came to realize something about his opponent during the tussle that night: he was able to bless Jacob and rename him. Then he is gone as quickly as he appeared. Jacob then states what readers ought to expect at this point in the story: that the mysterious stranger was God himself, whom Jacob had seen face-to-face. At sunrise the patriarch limps away, but not without having gained knowledge of God and of the steadfastness of his promises. So, too, readers who struggle with the enigmatic nature of this passage learn of God's unwavering commitment to all his people. They are now ready to move on to Jacob's meeting with Esau, more assured that God is able to see them through their challenges just as he will see Jacob through his reunion with Esau.

iii. Jacob meets Esau (33:1–20)

Context
Having moved through the enigmatic narrative of Jacob's grappling with a stranger, the storyline moves immediately to Jacob having to face Esau. Though still having some trepidation about the coming events, Jacob will confidently negotiate his entry into the land with his heretofore estranged brother.

Comment
1–3. Jacob eventually joined his family, and as they were travelling Jacob finally saw Esau and his entourage approaching. The narrative confirms the report of Jacob's messengers (32:6) that Esau was accompanied by four hundred men. Jacob's reaction is to divide his family among his wives. The narration first lists his wives in the order in which he married them: *Leah, Rachel, and the two slave women* (v. 1). However, Jacob arranged them according to his affection for them, with the slaves and their children first, Leah and her children behind them, and then his beloved wife Rachel and her son Joseph (v. 2). Those in the rear would have the greatest chance to escape should Esau and his men attack. This reminds the reader that even after providing Jacob with six sons and a daughter, Leah was still

unable to gain the emotional attachment from her husband that she craved (cf. 29:32; 30:20). Moreover, the mention of Joseph looks to the future of this rift that will continue to divide Jacob's family. Joseph, Jacob's most-loved son (cf. 37:3), is the only child of Jacob mentioned by name.

However, Jacob placed himself at the front of his family. His experience at Peniel and receiving of the divine blessing there had emboldened him. Previously he had sent his servants and then his family ahead of himself. Now he placed himself in the vanguard, acting according to his new name Israel instead of the old Jacob. As Jacob approached Esau, he prostrated himself, bowing before him seven times. This act serves to bring an ironic touch to the story of Jacob's life, since Isaac's blessing pictured nations bowing before Jacob (27:29). Instead, here Israel bowed before Esau, the ancestor of the Edomites.

4. Esau's lack of animosity towards Jacob is finally revealed by his actions that come rapid-fire as a string of five main verbs in this verse: *he ran . . . he embraced . . . he hugged*[22] *. . . he kissed . . . they wept.* This was not what Jacob expected, and the text makes a pun on Jacob's wrestling (Hebrew *'ābaq*) with a man the previous evening and Esau's embrace (Hebrew *ḥābaq*).

5–7. After their embrace, Esau turns his attention to Jacob's family. His question *Who are these with you?* (v. 5) was a request for introductions. Jacob's reply focuses on his children, not his wives, and on God's blessing, not on Jacob's effort. Jacob had arranged his family from those who enjoyed the least of his affection to those who enjoyed the most, and he presented them to Esau in the same order. The only names mentioned are those of Leah, Rachel and Joseph. The first two recall the rift in Jacob's family in Haran, while Joseph anticipates the rift that will continue in this family in Canaan and Egypt until Joseph brings it to an end (see 50:15–21).

8. Next Esau asked about the presents Jacob had sent ahead of him, calling them a *camp* (Hebrew *maḥăneh*). Here Esau makes a pun, since he knew they were a present (32:18; Hebrew *minḥâ*). But there

---

22. Hebrew 'he fell on his neck' is an idiom for a hug and is used also at Gen. 45:14; 46:29.

is more than a pun here: Esau is not acknowledging the property Jacob had sent ahead of himself as something he has yet accepted. Jacob, however, not only treated it like a present, but also states its purpose: *To find favour with you, my lord.* Jacob continued to use language that treated Esau as a superior, not as a brother. He made himself Esau's servant instead of his social equal or even the master he was prophesied to be (27:29).

9–11. Esau is not so easily bought, however. Accepting the present would place upon him the obligation to accept Jacob. Instead of being a gracious and forgiving brother as he ought, he would now be obliged to forgive. So Esau claims he has enough – an indirect way of saying to Jacob that, despite the stolen blessing, God has blessed him, too. He does not need Jacob to share his blessing, so *Keep what you have* (v. 9).

Yet Jacob has a heartfelt need to share his property – specifically calling the gift *my blessing* (v. 10). This sharing with his brother was a way of acknowledging and making amends for his own wrongdoing. So now Jacob urged Esau to accept the gift as a result of Esau's having treated Jacob favourably. No longer using it as a way of purchasing Esau's favour, Jacob now makes the lavish gift a means by which he can demonstrate his gratitude for being accepted again as Esau's beloved brother. Indeed, Jacob flatters Esau, telling him that seeing his face is like seeing God's face *since you have accepted me* (v. 10). Jacob had seen God's face, and he knew what it meant to be accepted by God. Esau was unaware of the full force of Jacob's words, but, nevertheless, he would have known that Jacob was telling him that his gracious acceptance of Jacob's return was a most godlike and virtuous act.

Jacob then pleaded with Esau to accept his gift as an acknowledgment of God's graciousness to him that had brought him all that he needed – Jacob's oblique way of confessing that he stole Esau's blessing. His present now became his way of demonstrating his contrition. This urging finally led to Esau's accepting the gift.

12–14. The conversation about the gift was concluded, so it was time to leave. Esau offered to lead the way, presumably to Seir. However, God had not instructed Jacob to go to Seir but to his homeland, Canaan (31:3, 13). At first Jacob offers a reason why Esau should not lead Jacob's family: the children and animals would slow

Esau's return home. They are too weak and vulnerable to travel at
the pace Esau would set. Instead, Jacob offers to follow slowly until
he arrives at Seir. This offer was intended to allow Esau to abandon
the idea that Jacob would spend some time living in Seir.

15. Esau, however, was not willing to give up the concept of two
brothers living side-by-side in peace. He offered to lend Jacob some
of his people to guide Jacob on the way to Seir. Jacob's reply is the
most direct in all of his conversation with Esau. He speaks now as
a brother in response to Esau's offer: *Why is this? Simply let me find
favour with you.* Jacob is indicating that he need not go to Seir to
establish a renewed relationship with Esau; it would be enough
if Esau simply acknowledged the restored brother-to-brother
bond.

16–17. Apparently Esau accepted Jacob's view. There was no
need for Jacob to go to Seir, so Esau returned to his home, while
Jacob went to Succoth. The name of that place means *shelters*. It
should not be confused with the Succoth mentioned in Israel's exit
from Egypt (Exod. 12:37; 13:20; Num. 33:5–6). Apparently Jacob
spent an extended period at this place – perhaps because his
children and animals actually needed some rest from the long trip
from Haran. He built himself a house and his animals' shelters,
which gave the place its name. Succoth would be the site of future
incidents in Israel's history (Josh. 13:27; Judg. 8:5–6, 8, 14–16; 1 Kgs
7:46; 2 Chr. 4:17). However, its exact location is unknown. Two sites
in the eastern Jordan valley north of the Jabbok River have been
suggested: Tell Deir 'Alla and Tell Ekhsas. The latter literally means
'mound of booths'.

18–20. Finally, the goal of Jacob's trip, the land of Canaan, was
reached. In his making Shechem his first home back in his native
land, we are told that Jacob paid 100 *kesitahs* of silver for a plot
of land. The 'kesitah' as a unit of weight is mentioned only here and
at Joshua 24:32 and Job 42:11. Its value is unknown.

The introduction of the *sons of Hamor, Shechem's father* not only
identifies someone who was willing to sell Jacob land but also
prepares readers for the horrendous events to follow in the next
chapter. For the present, however, Jacob is pictured as home in
Canaan and fulfilling the vow he had made when he left, that
Yahweh would become his God (28:20–21). The name of the altar,

God, the God of Israel, proclaimed his new relationship with God that was marked by the change of his name from Jacob to Israel.

Meaning

When he left the Promised Land, Jacob had pledged to make Yahweh his God if Yahweh brought him back safely (28:20–21). The account of Jacob's return is fraught with danger. Laban might well have destroyed Jacob had God not warned him against doing so. When nearing Canaan, Jacob became fearful of what his brother Esau might do to him, since twenty years earlier Esau had threatened to kill him soon after Isaac's anticipated death (27:41). On top of this, as Jacob spent a nearly sleepless night anticipating his encounter with Esau, he found himself in a wrestling match with a stranger. The return to his native land was neither easy nor uncomplicated.

But the journey to Canaan came at God's behest, and God made it possible. He kept Laban from harming Jacob. He sent his angels to welcome Jacob back to the land. He blessed Jacob and gave him a new name, ultimately giving Jacob the courage to meet Esau. On the surface this narrative could be read as a story about Jacob's perseverance despite adversity. However, it is more properly seen as the work of God. At stake was Yahweh's commitment to his promise to deliver all the children of Eve from the serpent's curse, his pledge to bless all peoples through this son of Isaac and grandson of Abraham. God's love for the world was coupled with his favour towards Jacob. This is an account of Yahweh delivering Jacob and the promise that he embodied from all harm and danger so that his plan for all humankind could continue in the Promised Land.

Yet that work of God took place primarily through the person of Jacob. We see him growing in faith, acknowledging to Esau that he had family and wealth only because of God's favour. Yet his faith also wavered at times. He acted on God's promises, prayed on the basis of those promises (32:9–12) and received assurance of those same promises even as he also feared Esau's wrath. In faith he clung to the man who wrestled with him and demanded a blessing before he would loosen his grip. In Esau he saw for a second time in two days the face of God – the acceptance based on forgiveness without any merit on Jacob's part. In fact, it was acceptance despite Jacob's faithless act of deceiving Isaac in order to steal Esau's blessing.

The story of Jacob's return, then, stands as a testimony to God's utter commitment to rescue a fallen world through Israel. It demonstrates the Almighty's single-minded dedication to love humanity and to implement his plan through flawed persons whom he has chosen to bear his holy guarantee of grace for everyone who will latch onto him as Jacob did. The struggle of Jacob serves, then, as a reminder of the challenge of all believers to be strengthened by God so that they can confidently assert, 'For I am persuaded that neither death nor life, nor angels nor rulers, nor things present nor things to come, nor powers, nor height nor depth, nor any other created thing will be able to separate us from the love of God that is in Christ Jesus our Lord' (Rom. 8:38–39, CSB).

19. THE FAMILY OF ISAAC: JACOB'S TIME IN CANAAN BEFORE ISAAC'S DEATH (34:1 – 35:29)

This last portion of the large section of Genesis devoted to the history of Isaac's family (25:19 – 35:29) gathers together various incidents relating to Jacob's residency in Canaan before Isaac's death. Most of this large section has been devoted to the story of one member of Isaac's family: Jacob. Isaac plays an important role only in the beginning with the account of the birth of Jacob and Esau (25:19–26), ending with his second blessing of Jacob (28:1–5). In this portion Isaac appears only at the end where he receives Jacob again, and then his death and burial are recounted (35:27–29).

The progress of Jacob towards a reunion with his father is slow, as shown by the narrative: he lived for some time in Shechem, which led to the unfortunate rape of his daughter Dinah and the murderous deceit of Simeon and Levi. Then the pace of the narrative quickens as Jacob went to Bethel at God's command. Afterwards, as he travelled towards Bethlehem, his beloved wife Rachel died in childbirth when Benjamin was born. He then settled for some time between Bethlehem and Hebron at a place called the Tower of Eder. Finally, Jacob was reunited with his father Isaac, and this long section of Genesis ends with Isaac's burial.

It appears as if Jacob's delays set the stage for some of the troubles he encounters: Dinah's rape (34:1–31) and Reuben's adultery (35:21–22a). Dinah's rape led to God commanding him to go to Bethel, where he had previously promised to make Yahweh his God if Yahweh would bring him safely back to his father's house (28:21). But once again Jacob delayed going to his father at Hebron by dwelling at the Tower of Eder, providing the setting for Reuben's adultery.

This section, then, provides an ending for the story of Jacob before the Genesis narrative switches its focus to Jacob's sons. It points backwards to his time in Paddan-aram (35:22b–36) and prepares the reader for what is to come: the blessing that will skip over Reuben, Simeon and Levi to land on Judah (49:3–12), as well as the pivotal role played by Benjamin in the account of Joseph's reunion with his brothers in Egypt.

A. The rape of Dinah (34:1–31)

Context

C.1902 BC

Perhaps the most disturbing event in the book of Genesis, and one of the most challenging for readers, this story tells of rape and murder. It reminds us that Jacob, like his father and grandfather before him, lived in a land of Canaanites and constantly had to negotiate his way through situations that made him feel as if there were no fear of God in Canaan (cf. 20:11). His reaction to the mistreatment of his daughter was passivity, which moved his sons to even more drastic action in deceiving and then slaughtering the male population of Shechem.

Comment

1–4. The narrative begins with a reminder of who Dinah is (v. 1; cf. 30:21). It is rare in the Old Testament that a person's lineage is traced through a mother.[1] At this point Dinah is old enough to be away from home on her own, and she went to socialize with the

---

1. There are seven instances in total: Gen. 34:1; 2 Sam. 3:3 (twice), 4 (twice); 2 Chr. 24:26 (twice).

other young women in the area where Jacob was living. This speaks to a considerable time that Jacob spent east of the Jordan at Succoth (33:16) and then at Shechem where he acquired land (33:18–19). Dinah could have been no more than five years old when Jacob left Haran, but here she is at least a teenager.[2] The man Shechem is introduced as the son of the most important man of this region. Hamor is identified as a Hivite, one of the ethnic groups descended from Ham's son Canaan (10:17). His rape of Dinah is described quickly and without embellishment: *he took her and raped her* (v. 2, CSB). Some have argued that Dinah was not forcibly raped, implying that she was seduced and that we should understand the text to say that Shechem 'took her and humbled her'.[3] That is, he did not follow the proper procedure to obtain her as a wife, thereby bringing shame upon her. However, Shemesh more recently has made a strong case that the account does portray the rape of Dinah, noting several textual and intertextual indications that Dinah was forcibly subjected to sexual intercourse:[4]

1. She is objectified by Shechem: he *saw her, and took her and lay with her and abused her* (v. 2). Only after having had sex with her does Shechem begin to treat her as a person: *his soul clung to her, he loved her and he spoke tenderly to her* (v. 3).
2. The narrator passes strong judgment on Shechem: *he committed an outrage in Israel by lying with the daughter of Jacob, and this is not to be done* (v. 7).
3. One can see some striking parallels when this story is placed against three other stories of rape in the Old Testament (the rape of the Levite's concubine at Gibeah [Judg. 19]; the rape of Tamar by Amnon [2 Sam. 13] and the attempted rape of the angels who visited Lot in Sodom [Gen. 19]):
   (a) In all four stories the rape or attempted rape occurs in the rapist's territory.

---

2. Steinmann (2011: 75–78).
3. Bechtel (1994); see also Hamilton (1995: 352).
4. Shemesh (2007); see also Mathews (2005: 592).

(b) In three of the stories the aftermath of the rape leads
     to confrontation and violence.
(c) In three of the stories revenge for the rape is
     accomplished through deceit (Gen. 34:13; Judg. 20:29;
     2 Sam. 13:23–29).
4. The stories have linguistic ties, including the use of the
   words *rape/humiliate* (Hebrew *'innâ*; Gen. 34:2, Judg. 19:24;
   20:5; 2 Sam. 13:12, 14, 22, 32) and *outrage* (Hebrew *nĕbālâ*;
   Gen. 34:7; Judg. 19:23, 24; 20:6; 2 Sam. 13:12).

Shechem's act was followed by his becoming attached to Dinah.
The only Old Testament use of the combined terms *soul* and *cling*
describing one person's emotional attachment to another is found
here (v. 3).[5] We are also told that *he loved the young girl*. The term *young
girl* is often used to describe a woman of marriageable age. In
addition, Shechem *spoke tenderly to her* – literally, 'he spoke upon the
heart of the young girl'. This expression, 'to speak upon the heart
of someone', is used nine times in the Old Testament and denotes
an attempt to win someone over, to give comfort or to encourage.[6]
Clearly, Shechem remained infatuated with Dinah, so much so that
he demanded that his father procure her as his wife.

5. We are not told how Jacob learned that Dinah had been
defiled. The reader expects Jacob to be outraged. Instead, we are
told that he did nothing until his sons returned from tending the
cattle. His silence leaves readers wondering about his reaction. Was
this stunned silence, or indifference to his daughter's plight? Did he
intend to press his case against Shechem when he had more
support, or was he afraid of the Hivites because they outnumbered
him and his sons?

6–7. Hamor responded to his son's demand fairly quickly, as
the narrative portrays him coming to Jacob as Jacob's sons were
returning from the field. Unlike the stoic Jacob, his sons were very

---

5. The two terms are used together at Ps. 63:8 to describe David's
   dedication to God.
6. Gen. 50:21; Judg. 19:3; Ruth 2:13; 2 Sam. 19:7; 2 Chr. 30:22; 32:6; Isa.
   40:2; Hos. 2:14.

upset and extremely angry. The author joins them in their anger, stating that Shechem committed an *outrage* against Israel by what he had done to Dinah (v. 7). By calling Dinah *Jacob's daughter* the author highlights the difference between Jacob's apparent lack of concern for Dinah and the brothers' intense indignation. The Hebrew word for *outrage* most often denotes a particularly heinous and wilful sin. Frequently it involves sins of a sexual nature (Deut. 22:21; Judg. 19:23, 24; 20:6; 2 Sam. 13:12; Jer. 29:23). Such sins rip apart the very fabric of society and violate Israel's social cohesiveness. That is why Moses adds the comment that *such a thing should not be done in Israel*. This is, perhaps, the first use of the name *Israel* to denote the people as a whole (in this case, Jacob and his sons).

8–10. Hamor addressed *Jacob's sons*, not Jacob, since he likely sensed that they were the ones who had to be placated (v. 8). Interestingly, he referred to Dinah as *your* [plural] *daughter*, thereby acknowledging Jacob's right as father but including the brothers in his request for Dinah to be given in marriage to Shechem. However, he offered no admission of wrongdoing on the part of his son, and offered no compensation for Shechem's shameful behaviour. Instead, he attempted to appeal to the brothers' self-interest: they could intermarry with the Hivites. Hamor was unaware that this family had no propensity to intermarry with Canaanites: Abraham had forbidden it for Isaac (24:2–4), and Isaac had forbidden Jacob to marry a Canaanite woman (28:1–2). When Esau had married Canaanite women, it had caused trouble in Isaac's family and brought his father's disapproval (27:46; 28:8). Later, Judah would marry a Canaanite woman and it would lead to problems in his family (38:1–30). Hamor's inducement was ineffectual. It was intended to cause Dinah's brothers to overlook Shechem's transgression. His second appeal, that Jacob and his sons make this area their permanent home, live among the Hivites and acquire property from them, was also misguided. God had promised to give this land to Jacob and his sons. They had no need to acquire property if they simply trusted God's promise. They did not need to switch their status from accepted resident aliens to fully fledged citizens.

11–12. Shechem was too anxious to allow the negotiations between his father and Jacob's sons to proceed. Perhaps he sensed the brothers' fury over what he had done. He appealed to them to set whatever price they wanted for Dinah, and offered them both *a bride price and a gift* (v. 12). While a bride price was expected in order to acquire a wife (cf. 29:18; 1 Sam. 18:25), the gift was an oblique way of offering compensation to Dinah for his disgraceful act.[7]

13–17. While the author clearly disapproved of Shechem's rape of Dinah (see v. 7), he also displays disapproval of the answer Jacob's sons gave to Shechem by noting its deceitful nature. At the same time, he also informs readers of the reason for their deception: Shechem had *defiled their sister Dinah* (v. 13). This is a resumption of the account of the brothers hearing of the news of their sister's misfortune, the last time the word *defiled* was used and the last time Dinah was mentioned by name. This resumptive language signals that they were still as outraged as they had been when they first heard about Shechem's act, and they were not disposed to accept the offers proffered by Hamor and Shechem. Their trickery is disguised in religious terms: they could not give their sister in marriage to an uncircumcised man. That would be a disgrace, and Dinah would be cut off from the covenant promise connected to circumcision (17:9–14). They stated that circumcision would allow them to intermarry, live among the Hivites and unite with them as one people. That, of course, was the heart of the deception, since Jacob's sons had no intention of allowing their children to inter-marry with Canaanites. Perhaps thinking that Hamor and Shechem would baulk at the thought of being circumcised, they proposed taking Dinah with them and leaving.

18–19. Hamor and Shechem, however, liked the idea of inter-marrying with Israel, and acted on it immediately. Shechem's desire for Dinah is emphasized once again, and his standing in Hamor's family as the most important would allow him to be most persuasive in appealing to his fellow Hivites.

20–23. Hamor and Shechem went to the place where all import-ant business was conducted – the city gate. The opening statement is telling: *These men are peaceful towards us.* They emphasize Jacob's lack of aggression and completely omit Shechem's aggressive rape of Dinah. It is interesting to note that although the deceptive nature

---

7. Wenham (1994: 313).

of the proposal offered by Jacob's sons is expressly pointed out by
the narrator (see v. 13), he simply allows the deception practised
by Hamor and Shechem. They fail to reveal their true motive,
thereby drawing the rest of the city into their circle of danger. Their
speech first appeals to the citizens of the city to allow what they had
proposed to Jacob and his sons: that Israel be recognized with the
full rights of natives instead of as resident aliens. They then reveal
the one condition Jacob's sons had made in their counter-offer: circumcision. That was a potential deal-breaker, so Shechem and
Hamor appealed to the men's greed: they could obtain Israel's
possessions and livestock if they would only agree to this one
demand.

24-26. The men who agreed to be circumcised are described as
all those who go out of his city, a way of referring to able-bodied men
who could serve in times of war.[8] Then on the third day (i.e. two
days later), when the men were most incapacitated, Simeon and Levi
attacked. These two sons of Jacob are described as *Dinah's brothers*
(v. 25). Like Dinah, Levi and Simeon were children of Leah, and
they had an especially strong motive for taking revenge. The city is
described as *unsuspecting*, the narrator's way of highlighting Simeon
and Levi's duplicity. Not only was every male killed, but the reader
is alerted especially to the deaths of Hamor and Shechem. It is only
at this point that the author reveals that Dinah had been kept in
Hamor's house. While not excusing the devious acts of Jacob's sons,
this may explain why they thought they had to use trickery to get a
measure of vengeance or justice for Dinah: the most powerful
family in the city had, in effect, held her captive, virtually forcing
them to come to some terms that would accede to Dinah's marriage
to Shechem.

27-29. We are then told that Jacob's sons came and plundered
the city, and their justification for doing so: *they* [the Hivites] *had
defiled their sister* (v. 27). The thoroughness of the plundering is
depicted in two categories. First, we are told that all the livestock
in both the city and the surrounding countryside (i.e. *the field*, v. 28)
was taken. Then we are told that all of the wives, children and

---

8. Speiser (1967: 83–88).

possessions were taken from the houses. In this way Jacob's sons exacted compensation for the rape of their sister.

30–31. Jacob's scolding of Simeon and Levi did not mention Dinah. Instead, he expressed concern that their action might unite the Canaanites and Perizzites, who could easily wipe out his entire family which was few in number compared with the inhabitants of Canaan (cf. 13:7). Interestingly, Jacob's words do not identify what transgression or transgressions he thought the two brothers had committed: breaking an agreement, murder or theft. In return, Simeon and Levi rebuked their father with a rhetorical question: *Should he treat our sister as a prostitute?* (v. 31). Jacob's reluctance to press a legal claim against Shechem showed that he was not demonstrating proper paternal concern for Dinah. They pointedly do not characterize her as 'your daughter' but as *our sister*, once again bringing to the foreground the rift in Jacob's family. As children of the less-loved wife Leah, it was left to them to defend Dinah, since their father, they implied, cared less for her and for them. In effect, they are blaming Jacob for forcing them to take action against Shechem.

B. Yahweh again blesses Jacob at Bethel (35:1–15)

Context

c.1902 BC

Genesis 35 brings to a conclusion the narrative's focus on Jacob with five incidents. Two look forward to the next episodes in the patriarchal family, while two bring to a close themes from previous chapters. One links the past narrative with the narrative to come:

1. Forward-looking: God blesses Jacob – a reminder of God's promises that will be fulfilled in the future (35:1–15)
2. Backward-looking: Rachel's death – the end of Jacob's marriage to his favourite wife (35:16–20)
3. Forward-looking: Reuben's sin – an attempt to usurp Jacob's position in the family that will lead to Reuben forfeiting family leadership (36:21–22a)
4. Backward- and forward-looking: Jacob's sons – Jacob's family from the past that will dominate the narrative concerning the events in the rest of Genesis (36:22b–26)

5. Backward-looking: Isaac's death – the end of the life
of Jacob's father (35:27–29)

While Jacob will continue to be part of the narrative of Genesis
until nearly the end of the book, this is the last chapter with him as
the main focus. Starting with chapter 37 the narrative emphasis will
shift to the actions of Jacob's sons.

Comment

1. Because of the actions of Simeon and Levi in killing the men
of Shechem, Jacob had feared for the safety of his family. God's
solution is to command Jacob to move to Bethel. The command
also includes the only time God instructed one of the patriarchs to
build an altar. The reminder that God had appeared to Jacob at
Bethel when he fled from Esau has an ironic twist to it: Jacob came
to Bethel as a result of his deceiving Isaac and stealing Esau's
blessing. Now Jacob returned to Bethel as a result of his sons'
deception involving the Hivites at Shechem.

2–4. In preparation for the trip where Jacob would pledge to
make the God who appeared to him at Bethel his only god, Jacob
ordered his family to get rid of their foreign gods. These certainly
must have included the teraphim that Rachel had stolen from her
father (31:19, 30), but may also have included others. It may be
shocking to readers that Jacob's household contained idols. However, idolatry was a constant temptation for God's people in
antiquity, since it was ubiquitous in the surrounding cultures. Note
that Abraham's ancestors worshipped pagan gods (Josh. 24:2,
14–15), and even David's household included teraphim (1 Sam.
19:13). To Jacob's credit, he had now come to the realization that
as Yahweh's chosen bearer of the messianic promise he could not
worship pagan gods or even tolerate the presence of their idols.
He then ordered everyone with him to purify themselves and
change clothes in preparation for their new dedication to Yahweh
alone. Purification often involved bathing the body, washing one's
clothes and shaving (Lev. 14:8–9; Num. 8:7). Jacob announced the
trip to Bethel by connecting it to the building of an altar to *the God
who answered me in my day of distress* (v. 3). This is essentially what
God had told Jacob, yet Jacob omits any reference to fleeing from

Esau. Jacob's newfound dedication to God stemmed from God's faithfulness: *He has been with me everywhere I have gone.* Because of this, Jacob was now obligated to worship God alone (cf. 28:20–21). Jacob's hiding the idols under an oak tree near Shechem placed them where the others could not be tempted to retrieve them and resume their idolatry. The reason for also hiding the earrings is not obvious from this context. It has been suggested that this was part of the purification process and the earrings may have been among the spoils plundered from the city of Shechem by Jacob's sons.[9] Alternatively, it has been suggested that the earrings came from the idols themselves, and, therefore, had pagan associations.[10]

5–7. The journey to Bethel was safe, and Jacob's fear of a Canaanite alliance attacking his family proved to be baseless (cf. 34:30). However, the author is careful to point to God's action in placing fear into the cities around them. In this way, he does not excuse the murderous actions of Levi and Simeon, but notes that, had it not been for God's protection, Jacob's fear of the Canaanites would have been justified. The old name of Bethel, *Luz* (v. 6), is consistently used in the Old Testament before Israel's conquest and resettlement by Israel (28:19; 48:3; Josh. 16:2; 18:13; Judg. 1:23). Jacob not only obeyed God by building an altar, but he also renamed the place El-Bethel, *the God of Bethel*. This emphasized that Jacob had committed himself to the God who had first appeared to him at Bethel years before (28:12–22, esp. vv. 20–21).

8. During Jacob's time at Bethel the death of Deborah took place. This woman is mentioned only here and at 24:59 when she accompanied Rebekah on her journey to Canaan to marry Isaac. She must have been quite elderly, since she was Rebekah's wet nurse. Her presence in Jacob's camp may indicate that she was sent to Jacob in Paddan-aram to bring him news of his mother's death. Rebekah's death is never mentioned in Genesis, although her burial place is noted (49:31). Jacob is never said to have enquired about his

---

9. Wenham (1994: 324). Compare Num. 31:19–20, 51; Deut. 7:25.
10. Hurowitz (2000).

mother when he returned to Canaan, which may be an indication
that he knew of his mother's death.

9–10. These verses indicate that with his residence at Bethel,
Jacob's return from Paddan-aram was complete. Here God blessed
him, and Jacob's change of name to *Israel* is once again stated. This
serves to identify the God who first appeared to Jacob at Bethel
with the God who renamed him and blessed him near the Jabbok
River (32:28–29).

11–13. God continued his words to Jacob by identifying himself
as *God Almighty* (v. 11), the name God used when he renamed
Abram (17:1–8) and gave him promises, most of which are repeated
here:

- A nation will come from him.
- An assembly of nations will come from him (cf. 17:4, 7).
- Kings will descend from him (cf. 17:7).
- God will give him the land promised to Abraham and Isaac
  (cf. 17:8).
- God will give the land to his descendants (cf. 17:8).

The one difference here is that a nation would come from Jacob
(i.e. Israel), but, in addition, *an assembly of nations* would come from
him (v. 11). Jacob's sons would produce only one nation – Israel –
so this promise would be fulfilled in some other way. In the New
Testament Jesus indicates that this will be fulfilled in God's
kingdom when many nations will share a banquet with Abraham,
Isaac and Jacob (Matt. 8:11; Luke 13:29). Then we are told that
God *went up from him* at that place (v. 13). This recalls Jacob's dream
at Bethel, where angels were going up and coming down on a
staircase (28:12).

14–15. Jacob's reaction to God's second appearance to him at
Bethel was similar to his reaction to the first: he set up a stone
marker (v. 14; 28:18), and in both cases he consecrated the stone by
pouring oil on it. There is one difference here, however: Jacob also
poured out a drink offering on the stone as an act of worship. The
drink offering consisted of wine or beer (Num. 28:7). Once again
Jacob named the place *Bethel*, reaffirming his belief that God had
appeared to him here.

C. Rachel's death (35:16–20)

C.1901 BC

16–18. Why Jacob left Bethel is not stated, though it seems that his goal was to go to Hebron where Isaac was. The reader is completely surprised by mention of Rachel's strained labour pains, since there has been no notice that she was pregnant. Her midwife sought to comfort her during her last moments by telling her that she had another son, fulfilling the wish Rachel had made at Joseph's birth (30:24). With her dying breath she named him *Benoni*, 'son of my sorrow' (v. 18). Jacob, however, named him *Benjamin*, son of a right hand. This is the only instance when Jacob named one of his children. It is unclear to what Jacob was referring when he chose this name. Since *right hand* can sometimes indicate the direction 'south', some have proposed 'son of the south', since he was born south of Paddan-aram where Jacob's other sons were born. The right hand can also signify the position of favour (e.g. 48:14–19). In this case, 'son of the favoured one' might refer to Benjamin as son of Rachel, Jacob's favoured wife. At any rate, the name will later also lend itself to irony, since the tribe of Benjamin will become known for producing men who are skilled with their left hand (Judg. 3:15; 20:15–16; 1 Chr. 12:2).

19–20. The burial place of Rachel is said to have been *on the way to Ephrath (that is, Bethlehem)* (v. 19). The Ephrathite clan of Judah was given territory just to the south of Benjamin, with its major cities being Kiriath Jearim and Bethlehem. Earlier we are told that the birth of Benjamin took place *some distance from Ephrath* (v. 16). The word for *some distance* may mean a distance that can be travelled in two hours, about 7 miles or 11 km.[11] That would place Rachel's grave north of Jerusalem. This would agree with later references to Rachel's tomb, which is said to be located in the territory of Benjamin on the border with Judah at a place called Zelzah (1 Sam. 10:2). Later the prophet Jeremiah would depict Rachel weeping for her children when they were led into captivity, noting that her voice could be heard in the Benjaminite city of Ramah, which would also

---

11. Vogt (1975).

be in the vicinity of her tomb (Jer. 31:15; cf. Josh. 18:25). Jacob's marker for Rachel's tomb is said to be there *to this day* (v. 20); that is, when this text was written, the tomb and marker were still able to be found by readers.

D. Reuben's sin (35:21–22a)

C.1900 BC

21. Jacob travelled beyond Rachel's grave to a place called *the Tower of Eder*, meaning 'tower of a flock'. The text appears to assume that the original readers would know the location. It must have been between Rachel's tomb and Hebron, but we cannot be certain where it was located. The prophet Micah later mentioned a tower of a flock near Jerusalem (Mic. 4:8). If this is understood as a place name, then this place may have been a village near Jerusalem.

22a. Reuben's incest with Bilhah, Rachel's maidservant, was not simply motivated by lust; it most likely was an attempt to usurp Jacob's place as leader of the family. Similar instances of sleeping with someone's concubine are mentioned elsewhere in the Old Testament as bids for power, often over one's father (2 Sam. 3:7; 16:20–22; 1 Kgs 2:22; 20:3–7). Reuben, being Leah's firstborn, and his choice of Bilhah, the maidservant of Rachel, once again points out the divide in Jacob's family due to his favouring one wife over the other. Nevertheless, Reuben's act was sinful and shocking. Such incest is condemned at Leviticus 18:8; 20:11; and Deuteronomy 27:20. For this reason Reuben would not receive the double share of Jacob's inheritance. That would be given to Joseph, the firstborn of Rachel, through his sons Ephraim and Manasseh (48:5–22; 1 Chr. 5:1–2). In addition, Reuben would later be passed over for his father's blessing when Jacob prophesied on his deathbed (49:3–4).

Jacob's silence about Reuben's offence mirrors his silence concerning the rape of his daughter Dinah (34:5). In the face of sexual sins, violence and a bid for family dominance, Jacob was passive. However, he did notice the sins of his sons and would pronounce judgment on them as he lay dying (49:3–7).

E. Jacob's sons (35:22b–26)

22b. This list of Jacob's twelve sons follows accounts depicting his youngest and eldest sons. It comes near the end of the long narrative about Isaac's family that has centred on Jacob and the events of his life before the death of Isaac.

23–25. The grouping of sons according to wives lists them in the order of Jacob's acquiring the wives. This is also the order found at Exodus 1:1–4. A different order is found later at 46:8–26, which lists Leah's sons, then Zilpah's, then Rachel's and finally Bilhah's. However, in each list Leah's sons are listed first.

26. The final note says that these sons were born to Jacob in Paddan-aram. However, Benjamin, who is included in the list, was not born there but, as just narrated, was born in Canaan. The inclusion of Benjamin in the list without separate notice of his birthplace was probably due to a desire to maintain a compactness in this list, since readers would have been well aware of this exception.

F. Isaac's death (35:27–29)

c. 1900–1886 BC

27. Jacob finally was reunited with Isaac at Kiriath-arba. Isaac must have moved there during the time Jacob was in Paddan-aram, since his residence was at Beersheba when Jacob fled Esau (26:23, 33; 28:10). The triple naming Mamre/Kiriath-arba/Hebron recalls Abraham's purchase of land there, the first parcel of land in Canaan owned by any patriarch (23:3–20).

28–29. Isaac's life lasted much longer than he, Esau or Rebekah expected, since they thought he would die when he was 100 years old (27:2, 4, 10, 41). Isaac's death at 180 meant that he lived through the selling of Joseph into slavery and died in the year when Joseph was freed from prison.[12] This also implies that Jacob lived at Hebron for about fourteen years before Isaac's death. There are a number of parallels between the notice of Isaac's death and the notice of Abraham's death:

---

12. Steinmann (2011: 73, 76).

- At Mamre (25:9; 35:27)
- The age at death is given (25:7; 35:28)
- *Took his last breath and died* (25:8; 35:29)
- *Gathered to his people* (25:8; 35:29)
- *Old and full of years* (25:8; 35:29)
- Buried by two sons (25:9; 35:29)

While it is not stated, this passage implies that Isaac was interred in the cave at Machpelah, and this is confirmed at 49:31.

This is the last mention of Esau in the Genesis narrative. He will appear again only in the genealogical material that follows. However, his presence with Jacob at the burial of Isaac serves once again to show that the two brothers were reconciled.

Meaning

This last part of the history of Isaac's family focuses on Jacob's time in Canaan after his return from Paddan-aram. The high point of this time is Jacob's devotion to God during his residency at Bethel. Before journeying there he ordered the members of his household to rid themselves of all idols, in effect adopting a strict monotheism that would acknowledge only the God who had been with him since he first revealed himself at Bethel (35:3). The contrast between God Almighty who had accompanied Jacob in all his journeys and the gods who could be secreted under an oak tree at Shechem and abandoned (35:4) is striking. Only the God of Bethel could be relied on to protect his people, keep his promises and maintain a relationship of mercy and grace towards them. God's acts brought Jacob to faith. The Almighty's faithfulness to Jacob even when Jacob fell short of acting in a morally just way demonstrated to the patriarch that this God and no other could be relied upon for all good things.

Yet in this life, no matter how strong a faith one has, there will be trials and tribulations, even in events that surround a powerful mountaintop experience of God's grace and favour. This is illustrated by Jacob's troubles in this section. Some of them came from events beyond his control: the rape of Dinah, the deaths of Deborah and then his beloved wife Rachel, and finally the death of his father Isaac. Jacob contributed to other troubles by his silence or by his favouring one wife over the other and one son over the rest. Such is the life of faith that must exist in a world beset with sin.

This narrative ends with the burial of Isaac, drawing clear parallels with the burial of Abraham. Isaac, therefore, shared in the rewards given to Abraham. He is counted as a true son of the great patriarch whom God called from Haran and to whom God gave great promises. His sonship was not only according to the flesh but, more importantly, according to faith (Rom. 4:13–16; Gal. 3:9). Thus, he is rightly recalled along with Abraham as one of the great patriarchs of Israel.

20. ESAU'S FAMILY: ESAU'S WIVES AND SONS (36:1–8)

Context

This the shortest of the major sections of Genesis tells about Esau's immediate family – his three wives and five sons – and how they came to live in Seir. This section naturally divides into two parts. The first part (vv. 1–5) records Esau's marriages and the births of his sons in Canaan. The second part (vv. 6–8) documents Esau's move from Canaan to Seir. There is some confusion over the names of Esau's wives as compared with those given at 26:34 and 28:9 (see Table 15 on p. 336).

The names of Esau's wives are confusing, since *Mahalath* is called *Basemath* at 36:3, and one of Esau's Hethite wives is called *Basemath* at 26:34 but *Adah* at 36:2. Perhaps Basemath, meaning 'balsamic' or 'fragrant', was a nickname applied to either woman. Another problem is presented by the fact that Esau is said to have married two Hethite women at 26:34, but only one Hethite woman is named at 36:2.[1] The

---

1. The Samaritan Pentateuch and LXX apparently attempted to solve this problem by changing the text of 26:34 to Basemath, daughter of Elon

Table 15 Names given of Esau's wives

Hethite wife	Judith, daughter of Beeri (26:34)	
Hethite wife	Basemath, daughter of Elon (26:34)	Adah, daughter of Elon (36:2)
Hivite wife		Oholibamah, daughter of Anah (36:2)
Ishmaelite wife	Mahalath, daughter of Ishmael (28:9)	Basemath, daughter of Ishmael (36:3)

most likely solution to this problem is that one of Esau's wives died without bearing children and that Esau married another Canaanite wife, Oholibamah. This time Esau chose a Hivite wife, perhaps because his mother Rebekah detested his Hethite wives (27:46). This would, then, give Esau four wives, just as his brother Jacob had four wives. However, due to God's blessing, Jacob's four wives provided him with twelve sons, whereas Esau's wives produced less than half that number of sons.

Another complication in this section is that several of the people mentioned here share names with the Horites listed at 36:20–30. While there have been attempts to equate some of these persons with the Canaanites in this section, it is best simply to assume that some of these names were popular and occurred among different ethnic groups who inhabited the Levant.

Comment

1. This opening follows the normal *tôlĕdôt* formula for opening major sections of Genesis (see the discussion in the Introduction). In addition, Esau's alternative name Edom is noted, since it will become the name of the nation descended from him.

2–3. Esau's wives are said to be Canaanite women. However, one of them – Basemath – was the daughter of Ishmael, who was ethnically Egyptian and married an Egyptian woman (21:21). Perhaps

---

(note 1 *cont.*) *the Hivite.* However, LXX translators of the Pentateuch often changed the text to ameliorate perceived problems. See Larsson (1983).

here Ishmael, who apparently spent his entire life in Canaan, is considered to be Canaanite by residence if not by ethnicity.

Adah was also the name of Lamech's wife (4:19). It was a common name in the Ancient Near East.[2] The name of her father, *Elon*, means 'large tree'.

Oholibamah means 'tent of a high place'. This name was also given to one of Esau's male descendants (36:41; 1 Chr. 1:52) and a Horite woman whose father was named Anah (36:25). The mother of Esau's wife Oholibamah was named *Anah* (36:20; 1 Chr. 1:38) and her grandfather was named *Zibeon*, which means 'hyena'.[3] Among the Horites there was an Anah who was a son of Zibeon (36:24; 1 Chr. 1:40), and there was another man, the brother of the Horite Zibeon, who also bore the name *Anah* (36:20, 25; 1 Chr. 1:38).

Basemath, which means 'balsam tree', was Ishmael's daughter and sister of Ishmael's oldest son Nebaioth (Gen. 25:13; 1 Chr. 1:29).

4–5. Adah's only son *Eliphaz* shared his name with one of his descendants who was a friend of Job (Job 2:11; 4:1; 15:1; 22:1; 42:7, 9). The name Eliphaz probably means 'God is fine gold'.[4]

Basemath's only son was named *Reuel*, 'friend of God'. He shared his name with Moses' Midianite father-in-law (Exod. 2:18; Num. 10:29) and a man from the tribe of Benjamin (1 Chr. 9:8).

Oholibamah was the only wife of Esau to bear more than one son. *Jeush* may mean 'may he [i.e. God] help'. This name was also given to two men from the tribe of Benjamin (1 Chr. 7:10; 8:39), a Levite (1 Chr. 23:10–11) and a son of Judah's King Rehoboam

---

2. *ABD* 1.60.

3. Esau's wife Oholibamah is sometimes identified with the Horite woman named Oholibamah (36:25). In order to make this identification two changes must be proposed at 36:2. First, *Hivite* must be conjectured to be a mistake for *Horite* (due to a confusion of the similarly shaped Hebrew letters *waw* and *resh*). Second, *Anah* must be understood to be the *son*, not the daughter, of Zibeon. Support for this is found in LXX and the Samaritan Pentateuch.

4. Other suggestions include 'God is victor', 'God is pure' or 'God is shining'. See *ABD* 2.471.

(2 Chr. 11:19). The meaning of the name *Jalam* is obscure. *Korah* perhaps means 'bald'. This name was also given to one of Adah's grandsons (36:16), a man from the tribe of Judah (1 Chr. 2:43) and, most famously, a Levite (Exod. 6:21) who in Numbers 16 led a rebellion against Moses.

6–7. Esau's move to Seir is attributed to his desire to move out of Canaan away from Jacob. The extensive list of people and types of property he took with him is a way of saying that he took everyone and everything that was his to Seir. The reason for Esau's departure from Jacob is similar to the reason given for Lot's departure from Abram (13:6).

8. This conclusion not only tells us that Seir became Esau's permanent home, but also ties the end of this section to its beginning by repeating that Esau was also called Edom.

Meaning
Following the report of Isaac's death (35:27–29), this brief section summarizes Esau's adult life in Canaan before he moved to Seir. It follows the general procedure of Genesis in presenting a collateral line of descent from one of the patriarchs before turning to the line that bore the messianic promise. For instance, note the placement of the discussion of Ishmael's descendants (25:12–18) after the report of Abraham's death (25:7–11) and before turning to the longer account of Isaac and his sons beginning at 25:19. This section not only tells readers about Esau's wives and their sons, but also explains how he came to live in the mountains of Seir, hinting once again that he despised his birthright as the firstborn of Isaac (25:34; Heb. 12:16–17).

21. ESAU'S FAMILY: ESAU'S FAMILY IN THE MOUNTAINS OF SEIR (36:9 – 37:1)

Context

This second section devoted to Esau's family not only informs readers about the various Edomite clans descended from Esau, but also sets forth the clans of the Horites that the Edomites displaced from the mountains of Seir (Deut. 2:12, 22). In an appendix, perhaps added later, there is a list of kings who reigned in Edom *before any king reigned over the Israelites* (v. 31). Finally, the last verse in this section notes that Jacob lived in Canaan, the land of his father, thereby contrasting Jacob and Esau and preparing for the last major section of Genesis, the history of Jacob's family (37:2 – 50:26).

Comment

A. Esau's sons and the chiefs of the Edomite clans (36:9–19)

This list of Edomites divides into two main sections. The first is a list of Esau's sons followed by a list of his grandsons organized by their matriarchal lines (vv. 10–14). It is followed by a list of the chiefs of Esau's sons, an indication of the various clans of Edom

(vv. 15–18). This also is organized along matriarchal lines. These two sections are framed by opening and closing verses that mention Esau (vv. 9, 19).

9–10. This section is headed by another *tôlĕdôt* formula similar to that in verse 1. However, here Esau is called *father of Edom* (i.e. the Edomites), and the location is *the mountains of Seir.* This implies that Esau's grandsons were born in Seir, although his sons were born in Canaan (cf. vv. 2–5). The sons of two of Esau's three wives are mentioned here (cf. v. 4).

11–12. This list includes five sons of Eliphaz. The name *Teman* may mean 'south'. The region of Teman (Hab. 3:3) would become known for producing wisdom (Jer. 49:7) and was an important site in Edom (Jer. 49:20; Amos 1:12; Obad. 9). Job's friend Eliphaz was a Temanite (Job 2:11).

Omar may mean 'lamb' or 'eloquent'. Several possible meanings have been proposed for the name *Zepho*, but it remains uncertain, as do the meanings of *Gatam* and *Kenaz.* Some have proposed that Kenaz may be related somehow to the Kenizzites mentioned at 15:19 or the Kenizzite clan of Judah (Num. 32:12), but neither is likely.

Special notice is given to Amalek, who was the son of Eliphaz's concubine Timna, whom Eliphaz obtained from the Horites. She was the daughter of Seir and sister of Lotan (v. 22). Sons of concubines, unlike the sons of full wives, were guaranteed no inheritance. This may explain why the Amalekites were a nomadic people living south of Edom. They are mentioned frequently in the Old Testament as a bitter enemy of Israel (Exod. 17:8–16; Num. 14:39–45; Deut. 25:17–19; 1 Sam. 15).

The mention of the matriarch Adah at the end of this list of men marks the end of this portion of the Edomite clans.

13. Reuel had four sons. The meaning of the name *Nahath* is unknown. This name was also shared by two Levites (1 Chr. 6:26; 2 Chr. 31:13). *Zerah* means 'dawn' or 'brightness'. His name was shared with the father of a king of Edom (v. 33) and a Cushite ruler (2 Chr. 14:9), as well as with one of Judah's sons by Tamar (Gen. 38:30). *Shammah* means 'heard'. David had a brother with this name (1 Sam. 16:9; 17:13) and two of his prominent soldiers also bore this name (2 Sam. 23:11, 25). The meaning of the name *Mizzah* is unknown. Once again, the name of the matriarch marks the end of this portion of the Edomite clans.

14. This list of Esau's descendants ends with Oholibamah's sons, repeating information from verses 2 and 5. Since her sons had no issue, she and her sons are separated from the other wives and sons of Esau.

15–17. A second list of *chiefs* among Esau's sons presents the organization of the Edomite clans. The organization is essentially along the lines of clans formed from each of Esau's grandsons and grouped according to Esau's sons. There are two interesting differences between the list of the Eliphaz clans and the sons of Eliphaz in verses 11–12. First, the order of two of the sons is reversed: in this list Kenaz comes before Gatam. Second, this list includes someone named *Korah*. This name does not appear in the Samaritan Pentateuch or in the list of Eliphaz's sons at 1 Chronicles 1:36. It is probably an intrusion into the text, perhaps being displaced from verse 14 or verse 18.

18. Oholibamah's sons are listed as chiefs, since they had no sons themselves.

19. This concluding verse links back to verse 9 through the mention once again of the name *Edom* and by noting that both the sons of Esau and *their chiefs* are listed.

B. Seir's sons and the chiefs of the Horite clans (36:20–30)

This list of Horites is organized like the previous section about Esau's descendants. It also covers three generations: Seir, his sons and his grandsons. The list is framed by lists of Seir's sons (vv. 20–21) and the chiefs of the Horites, the clan organization flowing from Seir's seven sons (vv. 29–30). Between these verses are seven lists of Seir's grandsons organized along patriarchal lines.

Twentieth-century scholarship tended to identify the Horites with an Indo-European people in the Ancient Near East known as the Hurrians whose native land was in Anatolia and northern Mesopotamia. However, this identification is unlikely, since the names of the Horites listed here are Semitic names, not Indo-European names.

20–21. The reason for including this list in this section about Esau's descendants in Seir is stated when the sons of Seir are introduced: they were *the inhabitants of the land* (v. 20) who were displaced by the Edomites (Deut. 2:12, 22).

The meaning of the name *Lotan* is unknown. *Shobal* may be related to the Hebrew word *shibboleth* (Judg. 12:6), meaning 'an ear of grain'. This name was also given to two Israelites, a descendant of Caleb (1 Chr. 2:50, 52) and a son of Judah (1 Chr. 4:1–2). *Zibeon* and *Anah* were also names of the grandfather and mother of Esau's wife Oholibamah (v. 2). *Dishon* denotes a type of deer or antelope. *Ezer* was a very common name, meaning 'help', and is related to the name Ezra, which means 'helper'. Others who bore this name include men from Judah (1 Chr. 4:4), Ephraim (1 Chr. 7:21) and Gad (1 Chr. 12:9), as well as a ruler of Mizpah (Neh. 3:19) and a post-exilic priest (Neh. 12:42). The meaning of the name *Dishan* is unknown.

This list of sons of Seir notes that they occupied *the land of Edom* (v. 21). This identification of the land mentioned in verse 20 is a subtle way of noting that these Horites were eventually displaced by the Edomites from the land once known as Seir that they had occupied since before Abraham's time (cf. 14:6).

22. The first of Lotan's sons was *Hori*. This was also the name of a man from the tribe of Simeon, one of the twelve spies sent into Canaan by Moses (Num. 13:5). Lotan's other son was *Heman*, who is called Homam at 1 Chronicles 1:39.

23. Shobal had five sons. *Alvan* is called Alian at 1 Chronicles 1:40, due to a confusion of the similarly shaped Hebrew letters *waw* and *yodh*. The name *Manahath* is related to the Hebrew word for 'rest' and the name of Samson's father Manoah (Judg. 13:2). *Ebal* is also the name of a son of Joktan (1 Chr. 1:22), although in Genesis this man is called *Obal* (10:28). *Shepho* is called Shephi at 1 Chronicles 1:40, once again due to the confusion of the letters *waw* and *yodh*. The name *Onam* may mean 'vigour', 'power', and was also the name of a man from Judah (1 Chr. 2:26, 28).

24. The first of Zibeon's sons was *Aiah*, a name which is the word for 'kite', a falcon-like raptor. The father of Saul's concubine Rizpah also bore this name (2 Sam. 3:7; 21:8, 11). *Anah* is the third person in this chapter with this name. To distinguish him from his uncle of the same name (v. 20) we are told that this Anah discovered hot springs in the wilderness while finding pasturage for his donkeys.

25. Anah had only one son, *Dishon*, who shared his name with one of his uncles (v. 21). However, Anah also had a daughter named *Oholibamah*, who shared this name with one of Esau's wives.

26. *Hemdan* was the first son of Dishon. At 1 Chronicles 1:41 he is called Hemran due to confusion of the similarly shaped Hebrew letters *resh* and *dalet*. The name means 'desired'. The meanings of the names *Eshban* and *Ithran* are unknown. Ithran was also the name of an Israelite from the tribe of Asher (1 Chr. 7:37). The name *Cheran* ('Keran' in some English versions) is otherwise unknown.

27. Among Ezer's three sons, *Bilhan* shared his name with a man from Benjamin (1 Chr. 7:10). *Zaavan* is a name occurring only here in the Old Testament. *Akan* occurs as *Jaakan* at 1 Chronicles 1:42. Once again, the difference in spelling is due to confusion of the letters *waw* and *yodh*. The names of two Edomite places incorporate his name: Bene-jaakan ('sons of Jaakan'; Num. 33:31–32) and Beeroth Bene-jaakan ('wells of the sons of Jaakan'; Deut. 10:6).

28. Dishan's first son was *Uz*, a name he shared with one of Aram's sons (10:23) and a son of Abraham's brother Nahor (22:21). Job was from the land of Uz (Job 1:1), which probably was a region in Edom. The name *Aran* is attested only here. However, it may be a variant of the name Oren (1 Chr. 2:25), meaning 'cedar tree'.

29–30. These verses set forth the tribal order of the Horites. They were organized through the sons of Seir.

C. The kings of Edom and the chiefs of the Edomite clans (36:31–43)

c.1096–c.976 BC

This is a list of eight kings of Edom who ruled *before any king reigned over the Israelites*. Each king except the first is introduced by a formula that includes the death of his predecessor, the new king's name and, when appropriate, the name of his father or other additional information (see vv. 32, 34, 35, 38, 39). This king list is probably a later appendix added during the time of David who subdued Moab and brought this line of kings to its end (2 Sam. 8:12). The king list is followed by a list of Esau's chiefs that differs from the one in verses

15–18, since it appears to be from a later time, probably the time of David's reign (1009–969 BC).

31. This is only the second mention of *the land of Edom* in the Old Testament (cf. v. 21). With this phrase Esau's children are treated for the first time as a nation.

32. *Bela*, Edom's first king, shared his name with two men from Israel: Benjamin's eldest son (46:21) and a Reubenite (1 Chr. 5:8). The meaning of the name is uncertain. His father's name *Beor* was also the name of Balaam's father (Num. 22:5; 24:3, 15; 31:8; Deut. 23:4; Josh. 13:22; 24:9; Mic. 6:5). Since Bela was the first of eight kings of Edom, he probably began his reign about 1096 BC, some 120 years before David subdued Edom.[1] The location of his capital city Dinhabah is unknown.

33. *Jobab* was a popular name that was also borne by a descendant of Shem (10:29), a king of Madon (Josh. 11:1) and two men from the tribe of Benjamin (1 Chr. 8:9, 18). Jobab's father was *Zerah*, a name he shared with a grandson of Esau (v. 13) and a Cushite ruler (2 Chr. 14:9), as well as with one of Judah's sons by Tamar (Gen. 38:30). Jobab's town *Bozrah* is modern Buseirah. It was an administrative centre in Edom for much of antiquity (Isa. 34:6; Jer. 49:13, 22; Amos 1:12). There was also a city in Moab with this name (Jer. 48:24).

34. *Husham* is the only person with this name in the Old Testament. This king was from *the land of the Temanites*, the area occupied by the descendants of Esau's grandson Teman.

35. *Hadad* shared his name with Edom's eighth king (v. 39) as well as with a later Edomite who rebelled against Solomon (1 Kgs 11:14–22, 25). His father's name *Bedad* is included to distinguish him from the later Edomite king. This early Edomite king Hadad is said to have defeated Midian in the field of Moab, a battle mentioned nowhere else.[2] Hadad is the name of an ancient Syrian deity who

---

1. David completed his palace in 976 BC and by that time God had given him rest from all his enemies (2 Sam. 7:1). Thus, he had probably conquered Edom by this time. See Steinmann (2011: 117–123).

2. *The field of Moab* may simply be a way of referring to Moab's territory. See Ruth 4:3 where Naomi is said to have returned to Bethlehem from the field of Moab.

is better known as Baal (meaning 'lord' or 'master'). At least three ancient Aramean kings mentioned in the Old Testament were named Ben-Hadad ('son of Hadad').

36. The meaning of the name *Samlah* is unknown. Moreover, the location of his hometown *Masrekah* is also unknown.

37. *Shaul* is the same name as that of the first king of Israel, Saul, and means 'asked [of God]'. This name was also given to two other men in the Old Testament: one a son of Simeon (46:10), the other a Levite (1 Chr. 6:24). He is said to have hailed from *Rehoboth on the River.* In the Old Testament 'the river' normally refers to the Euphrates, but that is not certain in this case. *Rehoboth*, meaning 'wide spaces', was also the name Isaac gave to one of the wells he dug (26:22).

38. *Baal-Hanan,* the name of Edom's seventh king, means 'Baal is gracious'. This name was also given to an Israelite man from Gedor who supervised King David's trees (1 Chr. 27:28). Baal-Hanan's father was *Achbor*, which was also the name of an official who served Judah's King Josiah (2 Kgs 22:12, 14; Jer. 26:22; 36:12).

39. Like Edom's fourth king, Edom's eighth king was named *Hadad*.[3] His capital city was Pau, whose location is unknown. Hadad's wife's name was *Mehetabel*, meaning 'God benefits'. This name was also borne by an ancestor of a certain Shemaiah who was a resident of Jerusalem in Nehemiah's day (Neh. 6:10). Mehetabel's mother was *Matred* and her grandfather (or grandmother) was *Me-zahab*, whose name meant 'waters of gold'.

40–43. This is a list of Esau's chiefs who are twice said to be linked to specific locations in Edom (vv. 40, 43). The emphasis on locations may indicate the administrative organization of the kingdom of Edom prior to David's conquest. Only two names from the previous list of Edomite chiefs recur here: Kenaz and Teman

---

3. Many Hebrew manuscripts read 'Hadar', a mistake caused by confusion of two similarly shaped Hebrew letters, *dalet* and *resh*. This name is given as Hadad at 1 Chr. 1:50, in some Hebrew manuscripts of Gen. 36:39 and in the Samaritan Pentateuch. LXX shows the same confusion of letters, and names this king Harad.

(cf. v. 15). *Timna* (v. 40) was also the name of Eliphaz's concubine (v. 12). *Alvah* and *Jetheth* are otherwise unknown names. *Oholibamah* (v. 41) occurred previously in verses 2, 5, 14, 18, 25. The name *Elah* means 'oak'. It was also the name of a king of Israel (1 Kgs 16:6), the father of Hoshea (2 Kgs 15:30), a descendant of Caleb (1 Chr. 4:15) and Uzzi's son (1 Chr. 9:8). The name *Pinon* is used only here, but may be the same as the place Punon mentioned at Numbers 33:42–43. *Mibzar* (v. 42) means 'fortress'. *Magidiel* (v. 43) means 'gift of God'. The name *Iram* is otherwise unknown. This section ends with a note that Esau was the father of the Edomites, bringing this treatment of the Edomite kingdom to a close and forming a contrast with the next verse.

Meaning

In keeping with the general pattern in Genesis, a line outside of the line of the messianic promise is treated briefly before proceeding to a more thorough narrative concerning persons whom God chose to bear the pledge of blessing for all nations. Esau did not receive the promise previously delivered to Abraham and Isaac, so we have a recounting of his descendants before moving on to the final major section of Genesis which will focus on Jacob's sons.

D. Jacob in Canaan (37:1)

Context

Having commented on the line of Esau, the narrative here transitions back to the main line of descent.

Comment

1. This notice serves to contrast Jacob's residence in Canaan, the land of Isaac, with Esau's abandonment of his birthright to live in the mountains of Seir (cf. 36:6–8). Canaan is called *the land where his* [i.e. Jacob's] *father had lived*. The word for *lived* denotes living as a resident alien, alluding to 17:8 where God promised Abraham this land where he was living as a resident alien. This emphasizes Jacob's faith in God's promise that had yet to be realized, although he was now the third generation to look forward to its fulfilment.

Meaning

This tenth *tôlĕdôt* section in Genesis serves two purposes. First, it explains the origin of an important neighbour of Israel, the Edomites, as well as identifying the Horites whom they had displaced. Second, and more importantly, it serves to demonstrate Esau's lack of concern for his birthright and, by contrast, Jacob's faith in God and his promises. If the names of later Edomite kings such as the two Hadads and Baal-Hanan are an indication, it demonstrates that Esau's abandonment of his birthright and marriage to Canaanite women was due not simply to a lack of family identity on his part, but to a lack of faith that led to his descendants adopting the pagan religion of Canaan. The appendix that lists the eight kings of Edom serves to further justify Isaac's prophecy that Esau would *live by the sword and . . . serve* [his] *brother* (27:40). Ultimately, it is God's people who will reign over the world (Dan. 7:27; 2 Tim. 2:12), and this section ending with Jacob in Canaan and implying David's later conquest of Edom is a foretaste of that future kingdom.

22. THE FAMILY OF JACOB: JOSEPH AS A YOUNG BOY IN CANAAN (37:2–36)

Context

This final major part of Genesis is the *tôlĕdôt* of Jacob, leading the reader to expect that it will focus on Jacob's sons, just as the *tôlĕdôt* of Terah (beginning at 11:27) focused on Abraham and the *tôlĕdôt* of Isaac (beginning at 25:19) focused on Jacob and, to a lesser extent, Esau. This section is often characterized as Joseph's story (37:2 – 50:26). However, this is misleading, since the narrative is not simply about Joseph. In fact, Joseph does not play a major role in a good part of the narrative.[1] Genesis 38 focuses on Judah. In Genesis 42 – 43 Joseph's brothers and his father Jacob are the main characters in the plot line. In Genesis 44 the storyline revolves mainly around Joseph's interaction with Judah, while Genesis 46 concentrates on Jacob, and Genesis 49 records Jacob's words before his death. Instead of being the story of Joseph, this final section is the story of Jacob's family and the rift caused by Jacob's favouring Joseph,

---

1. Smith (2005).

the son of his most-loved wife Rachel. It is the account of how that fracture in the family is used by God to preserve his people, and how healing and reconciliation brings the family together again in Egypt.

In these chapters the leadership of the family is represented by Jacob. When Jacob is absent his eldest son Reuben takes the role of leader (37:21–22, 29; 42:22, 37). The family's division is epitomized by the differing roles of Joseph and Judah. In fact, these four are the only members of Jacob's family whose words are recorded here.[2] The story of Jacob's family begins with Joseph and his dreams which drive another wedge into the family structure, further dividing them and leading to his separation from his father and brothers.

A. Joseph's dreams (37:2–11)

1899 BC
Comment
   2. This verse begins with the last of the eleven *tôlĕdôt* formulas in Genesis.[3] Immediately the narration turns to Joseph, and we are introduced to him through four comments. First, he was seventeen years old. Second, he tended sheep with his brothers, learning the family occupation (see 46:32; 47:3). Third, we are told that he was a *young man* – perhaps meaning an assistant or apprentice – with the four sons of Jacob's concubines.[4] Finally, we are told that he gave Jacob a bad report about his brothers. The word for *report* is often used of malicious rumours or gossip (see Ps. 31:13; Prov. 10:18; 25:10; Jer. 20:10; Ezek. 36:3), words that did not endear him to his brothers.

   3–4. The focus shifts next to Jacob and his affection for Joseph. His favouritism of Joseph is explained through Joseph being a son born in Jacob's old age. This appears a bit strange, since Benjamin

---

2. At times Jacob's sons are said to speak either collectively (e.g. 37:8) or individually (e.g. 42:28), but they are not identified by name.
3. The others are found at Gen. 2:4; 5:1; 6:9; 10:1; 11:10, 27; 25:12, 19; 36:1, 9.
4. Wenham (1994: 350).

was born much later than Joseph. However, it probably refers to Joseph among Jacob's grown sons, since Benjamin would have been only about two years old at this time. Unhidden favouritism seems to have run in this family: Isaac had favoured Esau over Jacob, Rebekah had favoured Jacob over Esau and Jacob had favoured Rachel over Leah. In this case also Jacob was not subtle about his favouritism in giving Joseph a special tunic. Some English versions describe this garment as many-coloured or ornamented (CSB, ESV, NIV, TNK). This description is as old as LXX, which called it 'variegated'. Other English versions call it a long robe or a robe with long sleeves (GW, NRSV). The last is probably correct. The term occurs in Aramaic for the palm of a hand or the sole of a foot (see Dan. 5:5, 24) and may be connected to the Hebrew words for 'end', 'extremity' and 'ankle'.[5] The same type of garment was later worn by the virgin daughters of David (2 Sam. 13:18, 19).[6]

Joseph's brothers had no trouble spotting Jacob's love for Joseph over all the other brothers. Their reaction was to channel their resentment towards Joseph, not their father. Both their inward bitterness (*they hated him*, v. 4) and their outward expression of it (*they could not speak peaceably to him*) is noted.

5–8. Joseph's first dream is introduced in a matter-of-fact way. Then, however, we are told that he related the dream to his brothers, and the result of his words: *they hated him even more* (v. 5). In Hebrew this forms a play on words with Joseph's name, heightening the tension between them. The dream clearly placed Joseph and his brothers in an unfamiliar setting: they were shepherds, not farmers. This, however, was a hint of what was to come: they would indeed later yield to Joseph in the matter of gathered grain when they came to Egypt (42:5–6). Their binding sheaves turned into a surrealistic vision as many dreams do. The sheaves became animated, with Joseph's standing and theirs gathering around and bowing.

---

5. Equating Hebrew *pas* (palm/sole) and *'epes* (end, extremity) may be found in the place name Ephes-dammim (1 Sam. 17:1), which was also called Pas-dammim (1 Chr. 11:13).

6. Note also that at 2 Sam. 13:18 LXX calls this type of garment a 'tunic to the wrists', not a multicoloured tunic.

The brothers immediately knew the meaning of the dream, and they mocked Joseph with questions about whether he really was going to rule them. For a third time we are told they hated Joseph, but we are now given two reasons. First, they hated him because of the dream. This implies that they knew the dream was more than simply a bizarre product of Joseph's mind – they may well have suspected that it was a vision from God. Second, they hated him *because of his words* (v. 8). This at least implies that Joseph was being foolish to fan the flames of their jealousy by telling them his dream. However, it may imply even more: that this younger brother was bragging about his status in the family.

9. Joseph's relating of his second dream is told in brief strokes. The scene is not given a setting as in the previous dream. This time Joseph simply relates the gist of the dream: sun, moon and eleven stars bowing to him. Note that in relating the dream Joseph does not mention his star but mentions himself directly (contrast this with the previous dream, where Joseph referred not directly to himself but to his sheaf). This indicates that Joseph understood the dream and was not asking for an interpretation. Instead, he was putting himself forward as the designated ruler of the family.

10–11. The inclusion of the sun and moon expanded the imagery to cover Jacob, and we are told that Joseph included Jacob in his audience (v. 10). Jacob rebuked Joseph, implying that Joseph may well have been perceived as impertinent. Jacob asks a question similar to that of the brothers: will the family bow down to him? Interestingly, Jacob clearly interprets the moon as *your mother*. Yet Rachel had died in childbirth, and Benjamin is certainly represented by one of the eleven stars. Probably the reference is to Leah as the living family matriarch and stepmother to Joseph and Benjamin. This time the brothers' reaction is characterized as jealousy, another indication that they believed the dream to be a sign of God's favour on Joseph. Jacob must have taken this even more seriously than his sons, since he *kept the matter in mind* (v. 11).

B. Joseph sold into slavery (37:12–36)

12–14. It is curious to read that Jacob's sons were pasturing his flocks at Shechem, the site of Dinah's rape and the murder of the

men of Shechem by Simeon and Levi. Perhaps after about three
years the animosity of the Canaanites had lessened, especially if
they had learned about the rape that caused the problems. The
patriarch is called *Israel* in these verses, and this name will be used
frequently for him in this last section, nearly as often as he is called
by the name Jacob.⁷ It is difficult to determine a reason for the
author's choice of names for him.

It is not clear why Joseph was not working with his brothers,
although it seems that Jacob was blind to the strong animosity they
held towards Joseph. Jacob knew where his sons were supposed to
be, as he instructed Joseph to go to Shechem. Joseph was to bring
word about his brothers' welfare back to Jacob. The word for *welfare*
here is the same word used of how the brothers could not speak
to Joseph *peaceably* (*šālôm*, v. 4). The use of this term may be a
forewarning to the reader of what will happen to Joseph. The
distance from Hebron to Shechem was about 50 miles. Interestingly,
we are told that Jacob sent Joseph *from the Valley of Hebron*, the only
occurrence of this phrase in the Old Testament.

15–17. Upon arriving in Shechem Joseph was unable to find his
brothers, and a brief conversation with an unnamed man is related
in order to tell the reader why Joseph moved on to Dothan to look
for them. Dothan was about 13 miles (21 km) north of Shechem. It
is mentioned only one other time in Scripture (2 Kgs 6:13).

18–20. Joseph's brothers recognized him from some distance –
perhaps because of his special tunic (cf. vv. 3, 23, 32). This gave
them time to plot his murder: in their initial scheme they were
simply going to kill him and throw his body into a pit. They would
then claim that he had been killed by a wild animal, a real possibility
in ancient Canaan where beasts would attack (Judg. 14:5–6; 1 Kgs
13:24; 2 Kgs 2:24). Their derisive reference to Joseph as a *dreamer*
(v. 19) is an example of their contempt for him, and they imagined
that by killing him they could make his dreams go unfulfilled.

---

7. He is called Israel thirty-two times in Gen. 37 – 50; he is called Jacob
   thirty-nine times. Also occurring are the phrases *sons of Israel* (42:5; 45:21;
   46:5, 8; 50:25), *sons of Jacob* (49:2) and *tribes of Israel* (49:16, 28). Three times
   the name Israel is used as an ethnic designation (47:27; 48:20; 49:7).

21–22. Reuben's first intervention into the brothers' conspiracy urged them not to *take his life* (v. 21). The construction 'take life' is often used in the Pentateuch's laws concerning homicide and manslaughter (Lev. 24:17; Num. 35:11, 15, 30; Deut. 19:6, 11; 27:25). Then Reuben suggested that they throw him into *this pit in the wilderness* – that is, outside inhabited cities where someone might find Joseph and rescue him. His suggestion was to avoid actively killing Joseph but instead to allow him to die in the pit, a passive type of murder. The author, however, twice emphasizes that Reuben was actually attempting to rescue Joseph. In the second instance he notes that his goal was to return Joseph to Jacob. This is the first time that Reuben takes on in a positive way the leadership responsibility expected of the eldest brother (cf. 42:37). Earlier he had attempted to assert his headship in a negative way by sleeping with his father's concubine (35:22). Later he would remind his brothers that he had warned them not to take Joseph's life (42:22).

23–24. The brothers' treatment of Joseph upon his arrival is told quickly. They stripped him of his tunic and threw him into the pit. Both items are amplified by descriptions: the tunic was Joseph's special tunic (cf. v. 3), and the pit had no water in it. For this reason some believe the pit to have been a cistern, though the Hebrew word does not necessarily denote a cistern. Though the narrative does not tell readers Joseph's reaction to his brothers' acts, later they would admit that he had begged them for mercy (42:21).

25. The brothers' callous treatment of Joseph is highlighted by their sitting down to a meal. But as they were eating something unexpected happened: they saw a caravan of Ishmaelites that had come from across the Jordan River in Gilead. Their camels were loaded with the aromatic gums and resins produced in Gilead. Some of these same items would be included later among Jacob's gifts sent to the man in charge of grain distribution in Egypt, who he did not realize was Joseph (43:11). The characterization of these traders as both Ishmaelites (vv. 25, 27, 28) and Midianites (vv. 28, 36) has been the occasion for much comment. It appears as if these terms overlap and at times are used interchangeably (37:36; 39:1; Judg. 8:22–28). It has been proposed that the term *Ishmaelite* was a general descriptor for nomadic tribes in the Levant, while *Midianite* was a more specific ethnic indicator, and this may well be the case.[8]

26–28. Judah developed a plan to use Joseph instead of allowing him to die in the cistern. It was a cynical trading on their brother as a commodity, noting that there was nothing to be gained by killing the boy and concealing his death (literally 'covering his blood', v. 26). The gain would come in selling Joseph and reaping a profit from him. Judah seeks to make this a better option by comparing it with slaying their brother, their own flesh. However, the law of Moses would condemn Judah's suggestion as equally abhorrent, requiring capital punishment for the offender as if he were a murderer (Exod. 21:16; Deut. 24:7). Nevertheless, the rest of the brothers agreed. So they sold Joseph for 20 shekels of silver, about 8 oz (227 g). This price was the average price for a male slave during this era.[9] Joseph is then removed from the narrative by a short notice that the Midianites took him to Egypt (v. 28).

29–30. We are not told where Reuben was when the transaction for Joseph was made. Instead, he is portrayed as returning to the pit and finding it empty. His reaction is one of shock and grief that anticipates Jacob's grief: he tore his clothes. He also asks, *Where can I go?*, implying that without Joseph he cannot go home to face Jacob. Once again Reuben was assuming the role of family head in Jacob's absence.

31–32. The brothers' response is to manufacture evidence of Joseph having been killed by a wild animal, just as they proposed initially (cf. v. 20). Their plot to deceive Jacob mirrors Jacob's plot to deceive Isaac: they used their brother's clothing and a goat (cf. 27:15–16). Then they sent Joseph's blood-stained special tunic to Jacob with the question whether this was Joseph's. Jacob's sons sought to distance themselves from Joseph's disappearance in two ways. First, they did not bring the robe to Jacob, but sent it to him, presumably using one of their slaves for the task. Second, they asked, *Is it* your son's *tunic?* (v. 32). They did not call Joseph their brother, but identified him as Jacob's son. In this way they also

---

8. Hamilton (1995: 423); Wenham (1994: 355).

9. Wenham (1978b: 264–265).

obliquely indicated their resentment over the favouritism Jacob had
shown towards Joseph.

33–35. Jacob immediately recognized the robe and came to the
conclusion they had hoped he would come to: Joseph had been
killed by a wild animal. Jacob's mourning showed that he was
inconsolable. Not only did he observe the outward mourning ritual
of torn clothes and donning sackcloth, but he also refused any
comfort his sons and daughters offered, and he wept. The mention
of *daughters* is curious. Since Jacob had only one daughter, Dinah,
the expression may include his daughters-in-law.[10] Jacob's mourning
was also excessive in that it lasted *many days* (v. 34), and he intended
to mourn until his death (v. 35). The brothers would have to
live with the realization that although they had eliminated Joseph,
Jacob would not subsequently transfer his doting attention to any
of them.

36. The sale of Joseph to Potiphar and the identification of him
as one of Pharaoh's officials is mentioned here. The word for *official*
can also mean 'eunuch' (e.g. Esth. 2:3, 14, 15), but that is not the
case here. He is also called *captain of the guards*. This title is very
similar to the title of the Babylonian official Nebuzaradan
mentioned in 2 Kings 25 and Jeremiah 39 – 43; 52.

---

10. One could argue that Jacob had other daughters and that Dinah
    alone was mentioned because of the account of her rape (34:1–31).
    However, the narrative concerning the births of Jacob's children during
    his first fourteen years in Haran (29:31 – 30:24) precludes the possibility
    of Leah, Rachel or Zilpah bearing daughters, and leaves only the
    possibility of Bilhah bearing one or two daughters (see 'Additional
    note on the chronology of the births of Jacob's children'). Thus, one
    would have to posit that during the remaining six years in Haran Jacob's
    wives gave birth only to daughters or that after his return to Haran,
    when they were nearing the end of their childbearing years, they bore
    him daughters. That is possible, but it is still peculiar that, in an overall
    narrative about Jacob that emphasizes God building him a large family
    (e.g. 33:5), there is no mention of the births of daughters – not even
    a general notice (see 5:4, 7, 10, 13, 16, 19, 22, 26, 30; 11:11, 13, 15, 17,
    19, 21, 23, 25).

Meaning

This opening chapter of the story of Jacob's sons concentrates on
the division in the family caused by Jacob's overt favouritism of
Joseph. In a way this was a continuation of his favouring Joseph's
mother Rachel over his first wife Leah. The division among the
brothers was learned behaviour – jealousy over Jacob's affection
among their mothers led to their jealousy caused by Jacob's affection
for Joseph. Jacob's misery at the end of the chapter is in part due to
his failure as a father to show proper concern for all of his family.

The narrative, however, begins to develop other themes –
especially the growth and maturity of three of Jacob's sons. The
first is Joseph. This lad of a mere seventeen years was imprudent
and immature in bragging about his dreams to his brothers. Perhaps
Joseph's boastful relating of his dreams was tinged with the naivety
of a boy near the end of his teenage years, making him not quite
conscious of the swagger that his brothers perceived in his words.
Nevertheless, combined with Jacob's outright doting on him, it was
a combustible mixture that became inflamed nearly to the point of
murder when the rest of Jacob's sons were far removed from their
father. Joseph would need to grow into a mature man who acted
more prudently, and his experience in Egypt would demonstrate
that growth.

The second son who needed to grow in godly behaviour was
Judah. For readers of Genesis their first real encounter with Jacob's
fourth son comes in this chapter where they see a cynically
opportunistic man who uses his brother for personal gain. This
behaviour will continue into the next chapter until Judah finally
begins to develop a compassionate heart that will show itself again
(44:8–10, 16–44).

The third son is Reuben. As firstborn he was expected to be the
leader of the next generation of the family, especially in Jacob's
absence. Earlier he had tried to usurp the family headship by sleeping
with Jacob's concubine Bilhah, the slave girl of Rachel (35:22). But
in this chapter he has matured and taken on real leadership – seeking
to rescue Joseph and return him to Jacob. He will continue to show
the responsibility of family leader later as well (42:37).

Yet despite the deep divide among Jacob's sons, there is an even
greater meaning to this chapter: the plan of God working despite

the schism among his chosen people. Although God is never mentioned in this chapter, it is clear that his plan was revealed in Joseph's dreams, and it is certain that, even in the cruel and evil act of Joseph's brothers when they sold him into slavery, God was still at work not only to keep his promise to what would become the nation of Israel, but also to keep his promise to bless all nations through Abraham's offspring who would come from Israel to deliver the world from Adam's sin. That God is not mentioned at all in this chapter makes his work appear all the more powerful when his plan comes to fruition in Egypt many years later.

23. THE FAMILY OF JACOB: JUDAH'S SONS BY TAMAR (38:1–30)

Context

Although readers of Genesis might expect to follow Joseph's movements down to Egypt, this chapter instead follows Judah's movements in Canaan. In the past some have thought Genesis 38 to be an intrusion into this part of Genesis, a somewhat out-of-place story inserted into a narrative about Joseph. A closer look at this chapter, however, reveals that it is at home both in the wider context of Genesis as a whole and in the closer context of the story of Jacob's family.

In the context of Genesis, this chapter further develops themes already encountered: childlessness is a major concern. Tamar's childlessness, however, takes on a new dimension. In this case it is not because she is barren (cf. 11:30; 25:21; 29:31) but because God killed her husbands (vv. 7, 10). Yet Tamar's determination to have children through the descendants of Abraham demonstrates a remarkable commitment, a dedication that God rewarded so that all the families of the earth could be blessed (Ruth 4:12; Matt. 1:3).

With the births of her children another frequent theme in Genesis comes to the fore: the Lord's preference for the younger child. Though Zerah was technically the firstborn (v. 28), Perez actually was fully born ahead of him (v. 29). He would be the son of the messianic blessing (Matt. 1:3; Luke 3:33).

In the closer context, there are a number of connections with the surrounding chapters of Genesis. In the previous chapter Jacob is sent Joseph's robe and told to examine/identify it, and he identified it (37:32–33). In this account Tamar sends Judah his seal, cord and staff and tells him to identify them, and he identifies them (38:25–26). At 37:31 goat's blood was used to stain Joseph's coat, while at 38:17 a young goat is the agreed-upon price for Tamar's services as a prostitute. There is also a contrast between the two chapters in that Jacob refused to be consoled after Joseph's presumed death (37:35), whereas Judah is consoled after his wife's death (38:12). Both chapters also involve deception: Israel's sons deceived him about Joseph (37:31–33) and Tamar deceives Jacob by dressing as a prostitute (38:14–18).

Connections with the next chapter of Genesis include the openings of both narratives: Judah *went down* from his brothers (38:1) and Joseph was *taken down* to Egypt (39:1). Both chapters feature a seductress: Tamar, who was successful in tempting Judah, and Potiphar's wife, who was unsuccessful in beguiling Joseph, thus producing a contrast between these two sons of Jacob.

Finally, note that there is a connection among all three chapters: the use of evidence to persuade someone. In Genesis 37 Joseph's bloodstained coat is offered as evidence of his demise. In Genesis 38 Judah's seal, cord and staff are tendered as proof pointing to the man who impregnated Tamar. In Genesis 39 Joseph's garment is used by Potiphar's wife as support for her claim that Joseph sought to sleep with her. In all three instances some property of each narrative's protagonist is used as evidence. In all three cases the evidence is linked to someone who was duped: Jacob and Potiphar were hoodwinked into believing a lie, while Judah was tricked into surrendering the evidence that would condemn his lustful and foolish pursuit of sexual pleasure as well as his refusal to behave as a dutiful father-in-law.

All of these links among these three chapters demonstrate that Genesis 38 is not out of place or an interruption to the main narrative of the story of Jacob's family. Instead, it is well integrated into the overall story that spans Genesis 37 – 50. Moreover, it is a necessary part of the story, for it tells readers about a major figure among Jacob's sons – Judah – who will appear several times again at pivotal points as the story of Israel develops in the subsequent chapters.

The chronological context of this account can be fairly well outlined.[1] About the time Joseph was sold into slavery (1899 BC), Judah married a Canaanite woman (38:1–2). Since Judah was about three years older than Joseph, he would have been about twenty. By this Canaanite woman he had three sons: Er (38:3), Onan (38:4) and Shelah (38:5). Judah's marriage can be dated to about 1900 BC, then the marriage of Er to Tamar (38:6) may have taken place about twenty years later in 1879 BC when Er was nineteen or twenty years old. Er died shortly after marrying Tamar (38:6–7), and Judah gave her Onan in a levirate marriage (38:8–10). This implies that Onan must have been born within a year or two of Er and was, perhaps, eighteen or nineteen years old at the time. Shelah, however, was too young to enter into a levirate marriage, but would have been old enough to fulfil this obligation in a few years (38:11). So Shelah may have been about sixteen years old at the time. After the deaths of Er and Onan, Judah's wife died (38:12). This led to his illicit assignation with Tamar and the births of Perez and Zerah (38:27–30). Since these boys were born in Canaan, they must have

Table 16 Chronology for Judah's family

c.1900	Judah marries	38:1–2
c.1899	Er born	38:3
c.1897	Onan born	38:4
c.1895	Shelah born	38:5
c.1879	Er and Onan marry Tamar	38:6–10
c.1878	Judah's wife dies	38:12
c.1877	Perez and Zerah born	38:27–30

1. See Steinmann (2011: 78–79).

been born before Jacob took his family to Egypt sometime in 1876 BC. Therefore, Judah's wife must have died about 1878 BC and Perez and Zerah were born in 1877 or early 1876 BC. The chronology for Judah's family is shown in Table 16 (see p. 360).

1896–c.1877 BC
Comment

1. The opening of this verse places Judah's departure from the rest of the family about the time that Joseph was sold to the Midianites. Judah moved north-west near Adullam, which is usually identified as modern Tell esh-Sheikh Madhkur. This city would become part of the inheritance of the tribe of Judah (Josh. 12:15; 15:35; 1 Sam. 22:1; 2 Sam. 23:13; 1 Chr. 11:15; 2 Chr. 11:7; Neh. 11:30; Mic. 1:15). We are not told how Judah came to befriend Hirah, but Hirah will play an important role in this narrative about Judah (vv. 12, 20, 22).

2–5. It was at Adullam that Judah *saw* and *took* (v. 2) a Canaanite woman. The conjunction of these two words in Genesis accompanies impetuous actions that often have undesirable outcomes (3:6; 6:2; 12:15; 34:2). Considering the preference among Abraham and his descendants to avoid intermarrying with Canaanites, Judah's marriage signals trouble to come. We never learn the name of Judah's wife, only the name of her father, *Shua*. This name was also the name of one of Asher's granddaughters (1 Chr. 7:32). Very quickly the narrative summarizes the births of Judah's sons. The first was named *Er*, which probably means 'watchful' (v. 3). The second was *Onan*, which may mean 'strength, vigour' (v. 4). The third son was named *Shelah*, meaning 'drawn out [from the womb]'. He would become the ancestor of the Shelanite clan of Judah (Num. 26:20). Shelah's birth is placed at Chezib, which is usually considered an alternative name for Achzib (modern Tell el-Beidai) just west of Adullam (Josh. 15:44; 19:29; Judg. 1:31; Mic. 1:14).

6–7. The narrative now passes over a number of years until Er was old enough to marry, making him about twenty years old. His wife Tamar (meaning 'date palm tree') presumably was a Canaanite. God's judgment fell on Er because he was evil. This forms a play on words with his name, since the Hebrew word for *evil* is an anagram of the name Er. Er's death is the first time in Scripture where it is said that God killed someone. We are not told what his offence against God was, but considering that he was the son of a Canaanite woman, it may have been any of the Canaanite abominations associated with their religious practices.

8–10. Judah then ordered Onan to perform his duty as a brother-in-law, known as a levirate marriage (from Latin *levir*, brother-in-law). In some Ancient Near Eastern societies, including Israel, a brother-in-law's duty to the childless widow of his brother was to marry her and have children who would then receive his brother's share of his father's estate. This custom is found in Middle Assyrian and Hittite laws, as well as in later Israelite law (Deut. 25:5–10).[2] Onan, however, did not want to produce any offspring for his brother so that any future inheritance could be entirely his. To frustrate the intent of the levirate custom Onan withdrew before ejaculation, thereby preventing Tamar from conceiving. Onan, however, was not simply frustrating the intent of the levirate custom, but his actions also ran counter to God's oft-repeated promise to the patriarchs that he would make them fruitful and multiply them (15:5; 17:6, 20; 22:17; 26:4; 28:3; 32:12; 35:11). This was also *evil in the Lord's sight* (v. 10; cf. v. 7), so the author notes that God also killed Onan.

11. At this point Judah was afraid to give his only remaining son to Tamar, fearing he might also be killed. Instead, he gave her the excuse that Shelah was not old enough for marriage. Until Shelah was given to her, she was to live as a widow in her father's household (cf. Lev. 22:13). Judah's action was fairly callous, since he was leaving Tamar as a widow with no husband or son to support her. Widows were among ancient society's poorest members and often needed help from others to provide for even their basic needs (Deut. 10:18; 14:28–29; 24:19–21; 26:12–13). In this case it appears that Tamar's father was still living and she could be supported by him for a time until Shelah reached adulthood.

12. The narrative now continues *after many days*, perhaps as much as a year later, with the death of Judah's wife. Sometime later, after mourning his wife, Judah and Hirah went to Timnah where Judah's

---

2. *ANET* 182, 196.

sheep were being shorn. This would place the events of verses
12–23 in April or May. There are two possible locations for Timnah.
One was a village on the border of Judah and Dan where Samson
would later be active (Josh. 15:10; Judg. 14:1–5). The other was in
the southern part of the territory of Judah (Josh. 15:57). If the
location of Enaim (v. 14) is the same as Enam (Josh. 15:34),
the northern location is more likely. Another factor in favour of the
northern village is that it would also have been closer to Adullam
and Chezib.

13–15. We are not told how Tamar learned of Judah's plans to
go to Timnah. However, we are shown her determination to make
her father-in-law responsible for providing for her. While the author
does not say that Tamar exchanged her widow's clothes for the
dress of a prostitute, he implies that she could easily have been
mistaken for one (see v. 15). Tamar clearly sought to intercept her
father-in-law and we are told that she positioned herself in clear
view *at the entrance to Enaim* (the town name means 'two springs').
This may be Enam in what was later part of the territory of Judah
(Josh. 15:34), placing it on the way to Timnah. If it is, the author
may have purposefully changed the name of the town from Enam
to Enaim in order to form a pun: the words *at the entrance to Enaim*
could also mean 'in the opening of eyes'. Judah's eyes were not
open to her identity when he met her, but they would be opened
later (see vv. 25–26). Her motive is clear. She knew that Shelah had
now reached his majority (about eighteen years old), but Judah
had not given her to him as wife. Judah clearly fell for her disguise,
and we are told specifically that this was because she covered her
face (v. 15) – that is, he did not recognize her.

16–19. Judah initiated the discussion with Tamar, propositioning
her. She, however, started the dialogue about the price for her
services, but left the price to him, making him feel that he was in
charge of the conversation. Apparently Judah had nothing of value
with him to offer her, so he promised her a young goat from his
flock. This was a logical choice, since he was headed for the flock
in Timnah. Tamar was not interested in promises – she wanted
something as a guarantee of payment. In reality, she was not
interested in payment at all, but wanted proof of the identity of
Judah. While she had allowed him to feel as if he were in charge

of the negotiations, she had deftly manoeuvred her father-in-law into a vulnerable position. When Judah asked what would serve as a pledge, Tamar sprang her trap: she asked for items that were markers of his identity. The seal could have been either a cylinder seal or a signet ring, since both are known from this era in Canaan. The cord would have been used to wear the seal around the neck. The staff was usually personalized and served as a sign of the owner as head of his clan. Once the price had been negotiated the narrative speeds up, noting their coupling, Tamar's conceiving by Judah and her return home to resume her identity as a widow.

20–21. The focus of the story now shifts to Judah who, it seems, had arrived at his flock in Timnah. Judah sent his Adullamite friend back to Enaim with a goat as payment. At sheep shearing it was important for the owner of the flock to be with the shearers and celebrate with them. This required Hirah to serve as Judah's emissary. By the time Hirah got to Enaim, Tamar was gone. He enquired about the *cult prostitute*. Since it appears that cult prostitution was accepted among Canaanites as a legitimate form of worship (see Deut. 23:18; Hos. 4:14), this may have been a more polite way of enquiring about the woman he was seeking than simply calling her a prostitute and thereby indirectly accusing the people of the village of tolerating harlotry. However, Enaim's men knew nothing about a cult prostitute.

22–23. The Adullamite's report to Judah is filled with bewilderment: he could not find the woman, and no-one knew anything about her. In response, Judah decided to give up on retrieving his items so that *we do not become a laughing stock* (v. 23). That is, it would become evident that Judah was taking advantage of a prostitute by not paying her and leaving her with items that were valuable to him but of no use to her. Pursuing the matter would have simply pointed out his lust and made him appear to be untrustworthy. He justified this by noting that he had made an effort to pay her, implying that it was the woman's fault that she did not receive what he had promised.

24. Once again the narrative skips forward – this time three months – to when it became evident that Tamar was pregnant. The assumption was that as she was pregnant, and since she had no husband, she must have been engaging in prostitution to support herself. Since Judah still had a claim on her for his son Shelah, he felt no compunction about condemning her to death. However, death by burning was a particularly harsh punishment. Later in Israel the normal punishment for illicit sexual behaviour was stoning (Deut. 22:21). Burning was reserved for the sexual impropriety of a priest's daughter, since defiling the priestly office was seen as particularly disgraceful (Lev. 21:9).

25–26. Once again Tamar outwitted Judah. He assumed he was in charge, but as she was brought out, she turned the tables on him. She asked him to recognize the evidence she had concerning the father of her unborn child. When Judah was confronted with the evidence, he knew that she was the injured party. He was responsible, since he had not fulfilled his duty to give her to Shelah. This marks Judah's first recognition of the consequences of his manipulating people for his own purposes without regard for their welfare.

27–30. The story skips forward one more time: to about a half-year later when Tamar gave birth. The phrase *there were twins in her womb* (v. 27) echoes the words used to describe Rebekah's labour with Esau and Jacob (25:24). Just as in the case of the earlier twins, these also engaged in a struggle. When the first put out his arm, the midwife tagged him as the firstborn by using a scarlet thread and declared him to have come out of the womb first, although he was not fully born. Then the second son emerged fully, and she exclaimed, *What a breakout you have made!* His name became *Perez*, meaning 'break out' (v. 29). His brother was named *Zerah*, meaning 'dawn', perhaps a reference to the red cord (v. 30). This was a popular name and is found elsewhere in the Old Testament as a name for an Edomite (36:13, 17, 33), a Cushite king (2 Chr. 14:9), a son of Judah's brother Simeon (1 Chr. 4:24) and a Levite (1 Chr. 6:21).

Meaning

This short account of Judah and his family spans the time between Joseph being sold into slavery and Jacob and his sons going down to Egypt. In the end, Judah finally comes to the realization that his manipulation of others for his own purposes had consequences in their lives. He had heartlessly condemned Tamar to death when he, by his own admission, was more guilty than she was. This recognition of his lack of compassion for others effected a transformation in him – a change that will be immediately evident in events that take place at nearly the same time as his change of heart. His sensitivity to Jacob's attachment to Benjamin and his taking responsibility for his youngest brother's welfare demonstrates this transformation (43:3–10; 44:16–34). The words of this renewed Judah would melt Joseph's heart, leading to the reuniting of the family in Egypt (45:1–13). Moreover, Judah would also gain stature in the eyes of his father, who would designate him as liaison with Joseph as they were entering Egypt (46:28). Ultimately, Judah's alteration from unfeeling exploiter of other persons' vulnerabilities to compassionate brother and son would lead to his being designated the heir of the messianic promise (49:8–12). Although at first blush this chapter appears to be a diversion from the main story of Jacob's family, it is a necessary component of the overall plot that demonstrates how God's plan unfolded in the lives of the sons of Jacob, the twelve patriarchs of the people of Israel.

24. THE FAMILY OF JACOB: JOSEPH IS BLESSED BY GOD IN EGYPT (39:1 – 41:57)

This next part of the story of Jacob's family covers about the same period of time as the previous part, the account of Judah and the birth of his sons. Just as that narrative demonstrates Judah's transformation, this part traces Joseph's transformation in Egypt from a slave of one of Pharaoh's servants to second in rank to Pharaoh himself. One signal of the parallel nature of Genesis 38 with Genesis 39 – 41 is the use of God's name Yahweh. Except for 49:18, the name *Yahweh* does not occur in the story of Jacob's family except in Genesis 38 and 39 where it is always used by the narrator (never by Joseph or by any of the other characters). In Genesis 38 Yahweh brings judgment on Judah's evil sons (38:7, 10). In contrast, here Yahweh brings blessing on Joseph and his master (39:3, 5, 21, 23). In both chapters Yahweh's acts further the progress of the unfolding promises to the patriarchs: in Genesis 38 by extirpating evil behaviour that would harm the fulfilling of his pledges, and in Genesis 39 by supporting the advancement of faithful Joseph's rise in Egypt.

To show the change that takes place in Joseph the narrative is divided into three distinct stories with three different physical settings:

Potiphar's house, the prison for the king's prisoners, and Pharaoh's court. In each of these places God was with Joseph (39:2–3, 21, 23; 41:16, 38). In each setting God's presence with Joseph elevated him to the second highest in authority with only the master he served higher than him (39:4, 6, 22; 41:40). In the first two stories Joseph suffered setbacks despite his faithful service, and at the end of both stories Joseph is in prison (39:20; 40:14, 23). Also in the first two stories people are imprisoned for offences against their master: Joseph for attempted adultery (alleged; 39:17–18), and the cupbearer and baker for an offence against Pharaoh (40:1). In the third story Joseph was successful, and his administrative competence is described in some detail (41:46–57). In these three stories the setbacks make Joseph's eventual elevation to second in authority over all Egypt possible: if Joseph had not been falsely accused by Potiphar's wife he would have been a successful steward, and would not have been placed in prison; and if Joseph had been freed from prison soon after Pharaoh's cupbearer was restored to his position, he would likely not have been easily located so that he could be brought to the royal court to interpret Pharaoh's dreams (see 41:14). Thus, although each of these three stories could be treated as a separate unit, they are not simply a collection of anecdotes about Joseph's time in Egypt. Instead, they combine to tell the chronicle of God's work to bring Joseph to the summit of power in Egypt in order to preserve his people and to keep his promises to Abraham, Isaac and Jacob (see 50:20).

A. Joseph in Potiphar's house (39:1–20)

Context
1899–c.1889 BC
The first verses of this section introduce Joseph's rise in Potiphar's household, thus returning readers to Joseph's story as it was left off at the end of chapter 37.

Comment
i. God blesses Joseph (39:1–6)
   1. In order to bring the reader back in time to the end of the events of Genesis 37, this verse begins with Joseph's being taken down to Egypt. Joseph's master is identified by name along with his

connection to Pharaoh's court, forming a clear link to 37:36. In addition, Potiphar is called *an Egyptian man*. The name *Potiphar* is probably a shortened form of Potiphera (41:45, 50; 46:20) and means 'he whom [the sun-god] Re has given'. The form of this name cannot be documented earlier than Egypt's nineteenth dynasty in the thirteenth century BC. However, since there is evidence for updating proper nouns throughout the Pentateuch, this may be another case in which the name was updated from an earlier form (see discussion in the Introduction).

2. Immediately Joseph's rise in Potiphar's household is attributed to the fact that Yahweh was with him. God's presence with those who are chosen to further his work of blessing all nations is a constant theme in Genesis, beginning with Abraham (21:22; 26:3, 24, 28; 28:15, 20; 31:3; 48:21).

3–4. Potiphar observed Yahweh's work in Joseph's life and that it made *everything he did successful* (v. 3). It brought Potiphar's favour also. He made Joseph his personal attendant (cf. the same characterization of Joshua as Moses' personal attendant: Exod. 24:13; Josh. 1:1). Thus, Joseph was elevated from simple slave to trusted member of Potiphar's staff. Since Joseph was made steward of all Potiphar's property, he would have learned valuable administrative skills that would prepare him for his future role as Pharaoh's right-hand man. Potiphar's estate must have been substantial, since he was highly placed in the royal court.

5–6. The blessing on Potiphar's household did not come until he had elevated Joseph. God responded by blessing those who blessed Joseph (cf. 12:3; 27:29). Moreover, the text emphasizes that the blessing extended to everything Potiphar owned, not simply the persons and things in his house. Joseph proved himself so trustworthy that we are told that Potiphar did not even concern himself with anything he owned. The lone exception was *the food he ate* (v. 6). While this has been interpreted in various ways, it probably refers to the fact that Egyptians did not eat with foreigners (cf. 43:32).[1] The next

---

1. See Herodotus, *Histories* (2.18, 41). Other interpretations of Potiphar's lack of concern except for his food include the following: it is a euphemism for Potiphar's sexual relationship with his wife (v. 9;

statement also shows God's favour on Joseph while at the same time preparing for his encounter with Potiphar's wife: he was *beautiful in form and beautiful in appearance*. The phrase *beautiful in form* is used elsewhere to describe David's wife Abigail (1 Sam. 25:3) and Esther (Esth. 2:7). The phrase *beautiful in appearance* is also used to describe Sarai (Gen. 12:11), David (1 Sam. 17:42) and David's daughter Tamar (2 Sam. 14:27). However, only one other person in all of Scripture is described by both these phrases: Joseph's mother Rachel (Gen. 29:17). This may indicate that Joseph bore a strong resemblance to his mother, and may also have furthered Jacob's unabashed favouritism towards Joseph (37:3–4).

ii. Joseph resists Potiphar's wife (39:7–20)

Having described Joseph's position in Potiphar's house, a complication is introduced into the account. As a result, Joseph will be placed in prison, frustrating his success as Potiphar's personal assistant.

7–10. These verses begin *after these things* (v. 7), indicating that Potiphar's wife only began to notice Joseph after he had achieved prominence in Potiphar's household. She looked at him with yearning.[2] Her entire invitation to Joseph is summarized in two words in Hebrew: *sleep with me*. Joseph's reply is recorded in many more words, and he gives his reasons for refusing her: Potiphar does not concern himself with anything in the house. Everything is under Joseph's authority – no-one is superior to him. Potiphar has withheld only his wife from Joseph. To do what she suggests is a grave evil (cf. 20:9), a sin against God. These reasons build on one another. The first (Joseph's authority) speaks to Potiphar's trust in Joseph – his vocation as servant. The second (Potiphar had withheld

---

(note 1 *cont.*) cf. Prov. 30:20; Mathews [2005: 733]); it is a way of referring to his private affairs (Wenham [1994: 374]); or it expresses the thought that Egyptians did not think foreigners were capable of properly preparing food (Hamilton [1995: 461]).

2. The Hebrew text uses the idiom 'lifted her eyes towards'. This idiom is used elsewhere to denote looking with longing or desire (Ps. 121:1; Ezek. 23:27).

only his wife) points to Joseph's vocation as household steward. The third calls on Joseph's moral responsibility as a child of God. Yet Joseph's reasons meant nothing to her, and we are told she kept after Joseph daily. However, Joseph refused to *lie beside her to be with her* (v. 10).

11-12. The narrative advances to a day when Joseph was working in the house without any other servants present. This notice implies that this was not normally the case. Are we to understand that Joseph was unaware that he was left alone with the woman? Are we to conclude that Joseph was oblivious to the danger this presented? We cannot be sure; perhaps the text is implying that Joseph was not acting with due caution. Potiphar's wife became emboldened by the situation, and this time she grabbed his garment and propositioned him. Joseph's startled surprise is signalled by three actions narrated in quick sequence: he left his garment, he fled and he went outside. Clearly Joseph was unprepared for this situation.

13-15. Immediately observing the result of Joseph's escape, Potiphar's wife decided that she needed to explain why she had Joseph's garment and why Joseph was gone. Her words to the household servants were the first part of her attempt to place the blame on Joseph. She pointed to her husband's introducing a Hebrew into the household, implying that he was guilty of poor judgment in bringing a foreigner into their midst specifically in order *to make fools of us* or *to fool around with us*. The Hebrew is ambiguous, and can take on a number of nuances. At 19:14 it depicts Lot's prospective sons-in-law as thinking that he was joking. At 21:9 it describes Ishmael's joking behaviour that Sarah found offensive. Then at 26:8 it is used to speak of Abraham caressing Sarah, a use with clear sexual overtones. It would appear that 1 Corinthians 10:7 also understands the use of this verb at Exodus 32:6 as having a sexual connotation. Finally, at Judges 16:25 Samson is brought into the temple of Baal where he 'performed' in their presence – that is, he entertained them. Although the presence of the household slaves may have caused Potiphar's wife to speak in less-than-direct terms, the sexual implication is also most likely present here in verses 14 and 17 where Potiphar's wife is depicted as holding Jacob's clothing and accusing Potiphar of bringing a *Hebrew man* into the household *to fool around with us*. This appears to be confirmed in her next statement when she accuses Joseph of making advances towards her. Her next claim is that she screamed. Interestingly, the narration does not mention any screaming when relating the actual event. Moreover, she summoned the servants and claimed only that Joseph had heard the scream and that is what caused him to flee. Clearly, she had no eyewitnesses and no-one who could honestly claim to have heard her shout.

16–18. After attempting to establish her story with the rest of the household servants, we are told that the woman *put Joseph's garment beside her* (v. 16). The author has introduced an irony here: Joseph refused to lie beside her, but she placed his garment beside her in order to accuse him of what he refused to do. She told Potiphar essentially the same tale she had fabricated for the servants. However, she changed it in subtle ways. While once again she pointed out that her husband had brought a Hebrew into their household, she did not say that Potiphar had brought Joseph to them *to fool around with me*. Instead, she blamed that idea directly on Joseph, whom she now called *a Hebrew slave*, thereby pointing out his lowly status and implying that her husband was foolish to put Joseph in charge of the household. She once again claimed to have screamed and scared Joseph off.

19–20. We are told that her accusation made her husband furious. However, if Potiphar was so angry at Joseph, it is strange that he did not have him executed, since that would have been the normal punishment for such an infraction. It may be that Potiphar already doubted his wife's story. After all, she indirectly blamed him for the problem, and she told the servants that Potiphar had intended Joseph to *fool with* the household. Nevertheless, he had to take some action, so he had Joseph placed in prison. The Hebrew term for this place of incarceration means 'round house' (v. 20) and is unique to the Joseph account in these chapters (39:21–23; 40:3, 5). It may suggest a fortress-like structure. However, this was no ordinary prison. It was the prison for the king's prisoners, perhaps adjacent to or in the vicinity of the royal palace. Moreover, 40:3–4 and 41:10 imply that this prison was under the authority of the captain of the guards, the very office that Potiphar held (37:36; 39:1)! All of this suggests that Potiphar suspected that Joseph may not have been guilty of propositioning his wife. Thus, the verse ends with the statement that Joseph was in the round house, presumably where Potiphar could keep an eye on Joseph's welfare.

Meaning
Despite being made a slave for an Egyptian official, Joseph prospered because the Lord was with him (39:2). Moreover, he was serving a man who was able to recognize that the Lord was with Joseph (39:3). Joseph's rise in Potiphar's household brought blessing to Potiphar, who was wise enough to place Joseph in charge of his affairs. Clearly, things went well for Joseph because the Lord was with him. However, God's favour on Joseph did not remove trouble and injustice from his life. Nevertheless, Joseph's difficulties would become another opportunity for God to bless him.

B. Joseph in prison (39:21 – 40:23)

Context
c. 1889–1886 BC
Joseph's being placed in prison may seem to have imperilled God's promises. However, although Potiphar's household now recedes into the background, these chapters carefully pick up on other elements from chapter 37, especially Joseph's understanding of dreams, to demonstrate that even in unexpected circumstances, God was still present with him.

Comment
i. God blesses Joseph (39:21–23)
21–23. These verses introduce Joseph's role in the prison and are clearly parallel to the introduction to Joseph in Potiphar's house (39:1–6). Some of the more prominent parallels are shown in Table 17 (see p. 374).

ii. Joseph interprets dreams in prison (40:1–23)
Just as the advances made by Potiphar's wife on Joseph introduced a complication into the previous story, so also the dreams of the cupbearer and baker introduce a complication into Joseph's time in prison. Both are introduced by the same phrase: *after these things* (39:7; 40:1), and both end with Joseph in prison.

Table 17 Parallels between Joseph's time in Potiphar's house
and in prison

Joseph in Potiphar's house	Joseph in prison
The Lord was with Joseph (39:1)	The Lord was with Joseph (39:21)
Joseph found favour with his master (39:4)	The Lord granted him favour with the prison warden (39:21)
All Potiphar owned was placed under Joseph's authority (39:4)	All the prisoners were placed under Joseph's authority (39:22)
His master as not concerned with anything (39:6)	The warden did not oversee anything (39:23)
His master saw that the Lord was with him (39:3)	because the Lord was with Joseph (39:23)
The Lord made everything he did successful (39:3)	The Lord made everything he did successful (39:23)

1–4. This section begins with *after these things*, that is, sometime after Joseph was made head trustee in the prison. We are told that the chief cupbearer and chief baker were in prison because *they offended* the king of Egypt (v. 1). The word for *offended* is the same as the word for *sin* at 39:9, inviting a comparison with Joseph. Were these men in prison for a real crime or simply for an alleged one? Twice Pharaoh is called *king of Egypt*, which is rare in the Old Testament when he is not also called Pharaoh.[3] Pharaoh placed them in prison in a fit of anger.[4] The text is careful to identify where they were held in custody by a threefold description of the jail: in the house of the captain of the guards (i.e. Potiphar; cf. 39:1), in the round house (cf. 39:20), in the place where Joseph was in custody (cf. 39:20). Since 39:20 has already told readers that this prison was where the king's prisoners were confined, it is not surprising that

---

3. *King of Egypt* occurs twice in Genesis, and thirty-five times in the entire Old Testament. *Pharaoh* occurs by itself 216 times and *Pharaoh king of Egypt* twenty-one times.

4. The Hebrew word used to describe Pharaoh's anger 'often concerns a quickly rising, forceful, and also quickly subsiding emotion'. *TLOT* 3.1157.

these two high officials of Pharaoh were put in this particular prison. Next we are told that Joseph was assigned to be their personal attendant, the same description of how he had served Potiphar (cf. 39:4). Finally, we are told that they were there *for some time*, with the Hebrew text implying a short period of time.[5]

5. The two men having a dream – both on the same night – is emphasized. It is also clearly stated that each dream had its own meaning. While there are three pairs of dreams in the stories from Joseph's life, only these two have separate meanings (cf. 37:7–8 with 37:9–10; see also 41:25–26).

6–8. In the morning Joseph immediately saw that they were distraught[6] – by this time he knew them well enough to recognize that neither man was his usual self. As their assigned attendant he may have considered himself responsible for enquiring about their welfare and tending to it if possible. Their reply was that both had had dreams, but they had no interpreter for them. The problem was not that they had dreamed but that they did not have access to the court interpreters who were trained in analysing and explaining signs and dreams and who were kept on staff by Pharaoh and also in other Ancient Near Eastern royal courts (cf. 41:8, 24; Dan. 2:2). Joseph, however, challenged their belief that real dream interpretation could come through human training and effort. Instead, *interpretations belong to God* (v. 8), and only God's revelation could explain a dream's meaning. Joseph immediately asked them to tell him their dreams – because God was with him, even in prison (39:21, 23).

9–11. The cupbearer's dream relied heavily on groups of three. The vine he saw had three branches. The vine did three things:

---

5. The Hebrew literally says 'and they were days there' (v. 4). This is a unique phrase in the Old Testament. For long periods of time the usual phrasing is 'many days' (Gen. 21:34; 1 Kgs 17:7; 18:1; Jer. 13:6; and twenty more times). At other times a specific time period may be specified (Gen. 41:1; Josh. 3:2; 9:16; 2 Sam. 13:23; 2 Chr. 20:25; Jer. 42:7; Ezek. 3:16).

6. The word is used only twice in the Old Testament and both times signifies persons who are visibly unwell (cf. Dan. 1:10).

budded, blossomed and ripened. In the dream the cupbearer did
three things: he took the grapes, squeezed them into Pharaoh's cup
and placed the cup in Pharaoh's hand.

12–13. Joseph did not hesitate in offering an interpretation.
Some elements of the dream were symbolic: the three branches
were three days. This symbolized the time when Pharaoh would *lift
up* the cupbearer's head. In Hebrew the phrase 'lift up [someone
else's] head' can denote elevating a person from a lowly position to
an honoured one (2 Kgs 25:27; Jer. 52:31).[7] Joseph does not explain
the cupbearer's taking the grapes from the vine and squeezing
them, since this obviously symbolized him preparing Pharaoh's
wine. Handing Pharaoh's cup to him was not a symbolic part
of the dream but what the cupbearer would actually do in three
days.

14–15. Joseph was so confident that God had given him the
correct interpretation that he asked the cupbearer to reciprocate.
He used four imperatives to make his request: *remember me, do me a
favour, mention me to Pharaoh* and *get me out of this prison* (v. 14). To these
he added a brief account of how he came to be imprisoned. In
it he characterized his brothers' actions as kidnapping (literally,
'stealing'). He noted that he was not from Egypt but from *the land
of the Hebrews* (v. 15), an expression unique to this verse but which
serves to contrast his homeland with *here* (i.e. Egypt), where he
noted that he was unjustly imprisoned in *the pit*. Joseph's characterization of prison as a pit introduces an ironic touch: his brothers
had thrown him into a pit (37:24) and he had pleaded with them
(42:21), and once again he is in a pit and is again pleading for a
favour. It appears that Joseph's request to the cupbearer was not for
him to mention how well Joseph could interpret dreams but to
allow Joseph to appeal his case to Pharaoh by setting forth his story
as he did briefly with the cupbearer.

<hr>

7. The other meanings of lifting up someone else's head include taking
a census (Exod. 30:12; Num. 1:2; 4:2, 22; 26:2; 31:26, 49) or beheading
someone (1 Chr. 10:9). This is distinct from lifting up one's own head,
which means to act with confidence or boldness (Judg. 8:28; Job 10:15;
Pss 24:7, 9; 83:2; Zech. 1:21).

16–17. The baker may have been reluctant to tell his dream, but the positive meaning of the cupbearer's dream may have encouraged him. After all, his dream had some elements in common with his companion's dream: the use of three items (bread baskets)[8] and the presence of objects associated with his former position in Pharaoh's court (baked goods in the topmost basket). The only possibly troubling element was the birds eating the baked goods. Was this a good sign or a bad one? For instance, this could have been a good sign, since in Egyptian mythology the god Horus, the patron god of the pharaohs, was often depicted as a falcon.[9] Thus, the dream might have meant that the baker would return to his post and once again provide food for the royal table.

18–19. Joseph's interpretation of the baker's dream starts like the previous one, with a symbol for three days. It continues with Pharaoh lifting up the baker's head, as in the previous interpretation. But then it takes a turn for the worse: the head-lifting this time means decapitation as Joseph says *lift up your head from upon you*.[10] Then Joseph adds an element not depicted in the dream: the baker's body will be hung on a tree. In antiquity displaying a corpse in a public place signalled an ignominious death (Deut. 21:22–23; Josh. 8:29; 10:26; 2 Sam. 4:12; 21:12; Esth. 2:23; 5:14; 6:4; 7:9–10; 8:7; 9:13, 25).

20–22. The narrative skips forward to the third day, and one reason for Pharaoh's actions towards the two royal prisoners is revealed: it was his birthday, a day of feasting for his servants. Readers now encounter the use of the idiom from Joseph's interpretation of the dream: Pharaoh *lifted up the head of the chief cupbearer and the head of the chief baker among his servants*. Once again there is an ironic twist in the narration, since *lifted up the head* means two different things for these two servants: the cupbearer became an

---

8. While many English versions call them 'baskets of bread', implying that there was bread in all three baskets (CSB, GW, NET, NIV), it is more likely that the phrase means 'baskets for bread', i.e. bread baskets.

9. Zakovitch (2005: 41); Bailleul-LeSuer (2012).

10. Note the use of 'lift up [someone else's] head' for decapitation at 1 Chr. 10:9 where Saul's corpse was beheaded.

example of pardon from Pharaoh and the baker an example of Pharaoh's condemnation. These communicated both positive and negative messages for the rest of Pharaoh's courtiers. The fulfilment of the dreams is related in terms exactly matching the explanations given by Joseph: *just as Joseph had interpreted for them* (v. 22).

23. The story ends with a simple statement that the cupbearer did not remember Joseph but forgot him. Thus, the other three things Joseph requested did not happen: the cupbearer did not do Joseph a favour, he did not mention him to Pharaoh and he did not get him out of prison (cf. v. 14).

Meaning
Apart from the description of the dreams of Pharaoh's imprisoned officials with their interpretation and fulfilment, Joseph's time in prison is barely described in this chapter. As in Potiphar's house, Joseph was successful because the Lord was with him. Also as in Potiphar's house, subsequent developments led to misery. Despite the fact that Joseph could interpret the dreams, the cupbearer showed little concern for the Hebrew who had helped him.

One important point made by this chapter is that *interpretations belong to God* (40:8). The baker and cupbearer despaired because they did not have their former access to the royal sages of Pharaoh's court who might have offered them an interpretation of their dreams. However, Joseph's words serve to remind the reader that the future belongs to God and only he can reveal it. Indeed, seeking to know the future through occult means is thoroughly condemned throughout Scripture (Deut. 18:10–12). Thus, readers of Genesis are reminded that they must leave the future in God's hands and trust him (Jas 4:13–14). Indeed, Joseph had no idea how he would be delivered from prison even though God had revealed to him the future of Pharaoh's servants.

C. Joseph becomes Pharaoh's administrator (41:1–57)

Context
The notice that two years had passed since the cupbearer was freed from prison (v. 1) not only gives a chronological marker for this new narrative, but it also connects it to the previous one. It also evokes

the reader's sympathy for Joseph who languished in custody. In addition, it communicates something much more subtle, given the outcome of the events narrated in this chapter: the timing of events was determined by God's plan, not by Joseph's desire or the forgetfulness of the cupbearer (cf. 40:23). Had the cupbearer effected Joseph's release from prison earlier, Joseph may well not have been available to interpret Pharaoh's dream and, in turn, he may not have saved his family during the coming famine (cf. 50:20).

This chapter sees Joseph made a member of the Egyptian court and assimilated into Egyptian culture. He shaved (v. 14): Egyptian men normally sported no facial hair. He was clothed in Egyptian garments (v. 42). He was given an Egyptian name and an Egyptian wife (v. 45). To highlight this assimilation of Joseph into Egypian society, this chapter contains a number of words of Egyptian origin. The Hebrew words for *Nile* (vv. 1–3, 17–18), *reeds* (vv. 2, 18), *magicians* (vv. 8, 24), *fine linen* (v. 42) and the word *'abrēk* (v. 43), whose meaning is unknown, are all loan words from ancient Egyptian and occur only here in all of Genesis.[11] This transformation of Joseph from a Hebrew slave (v. 12) to the second most powerful man in Egypt prepares readers for his brothers' inability to recognize him when they come to Egypt during the famine (42:8).

1886–1879 BC

Comment

i. Joseph interprets Pharaoh's dreams (41:1–36)

1–4. The chapter begins with a description of Pharaoh's dreams. The first dream is filled with Egyptian connections, most notably that in the dream Pharaoh was standing beside the Nile, the river that virtually defined ancient Egyptian life. He saw seven cows come out of the Nile and graze on reeds. Egyptians often pastured cows along the Nile in areas that were not suited for agriculture, especially the delta. One of the more important deities of Egypt, Hathor, was often depicted as a cow. She was the goddess of joy, music, dance, feminine love, fertility, motherhood and foreign lands. These first seven cows are described as *beautiful in appearance and plump* (v. 2). The

---

11. Perhaps also the word for *signet ring* (v. 42), although this is less certain.

seven cows that came out of the Nile after them are described as *abysmal in appearance and thin* (v. 3). The ill-fed cows ate the well-fed ones. We are told that Pharaoh awoke at the end of this dream. This is in keeping with human sleep patterns before the advent of modern electric lighting that now enables people to stay awake beyond sunset without having to burn relatively expensive oil. Since darkness could often last eleven to thirteen hours, the typical pattern was segmented sleep.[12] This consisted of a period of deep sleep until the middle of the night. During this first segment dreams were most common. After a period of wakefulness, when there might be activity in or out of bed, there usually followed a second sleep when dreams were less often experienced. Several biblical passages suggest that this sleep pattern was expected and normal (Ruth 3:8–14; Song 3:1–5; 5:2–8; Ps. 119:62; Matt. 25:1–13; Luke 12:36–38; Acts 16:25). Thus, Pharaoh's first dream came in the expected part of the night.

5–7. Next we are told that Pharaoh fell asleep and *dreamed a second time* (v. 5). This would have been an unexpected dream. This time he saw a single stalk of grain grow, and it had seven heads of grain. The heads are described as *plump and good*. The word for *plump* (vv. 5, 7) is used elsewhere in the Old Testament to describe only animals or humans (cf. the cows in v. 2). This is the only use of it to describe plants. Its use here is most likely purposeful in order to connect these seven heads of grain with the first seven cows in the previous dream. The next seven heads of grain are described differently from the first seven. Not only are they *thin* (vv. 6, 7) like the second set of seven cows (cf. vv. 3, 4), but they were *scorched by the east wind*, completely useless as food. As in the previous dream the second seven consumed the first seven, this time described as *swallowed* (v. 7) rather than *ate* (v. 4). Not only are we told that Pharaoh woke after this dream, but it is stated that *it was [simply] a dream* (see CSB, GW). This statement may have been included because a dream during one's second segment of sleep at night was not usual.

8. Pharaoh was *troubled* by the dreams.[13] This expression occurs only one other time in the Old Testament – when Nebuchadnezzar

---

12. Holladay (2007).

13. Literally, 'his spirit was troubled'.

was troubled by a dream (Dan. 2:3). Pharaoh summoned *all the magicians of Egypt and all its wise men.* The use of the word *all* twice emphasizes the seriousness of Pharaoh's concern. This was likely caused by both dreams containing seven items twice and by the fact that he dreamt the second dream in his second sleep segment. Although many English versions say that *Pharaoh told them his dreams*, the Hebrew text uses the singular *dream* (also vv. 15, 17, 22, 25, 26, 32) and then states that *no-one could interpret them* (plural). In this way the text subtly but repeatedly signals that Pharaoh believed the two dreams were one in meaning.[14]

9–13. When no-one could supply Pharaoh with an interpretation, the chief cupbearer spoke up, initiating his speech with an admission of his fault. He admitted to having been imprisoned but did not openly admit that he had forgotten Joseph. The cupbearer summarized the story of his and the baker's dreams in terms that presented the content of the previous chapter without distortion but also in a way that placed himself in the best light possible. However, he added some information about Joseph: that he was a Hebrew slave of the captain of the guards in the prison run by the captain of the guards. Nowhere in Genesis 40 is Joseph depicted as speaking about his relationship with the captain of the guards. The cupbearer noted that Joseph interpreted each dream and that each had its own interpretation. Then he added that Joseph's interpretation aligned with the subsequent events.

14. It is emphasized that Pharaoh's orders were carried out with haste. It is interesting to note that Joseph is said to have been brought *from the pit,* since that was the word Joseph used to characterize the prison when he asked the cupbearer to get him released (see 40:15). Joseph was shaved. While it was common for Semitic peoples including the Hebrews to sport facial hair (Lev. 14:9; 19:27; 21:5; 1 Sam. 21:13; 2 Sam. 10:4–5; 20:9; 1 Chr. 19:5; Ezra 9:3; Ps. 133:2; Isa. 7:20; 15:2; 50:6; Jer. 41:5; 48:37; Ezek. 5:1), Egyptians were clean-shaven. So Joseph shaved and changed his clothes in order to be presentable to Pharaoh.

---

14. Wenham (1994: 391).

15–16. Pharaoh opened his conversation with Joseph by explaining the situation and then stating that he had been told that Joseph could *hear a dream and interpret it* (v. 15). In his reply Joseph denied that he would interpret the dream but said that God would give Pharaoh a *favourable answer* (v. 16; see CSB, ESV, NRSV). This is the Hebrew word *šālôm* which means 'peace', 'wholeness' or 'welfare'. Here it indicates an answer that would ensure the welfare of Pharaoh.

17–21. Pharaoh's retelling of his dreams to Joseph faithfully tracks the narrator's version (cf. vv. 1–7). Yet Pharaoh's version includes a number of slight differences as well as Pharaoh's own comments about what he saw in his dream. These changes and additions taken together indicate that he understood the dreams as menacingly foreboding. In addition, he always refers to the two dreams as being essentially one by using the word *dream* (i.e. singular; vv. 17, 22; cf. v. 15). In reference to the first seven cows in his initial dream he called them *plump and beautiful in form* (v. 18), reversing the description used by the narrator and exchanging *beautiful in form* for the narrator's *beautiful in appearance* (v. 2). He described the second seven cows more unfavourably than the narrator had: *poor, very abysmal in appearance and thin* (v. 19; cf. v. 3). Then he commented that he had never seen such sickly cows in Egypt. In addition, after describing the sickly cows' consumption of the plump ones, he observed that the emaciated cows looked none the better for having eaten the well-fed ones.

22–24. In turning to his second dream Pharaoh's description tracks more closely to the narrator's version, with fewer changes. He described the first ears of grain as *full and good* (v. 22), instead of the narrator's *plump and good* (v. 5). Like his description of the second seven cows, he described the second seven ears more fully: *withered, thin and scorched* (v. 23; cf. v. 6). He depicted the seven thin ears of grain swallowing the *good* ones (instead of the narrator's *plump and full*, v. 7). He then repeated that he told the magicians his dream but no-one could offer a meaning for it.

25. Joseph began his interpretation by making two statements that he would repeat: first, he said that the two dreams were one, meaning that they conveyed the same message (cf. v. 26); then he stated that *God has revealed to Pharaoh what he is about to do* (cf. v. 28, where the synonym *shown* is substituted for *revealed*). Joseph interpreted the dreams in two parts (vv. 26–27 and vv. 28–31) corresponding to these two statements.

26–27. In the first part of his interpretation Joseph identified the seven good cows as seven years and the seven good ears of grain as seven years. In this way he demonstrated that *the dreams are one* (v. 26). Note that Joseph dispensed with the full description of these years and only described them as *good*. By dispensing with fuller characterizations of these years he signalled that they were not the important part of the dream – they simply gave time for preparation for the next heptad of years (cf. vv. 34–35). Then he identified the seven *thin, bad* cows as seven years and the seven *worthless, scorched* heads of grain as seven years *of famine* (v. 27). Note again that the emphasis is on the famine years. Although he characterized the second set of seven years as famine years, the first seven years were not characterized by Joseph as years of abundance, as he would do later (see vv. 29, 34).

28–31. Joseph next transitioned to explaining that God had shown Pharaoh what he was about to do. Joseph called the first seven years *years of great abundance* (v. 29), clearly a reference to the very appealing appearance of the first seven cows and the fullness of the first seven ears of grain. Then he noted two things about the seven famine years to follow, alternating them in verses 30–31. First, the abundance would be *forgotten*; it would not be *remembered*. Note that this is the opposite order to what the cupbearer did: in his abundance after being released from prison he did not *remember* Joseph but *forgot* him (40:23). Second, the famine would devastate the land since the famine would be so severe. Note once again that

Table 18 Statements describing years of abundance and famine

Years of abundance	Years of famine
seven years of abundance throughout the land (v. 29)	after them will be seven years of famine (v. 30)
	the abundance will be forgotten (v. 30)
	the famine will devastate the land (v. 30)
	the abundance will not be remembered (v. 31)
	the famine will be severe (v. 31)

Joseph emphasized the seven years of famine. There is only one statement characterizing the years of abundance, but there are five that describe the years of famine (see Table 18 on p. 383).

32. Joseph added a final note to explain why Pharaoh had two dreams: God had determined the matter and it would be implemented immediately.

33–36. Although Joseph was not asked what to do about the dream, he nevertheless took this opportunity to advise Pharaoh as to a course of action. This advice shows Joseph's administrative and planning skills that he had developed as administrator of Potiphar's household and as chief trustee in the royal prison. Joseph urged Pharaoh to appoint a *discerning and wise* man over Egypt (v. 33). Proverbs 16:21 describes a person with a wise heart as discerning and able to instruct with sweet lips, and this is an apt description of Joseph's discernment as exhibited in his skilful explanation of the dream to Pharaoh. This also is a subtle condemnation of Egypt's wise men (see v. 8) who could not explain the dream.

While the project Joseph was proposing required a wise leader, it also required more administrators to implement it, so Joseph called for Pharaoh to appoint *overseers over the land* (v. 34). They were to *take a fifth [of the harvest]*. The Hebrew verb which is derived from the number 'five' is generally understood to mean to take one-fifth of something, as widely reflected in English versions.[15] However, some commentators understand it to mean 'organize' or 'organize [the land] into five districts'.[16] Considering that Joseph actually set aside a fifth of Egypt's harvest each year (47:24, 26) and that there is no firm evidence that Egypt was organized into five agricultural districts during this era (the twelfth dynasty during the Middle Kingdom period), the verb almost certainly means to take a fifth of something. Joseph's plan to gather and store the excess during the years of abundance (v. 35) was for the purpose of having a reserve for the famine years and thereby avoiding the devastation of Egypt (v. 36). Without any central planning such as this, the normal human

---

15. This understanding is as old as LXX, which translates it as 'collect one-fifth'.

16. Wenham (1994: 394); Hamilton (1995: 498, 500).

tendency is to overindulge when there is plenty, leaving no reserve for future needs. Joseph's advice was wise because it ran counter to the unbridled enthusiasm that can accompany a windfall but is foolishly short-sighted.

Additional note on paired dreams in Joseph's life

One of the recurring features of the extended narrative about Joseph's rise to power in Egypt is the pairs of dreams and their interpretation. Joseph had two dreams about his ascent to a position above the rest of his family (37:5-11). In prison the chief cupbearer and chief baker both had dreams in the same night (40:5-19). Then Pharaoh had two dreams in the same night (41:1-32). These six dreams are the only paired dreams in Genesis.[17]

In each case the paired dreams are somehow connected. In the case of the first two dreams they are joined in that both were dreamt by the same person: Joseph (37:5, 9). The second pair of dreams are linked in that they were both dreamt in the same night (40:5). The third pair of dreams are coupled in both ways: they were dreamt in the same night and by the same person – Pharaoh (41:1, 4, 7). The fact that Pharaoh's visions combine both ways of pairing dreams signals that they come at the climax of Joseph's rise to prominence.

Joseph's dreams in particular are different from the other two pairs. First, Joseph's dreams did not reveal the immediate future. Instead, they revealed how his family would acknowledge his status more than two decades later (42:6; 43:26; 47:31). Second, they are the only dreams for which Joseph did not offer an interpretation. His brothers interpreted the first dream (37:8), and Jacob interpreted the second one (37:10). The import of this is not apparent until the later dreams find no-one in Egypt to interpret them (40:8; 41:8, 15). In both instances Joseph asserts that dream interpretation belongs to God (40:8; 41:16). This implies that God was not only with Joseph but also with Joseph's family, and that he revealed the meaning of Joseph's dreams to his brothers and his father.

_____

17. For single dreams, see 20:3, 6; 28:12; 31:10-11, 24.

Another lesson learned from the paired dreams of Joseph and of Pharaoh is the last interpretive principle that Joseph enunciated to the Egyptian king: the dream was given twice to convey the message that *the matter has been determined by God* (41:32). Thus, the twinned dreams of Joseph also communicated this message. Once this principle has been revealed in the text of Genesis, it prepares readers for what they now understand is the inevitable consequence of Joseph's rise to power in Egypt that will be revealed in the ensuing chapters: Joseph's family will bow before him and acknowledge that he does indeed rule over them (cf. 37:8; 50:18).

But what of the other set of dreams that conveyed not one message like the dreams of Joseph and Pharaoh, but two messages (41:12) – the dreams of the chief cupbearer and the chief baker? These messages are conjoined in a different way.[18] This is signalled in five ways. First, the cupbearer and baker are initially presented as a pair of officers who committed a single offence against Pharaoh (40:1–4). Second, they dreamt their dreams in the same night (40:5). Third, they told Joseph, *We had a dream but there is no-one to interpret it* (40:8), as if their two dreams were one.[19] Fourth, the initial impression given by the dreams is that each predicts the same thing, since each involves three items related to each man's occupation. Finally, Joseph's interpretation of both dreams employs the phrase *lift up your head* (40:13, 19), though with two very different meanings. So, while these two dreams had different meanings, they clearly were intended to complement each other. In the story of Joseph's rise they serve to demonstrate that with God's guidance Joseph was able to discern subtle differences in the meaning of dreams, thereby convincing Pharaoh's cupbearer of his advanced skill in dream interpretation (41:13).

In addition, the story of Pharaoh's cupbearer and baker and their dreams invites readers to consider the untold backstory of conspiracy in Pharaoh's court. While no-one can be certain why

---

18. Grossman (2016: 723–725).

19. Most English versions read 'dreams . . . them', but the Hebrew text employs singular forms, not plural forms.

Pharaoh had them imprisoned, it appears as if Egypt's king chose to punish the two men in charge of his food and drink perhaps because of an attempt to poison him. This episode conjures up images of palace intrigue in which Pharaoh incarcerated both men until he could determine who was at fault. The cupbearer was exonerated, but the baker was found guilty and executed. While this may not be a completely accurate reconstruction of the circumstances that led to the imprisonment of these two men, the text's provoking readers to think about this also encourages them to see God's hand working even among Pharaoh's servants in order ultimately to elevate Joseph over all Egypt so that he could save Jacob's family.

ii. Joseph given high rank by Pharaoh (41:37–45)

37–38. Joseph's interpretation of the dream was not good news for Pharaoh, since seven years of famine were truly enough to wipe out the land (see v. 36). Yet Pharaoh's reaction was favourable, probably because he had already concluded that the dreams were not favourable portents. More importantly, *the matter pleased Pharaoh and all his servants* (v. 37). While many English versions take this to mean that Pharaoh was pleased by Joseph's advice, his proposal for averting disaster, the Hebrew is much more general and probably applies both to the dream interpretation and to the advice. Pharaoh immediately asked whether there was anyone else like Joseph, a rhetorical question that assumes there was none other. He described Joseph as having *God's spirit* (v. 38). However, this ought not to be taken to mean that Pharaoh had adopted Joseph's belief in Yahweh. In fact, the Hebrew text allows for Pharaoh's words to mean that Joseph had 'a spirit of the gods', in keeping with ancient Egypt's polytheistic practices.

39–41. When addressing Joseph, Pharaoh called him *discerning and wise* (v. 39), the very same words Joseph had used to characterize the man who should be set over the land of Egypt (see v. 33). Pharaoh then placed Joseph over his house (i.e. the palace). Thus, having been freed from prison Joseph had gone from being over Potiphar's house to being over Pharaoh's house. Moreover, everyone in Pharaoh's house was subject to Joseph. The Hebrew expression used here for this is *all my people will kiss your mouth* (cf. Ps. 2:12).[20] In fact, Pharaoh exempted only himself from Joseph's authority. Yet being over Pharaoh's house was not the extent of Joseph's authority, Pharaoh addressed Joseph a second time and placed him over the entire land of Egypt. Thus, Joseph was made one of ancient Egypt's viziers. A vizier's responsibilities included the running of the country, much like a prime minister. Lesser officials would report to the vizier. Viziers oversaw the political administration of the kingdom, and all official documents had to have the vizier's seal on them (see v. 42). Traditionally they also managed the taxation system and monitored the supply of food – something that is emphasized among Joseph's responsibilities (vv. 47–49, 53–57). The vizier also ran the pharaoh's household.

42–43. Pharaoh's investiture of Joseph with authority included the trappings of authority: signet ring, fine linen clothing and a gold chain. Joseph's position was publicly acknowledged by having him ride in a chariot behind Pharaoh. The proclamation made in front of Joseph is the obscure Egyptian word *'abrēk* (v. 43). Several proposals have been made for its meaning, including *Make way!* or *Kneel!*[21]

44. Pharaoh explicitly placed Joseph in charge of everyone's activities since *no-one will be able to raise his hand or foot* without Joseph's permission.

45. Joseph's integration into the Egyptian court was completed by his receiving a new name and his marriage. The meaning of the name given to Joseph is disputed.[22] His wife's name was *Asenath*, which probably means 'belonging to [the goddess] Neith'. His father-in-law's name *Potiphera* was essentially the same as his former master's name. That Joseph married into the family of a priest of On was another part of his integration into the highest level of Egyptian society. On, near present-day Cairo, was the centre of worship of the Egyptian gods associated with the sun. Thus, the

---

20. For a discussion of other proposed meanings for this phrase, see Hamilton (1995: 504–505).

21. For a discussion of proposed meanings, see Mathews (2005: 763) and Hamilton (1995: 506).

22. Hamilton (1995: 507–508).

Greeks called it Heliopolis, 'Sun City' (Jer. 43:13). The final sentence in this verse says that *Joseph went out over the land of Egypt*, signifying that when he left the palace he was now in charge of the entire kingdom.[23]

iii. Joseph as administrator (41:46-57)

46. Joseph's age is an indication of his maturity. When his age was last given he was a brash young man of seventeen on whom his father doted (37:2). Now through experience in Potiphar's house and in prison, and, more importantly, through the blessing of God, he is a mature man. His thirteen years in Egypt have brought him to the pinnacle of service in the ancient Mediterranean world of his day: service to Pharaoh. The Hebrew text uses a figure of speech to speak of Joseph's entering Pharaoh's service: *he stood before Pharaoh, king of Egypt*. This is the only occurrence of the phrase *Pharaoh, king of Egypt* in Genesis, although it is used twenty more times in the Old Testament. Here it likely is employed to emphasize the power of the throne that now was at Joseph's disposal as he administered the land on Pharaoh's behalf. Joseph, it is emphasized, was a hands-on administrator. He *travelled throughout the land of Egypt* and did not simply issue orders from the confines of the palace.

47-49. The fruitfulness of the land is emphasized in three ways. First, the phrase *the seven years of abundance* (v. 47) in Hebrew employs assonance: each of the three words in the phrase contains a sibilant. Second, this phrase also uses a pun: the words for *seven* and *abundance* are nearly identical. Finally, the land is said to produce *in abundance*, which is literally 'by the fistful', probably referring to the fullness of each head of grain as large enough to fill one's hand. The description of Joseph's execution of his plan to provide for the coming famine years notes that he stored the grain in the nearby cities. Placing the granaries in centres of population made the most sense and demonstrated Joseph's character as *wise and discerning* (vv. 33, 39):

---

23. The expression *went out over* is clearly an idiom and is found with this meaning only here and at Ps. 81:5, which is a reflection of this verse. Normally this idiom means 'to attack' as in warfare, a meaning not appropriate in this context.

there would be a ready source of personnel to service the granaries and yet distribution would not be a problem, since the stores in each city could provide for the immediately adjacent countryside. The abundance of the harvests from which Joseph sequestered one-fifth was so great that it was futile to measure it. The abundance is described as *like the sand of the seashore* (v. 49), a phrase that earlier was used to describe the promise to Abraham and Jacob of the abundance of their descendants (22:17; 32:12). This prepares for the content of the next verses: the births of Joseph's sons.

50–52. During these seven years before the famine we are told that Joseph had two sons, and it is emphasized that they were borne by his wife – perhaps a subtle reference to Joseph's commitment to the sanctity of marriage (v. 50; cf. 39:9; 46:20). The name of Joseph's firstborn, *Manasseh* (v. 51), means 'caused to be forgotten' and fits well with Joseph's explanation that God had made him forget two things: his hardship (i.e. slavery and imprisonment) and his family. Here *forget* does not mean to lose all knowledge of something, but instead to cease actively thinking about something (cf. Job 11:6).[24] In naming his second son *Ephraim*, perhaps meaning 'doubly fruitful' (v. 52), Joseph acknowledged God's work in his life even through his times of affliction. In naming both sons, Joseph mentioned the adversity that had beset him. In the second case he spoke of *affliction*, a word that presages Israel's later affliction upon being enslaved in Egypt (Exod. 3:7, 17; 4:31; Deut. 26:7).

53–55. Following the birth of Ephraim the seven abundant years ended and the seven famine years began *just as Joseph had said*. This confirmation of Joseph's interpretation of Pharaoh's dream not only justified the recommendation of the cupbearer (see v. 13) but more importantly demonstrated that Joseph was acting as Yahweh's prophet as he communicated the unalterable and utterly reliable word of God. This presence of God in Joseph's life was reflected in the blessing he brought to Egypt, just as he had brought blessing to Potiphar's house and even to the royal prison (39:3, 5, 23). To emphasize God's blessing through Joseph the text draws a contrast

---

24. Obviously it does not mean that Joseph no longer had knowledge of his affliction. Note his mention of it in v. 52.

between famine *in every land* and food *in the whole land of Egypt* (v. 54).
When Pharaoh's people demanded food, with all confidence he sent
them to Joseph and instructed them to *do whatever he tells you.*

56–57. Joseph's distribution of grain was by sale. This, too,
demonstrated his wise and discerning character. Had he simply
given out grain without charge the Egyptians would have developed
a tendency to use more grain than they needed, perhaps even to
engage in easy profiteering by selling grain to foreigners. However,
if they had to use their own resources to obtain food, they would
be much more restrained. Indeed, the famine brought people from
other lands to Egypt in search of grain *since the famine was severe*
[literally 'grew strong'] *in every land* (v. 57). This last statement
prepares for the next part of the story of Jacob's family: Joseph
once again would have to deal with his brothers.

Meaning

Is God with his people even in the midst of trial and adversity? It
is a question that many a believer has raised when trouble strikes –
especially trouble that appears to be undeserved or unjust. In these
three accounts of Joseph in Egypt we see that God keeps his
promise to be with those who trust in him. Joseph found himself in bondage in Potiphar's house, and God was with him. He
prospered and even was elevated to chief steward. Yet even though
God was with him, Joseph was not immune to setbacks and difficulties. Despite the seductive invitation of Potiphar's wife, he
refused to commit an offence against his master and against God.
For his righteous behaviour he was punished. In prison he proved
to be a model prisoner, and his interpretation of the dreams of the
cupbearer and baker demonstrated that God had given him extraordinary ability to proclaim God's dream messages. Yet we can only
imagine Joseph's despair as he sat in prison for two more years
(40:14–15, 23). God, however, had told both Joseph and his family
that he had been chosen for great things (37:5–11), and God kept
his word. It took the maturity gained during thirteen years of
slavery and imprisonment to bring Joseph to the right time and
place so that Yahweh could use him to provide not only for the
people of Egypt but also for people from other lands (41:53–57).
Not all of the misery experienced by Christ's people will be a

stepping stone to earthly glory as it was for Joseph. Some will die a martyr's death, as did Stephen, Paul and Peter. Others will live lives in earthly obscurity, though their faith and works are surely known to God. Yet Joseph's story ultimately also demonstrates to all of them that there is a glorious future stored up for them as God has promised (Heb. 11:35–40). Faithful believers find their ultimate hope not in earthly rewards but in the goal of God's work in Joseph's life that preserved the people of Israel: the bringing forth of a Saviour to bless people from all nations. For victory over adversity they look to Christ and God's promise in him (Heb. 12:1–11).

Additional note on parallels between Joseph and Daniel

One of the most prominent scriptural parallels to the story of Joseph is the story of Daniel. Both were taken by force to a foreign country (Gen. 37:12–36; Dan. 1:1–7). God was with them in their punishment that came to them because of their loyalty to God (Gen. 39; Dan. 6). Joseph and Daniel served as advisors to foreign royal courts (Gen. 41:46; Dan. 1 – 6). Both men interpreted dreams for kings (Gen. 41:1–38; Dan. 2; 4). Both were promoted to the highest office below the king (Gen. 41:39–45; Dan. 6:1–2).

However, the similarities between Joseph and Daniel extend beyond these obvious parallels. The vocabulary used in Daniel is similar to that used in the narratives concerning Joseph. For instance, the term for 'magician' occurs in both to describe the king's advisors (Gen. 41:8, 24; Dan. 1:20; 2:2). This word is an Egyptian loanword used elsewhere in Scripture only in Egyptian settings (Exod. 7:11, 22; 8:7, 18–19; 9:11).

Another similarity is the use of Hebrew (Gen.) and Aramaic (Dan.) cognate roots for 'interpret' and 'interpretation' (Gen. 40:8, 16, 22; 41:12–13, 15; Dan. 5:12, 16). This similarity is all the more striking because these Hebrew words occur in the Old Testament only in Genesis 40 – 41, and except for Ecclesiastes 8:1, the Aramaic terms occur only in Daniel.

The phrase 'one's spirit is troubled' to describe the distress that kings experienced because of dreams is used in both Genesis (41:8) and Daniel (2:1, 3). Both the Joseph and Daniel narratives refer to men who appear to be downcast or sickly using the same word – the only uses of this word in this sense (Gen. 40:6; Dan. 1:10).[25] Moreover, it ought to be noted that royal attendants described by the word for 'king's servant' or 'eunuch' play important roles in the lives of both men (Gen. 37:36; 39:1; 40:2, 7; Dan. 1:3, 7–11, 18).

More significant parallels connect the divine gift of insight and wisdom of both Joseph and Daniel. Both were endowed with a 'spirit of [holy] god[s]' (Gen. 41:38; Dan. 4:8–9; 5:11, 14). Both recognized that God had used dreams to reveal the future to kings (Gen. 41:25, 28; Dan. 2:28). Joseph and Daniel alike admitted that their ability to interpret dreams was a gift from God (Gen. 40:8; 41:16; Dan. 2:28).

These connections are too numerous and too vital to the stories of both men to be simple coincidence or the result of similar life experiences. Instead, clearly Daniel modelled the telling of his story on the narrative about Joseph to draw his readers' attention to the similarity between his situation and Joseph's. Daniel is telling his readers that God had not lost control of the world or abandoned his people in Babylon any more than he had in Joseph's day. Just as God was present with Joseph and used him to keep many people alive (Gen. 50:20), so he used Daniel and other captive Judeans to preserve and prosper his people in Babylon.

---

25. Elsewhere the word means 'be angry', 'be in a rage'.

25. THE FAMILY OF JACOB: THE FAMINE BRINGS JOSEPH'S BROTHERS TO EGYPT (42:1 – 45:28)

This portion of Genesis resolves the tension in the narrative that has built since Jacob first favoured Rachel over Leah and then Rachel's son Joseph over his brothers. As such it contains a number of links back to previous chapters, especially Genesis 37 and 41. The need for Jacob to send his sons to Egypt (42:1–4) presupposes 41:54–57. That they must return a second time for more food despite Jacob's reluctance to send them with Benjamin (43:1–14) recalls the split in the family because of Jacob's favouring Rachel and her sons over Leah and her sons. Joseph's lordship over the land (42:6) assumes the events narrated in 41:40–45. Joseph remembers his dreams when he sees them fulfilled (42:6, 9). Joseph's brothers recall their shameful treatment of him (42:21–22; cf. 37:14–36). Their being released from custody on the third day recalls the custody of the chief cupbearer and chief baker that ended three days after Joseph spoke to them (42:18; 40:20). Jacob's bitter remembrance of Joseph and clinging to Benjamin in his absence (42:36–38) demonstrates that even after two decades he was still mourning the loss of Joseph (37:33–35).

The climax of this story is the long plea for Benjamin by Judah (44:18–34). His words recapitulate the history of the brothers' interaction with Jacob concerning his youngest son. It is Judah's concern for his father's well-being and his unselfish offering of himself in place of Benjamin that finally breaks through Joseph's reluctance to effect a total reconciliation with his brothers.

This portion of the story concludes with Pharaoh's invitation for his father to come to Egypt (45:16–28), which prepares for much of the rest of the book: Jacob's time in Egypt from his descent to the land of the Nile to his death. Israel will be welcomed into the land (47:1–12). Jacob will see Joseph and bow before him (47:31), bless Ephraim and Manasseh (48:1–22), prophesy about the future tribes of Israel (49:1–28) and charge them concerning the interment of his body in Hebron (49:29–33).

The events of this portion of Genesis take place during the first two years of the famine (see 45:6, 11). Since the birth and death of Jacob can be securely dated, and since Jacob lived seventeen years in Egypt before his death, these events took place between about 1878 and 1877 BC.[1]

A. Jacob's sons' first trip to Egypt (42:1–26)

Context
c.1878 BC
Having traced Joseph's rise from his enslavement and subsequent imprisonment to his position as vizier, this portion of the narrative returns to his brothers, beginning the process of reuniting them.

Comment
1–4. With the beginning of this chapter the narrative abruptly but briefly shifts to Jacob and his sons in Canaan. We are not told how Jacob learned that there was grain for sale in Egypt. He took the initiative to send his sons to Egypt, asking why they were *looking at each other* (v. 1) – that is, dithering instead of taking action when the famine affected them. Jacob, however, was still the head of the

---

1. Steinmann (2011: 74–80).

family and here acted decisively, informing them of his knowledge and ordering them to go to Egypt for grain *so that we might live and not die* (v. 2). The construction *live and not die* is a tautology that pairs a word and its negated opposite. Tautologies formed in this way are common in biblical Hebrew. This one occurs twice more in Genesis with the telling of stories connected to the famine (43:8; 47:19).[2]

Note that Jacob's sons are called *Joseph's brothers* when they go down to Egypt (v. 3). This anticipates their role in the next scene when Joseph recognizes them (vv. 6–7). Jacob's refusal to send Benjamin shows that he still valued Rachel's child over the children of the rest of his wives. His worry that *an accident* (v. 4) might happen to him is an oblique reference to Joseph's assumed death from a wild animal (37:33). He will use the word *accident* twice more to express his fear of losing Benjamin (42:38; 44:29).

5–6. Verse 5 resumes the line of thought begun at 41:57 after the brief interruption of 42:1–4. Readers were told that the famine was in every land, and now it is explicitly stated that *the sons of Israel* came *because the famine was severe in the land of Canaan* (v. 5). Joseph, the son of Israel who was already in Egypt, is called *the ruler of Egypt*, and his role in this narrative is defined as being the one who sold grain to the people. Perhaps this double identification of Joseph as both ruler and dispenser of grain is meant to evoke readers' memories of his two dreams, where he was ruler (the stars bowing to him) and the most important gatherer of grain (the sheaves bowing to his sheaf). This impression is reinforced with the statement that Joseph's brothers bowed before him. Therefore, readers remember Joseph's dreams before they are told that he remembered them (see v. 9).

7. Joseph's recognition of his brothers is masked by his *treating them as strangers*, an ironic statement in Hebrew since the same root is used for both 'recognize' and 'treat as strangers'. His speaking harshly to them is not explained by the text, and readers are left to wonder what motivation lay behind Joseph's severity. No matter

---

2. It is also used at Num. 4:19; Deut. 33:6; 2 Kgs 18:32. Another example of a tautology formed in this manner is 'remember and not forget' (Deut. 9:7; 1 Sam. 1:11).

what Joseph's motivation was, there is no doubt that his brothers recognized his harsh tone, even through an interpreter (see vv. 23, 30). Joseph initiated what would be the first of three dialogues with his brothers, dialogues that would enable him to surmise whether he could learn to trust them in order to reveal his identity to them and be reconciled to them.

8–11. The recognition, we are told, was not mutual. They were kept from recognizing him, perhaps because Joseph had been assimilated into Egyptian culture: he was probably clean-shaven and dressed in Egyptian garb. In addition, they assumed that he was now dead (see v. 13). Joseph, however, not only recognized them, but he also remembered his dreams (37:5–11). How this prompted his accusation against his brothers is not made clear, but he was clearly accusing them of lying when they said they had come to buy grain. Instead, he said their real purpose was to see the vulnerability (literally, 'nakedness') of the land. The brothers' reply further fulfilled Joseph's dream as they addressed him as *my lord* (v. 10) and later referred to themselves as *your servants* (vv. 11, 13), acknowledging his superior position but still insisting that their only purpose was to purchase food. As supporting evidence for this they revealed that they were *the sons of one man*, since it was unlikely that ten spies would all be from the same family. Then they stated, *We are honest*, meaning that they were not lying about their reason for being in Egypt.

12–13. Joseph, however, repeated his accusation to draw out his brothers. They took the bait and further described their family. They gave several more facts to allay any suspicion that they were spies: they were originally twelve sons of one man in Canaan. They clarified why there were only ten of them present: the youngest was with their father and one *is no more* (v. 13) – an oblique way of saying that he was presumed dead. While this explanation was meant to convince Joseph that they were not lying about coming to Egypt to purchase food, it told Joseph two things: they did not recognize him, and his father and younger brother Benjamin were still alive.

14–17. Joseph's continued accusation now resulted in what he presented as a test: if they were telling the truth, they could produce their youngest brother. Joseph even took an oath by Pharaoh's life to demonstrate the seriousness of his accusation.[3] Joseph's proposed test was to imprison his brothers and send only one back to fetch Benjamin. Benjamin's presence would confirm their claim. Clearly, however, Joseph desired to see his brother who had been only a toddler when Joseph was sold into slavery. Joseph also gave his brothers a taste of the misery he had lived through by placing them in prison for three days.

18–20. The narrative skips to the third day, when Joseph addressed them again. He told them what to do in order to remain alive: only one brother would be kept in custody, while the others would take grain to their families. Joseph did this, he said, because he feared God. The God-fearing person cares for those who are in need and are hungry (Job 29:12–13; Prov. 31:20, 30). Since the famine was severe, Joseph's change of heart allowed more grain to be taken back to Egypt, since the grain one man could have taken would hardly have been enough to feed everyone (v. 19). But Joseph reminded them that they needed to bring Benjamin back to confirm their contention that they were honest in stating their reason for coming to Egypt. Then we are told that they consented to this arrangement.[4]

21–23. A discussion among the brothers ensued. They now felt that they were being punished for their actions against Joseph years earlier. Their words imply that they believed God was at work behind the scenes to bring about their unpleasant experiences

---

3. Note that Joseph clearly maintained his character as an Egyptian so that his brothers would not recognize him. Whereas it was common for Israelites to swear by God's life (Judg. 8:19; Ruth 3:13; 1 Sam. 14:39, 45; 19:6; 20:3, 21; 25:26; 26:10, 16; 28:10; 29:6; 2 Sam. 4:9; 12:5; 14:11; 15:21; 1 Kgs 1:29; 2:24; 22:14; 2 Kgs 2:2, 4, 6; 4:30; 5:16, 20; 2 Chr. 18:13; Jer. 4:2; 5:2; 12:16; 16:14–15; 23:7, 8; 38:16; Hos. 4:15), Joseph swore by the life of Pharaoh, who in ancient Egyptian religion was considered to be the intermediary between the gods and the people, thereby making him divine.

4. The Hebrew text says, 'They did this.' However, since there was nothing that they did immediately, the sense is that they agreed to Joseph's demands (see CSB, GW, NRSV).

(cf. v. 28). Their words here are the only time in Genesis that we hear of Joseph's anguish and pleas to his brothers when they put him into the pit. They also admitted that they heartlessly refused to listen to him. Reuben's words accuse his brothers of not listening to him, either. He had told them not to harm Joseph (cf. 37:22), and now Reuben claimed that they would be held accountable for Joseph's blood (cf. 4:10–11; 9:6). We are told that Joseph understood what they said but that they did not realize this, since he had spoken to them through an interpreter – which may also help explain why they did not recognize him (see v. 8).

24. Joseph's reaction to his brothers' words is poignant. His weeping may have been partly because he did not realize that Reuben was not complicit in their actions and partly because of his empathy for them: they now were as frightened as he was when they had power over him. Nevertheless, Joseph was not yet ready to reveal himself to them. He wanted to see whether they had truly changed. So he had Simeon bound. The choice of Simeon, Jacob's second son, may have been the result of Reuben's words. It would have been logical to hold back the firstborn son – presumed to be the most important son in the family in the culture of the Ancient Near East. However, Joseph now knew that Reuben was not responsible for what had happened to him, so he spared this oldest son of Jacob and took Simeon instead. Joseph was probably confident that they would return to Egypt. He knew that the famine would last about six more years (see 45:6, 11) and that they would be forced to return for more grain.

25–26. Joseph may not have been ready to reveal himself to his brothers, but he was generous to them. He not only gave them grain but also returned the silver that they had used to purchase it.[5] In addition, he gave them provisions for their trip back to Canaan. The return of their silver has been seen as either a trap set by Joseph or a sign of generosity. If it were intended as a trap, it is

---

5. Technically, this was not money, since coinage was not invented until the early seventh century BC. Prior to the minting of coins silver was used as a medium of exchange and was weighed at the point of purchase.

curious that Joseph never mentioned it or accused them of theft (contrast 44:3–10).

Meaning
Previous experiences with people affect our later behaviour around them. Joseph was no exception to this. His first encounter with his brothers in Egypt reveals him to have been cautious and perhaps suspicious of them. Therefore, he did not immediately reveal his true identity to them. Nevertheless, he was anxious to learn about his father and his brother Benjamin, quizzing them by means of a ruse: his scepticism towards their denial of being spies. Yet Joseph was also poignantly touched by Reuben's words as he learned of his eldest brother's previous attempt to keep the others from harming him. That, however, did not keep him from taking Simeon into custody in order to ensure their return to Egypt with Benjamin.

B. Jacob's sons return to him (42:27–38)

Context
c.1878 BC
Although Joseph's brothers have now met him, the connection with his father has not yet been re-established. Accordingly, this section follows the brothers as they return to Jacob, initiating the process by which the family will be reunited, though at this stage fear is the more prominent element.

Comment
27–28. The next scene takes place at a lodging stop on their way back to Canaan. An unnamed brother found silver in his sack when he opened it to get feed for his donkey. Their dismay at this discovery is conveyed by the Hebrew idiom *their heart went out*, which occurs only here. Jacob's sons now voiced what they must have been thinking when they assumed that they were being punished for selling Joseph into slavery (vv. 21–22): God had brought this about. Interestingly, there were no recriminations addressed to the brother in whose sack the silver was found. They did not suspect one another of thievery.

29–34. Upon returning to Jacob *they told him everything that had happened to them* (v. 29). This does not mean that the content of their words in the following verses is a recapitulation of every detail of their encounter with Joseph. Instead, it means that they gave an accurate, though compressed, account. Twice they refer to Joseph as *the man, the lord of the land* (vv. 30, 33), thereby revealing to the reader that they had not recognized Joseph but had unknowingly fulfilled the prophecy in his dreams. They omit a few facets of their experience: that they were imprisoned for three days, that Joseph indirectly threatened to have them executed if they returned without Benjamin (cf. v. 20) and that one of them had discovered his silver in his sack. They also softened the mention of Simeon's imprisonment, quoting Joseph as saying *leave one brother with me* (v. 33) instead of mentioning his being imprisoned (cf. v. 19).

35–36. Later, as they were opening their sacks, all the brothers discovered that their silver had been returned to them. The reaction of fear now struck not only the brothers but also Jacob. The brothers most likely were afraid that God was punishing them for what they had done to Joseph. However, Jacob expressed his fear: he had lost Joseph and now he believed he would never see Simeon again. He also accused his sons of wanting to deprive him of Benjamin. His last words, though, are selfishly unconcerned with his other sons: *everything has happened to me!* (v. 36).

37–38. As eldest son, Reuben offered his two sons in place of the two sons Jacob would have lost should he not return with Benjamin. Reuben, however, had four sons (46:9; Exod. 6:14; Num. 26:5–6; 1 Chr. 5:3). The offer was probably for two of these sons. Reuben to this point is the only son who has voiced concern for his brothers and has tried to protect them – first Joseph (37:21–22, 29–30) and now Benjamin. However, Jacob would have had no interest in executing two of his grandsons, so he rejected Reuben's offer. Moreover, he appeared to favour Benjamin over all of his other sons, just as he had favoured Joseph. He pointedly called Joseph *his* [i.e. Benjamin's] *brother* (v. 38) and not 'your brother'. Any harm to Benjamin would, he said, *bring my grey hair down to Sheol* (cf. 44:29, 31). He did not express the same affection for the imprisoned Simeon, whom he considered lost (see v. 36).

Meaning

Fear often leads us to do things we otherwise would not consider doing. Fear's weight upon Jacob led him bitterly to accuse his sons of depriving him of Simeon and wanting to risk great harm to Benjamin. He was withdrawing into himself, showing scant compassion for the obvious distress shown by his sons. In turn, the brothers were in a sense reliving the consequences of their selling Joseph into slavery and deceiving Jacob by faking Joseph's death. Thus, Jacob was wrong: everything was not happening to him – everything was happening to him and his sons in a way that he could not have understood at this point as God was behind these events that would lead to his family being reunited in Egypt.

C. Jacob's sons return to Egypt with Benjamin (43:1–34)

Context

c.1877 BC

The gradual process by which Jacob's family is brought together again continues here as Benjamin joins his brothers in travelling to Egypt and meeting Joseph, though by the end of this chapter the brothers still do not know Joseph's full identity, and the motif of fear which emerged in the previous chapter now comes to prominence. In all this, the narrative carefully demonstrates the ways in which Joseph's dreams are being fulfilled.

Comment

1–2. This is the fourth of seven times that the severity of this famine is mentioned in Genesis (cf. 41:31, 56, 57; 47:4, 13, 20). In this case the severity of the famine explains why Jacob's family had eaten all the grain they had obtained in Egypt so quickly (in less than a year; cf. 45:6, 11) – there was none to be had in Canaan. It also explains why Jacob was willing to send his sons back for more food even though on the first trip he had lost Simeon (42:36).

3–5. While Jacob had suggested that they return to Egypt for more food, he had not offered to send Benjamin with them, though he knew this was required (42:33). Judah, the oldest son in good standing with Jacob, now took the lead and emphasized Joseph's warning not to return without their youngest brother. Judah emphasized their relationship with Benjamin as *our brother* (v. 4) and their service to Jacob: Jacob had said *buy us a little food* (v. 2), but Judah said they would *buy food for you* (v. 4). To reinforce his insistence on taking Benjamin with them, Judah twice repeats Joseph's threat: *You will not see me again unless your brother is with you* (vv. 3, 5). While these words are not recorded in the previous chapter, they are certainly an accurate portrayal of the situation and may have been said though omitted in the recounting of the conversation in the previous chapter.

6–7. Jacob did not directly state his objection to sending Benjamin to Egypt as he had done earlier (see 42:38). Instead, Jacob voiced his frustration with having to send Benjamin to Egypt; why had they mentioned Benjamin to the man? However, this simply delayed the inevitable. The brothers backed up Judah's assertion and defended themselves by stating that the man had peppered them with questions and that they could not have anticipated his demand to bring Benjamin when they returned.

8–10. Despite Jacob's oblique objection, Judah directly addressed his father's concern and took responsibility by asking him to *send the boy with me* (v. 8). Judah offered a threefold argument in favour of sending Benjamin as Joseph had required. First, the main priority was that *we may live and not die* (v. 8), an echo of Jacob's original reason for sending his sons to Egypt (see 42:2). He emphasized the number of those who would benefit: *we, you and our children* (v. 8). Second, in the boldest language possible Judah assumed responsibility for Benjamin. His three older brothers had lost favour with Jacob due to their actions that had brought disgrace upon him and threatened his household (34:30; 35:22). Judah was, therefore, Jacob's presumed primary heir. In effect, he was pledging his status within the family as a guarantee for Benjamin's safety. Third, he noted that they had delayed returning to Egypt for more food – implying that Jacob's intransigence was the reason. They could have made two trips, and yet they had made none.

11–14. Once Jacob consented to Judah's wishes, he was keen to ensure that the man in Egypt would look favourably upon his sons so that they would return to him with Simeon. His present included the same aromatic resins from Gilead that the Ishmaelites were taking to Egypt when they bought Joseph (37:25). However, Jacob also added honey, pistachios and almonds. Jacob included several foods in his present even though the famine was severe and food was scarce. This may be an indication of how desperate he was that his sons make a good impression on the Egyptian lord of the land. In addition, he instructed his sons to take twice the silver they needed so that they could return the silver found in their bags. Jacob's supposition that the silver returned to their bags might have been a mistake may have been a suggestion as to what to say when they gave it back to the man (cf. vv. 21–22). Finally, Jacob gave them permission to take Benjamin – delaying it to the last possible moment. Then he expressed his blessing that *God Almighty* (v. 14) might make the man merciful to them and release Simeon and Benjamin. Elsewhere in Genesis the name *God Almighty* is associated with the promise of descendants for the patriarchs (17:1; 28:3; 35:11; 48:3), so it was an appropriate title for Jacob to invoke in his wish that all of his sons might return to him. Despite this, Jacob was resigned to the possible loss of two more sons.

15–17. The pace of the narrative briefly quickens when the brothers' departure and arrival in Egypt is quickly summarized. The author emphasizes that they took with them the three things Jacob had sent with them: the gift, double the silver, and Benjamin, all of which will be mentioned in the opposite order in the coming encounter with Joseph (vv. 16, 20–22, 25). With the Egyptian setting the narrative slows. When Joseph saw Benjamin, he was obviously pleased and ordered his household steward to take them to his home and to prepare for a noon meal. Since in antiquity there were no electric lights by which to eat an evening meal, the major meal on most days was eaten at noon.

18–19. Despite the welcome they had received, the brothers were afraid of what might be done to them because of the money in their bags. Why they thought this would be done at Joseph's house and could not have been done when they first were presented before Joseph is not stated. Interestingly, they not only envisaged themselves being enslaved, but they also mentioned their donkeys being seized. In order to pre-empt any action after they were inside the house, the brothers spoke to the steward at the doorway.

20–22. The words of Jacob's sons are not attributed to any particular brother but are portrayed as coming from all of them. In this

way the text emphasizes their common fear of what might be done
to them. Their portrayal of the discovery of the silver in their sacks
collapses two events into one. They speak of it happening at the
lodging place on the way back to Canaan. However, only one
brother discovered the silver then (42:27); the other brothers
discovered their silver when they were back in Canaan (42:35). They
may have thought that the details of their discovery were not
important. Instead, they emphasized their innocence in three ways.
First, they asserted that they *really did come down here the first time only
to buy food* (v. 20). Second, they stated that they had brought the silver
back as well as additional silver to purchase more food. Finally,
they claimed ignorance concerning how the silver had got into
their bags.

23. The steward's reply must have put them at ease. However,
his words must have seemed enigmatic. How did their God and
the God of their father (v. 23) provide the silver in their bags? The
mention of the God of one's father in Genesis is often used in
the context of God's protection (26:24; 31:5, 29, 42; 32:9; 46:3;
49:25), and it is coupled here with the steward's assurance that
everything was fine (literally, 'peace to you'; v. 23), so *do not be afraid.*
Was the steward saying that God was behind a human agent who
had put the silver there? This is not far from the truth, since Joseph
was God's agent to benefit them (50:20–21). The steward referred
to the silver as *treasure* (v. 23). This word, which is from the same
root as the Hebrew word for 'bury', often refers to hidden wealth
that is a boon to those who discover it (Job 3:21; Prov. 2:4; Isa.
45:3; Jer. 41:8). Moreover, the steward said that he had received
their silver, indicating that he was part of Joseph's team that
oversaw grain sales.

24–26. The scene now shifts to inside the house and the common
courtesies extended on the part of both parties. Joseph's brothers
were given water to wash their feet (18:4; 19:2; 24:32; 1 Sam. 25:41;
2 Sam. 11:8). For their part, the brothers prepared their gift in
anticipation of Joseph's arrival for the noon meal and then
presented it to him and bowed before him. This time there were
eleven brothers to bow to Joseph as well as the present from Jacob
which also acknowledged Joseph's supremacy. This matched well
Joseph's second dream (37:9–10).

27–28. Joseph's concern turned now to his father, though he stayed in character, referring to Jacob as *your elderly father whom you told me about* (v. 27). The brothers once again acknowledged Joseph's superior position by referring to Jacob by the polite and deprecating phrase *your servant* (v. 28) and then, after stating that Jacob was still alive, they knelt and prostrated themselves.

29–31. Joseph's acknowledgment of Benjamin in the form of a question and then his blessing Benjamin before anyone replied must have made it seem to the brothers as if Joseph knew more about them than they had suspected. Joseph, for his part, was overcome with emotion because of Benjamin and had to leave the room to conceal his weeping from his brothers. Joseph then washed his face to make himself presentable for the meal (cf. Matt. 6:17). Interestingly, this is the only mention in the Old Testament of someone washing his or her face.

32. Joseph and the Egyptians did not eat with Jacob's sons. The text explains that Egyptians viewed eating with foreigners as *detestable*. This term indicates a strong revulsion and is often used to characterize God's rejection of certain sins (Deut. 18:12; 23:18; 25:16; 27:15; 32:16). The Pentateuch also mentions other practices that Egyptians found detestable: raising sheep (46:34) and certain Israelite sacrifices (Exod. 8:26). According to the later Greek historian Herodotus, Egyptians would not eat or sacrifice cows, which were considered sacred since they were associated with the goddess Hathor.[6]

33–34. Joseph's knowledge of the brothers was revealed even more blatantly when they were seated in birth order. The brothers' reaction is described as wordless astonishment conveyed only in looks at each other. This is the only use of the word 'astonish', 'astounded' in the Pentateuch, emphasizing their utter bewilderment at Joseph's insight into their family's history. The favour of a fivefold portion given to Benjamin was perhaps aimed at discovering whether the older brothers would express jealousy towards him as they had done towards Joseph years earlier. However, they did not. Instead they enjoyed the meal with Joseph and drank to the point of intoxication.

---

6. *Histories* 2.18, 41, 42, 46.

Meaning
This scene begins with fear and ends with drunkenness. Jacob's fear
led him to delay a return to Egypt for much-needed food. His sons'
fear was in evidence in their behaviour and their suspicions about
the real reason why they had been invited to dine with Joseph at his
home. It would appear that their fears were assuaged, since they
became relaxed enough to drink and become drunk in Joseph's
presence. Thus, like Joseph's brothers who have been lulled into
complacency, the easing of the tension accomplished in this part of
the narrative also lulls readers into expecting that the final steps in
reuniting Joseph with the rest of his family will be accomplished
without further complications.

D. Joseph is reunited with his brothers (44:1 – 45:28)

Context
c.1877 BC
The gradual process by which Joseph's dreams are being fulfilled
comes to its climax in these chapters as Joseph is finally led to reveal
his identity to his brothers. Nevertheless, by the end of this section
Jacob is still not reunited with Joseph, though all preparations for
this are in place. Throughout this, the narrative works towards the
goal of showing how God has been at work to achieve his purposes.

Comment
i. Joseph accuses his brothers of theft (44:1–17)
1–2. Joseph's command to fill each man's bag to capacity and to
return their silver appears to extend his magnanimity. Moreover, the
placing of his silver goblet into Benjamin's bag along with returning
Benjamin's silver furthers his preferential treatment for his brother
– or so it seems.

3–5. The early morning departure would not have been out of
the ordinary and fits the travel pattern elsewhere in Genesis (21:14;
22:3; 26:31). The text emphasizes that Jacob's sons had not travelled
far when Joseph ordered his servant to pursue them. However,
his orders must have seemed strange, even to Joseph's steward. The
accusation was that the brothers had *repaid evil for good* (v. 4). This
phrase denotes not simply a breach of etiquette or some unspecified

type of wrongdoing, but a cynical and vicious exploitation of someone's kindness (1 Sam. 25:21; Pss 35:12; 38:20; 109:5; Prov. 17:13). The discovery of the cup is assumed in Joseph's words, phrased as a rhetorical question. The cup is presented as special to Joseph for two reasons: it was his drinking cup, and he used it for divination. Lecanomancy, the observation of liquids in a container, was practised throughout the Ancient Near East. However, Joseph is never portrayed elsewhere as using divination, which is forbidden in the laws of Moses (Lev. 19:26; Deut. 18:10). It would appear that Joseph probably did not engage in any occult practices. Instead, he was intent upon maintaining his character as an Egyptian in Pharaoh's court and explaining how he knew about Jacob's sons, including details such as their birth order and now their theft of the cup. Joseph, however, makes no mention of the silver in each man's sack. There is no thought that the silver was stolen, just as no such accusation was made about the silver in the bags from the last trip (cf. 43:20–23).

6–9. While the narrative does not directly quote the steward's repetition of Joseph's words when he overtook the brothers, it does record their surprise at the accusation and their defence. First, they simply denied doing what they were accused of doing, using a Hebrew oath formula to make this a solemn statement (v. 7). Second, they stated that they had returned the silver from their first trip to Egypt, so why would they steal this time? Finally, they made a confident statement of offering themselves as slaves and approving of the execution of the one found in possession of the goblet. Clearly, they did not believe that any of them had stolen the goblet, or they would not have made such a proffer. Note the similarity of their offer to Jacob's statement when Laban accused him of theft (31:32). Jacob had placed his beloved wife Rachel at risk, although she cleverly escaped (31:34–35). This time the youngest son of Rachel was placed in danger.

10. Immediately Joseph's steward changed the punishment so that only the man with the cup would be enslaved. This fits well with Joseph's purpose in putting the cup in Benjamin's sack in order to drive a wedge between the brothers and to observe whether they would abandon Benjamin. Thus, it would appear that the steward knew Joseph's plan.

11–13. The narrative pace quickens as the brothers open their sacks and the steward examines them. For the second time mention is made of the birth order of Jacob's sons, which once again indicates that Joseph had told his steward about the family. Of course, for the purposes of the narration, this leaves the tension to build, because Benjamin's sack will be the last one examined. The brothers' tearing their clothes at the discovery of Benjamin's misfortune recalls the tearing of clothes by Reuben (37:29) and Jacob (37:34) at Joseph's similar tragedy. At that time there was a rift in the family, but now there is family solidarity as all the brothers express their shock and grief. In addition, they did not abandon Benjamin but loaded their donkeys again and returned to the city.

14–15. Their arrival at Joseph's house is described as the arrival of *Judah and his brothers*. This foregrounds Judah's role as the one who had pledged to protect Benjamin (43:8–10) and anticipates his plea for his youngest brother. Knowing that they could only beg for mercy, the brothers are depicted as falling face down in front of Joseph. Yet Joseph showed no mercy. He asked them how they could have thought to defy him because he was an expert diviner.[7] The irony is, of course, that he was without his divining cup and thus unequipped to do what he claimed. This is another clue that Joseph's claim of practising divination was simply a ploy to apply pressure on his brothers in one last test of their sincerity.

16–17. Judah's reply begins with three rhetorical questions climaxing with *How can we justify ourselves?* (v. 16). They cannot offer any real defence, because *God has exposed your servants' iniquity* (v. 16), a statement that in context refers to the supposed theft of Joseph's goblet but strikes readers of the wider narrative as a statement about their earlier mistreatment of Joseph. Having no adequate way to refute the charge of robbery, Judah presented all of his brothers – not simply the one in whose possession the cup was found – as Joseph's slaves. The family solidarity could not be broken, and the brothers would stay with Benjamin. Joseph's reply, however, employed the same oath formula that his brothers had used when

---

7. The Hebrew text is emphatic when describing Joseph's ability at divination.

denying the theft (v. 17; cf. v. 7). He insisted on punishing only the man who had his cup and sending the rest of them off peaceably. In this way Joseph was forcing the wedge he had driven between Benjamin and his brothers to become even deeper in order to see whether they would act in their own selfish interests – perhaps reluctantly – and abandon Benjamin.

ii. Judah's plea for Benjamin (44:18–34)

These verses contain the longest speech in Genesis. They are the high point of the tension in the story of Joseph and his brothers. Here we see the reformed Judah, the Judah who had learned to have compassion as a result of the fairly recent birth of his twin sons to Tamar (38:1–30). His compassion for his father comes to the fore at the end of his speech. He uses the word *father* fifteen times.[8] Throughout this speech Judah uses respectful language to the point of obsequiousness. He refers to himself, his brothers and Jacob as Joseph's *servant*[s] ten times. He always refers to Joseph as *my lord* (seven times). Much of his appeal to Joseph is the recounting of past conversation: the words of Joseph (vv. 19, 21, 23), of the brothers (vv. 20, 22, 26), of Jacob (vv. 25, 27) and of Judah himself (v. 32). In this way he allows the Egyptian overlord to hear the story from the viewpoint of every participant, hoping thereby to draw Joseph into a sympathetic understanding that will lead to a favourable granting of his request (v. 33).

18. Judah's being the one to approach Joseph singles him out from the other brothers both as the leader and as the one who will offer to substitute himself for Benjamin. His words *do not be angry with your servant* are a request that Joseph listen to his appeal and not reject it out of hand (compare Abraham's appeal to God on behalf of Sodom at 18:30). His statement that Joseph was like Pharaoh acknowledged not only Joseph's absolute power over them but also his right to refuse to consider Judah's plea.

19–20. Judah began by relating their first encounter with Joseph, the fourth account of their meeting during their first trip to Egypt

---

8. Vv. 19, 20 [twice], 22 [twice], 24, 25, 27, 30 [twice], 31, 32 [twice], 34 [twice].

(42:9–20, 29–34; 43:3–7). Diplomatically, he omitted Joseph's accusation that they were spies and instead placed the mention of a brother and father into a question attributed to Joseph instead of into statements offered by the brothers (cf. 42:11, 13). Judah then recounted their reply, noting an elderly father and a younger brother. Here Judah described Benjamin as a child of Jacob's old age, a description earlier used by the narrator to describe Joseph (37:3). Moreover, he stated that *his father loves him*, pointing out Jacob's favouritism of Rachel's son without any hint of jealousy on the part of the other brothers. Judah also said that Benjamin's older brother was dead (a direct statement instead of the more oblique *he is no longer* used previously at 42:13). For the reader this is an ironic statement, since the reader understands that Joseph obviously knew that Judah's assumption concerning Joseph's death was false. Then Judah described Benjamin as the only remaining son of his mother, revealing a new portion of the family dynamic that was not stated earlier: that Jacob had more than one wife.

21–22. Next Judah quoted Joseph as demanding that Benjamin be brought to Egypt so that Joseph could see him. Once again, Judah couched his recollection diplomatically, omitting the imprisonment of Simeon which ensured that the brothers brought Benjamin with them. This time he expanded the description of the bond between Jacob and Benjamin by quoting the brothers as telling Joseph that Benjamin could not leave Jacob, since if he left, Jacob would die.

23. Finally in this account of their first meeting, Judah included one more quotation of Joseph in which he insisted on seeing Benjamin if they returned to Egypt. Again, no mention is made of Simeon or of Joseph's threat of death if they did not comply (cf. 42:20). In deference to Joseph's status, Judah allowed his account of their first conversation to end with Joseph's words, thereby giving the Egyptian potentate the first and last statements.

24–26. In his recollection of events Judah then shifted the scene to their return to Jacob and their recounting of Joseph's words. The first quotation he included was Jacob's order that they return to Egypt for more food. He followed this with their reply that pointed out the requirement that Benjamin accompany them – stating this twice for emphasis.

27–29. Judah slowed his retelling of the scene in Canaan by included a longer quotation of Jacob that mentioned the birth of two sons to Jacob's wife (Rachel, the beloved wife, the only wife mentioned). Here through Judah's words Joseph learned for the first time that Jacob thought that he had been killed by a wild animal. Then Judah used Jacob's own phrase for his demise should something happen to Benjamin: *you will bring my grey hair down to Sheol in sorrow* (v. 29). This is the third time Judah emphasized the strong affection of Jacob for Benjamin, and he once again amplified it in an attempt to evoke sympathy for Jacob and leniency towards Benjamin.

30–31. Judah then skipped forward to the theoretical future. If he should return without Benjamin, Jacob – whose *life is wrapped up with the boy's life* (v. 30) – would die. This is the closest description of the connection between father and son and notes that the loss of one will lead to the loss of the other. The blame for Jacob's death, however, would not be placed on Joseph or on Benjamin but on the other brothers: *your servants will have brought the grey hair of your servant our father down to Sheol in grief* (v. 31).

32–34. Finally, having summarized the situation and slowly ratcheted up the description of the close bond between Jacob and Benjamin, Judah made his appeal. He had made himself responsible for Benjamin and assumed the guilt should the young man not return. Instead, he offered himself in Benjamin's place as Joseph's slave so that Benjamin could return. Of course, this was not an even swap: as a younger man Benjamin made a more valuable slave, since he was likely to be in servitude for more years. Nevertheless, Judah had carefully played to the sympathies of the Egyptian magistrate who stood before him. So he ended his appeal with another rhetorical question and a statement: how could he go home without the boy? He could not bear to see his father's sorrow and its inevitable effect. This is Judah's first mention of his connection with his father, and it is one of compassion, sympathy and tenderness. It was not only Jacob who would suffer grief and sorrow if Benjamin did not return; Judah also would be overwhelmed with heartache.

iii. Joseph reveals himself to his brothers (45:1–15)

1–2. Judah's appeal that emphasized Jacob's attachment to Benjamin finally broke through Joseph's facade. His composure lost, he ordered his attendants to leave so that he could reveal his identity to his brothers in private. The exact words of his order are reproduced in only one other place in Scripture: when Amnon ordered his attendants to leave him so that he could be alone with Tamar (2 Sam. 13:9). The author emphasizes that no-one was with Joseph when he made his revelation to his brothers. Despite the private nature of the meeting we are told that *the Egyptians* (v. 2) heard him weeping. This must be a reference to Joseph's attendants who were ordered out of the room. We are also told that *Pharaoh's household* heard his weeping, indicating that Joseph's house was very near Pharaoh's. This would have been most practical considering Joseph's position as second only to Pharaoh, which would require him to meet frequently with the Egyptian king. It appears as if verses 1–2 are a summary of Joseph's private time with his brothers from the viewpoint of the Egyptians outside the room, making verses 3–15 an account from inside the room. Note that both accounts end with Joseph weeping (cf. vv. 14–15). This is the third time Joseph was moved to tears by his brothers (42:24; 43:30).

3. This was a family moment not to be shared with others. Joseph's first words were simple: *I am Joseph.* Clearly at this point Joseph must have spoken in Hebrew to his brothers, and not through an interpreter (cf. 42:23). They surely were stunned to hear their own language being used by this high Egyptian official. Joseph also asked, *Is my father still living?* Perhaps the thought of possibly seeing his father again was too overwhelming to seem true. No-one ever answered this question, and Joseph assumed that Jacob was still alive (vv. 9–11, 13). This may imply that these words were more of an emotional statement than an actual question. At any rate, the brothers were unable to answer him because *they were terrified in his presence.* The word *terrified* occurs elsewhere to speak of a paralysing fear (Exod. 15:15; Judg. 20:41; 1 Sam. 28:21; Ps. 2:5). In this case they may have been afraid of Joseph's power that he could have used to exact revenge on them. Certainly, Joseph felt the need to address them about this and to assure them that he was no threat to them (v. 5; 50:19–21).

4–8. While Judah earlier had approached Joseph, now Joseph invited the rest of his brothers to come near – to see him close up and verify his identity. This time he again identified himself and supplied information that only he and they would know: that they had sold him into Egypt. However, to assure them that he held no grudge against them and to relieve them of the guilt they had because of it (see 42:21), he talked about God's actions, not theirs. Three times he emphasized God's work:

- God sent him ahead in order to preserve life (v. 5).
- God sent him ahead in order to establish a remnant, to keep them alive (v. 7).
- They did not send him to Egypt – God did, and he made Joseph a father to Pharaoh (v. 8).

The first statement uses the same root for *preserve life* that is employed in the ark narrative for preserving animal life during the flood (6:19–20). Joseph was like Noah, preserving life in the face of a severe natural disaster. He stated as much when he told his brothers that there would be five more years of famine. After two years of famine, farming had become nearly impossible, so for the next five years there would be no *ploughing or harvesting* (v. 6).

The second statement emphasized the remnant of God's people, an indirect reference to the promises of God that had passed from Abraham to Isaac to Jacob, and now were preserved through Jacob's children and grandchildren. This remnant held the promise to benefit people from all nations and must be preserved (18:18; 22:18; 26:4).

The third statement is a conclusion about God's actions and Joseph's rise in Egypt. All this was God's work, and because of God Joseph had become a *father to Pharaoh, lord of his entire household, ruler of the entire land of Egypt* (v. 8). These three titles summarized Joseph's position and authority that God would use to preserve Jacob's family. The title *father to Pharaoh* indicates his status as a trusted advisor to the king.[9] It may correspond to the Egyptian title borne by some of ancient Egypt's viziers (i.e. prime ministers): 'father of the god' (where Pharaoh is portrayed as a living god).[10] The title

9. See similar use of 'father' at Judg. 17:10; 18:19; 2 Kgs 6:21; 13:14.
10. Ward (1957: 51–52).

lord of his entire household probably suggested his status in Pharaoh's court as his top official, while *ruler of the entire land* emphasized his superiority over all officials outside Pharaoh's court.

9–11. For the first time Joseph is quoted as calling Jacob *my father* (vv. 9, 13) as he instructs his brothers as to what they are to do. Joseph is anxious to see Jacob before Jacob dies, so he urges his brothers to act quickly (vv. 9, 13). His message to Jacob is also not to delay (v. 9). In stating that God had made him *lord of all Egypt* (v. 9), Joseph may have been seeking to allay any fears that Jacob may have had of abandoning the land of God's promise. There are other items in his invitation that Joseph used to induce Jacob to move to Egypt. First, as a positive inducement Joseph offered Jacob a place in the land of Goshen. The exact location of Goshen is not known, but it appears to be in the Nile Delta from the times it is mentioned in Genesis and Exodus (46:28–29, 34; 47:1, 4, 6, 27; 50:8; Exod. 8:22; 9:26). It is often said to be in the eastern Delta near the Wadi Tumilat.[11] Goshen is said to be near Joseph but also able to accommodate Jacob's children and grandchildren. Joseph also mentioned Jacob's herds and flocks, and the eastern Nile Delta is mentioned during the reign of Pharaoh Merneptah as a place for Semitic and Bedouin tribes of herdsmen.[12] Second, as an added incentive Joseph noted the negative impact of the famine: there would be five more years of famine, and in Canaan *you, your household and everything you have will become destitute* (v. 11).

12–13. Joseph then called on his brothers to be eyewitnesses to Jacob confirming that he was alive. Moreover, they could testify about his exalted status, what English versions render as his *glory* or 'honour' (v. 13). This also was part of Joseph's appeal to Jacob, demonstrating that he could do for his father what he promised. Joseph closed his instructions to his brothers as he had opened them, urging them to act quickly.

14–15. Joseph's concern for his brother Benjamin had been evident in his insistence that the young man be brought to Egypt (42:20). It is not surprising, therefore, that Joseph now went first to

---

11. Wenham (1994: 429); Hamilton (1995: 580); Mathews (2005: 815).
12. De Vaux (1978: 302).

Benjamin. Joseph and Benjamin are the only men in this scene who are said to have wept. In the Ancient Near East kisses were often exchanged between close family members as well as between close friends as a sign of affection (31:28; 1 Kgs 19:20; Matt. 26:48; Mark 14:44; Luke 7:45; 22:47–48; Rom. 16:16; 1 Cor. 16:20; 2 Cor. 13:12; 1 Thess. 5:26; 1 Pet. 5:14). So Joseph also kissed his brothers. Lastly, the scene ends with Joseph's brothers speaking with him. The rift between Joseph and his older brothers, who formerly could not speak civilly with him (37:4), is now healed.

iv. Pharaoh invites Jacob and his sons to live in Egypt (45:16–28)

16. The news of the arrival of Joseph's brothers pleased not only Pharaoh but also his servants. This and 41:37 are the only places in Genesis where both Pharaoh and his servants are mentioned together, and in both places Joseph garners the approval of both the king and his courtiers.

17–18. Pharaoh's invitation is more generous than Joseph's. The invitation mentions the brothers' father and families and offers them *the best of the land of Egypt* (v. 18), not simply Goshen. Moreover, they will be able to enjoy the finest produce of the land, *the fat of the land*.

19–20. Pharaoh followed his general invitation with more detailed instructions. They were to be given wagons to transport their wives and children on the journey. They were also to bring Jacob with them. However, Pharaoh told them there was no need to bring their belongings, because he would give them the best of Egypt. The word for *belongings* indicates inanimate objects, not animals such as cattle, sheep or goats. In fact, the family would bring their animals with them, and Joseph would instruct them to ask to be given land in Goshen because of this (46:31–34).

21–24. The author quickly affirms that *the sons of Israel* (v. 21) took wagons and provisions just as Pharaoh had commanded. The use of the phrase *sons of Israel* instead of 'sons of Jacob' looks forward to the nation of Israel that will prosper and grow in Egypt. Joseph also gave presents to his brothers: each received a change of clothes. Joseph, who had been stripped of clothing by his brothers (37:23), now did the opposite for them, again signalling that he held no grudge against them. Benjamin is once again singled out for special treatment with a gift of silver and five changes of clothes (similar to the fivefold portion of food that he was given at the banquet in Joseph's house at 43:34). Joseph also lavished gifts on his father. The ten male donkeys with the finest products of Egypt must have been meant to convince Jacob that Joseph did actually occupy a high position in Egypt. The ten female donkeys carried a more mundane cargo – food and provisions for the journey to Egypt. Joseph's final words to his brothers as they left to fetch Jacob have been understood in two ways, owing to the ambiguity of the Hebrew verb which generally means 'be stirred up, tremble'. Many commentators and English versions quote Joseph as saying, 'Do not argue' (v. 24), based on the supposed meaning of the verb at Proverbs 29:9.[13] However, that meaning is not necessary in Proverbs and probably means 'rant' in that context.[14] Others understand Joseph to have told his brothers 'Do not be fearful', which better fits the wider context of the narrative, considering the fear of Joseph and his authority that they had shown throughout most of their time in Egypt. Perhaps Joseph was concerned that they might be afraid to return to Egypt for fear that he would seek revenge (cf. 50:16–18).[15]

25–27. The journey to Canaan is once again summarized quickly, and then the narrative slows to report the delivery of the news of Joseph to Jacob. The brothers began by giving two pieces of information: Joseph was alive and he was ruler of Egypt. Jacob's reaction is described as a stunned numbness. How was he to believe either statement when for so long he had been mourning Joseph's death (see 37:35)? This type of shock is similar to the reaction of Jesus' disciples when they were told that he had risen from the grave (Luke 24:11). Jacob, however, was convinced by two pieces of evidence: the brothers' report of Joseph's words and the wagons that Joseph had sent. In this way *his spirit was revived* (v. 27). Perhaps for the first

---

13. See NET and LXX; Hamilton (1995: 587).

14. CSB, ESV, GW, NIV, NRSV, TNK; Steinmann (2009: 566).

15. For this verb denoting fear see Exod. 15:14; Deut. 2:25; 1 Sam. 14:15; Isa. 64:1; Joel 2:1; Mic. 7:17; Hab. 3:7.

time since he had seen Joseph's bloodstained special garment he again had the spirit of the Jacob who had prospered in Haran.

28. Jacob now not only believed the report about Joseph, but he also was to *go to see him before I die.* While Jacob may have been considered elderly and frail (43:27; 44:20), he would not only see Joseph before he died, but would live another seventeen years in Egypt (47:28).

Meaning

This long section that tells how Joseph was finally reunited and reconciled with his brothers emphasizes a number of themes concerning Jacob's family that are resolved or at least mostly resolved in order to bring Jacob and his descendants to Egypt. Clearly Joseph was wary and distrusting of his brothers when he first encountered them as they sought to buy grain during the famine. This distrust not only reflected the ill-treatment he had received from his brothers, but also indicated the consequences of a larger theme that runs through Genesis: the sinfulness that dwells in every human heart as a result of the first sin of Adam and Eve (6:5; 8:21). Because Joseph was especially aware of the sinfulness of his brothers he was cautious about revealing himself to them. First he tested them to see whether they would betray one of their own to prison when he took Simeon into custody (42:24). Would they abandon Simeon to the ravages of imprisonment in Egypt as they had abandoned Joseph when they sold him into slavery? During this test he discovered that not all of his brothers were part of the plot to sell him into slavery. Reuben, his oldest brother, had defended him and urged the others not to harm him (42:22).

Joseph had no way of knowing that their delay in returning for Simeon was due to Jacob's reluctance to send Benjamin to Egypt. Then after they returned with Benjamin and Simeon was freed, Joseph was still suspicious of them: perhaps they would turn their backs on the other son of Rachel as they had turned their backs on him. Yet Joseph learned that they would not abandon Benjamin. All of his brothers returned to Joseph's house when Benjamin was found to have Joseph's silver goblet. Judah, who had callously suggested that Joseph be sold into slavery (37:26–27), now pleaded for Benjamin and offered to substitute himself and bear Benjamin's punishment.

But most of all, Joseph's heart was melted by Judah's appeal to the welfare of his father Jacob. No longer was there resentment of Jacob for his favouring one wife's son over the sons of his other wives. Instead, there was only compassion for him and a plea that nothing be done to hasten Jacob's demise. In all of this Joseph learned that time, and, by implication, the acts of God in time, had changed his brothers. They were not the same fractured family he knew as a youth of seventeen years.

Judah also came to view his family with empathy and compassion. The events that had transpired concerning his sons and his daughter-in-law Tamar had made him more sensitive to others so that he could become the leader of the sons of Jacob, a leadership that had been forfeited by Reuben, Simeon and Levi. Judah would later be acknowledged as the family leader among the sons of Israel even by Jacob, who would send his fourth-oldest son ahead of him to Joseph to prepare for his arrival in Egypt (46:28).

Finally, another overarching theme from Genesis is present in this section: God's promise to send someone into the world to crush the serpent's head and deliver humankind from the curse of sin (3:15). That promise had been passed to Jacob, and to preserve that promise the sons of Israel had to survive the famine. Joseph came to realize that God had sent him to Egypt for just that purpose (45:5–8). God was also active in Judah, though the narrative at this point is less explicit than it will be later about his role as the bearer of the family promise of a saviour (49:8–12). Nonetheless, his rise as leader of the next generation of Abraham's descendants is documented here, preparing for the pre-eminence of the tribe of Judah in the subsequent history of Israel and for the bringing forth of Jesus who would ultimately fulfil all the promises to the patriarchs (Heb. 7:14–22; Rev. 5:5; 7:5).

26. THE FAMILY OF JACOB: JACOB'S TIME IN EGYPT (46:1 – 47:27)

Context

Jacob would spend seventeen years in Egypt before his death (47:28). Genesis 46:1 – 47:27 concentrates on his arrival in Egypt, while Genesis 47:28 – 49:33 will relate events during the final year of his life. Little is said about Jacob's family during the intervening years. However, the effect of the third to seventh years of the famine on the people of Egypt is discussed (47:13–26).

Jacob's family journeyed to Egypt with God's blessing (46:3–4) and with Pharaoh's approval (47:1–6). This is quite the opposite of Abraham's sojourn in Egypt which God never sanctioned and which Pharaoh found to be irksome (12:10–20). While Jacob and his sons acquired land in Egypt (47:11, 27), the native Egyptians would be losing their land to Pharaoh (47:20–26).

This portion of Genesis also gives a complete list of Jacob's descendants who came to Egypt (46:8–27). Like the list of Esau's descendants that lists the chiefs of Edom (36:9–19), this list demonstrates the organization of the nation of Israel into tribes and clans. This migration to Egypt is the beginning of the great nation promised to Abraham (12:2; 17:20; 18:18), a nation that will be produced during the four-hundred-year sojourn there (46:3; cf. 15:13).

A. Jacob goes to Egypt (46:1 – 47:12)

1876 BC
Comment
i. God sends Jacob to Egypt (46:1–7)

1. The narrative of the journey to Egypt begins with *Israel*, the name given to Jacob by God that will also become the name of the nation. The only stop recorded on the journey is at Beersheba, the place associated with the wells of Abraham and Isaac (21:22–33; 26:23–33). Jacob's grandfather and father had worshipped there (21:33; 26:25), and God had appeared to Isaac there (26:24). Jacob offered sacrifices to *the God of his father Isaac*, the only time in Genesis that this phrase is used, though Jacob frequently referred to Yahweh as *the God of my father* (31:5, 42; 32:9). Note that Jacob's sacrifices at Beersheba were a spontaneous act of worship without any prompting by God. Beersheba was the southernmost easily habitable place in Canaan (see Judg. 20:1; 1 Sam. 3:20; 2 Sam. 3:10; 17:11; 24:2, 15; 1 Kgs 4:25; 1 Chr. 21:2; 2 Chr. 30:5). Thus, it was appropriate for Jacob to worship there, since it was the exit point from the Promised Land as one headed towards Egypt.

2–4. God's appearance to Jacob that evening is called a *vision*, the only use of this word in this sense in Genesis. Elsewhere, appearances of God at night are called dreams (20:3; 31:24) or it is simply said that God appeared at night (26:24). While the narrator called the patriarch *Israel*, God addressed him as *Jacob* (v. 2). He had not yet become the great nation that would be called *Israel*. Jacob's reply, *Here I am*, was often simply a response that acknowledged someone's call (22:1, 7, 11; 27:1, 18; 31:11; 46:2). Just as Isaac had worshipped the God of his father, Yahweh now identified himself to Jacob as *the God of your father*, similar to the way he had identified himself to Isaac when giving him a promise like the one spoken here (26:24). Jacob is told not to be afraid of going to Egypt. Any fear that Jacob may have had might have been due to the ominous note in the earlier message from God to Abraham that his descendants would be enslaved in a foreign land (15:13). Nevertheless, the promise of a great nation that had been given to Abraham would be realized in Egypt (12:2; 17:20; 18:18). Another fear may have been due to the fact that Jacob was again leaving the Promised Land and once again might have been concerned that God would not be with him. Yet just as God pledged to be with Jacob when he left Canaan for Haran and to bring him back (28:15), so he gives the same guarantee here. The reader is left with the question as to what God means by *I will also bring you back*. Was Yahweh referring to Jacob's body (50:13) or to Jacob's descendants (15:16)? The ambiguity is not resolved here. However, Jacob is told in an indirect way that he will die a peaceful death in Egypt with Joseph at his side to *put his hands on your eyes* (v. 4), a reference to Joseph closing Jacob's eyes at death (see 49:33 – 50:1).

5–7. When Jacob left Beersheba we are told that the sons of *Israel* took *their father Jacob* (v. 5). The striking juxtaposition of both names for the patriarch notes the promised-but-not-yet nature of the great nation that God had pledged. Jacob is not the nation of Israel, but the makings of the nation are present in his sons. The wagons that Pharaoh had sent were used for the purpose for which they were given, transporting the elderly Jacob and the young children and wives (cf. 45:19). However, contrary to Pharaoh's urging, they brought their cattle and possessions (cf. 45:20). The author is careful to emphasize that all of Jacob's offspring accompanied him to Egypt. Note the envelope formed by the phrase *all his offspring* (vv. 6–7): all his offspring *with him, his sons and his grandsons with him, his daughters and his granddaughters, that is,* all his offspring.

ii. Jacob's family as they enter Egypt (46:8–27)

This genealogy of Jacob's family has six parts. There is an introduction (v. 8a), followed by the descendants of Leah (vv. 8b–15), the descendants of Zilpah (vv. 16–18), the descendants of Rachel (vv. 19–22) and the descendants of Bilhah (vv. 23–25). The genealogy closes with a summary (vv. 26–27). Each section that sets forth Jacob's descendants by one of his wives ends with its own summary (vv. 15, 18, 22, 25). The sections that list the descendants of Jacob's concubines note that Zilpah was given to Leah by Laban (v. 18) and Bilhah was given to Rachel by Laban (v. 25).

The section that records Rachel's descendants has several features that set it apart and thereby emphasize her as the beloved wife of Jacob. It is the only section that includes an introductory formula: *The sons of Rachel, Jacob's wife* (v. 19). Joseph is the only son whose wife is listed (*Asenath*, v. 20), and his sons are the only grandsons whose birthplace is noted (v. 20; cf. v. 27). This highlights Joseph's separate arrival in Egypt and his time there before Jacob's arrival. It also allows Joseph and his sons to be included in the list, but not in the numeric totals (vv. 26–27).

Another interesting feature of this list is the number of persons mentioned. A total of seventy-six names of people including Jacob and those descended from Jacob are listed. (This does not include the Egyptians in the list: Asenath, Joseph's wife and her father Potiphera; v. 20.) Of those seventy-six persons, three died in the land of Canaan: Rachel (35:19), Er (38:7) and Onan (38:10). Another three were already in Egypt when Jacob arrived: Joseph and his sons Manasseh and Ephraim (v. 20). Thus, seventy people came to Egypt from Jacob's family, including Jacob himself (v. 27; Exod. 1:5). By excluding Jacob's wives, the total is sixty-six people (v. 26). Among the descendants of Leah, a total of thirty-two persons settled in Egypt. For her slave girl Zilpah the total is exactly half of Leah's total: sixteen persons. The descendants of Rachel who lived in Egypt, including Joseph and his sons, totalled fourteen. For her slave girl Bilhah the total is once again half of that of her mistress: seven persons.

Of those included among Jacob's family are seventy men and six women. The women are his four wives, his daughter Dinah and his granddaughter Serah (v. 17). The inclusion of Dinah among Jacob's children is probably due to her having already been introduced to readers at her birth (30:21) and in the account of her rape (34:1–31). It seems unlikely that among Jacob's grandchildren there was only one granddaughter among fifty-four grandsons. Instead, it appears that Serah alone was listed among the granddaughters of Jacob in order to provide for seventy persons coming to Egypt and to provide Zilpah with exactly half the number of descendants as Leah. Four great-grandsons of Jacob are also listed: two sons of Perez (v. 12) and two sons of Beriah (v. 17).

The persons listed who *came to Egypt* (vv. 8, 26, 27) must include several who were born after Jacob entered the land. Benjamin, who was about twenty-five years old at the time, was unlikely to have already fathered ten children (v. 21).[1] Moreover, Perez and Zerah were born only about one year before Jacob entered Egypt, making it impossible for Perez to have had sons at that time (v. 12).[2] The inclusion of these grandsons of Jacob may have been prompted by the desire to have a total of seventy persons in the list to mirror the seventy nations said to have descended from Noah as listed in the Table of Nations (10:1–32). In this way the sons of Israel who would bring blessing to all nations (12:3; 18:18; 22:18; 26:4; 28:14) were made to mirror those nations. In addition, by including Perez's sons and all of Benjamin's sons, the list is able to attribute twice as many sons to each of Jacob's wives than are attributed to each of his concubines. Wenham has suggested that those who were yet to be born when Jacob entered Egypt may have been included as those who came to Egypt 'still in the loins of their ancestor' (see Heb. 7:10).[3]

The information in this list is expanded later in two lists of the descendants and clans of Israel: Numbers 26:5–50 and 1 Chronicles 2 – 8. There are a number of places where these lists differ in details from the roster of Jacob's descendants given here in verses 8–27.

8a. The opening of this genealogy is identical to the opening of the book of Exodus: *These are the names of the sons of Israel who came to Egypt*. This is followed by defining *sons of Israel* as *Jacob and his sons*. It may seem peculiar that Jacob is included among the *sons of Israel*, but this phrase is often used in the sense of people from the nation called *Israel* (i.e. 'Israelites' – e.g. 32:32; 36:31), so it is appropriate that Jacob is included.

8b–9. Reuben is the only son of Jacob who is given a descriptive label: *firstborn* (v. 8b). *Henoch* (v. 9; Exod. 6:14; Num. 26:5; 1 Chr. 5:3) is in Hebrew the same as the name *Enoch*. He shared his name with

---

1. Steinmann (2011: 80).

2. Steinmann (2011: 78–79).

3. Wenham (1994: 444); see also Mathews (2005: 834).

the son of Cain (4:17), with the well-known descendant of Seth (5:19–24; 1 Chr. 1:3; Luke 3:37; Heb. 11:5; Jude 1:14) and with a Midianite (1 Chr. 1:33). *Pallu* (v. 9; Exod. 6:14; Num. 26:5, 8; 1 Chr. 5:3), whose name means 'marvellous' or 'wonderful', was the ancestor of Dathan and Abiram, the men who rebelled against Moses' authority (Num. 26:8–10). *Hezron* (v. 9; Exod. 6:14; Num. 26:6; 1 Chr. 5:3) shared his name with a grandson of Judah (v. 12). *Carmi* (v. 9; Exod. 6:14; Num. 26:6; 1 Chr. 5:3), whose name means 'my vineyard', was the ancestor of the infamous Achan (Josh. 7:1, 18). The name Carmi was also borne by a descendant of Judah (1 Chr. 4:1).

10. Simeon's son *Jemuel* (Exod. 6:15) is called *Nemuel* at Numbers 26:12 and 1 Chronicles 4:24.[4] *Jamin* (Exod. 6:15; Num. 26:12; 1 Chr. 4:24), whose name means 'right hand', is also the name of a later man from Judah (1 Chr. 2:27) and a post-exilic Levite (Neh. 8:7). *Ohad* (Exod. 6:15) is not listed among Simeon's sons in Numbers 26 or 1 Chronicles 4, which may indicate that his line produced no clan in Israel. *Jachin* (Exod. 6:15; Num. 26:12) means 'let him establish'. A post-exilic priest also bore this name (1 Chr. 9:10; 24:17; Neh. 11:10). It was also the name given to one of the pillars erected near the entrance to the temple built by Solomon (1 Kgs 7:21; 2 Chr. 3:17). *Zohar* (Exod. 6:15) was also the name of the father of Ephron the Hethite (Gen. 23:8; 25:9). He is called *Zerah* at Numbers 26:13 and 1 Chronicles 4:24. The difference appears to be an accidental metathesis of the Hebrew letters *resh* and *ḥet*. *Shaul* is the same name as that of the first king of Israel, Saul, and means 'asked [of God]'. This name was also given to two other men in the Old Testament: one a king of Edom (Gen. 36:37–38), the other a Levite (1 Chr. 6:24).

11. Levi's sons *Gershon*, *Kohath* and *Merari* (Exod. 6:16; Num. 3:17; 1 Chr. 5:27; 6:1) formed the three great Levite families. *Kohath* was the ancestor of Moses (Exod. 6:20; Num. 26:58–59).

12. *Er* (38:3, 6–7; Num. 26:19; 1 Chr. 2:3), Judah's firstborn, was also the name of one of Judah's grandsons (1 Chr. 4:21) and of an

---

4. The difference is probably due to a copyist's error that confused the similarly formed letters *nun* and *yodh*.

ancestor of Joseph (Luke 3:28). Judah's second son was *Onan* (38:4, 8–9; Num. 26:19; 1 Chr. 2:3). These two sons were included for the sake of completeness, but the middle of this verse reminds us that they died in Canaan (38:3–9). *Shelah* (38:5, 11, 14, 26; Num. 26:20; 1 Chr. 2:3) was Judah's other son by his wife. In Hebrew his name is spelled differently from the Shelah who was the father of Eber (10:24; 11:12–15). *Perez* and *Zerah* are listed without reference to the circumstances of their conception and birth to Judah's daughter-in-law (38:1–30; Ruth 4:12; 1 Chr. 2:4; Matt. 1:3). *Hezron*, who is mentioned rather frequently in the Bible (Num. 26:21; Ruth 4:18, 19; 1 Chr. 2:5, 18, 21; 4:1; Matt. 1:3; Luke 3:33), shared his name with his cousin, the son of Reuben (Gen. 46:9). Unlike his brother Hezron, *Hamul* is seldom mentioned in the Old Testament (Num. 26:21; 1 Chr. 2:5).

13. Issachar's son *Tola* (Num. 26:23; 1 Chr. 7:1) shared his name with a later judge of Israel (Judg. 10:1). His name means 'scarlet'. *Puvah* (Num. 26:23) is called Puah at 1 Chronicles 7:1. This was also the name of the father of the judge Tola (Judg. 10:1). The name *Jashub* (Num. 26:24; 1 Chr. 7:1) means 'may he return'. The Hebrew text has the name as *Yob*, but on the basis of SP and LXX most English versions consider this a copyist's error and emend the name here to match its occurrences elsewhere in the Old Testament. The name was also borne later by one of the Judeans in Ezra's day who had married a foreign wife (Ezra 10:29). *Shimron* (Num. 26:24; 1 Chr. 7:1) was also the name of a Canaanite town (Josh. 11:1; 12:20) and a city in the territory of Zebulun (Josh. 19:15). The Hebrew name for Samaria (*Shomron*) is probably a variant of this name.

14. Zebulun's sons *Sered, Elon* and *Jahleel* (Num. 26:26) are the only persons in the Scriptures with these names. *Elon* means 'oak'. *Jahleel* means 'let [him] wait for God'.

15. This summary of Leah's sons notes that they were born in Paddan-aram, a statement that obviously does not apply to the grandsons listed here. It is a reminder of how Jacob came to be married to Leah, though he had been promised Rachel (29:21–27). Dinah is included in this summary, since she was among those born to Leah in Paddan-aram that forms the story of the rivalry between Leah and Rachel. Ironically, the total of thirty-three persons includes Jacob with the sons of his less-favoured wife.

16. Gad's son *Ziphion* is called Zephon at Numbers 26:15. This name is also part of the place name Baal Zephon (Exod. 14:2, 9; Num. 33:7). *Haggi* (Num. 26:15) means 'feast' and is a variant of the name borne by the post-exilic prophet Haggai. *Shuni* (Num. 26:15) is the only person with this name in the Bible. *Ezbon* (perhaps meaning 'finger [of God]') is called Ozni (meaning 'my ear') at Numbers 26:16. Ezbon was also the name of one of Benjamin's grandsons (1 Chr. 7:7). *Eri* (Num. 26:16) may mean watchful. *Arodi* is called Arod at Numbers 26:17. *Areli* (Num. 26:17) is the only person to have this name in the Scriptures.

17. Asher's first son *Imnah* (Num. 26:44; 1 Chr. 7:30) shared his name with a later Levite (2 Chr. 31:14). The name *Ishvah* (1 Chr. 7:30) is unique to this son of Asher. He is not listed at Numbers 26:44, which may indicate that his line did not produce a later Israelite clan. *Ishvi* (Num. 26:44; 1 Chr. 7:30) was also the name of one of King Saul's sons (1 Sam. 14:49). *Beriah* (Num. 26:44; 1 Chr. 7:30) was also the name of a descendant of King Saul (1 Chr. 8:13, 16) and a Levite (1 Chr. 23:10–11). *Serah* (Num. 26:46; 1 Chr. 7:30) is the only granddaughter of Jacob to be included among those said to have come with him to Egypt. Beriah's son *Heber* (Num. 26:45; 1 Chr. 7:31–32) was given a popular name that was also borne by the Kenite husband of Jael (Judg. 4:11, 17, 21; 5:24) and by men from the tribes of Judah and Benjamin (1 Chr. 4:18; 8:17). *Malchiel* (Num. 26:45; 1 Chr. 7:31) means 'my king is God'.

18. The summary for the sons of Zilpah is also a reminder of Jacob's time in Paddan-aram, since it mentions Laban's wedding present of this maidservant to his daughter Leah.

19. Rachel is the only woman in this list of persons who is called *Jacob's wife*, another reminder of Jacob's life in Paddan-aram. In addition, her sons are the only sons of Jacob who are listed twice: once with their mother and again with their sons.

20. This mention of Joseph's sons includes the explanation of Joseph's circumstances in Egypt before the arrival of Jacob. *Asenath daughter of Potiphera* (41:45, 50) is the only wife of a son of Jacob mentioned in this genealogical list.

21. Benjamin's son *Bela* (Num. 26:38; 1 Chr. 7:6; 8:1) shared his name with a king of Edom (Gen. 36:32–33; 1 Chr. 1:43–44) and a descendant of Reuben (1 Chr. 5:8). It was also the earlier name of

Zoar, one of the Cities of the Plain (Gen. 14:2, 8). *Becher* (1 Chr. 7:6) means 'young male camel'. This was also the name of one of Ephraim's sons (Num. 26:35). However, there is no clan from Becher listed in Numbers 26, indicating that Benjamin's son failed to produce an Israelite clan. *Ashbel*, meaning 'man of the master/Baal' (Num. 26:38; 1 Chr. 8:1), appears to be called Jediael (meaning 'God knows') at 1 Chronicles 7:6. Perhaps this was a scribal substitution of a more acceptable name for one that could have been perceived as honouring the Canaanite god Baal.[5] *Gera* is missing in the Benjaminite genealogies at Numbers 26:38 and 1 Chronicles 7:6. At 1 Chronicles 8:3, 5 there are two persons named Gera who are said to be sons of Bela. In addition, Gera was the name of the father of the judge Ehud (Judg. 3:15) and of a descendant of Saul (2 Sam. 16:5; 19:16, 18). *Naaman* means 'pleasantness' (see also the similar name Naomi; Ruth 1:20–21). At Numbers 26:40 and 1 Chronicles 8:4 Naaman is listed as a son of Bela. The name is recorded again as a son of the Benjaminite Ehud at 1 Chronicles 8:7. Naaman was also the name of an Aramean (2 Kgs 5:1–27). The names of the five remaining sons of Benjamin, namely *Ehi, Rosh, Muppim, Huppim and Ard*, present problems when compared with the parallel genealogies in Numbers 26 and 1 Chronicles 8. Numbers 26:38–39 may provide three of them with alternative names – Ahiram, Shupham and Hupham – while 1 Chronicles 8 has Aharah (instead of Ahiram; 1 Chr. 8:1) and records Shephuphan (instead of Shupham) as a son of Bela (1 Chr. 8:5). *Ard* is listed as a son of Bela at Numbers 26:40 and perhaps is listed as Addar, son of Bela at 1 Chronicles 8:3. *Rosh*, meaning 'head, leader', does not appear in either Numbers 26 or 1 Chronicles 8.

22. This summary statement for the sons of Rachel is the shortest of all four, owing to the expanded introductory statement (v. 19).

23. *Hushim* (1 Chr. 7:12) was the only son of Dan. At Numbers 26:42 his name is Shuham, probably a copyist's mistake that resulted in the metathesis of the Hebrew letters *shin* and *ḥet*.

---

5. *ABD* 1.447. For similar substitutions that were made in the book of Samuel, see Steinmann (2017d: 28–30).

24. *Jahzeel* (Num. 26:48) means 'may God divide' and is spelled Jahziel at 1 Chronicles 7:13. *Guni* (Num. 26:48; 1 Chr. 7:13) shared his name with a man from the tribe of Gad (1 Chr. 5:15). *Jezer* (Num. 26:49; 1 Chr. 7:13) means 'formed [by God]'. *Shillem* (Num. 26:49) is called Shallum at 1 Chronicles 7:13. Since Shallum was a popular name borne by eleven persons in the Old Testament, the name in 1 Chronicles 7 may be a copyist's mistake that substituted the more common name for the less common one.

25. Like the summary statement for Zilpah's sons (v. 18), this statement for Bilhah's sons is a reminder of Jacob's time in Paddan-aram through the mention of Laban's wedding gift of Bilhah to Rachel.

26–27. The summary for the entire family of Jacob begins with the total number of his direct descendants (literally 'those who came out of his loins', v. 26). The sixty-six persons include everyone who came with him to Egypt apart from his wives and Jacob himself. This total excludes Er and Onan, who died in Canaan, as well as Joseph and his sons, who were already in Egypt. The next total gives the number of sons born to Joseph in Egypt as two. The final total of seventy persons from Jacob's household who came to Egypt includes Jacob and his three wives Leah, Zilpah and Bilhah.

iii. Joseph prepares for his family to meet Pharaoh (46:28–34)

28–29. Jacob's new-found trust in Judah, who had kept his pledge to bring Benjamin back to Canaan, is now shown in his sending Judah ahead of him. While the Hebrew text is difficult, it appears that Judah's mission was to prepare the way for the family's arrival in Goshen, where Joseph had invited them to settle (45:10). It is ironic that Judah, who had played a key role in separating Joseph from his father (37:26–27), now facilitated their reunion. Joseph somehow was informed of their arrival. We are told that *he hitched his horses to his chariot*. This seemingly unneeded bit of information not only serves to tell the reader of Joseph's anxiousness to see his father as well as his haste to meet him, but also is another indicator of his impressive power and authority in that he had a chariot at his disposal. Joseph went to Goshen to meet Jacob – he did not wait for Jacob to come to him. We are told that Joseph did three things: he presented himself to Jacob (literally, 'he was seen by him', v. 29), he hugged Jacob (literally, 'he fell on his neck') and he wept for a long time (literally, 'he wept on his neck'). The first action is the only time this phrase is not used in Genesis of an appearance by God (cf. 12:7; 17:1; 18:1; 26:2, 24; 35:9). The only other time its use involves Jacob is when Jacob saw God at Bethel after he arrived back in Canaan (35:9). Now Jacob had arrived in Egypt and Joseph, God's agent to save him and his family from the famine, appeared before him. Just as Joseph had hugged Benjamin and wept on his neck (45:14), so now he hugged and wept on Jacob.

30. Jacob's reaction was that he could now die – presumably die in peace (cf. 37:35) – because he had seen Joseph's face. Seeing someone's face is a repeated motif in the life of Jacob. Seven times Genesis mentions Jacob seeing someone's face, always at pivotal moments in his life. He saw disapproval in Laban's face (31:2, 5). He sought to see Esau's face to determine whether his brother would forgive him (32:20; 33:10). He saw God face-to-face at Peniel (32:30). Now he had seen Joseph's face, a face he had thought he would never see again (48:11).

31–34. Joseph now unveiled his plan for obtaining Pharaoh's permission to settle the family in Goshen. Pharaoh had not been specific about where Joseph's family would live; he had simply offered them *the best of the land* (45:18, 20). Joseph's plan was to report to Pharaoh and then present his family to them. He advised them that they ought to coordinate their statements to impress upon the Egyptian king their need for pasturage. Joseph's description of them as being shepherds, raising other livestock and having brought their animals was part of this plan. It not only signalled that the family needed suitable land but also indicated that they would not be a burden on the Egyptian kingdom. They would not seek occupations in the pharaonic administration. Joseph then anticipated Pharaoh enquiring of his brothers concerning their occupation. They were to confirm that they raised livestock, but they were to add that *both we and our ancestors have raised livestock from our youth until now* (v. 34). This was not an exaggeration, since Abraham, Isaac and Jacob had had flocks and herds. Finally, Joseph concluded by saying that if they followed these directions they would be allowed to live in Goshen *since all shepherds are detestable to*

Egyptians. It is often stated that there is no ancient record of Egyptians having an aversion to shepherds, but that this might reflect the antipathy that urban dwellers have towards nomads.[6] However, it may be that the Egyptians detested shepherds simply because their sheep and goats tended to eat all vegetation to the ground within their pasturage. Since much of Egypt outside the Nile had limited arable land (usually only in the immediate vicinity of the Nile), shepherds and their flocks would have been unwelcome.

iv. Pharaoh welcomes Jacob (47:1–12)

1. Joseph's report to Pharaoh approximates what he told his brothers he would say to the Egyptian king. The main differences are that he referred to his father instead of his father's family (46:31), he did not explicitly mention their occupation (46:32) and he added that they were in Goshen.

2–4. Joseph took only five of his brothers to present to Pharaoh, though no reason is stated for this, and we are not told which five. The entire conversation between Pharaoh and the brothers is not recorded. The text focuses on Pharaoh's question concerning their occupation. They politely respond as *your servants* and confirm that their ancestral occupation is shepherding. We are also told that they revealed their intent in coming to Egypt: to live as resident aliens. By this the brothers were asking permission to be in the land and stating that they did not view their move to Egypt as permanent. Moreover, this statement also links to God's words to Abraham at 15:13 that his descendants would live as resident aliens in a foreign land. The brothers' motivation for coming to Egypt was that *the famine in the land of Canaan has been severe* (v. 4). They asked to be allowed to live in Goshen, where they already were.

5–6. To fulfil the brothers' request, Pharaoh turned to his administrator Joseph and ordered him to settle his brothers *in the best part of the land* (cf. 45:10, 18), specifically giving them permission to live in Goshen. Moreover, if Joseph knew that any of his brothers were *capable men*, that is, highly skilled at their craft, Joseph was to appoint them as royal stewards of Pharaoh's livestock. This

---

6. E.g. Vergote (1959: 188–189); Wenham (1994: 445); Hamilton (1995: 604).

indicates that much of Pharaoh's livestock was kept in Goshen. Some of Jacob's sons were, in effect, to become royal administrators and thereby be afforded legal protections not normally available to foreigners.[7] However, we are not told whether Joseph actually appointed any of his brothers to such positions.

7–10. The presentation of Jacob to Pharaoh appears to have been more of a courtesy visit by the patriarch than the granting of permission to live in Egypt as it was with Joseph's brothers. Both at the beginning and at the end of their meeting we are told that Jacob blessed Pharaoh. This is the only place in Genesis where one of the patriarchs is said to have blessed a foreigner, and it implies that Jacob assumed a position superior to Pharaoh, perhaps because of his status as the elderly head of a clan.[8] Pharaoh's question concerning Jacob's age confirmed Jacob's superior status, since the aged were held in high esteem in the Ancient Near East. Jacob referred to his lifespan as the *years of his living as a resident alien*, an expression of eschatological hope that he had a better home prepared by God (Heb. 11:13–16). Jacob's 130 years would have been seen as extraordinary. For instance, the nineteenth-dynasty pharaoh Rameses II, who died in mid-1213 BC at the age of ninety, was thought to have lived a very long life. In some Egyptian texts the ideal long lifespan was considered to be 110 years.[9] Neverthe-less, Jacob noted that his years had been *few and hard*. His struggles with his brother and with his uncle Laban, and his troubles with his sons, surely made them hard. They were also few in comparison with those of his father Isaac, who lived to be 180 years old, and of his grandfather Abraham, who lived to the age of 175 years.

11–12. Joseph carried out Pharaoh's orders not only by settling his father, brothers and their families in Goshen, but also by granting them ownership of property there. Here Goshen is called *the land of Rameses* after a later name for one of the cities in the

---

7. Sarna (1989: 319).

8. Note Melchizedek's blessing of Abram, which implied his superiority due to his office as priest of the Most High God (14:18–20; cf. Heb. 7:7).

9. E.g. *ANET* 414. See also Vergote (1959: 200–201).

Nile Delta.[10] This appears to be a later scribal gloss to explain the location to readers in late antiquity who may not have known the location of Goshen (see the discussion of scribal additions to the Pentateuch in the Introduction). Joseph's provision for his father, brothers and their families fulfilled the promise he had made to them (cf. 45:11).

Meaning

Jacob, who had fled from the land of his birth in the face of Esau's threat, now had received God's blessing on his leaving the land of Canaan (contrast God's words to him at 46:3 with his words to Isaac at 26:2). Moreover, this account of Jacob's entering Egypt and his family settling there resolves a number of concerns from previous narratives: Jacob now has the large family that God promised him; Joseph is reunited with his father; and Jacob's family no longer has to worry about survival during the remaining years of the famine.

B. Contrast between Jacob's family and the native Egyptians during the remaining years of famine (47:13-27)

Context

This section of Genesis 47 not only depicts the severity of the remaining years of famine and its effect upon ordinary Egyptians, but it also serves as a contrast through the delivery of Jacob's family from the famine's ravages as Joseph was able to provide for them out of Pharaoh's resources.

Comment

i. Pharaoh acquires all of the land in Egypt (47:13-26)

1876–1871 BC

13-14. The contrast between verse 12, with Joseph providing his father, brothers and their dependants with food, and verse 13 is stark. There was no food in the entire region – Egypt and Canaan (that is, there was no food except that which Joseph had placed in storage). Silver was the most common medium of exchange in the

---

10. Hoffmeier (1997: 121–122). The city was named after Rameses II.

Ancient Near East, and we are told that in the early part of the
famine it was used to buy grain. In addition, the text is careful to
note that Joseph was faithful in placing the silver into the palace
treasury. He was faithful in his duties and did not unjustly profit by
withholding a portion for himself.

15–17. However, at some point during the seven years of famine,
all of the silver to be had in Egypt and Canaan had been collected
by Joseph. The Egyptians now begged Joseph to give them food.
Their argument as to why Joseph ought to provide for them was
twofold. First, there would be no profit from their starvation. What
good would it do for Pharaoh to reign over a depopulated land?
Second, they had no silver left with which to purchase more grain.
Joseph, however, saw no wisdom in simply handing out food. Food
that was obtained without price could lead to problems – not
only indolence on the part of the population, but perhaps also
profiteering that would lead to a black market where food was sold
to foreigners. So Joseph proposed a new medium of exchange:
livestock. The types of livestock are listed: *horses, flocks of sheep, herds
of cattle and donkeys* (v. 17). This is the first mention of horses in the
Bible. Since shepherds were detestable to Egyptians (see 46:34),
presumably the sheep came from Canaanites who came to Egypt
for food. While cattle and donkeys are mentioned, it is interesting
to note that camels were not considered among the livestock in
Egypt or Canaan. In fact, camels had been domesticated and used
in Mesopotamia and Arabia for centuries before Joseph's day.
However, they were not commonly owned pack animals in either
Canaan or Egypt. In Genesis ownership of camels is confined to
those who had lived in Mesopotamia (e.g. Abraham and Jacob;
24:10–11; 31:17) or who came from the Arabian Desert (e.g. the
Ishmaelites; 37:25). The text emphasizes that Joseph bought *all their
livestock*.

18–19. Since the livestock purchased only one year's provisions,
the next year the people came again to ask for more food.[11] This

---

11. In the Hebrew text this is literally 'the second year', meaning the second
    year after the silver had been exhausted, not the second year of the
    famine. It was probably the last year of the famine (cf. vv. 23–24).

time they did not have any expectation that Joseph would simply distribute grain free of charge. They proposed an exchange: their bodies and their land for food. Again, they offered an argument as to why Joseph should accept this arrangement: *Why should we die before your eyes, both we and our land?* (v. 19). If Joseph gave them food, the land would not be depopulated and, therefore, become desolate.

20-22. While the people offered themselves as Pharaoh's slaves, the text concentrates on the acquiring of the land for the crown. The severity of the famine is underscored by the statement that *every Egyptian sold his field* (v. 20). Verse 21 is difficult. Some English versions follow the Hebrew MT which says that Joseph moved all of the people to cities (e.g. CSB, GW, TNK). However, other versions follow the SP, LXX and the Latin Vulgate which say that Joseph made the people slaves. Though these two readings appear to be quite different in English, they involve only slight changes in the Hebrew underlying the various ancient texts.[12] Most probably the reading in SP, LXX and the Vulgate is correct, since it would make little sense to depopulate the countryside – exactly what the Egyptian people were arguing would happen if Joseph did not provide food for them (vv. 15, 19–20). In addition, in verse 23 Joseph clearly states that he had acquired both the people and their land for Pharaoh (also see v. 25). Last of all, we are told of an exception: the Egyptian priests did not sell their land (and, presumably, themselves). Instead, in keeping with respect for traditional Egyptian religion, they were given food from the royal storehouses, with the result that they were able to retain their property.

23-24. Joseph's words to the people defined the terms of their servitude to Pharaoh, and it involved more than simply food. Joseph gave them seed, and they were to sow it. This may well indicate that Joseph expected a harvest the next year, indicating that

---

12. There are two differences. The MT has the Hebrew letter *resh* where the SP has the very similar consonant *dalet* (twice). In addition, the MT is missing the letter *beth*, producing the word 'cities', whereas it is present in the Hebrew text in SP, making that word 'servants, slaves'.

this was the seventh year of the famine. The agreement was that one-fifth of the harvest was to be paid to Pharaoh. The remainder would be for future seed and for food for those who farmed the land.

25–26. The people expressed gratitude to Joseph and agreed to be Pharaoh's slaves. In fact, they saw Joseph as having dealt generously with them: they had *found favour with our lord* (v. 25). Joseph's actions may seem to be harsh by modern standards, especially in reducing the people to slavery to the crown, but, obviously, it was not viewed quite so harshly by the Egyptians themselves. We ought to bear in mind that in antiquity the economic system was quite different from today's, so such comparisons are somewhat unfair. In addition, it ought to be noted that Joseph limited the people's obligation to Pharaoh to providing 20% of their harvest. This was not the chattel slavery to which Joseph himself was subjected when he was sold to the Ishmaelites and then to Potiphar. Instead, their slavery was limited to 20% of their labour in the fields. Moreover, the requirement of one-fifth of the yield of their crops was quite modest by Egyptian standards. For instance, in the ancient Mesopotamian Code of Hammurabi, an indentured farmer was required to pay between one-half and two-thirds of the produce of his land (after expenses), and interest rates on loans for farmers' crops were often as high as one-third (33%).[13] Joseph's arrangement was not simply for one year, as we are told that his agreement with the people became law *to this day* – that is, to the time of the writing of the book of Genesis some centuries later. Again it is emphasized that the law exempted the priests' landholdings.

ii. Israel settles in Goshen (47:27)
1876 BC

27. Here we are told that *Israel settled in the land of Egypt*. This is only the second time in Genesis that the name *Israel* is used to designate the entire nation, and not simply as a reference to Jacob (cf. 34:7). This verse is parallel to verse 11. Thus, the *land of Goshen*

---

13. Sarna (1989: 332).

is the same as *the land of Rameses*. Moreover, *they acquired property*.
There is an irony here in that as the Egyptians lost their property,
Israel acquired holdings in Goshen, a statement that precedes and
follows the account of how Pharaoh came to acquire all the land
of Egypt. Finally, we are told that they *became fruitful and very
numerous*, fulfilling the promises made to the patriarchs, especially
Jacob (17:6; 26:4; 35:11; see also 48:4; Exod. 1:7; Deut. 26:5; Acts
7:17).

Meaning
The entry of Jacob and his family into Egypt marks the beginning
of the fulfilment of God's promises to Abraham, Isaac and Jacob.
At the beginning of this section Yahweh appears to Jacob at
Bethel and repeats the promise that Jacob will become a great
nation in Egypt (46:2–4), although they enter as only seventy
persons (46:8–27). At the end of this section we are told that
Israel settled in Egypt and became numerous (47:27). Thus, this
entire narrative of the beginning of Jacob's sojourn in Egypt is
framed by the first floret of God's promise. The absolute reliability
of God's pledges is confirmed as one of them approaches its goal.
In turn, this points forward to other promises of God yet to be
fulfilled, especially the possession of the land of Canaan and the
blessing of all nations through the seed of the patriarchs. Those
promises are also emphasized, but only as items for the future or
items prefigured. Thus, Jacob will come back to the land of
Canaan (46:4), and Jacob's brothers acknowledge that they have
come to Egypt as temporary residents (47:4). There is also a
foreshadowing of the blessing for all nations in Joseph's being
the saviour of the Egyptian people from starvation. In fact, the
Egyptians themselves acknowledged this: *You have saved our
lives* (47:25). Pharaoh's welcome of Joseph's brothers and his
meeting with Jacob were also a result of Joseph's being a blessing
to Pharaoh and his people. In addition, Jacob himself twice blessed
Pharaoh (47:7, 10).

In the midst of this narrative about Jacob's family in Egypt is an
account of Joseph providing for the Egyptians and acquiring the
land of Egypt for the royal house (47:13–26). To some, this story
appears to be out of place, an insertion into an otherwise unified

narrative about Israel.[14] However, this story of Joseph's distribution of grain to the Egyptians is not ill-fitted to the context. Instead, it serves several purposes. First, as noted already, it shows God's promise to bless all nations through Abraham's descendants. Second, it shows God's overwhelming blessings on Israel in contrast to his lesser blessings on other nations. Israel acquired land during the famine (47:11, 27), whereas the Egyptians were forced to exchange their land for food (47:20). Both were fed during the famine (47:12, 22). Third, it emphasizes how Jacob and his family avoided being reduced to penury (cf. 45:11), and even the Egyptians were treated with compassion, having to pay only one-fifth of their harvest to Pharaoh's treasury – a very generous offer on Joseph's part.

---

14. Even Westermann, who is inclined to read the entire Joseph narrative as a unified account, sees 47:13–26 as originating from a different source and marking a secondary insertion into the Joseph story (Westermann [1986: 173–174]). See also Coats (1983: 298–300).

27. THE FAMILY OF JACOB: JACOB'S AND JOSEPH'S LAST ACTS (47:28 – 50:26)

This final section of the story of Jacob's family brings readers to the end of Jacob's life and prepares for the continuation of Israel's story in Exodus and beyond. It begins with Jacob's provision for his burial in Canaan (47:29–31), which will be repeated as his last words (49:29–33) and which was completed by Joseph (50:1–14). Genesis 48 relates Jacob's adoption of Joseph's sons as his own and his blessing of Joseph. This explains why Israel had a tribe for each of Jacob's sons, but there was no tribe of Joseph, since there were tribes for each of Joseph's sons, Ephraim and Manasseh (Num. 1:32–35; Josh. 14:4). Genesis 49 records Jacob's deathbed address to his children, a prophecy concerning the descendants of each of his sons from the eldest to the youngest. Finally, the life of Jacob ends with his restating his desire to be buried in the land of Canaan, pointing the reader beyond Israel's four hundred years in Egypt.

A. Jacob makes Joseph promise to bury him in Canaan (47:28–31)

Context

c.1858 BC

Although Joseph and Jacob have finally been reunited, the text gives little attention to this, focusing instead on events at the end of Jacob's life. In doing so, the focus begins to look beyond the time in Egypt to the point when Israel will settle in their own land.

Comment

28. This notice of Jacob's life is similar to the notices in the genealogies of 5:3–32 and 11:10–26. Jacob's time is Egypt is simply summarized as seventeen years, and any other incidents from his life during this time are skipped over in silence. However, there is symmetry in Jacob's life with Joseph's: his time with Joseph in Canaan was seventeen years (37:2) and his time with Joseph in Egypt was seventeen years. It is interesting that the notice of Jacob's total years of life is not presented with the account of his death (49:33) as it was with Abraham (25:7–8) and Isaac (35:28–29). Instead, Jacob's years of life are presented immediately before his preparations for his death, including his adoption of Joseph's sons (48:1–22) and his last words to his sons (49:1–32).

29–30. Now knowing that he did not have long to live, Jacob summoned Joseph. Jacob's opening words, *If I have found favour in your eyes* (v. 29), treat Joseph as a superior – perhaps now the default leader of the family – and recognize that Joseph's goodwill is necessary to fulfil his request. He asked Joseph to show him kindness and faithfulness, a word pair that denotes both compassion for and commitment to someone. They are often said to characterize Yahweh (Exod. 34:6; 2 Sam. 2:6; 15:20; Ps. 25:10; 86:15). The placing the hand under the thigh was a sign of the absolute seriousness of the vow Jacob was asking Joseph to make. Abraham required the same of his servant before sending him to Haran to find a bride for Isaac (24:2, 9). In these cases the thigh is most certainly a euphemism for genitalia[1]

---

1. For a parallel Mesopotamian custom, see Malul (1987).

(cf. 46:26; Exod. 1:5, where Jacob's descendants are said to have come out of his thigh; and Judg. 8:30, where Gideon's sons are characterized by the same phrase). Jacob's concern was that he not be buried in Egypt. He had struggled mightily to receive the birthright from his father, and that included the promise of the land of Canaan. Jacob used a common Old Testament euphemism for death: to rest with one's fathers.[2] The choice of this euphemism matches his concern: to be buried in their burial place. Joseph readily agreed to this. It is noteworthy that besides kings in the Old Testament, only two persons are said to have rested with their fathers: Jacob and Moses (Deut. 31:16).

31. Jacob, however, wanted to make this a solemn promise, so he asked Joseph to swear an oath to do what he had promised. Oaths were the most serious and respected promises one could make, and this oath assured Jacob that his wishes would be honoured. Then we are told that *Israel bowed at the head of his bed*. This was another fulfilment of Joseph's dream (37:9–11). However, LXX understood this sentence differently and translated it 'Israel worshipped on the head of his staff', an understanding that is repeated at Hebrews 11:21.[3]

B. Jacob blesses Joseph's sons (48:1–22)

Context
1859 BC
This vignette from the life of Jacob is told in three parts. Verses 1–12 portray Joseph's visit to his father and their conversation, which is largely dominated by Jacob's words adopting Ephraim and

---

2. This expression occurs forty-one times in the Old Testament, most often in 1–2 Kings and 2 Chronicles. This is its only occurrence in Genesis.

3. The difference is a slightly different construal of the Hebrew text. The verb can mean either 'bow' or 'worship'. The words for 'bed' (*miṭṭâ*) and 'staff' (*maṭṭeh*) differ only in the vowels, which were not written, since in ancient Hebrew only consonants were written, and the reader was expected to supply the vowels.

Manasseh as his heirs. Verses 13–20 describe Jacob's blessing on Joseph's sons. Finally, verses 21–22 depict Jacob's grant of land in Canaan to Joseph.

This chapter serves to explain the prominence of the tribes of Ephraim and Manasseh in Israel and simultaneously to clarify why there were two Joseph tribes while each of the other sons of Jacob accounted for only one tribe. The counting of twelve tribes of Israel (not thirteen, with the expansion of Joseph into two tribes) will come at the expense of Jacob's two disgraced sons, Simeon and Levi. For instance, the Blessing of Moses (Deut. 33:1–29) omits the tribe of Simeon (which was apparently subsumed under Judah, whom Moses mentioned second – the spot that should have been Simeon's, Deut. 33:7).[4] In the division of the land envisioned by Ezekiel, Palestine is divided into twelve areas (Ezek. 48:1–7, 21–29), with a thirteenth area given to Yahweh (Ezek. 48:8–20). However, no land is given to the tribe of Levi (Ezek. 44:28).

Finally, it ought to be noted that Joseph's sons were not young lads at this time, but had grown to maturity. Since Jacob had been in Egypt for seventeen years (47:28), having come during the third year of the seven-year famine (45:6), and since Joseph's sons were born before the famine began (41:50–52), Ephraim would have been at least twenty years old at this time, and Manasseh would have been at least twenty-one. However, since they were born sometime during the seven years of bountiful harvest, Manasseh could not have been older than twenty-eight, nor Ephraim older than twenty-seven.

Comment

1–2. The opening of this story, *Some time after this* (v. 1), sets it after 47:29–31 in the period when Jacob was preparing for his death, but probably not more than a year after his previous instructions to Joseph about his burial. Joseph somehow received word that his father was weaker. He took Manasseh and Ephraim with him, and the text implies that he had to travel some distance – that he was

---

4. Note that Simeon received land within Judah's inheritance (Josh. 19:1–9).

not living in Goshen, but continued to live near Pharaoh's palace as his chief administrator. It is interesting to note that Joseph's sons are mentioned here according to their birth order, the last time they will appear in this order in Genesis.[5] Just as Joseph was told of Jacob's condition, Jacob was told of his son's arrival, but not of the arrival of his grandsons. Thus, by the use of the terms *father* and *son*, the narrative highlights the paternal bond that has characterized their special relationship since the beginning. The bond was so strong that it enabled Jacob to rally his strength and sit up in bed.

3–6. Some commentators view verses 3–6 as interrupting the narrative.[6] However, these verses are crucial to establishing Jacob's reasons for adopting Ephraim and Manasseh as his heirs and granting Joseph a portion of the land of Canaan. Without verse 4, readers would not be prepared for the blessing of fecundity given to Jacob's grandsons (v. 16). Without verses 5–6, the blessing in verse 16 that Ephraim and Manasseh would be called by Jacob's name would make little sense. Moreover, without verses 5–6, Jacob's mention of Rachel's death (v. 7) makes little sense.

Jacob began his words with a remembrance of God's appearance to him at Luz, which he had renamed Bethel (28:19; 35:6). Jacob's body may have been frail, but his memory was sharp. He remembered the way in which Yahweh had identified himself at Luz: *God Almighty* (v. 3; 35:11; see also 17:1; Job 13:3; Ezek. 10:5). *Almighty* (Hebrew *šadday*) is an ancient understanding of this name, and its meaning is debated. What is clear is that in Genesis this name of God is always associated with God's promise of children and fertility.

Jacob pointedly said that God had blessed him at Luz. The verb *bless* and the noun *blessing* are key terms throughout Genesis.[7] The

---

5. The two men or the tribes derived from them are mentioned together thirty-seven times in the Old Testament, and Ephraim is mentioned first in over two-thirds of cases. Only at 46:20; 48:1; Num. 26:28; Josh. 17:8; 2 Chr. 34:6, 9; Pss 60:7; 108:8; Isa 9:21 [first occurrence]; and Ezek. 48:5 is Manasseh mentioned before Ephraim.

6. As noted by Mathews (2005: 874).

7. They occur a total of eighty-five times, first at 1:22 and last at 49:28.

verb is used six times in this chapter (vv. 3, 9, 15, 16, 20 [twice]). God's blessing on Jacob at Luz was now being passed on to Joseph's sons. Jacob recounted three promises of God: that he would be fruitful and numerous (35:11), that many nations would come from him (35:11) and that he would be given Canaan as a permanent possession (35:12). The mention of possession of the land stands in contrast to the possession of Goshen in Egypt (47:27; 48:4), which was to be temporary. However, Jacob did not mention the new name *Israel* that God had given him (35:10), since he was instead emphasizing the future role of Joseph's sons in fulfilling God's pledges given at Luz.

Next Jacob adopted Joseph's sons as his own for the purpose of inheritance.[8] Again, Jacob's mind is keen, even as his body is failing. He not only could name Joseph's sons but also knew that they had been born before he came to Egypt. Jacob called them *Ephraim and Manasseh* (v. 5), reversing their birth order and subtly indicating the future superiority of the younger over the elder (cf. vv. 17–20). Jacob's comparison of their status as his sons to that of Reuben and Simeon is not a random choice of names among his twelve sons. Instead, he is comparing Joseph's first two sons to his first two sons. The prominence of Jacob's eldest two sons was being transferred to these two adopted sons.

Finally, Jacob noted that any sons born to Joseph after Ephraim and Manasseh would be counted as Joseph's and would be enrolled in the tribes of either one of their brothers. However, neither Genesis nor the rest of the Bible records any other sons of Joseph. Interestingly, however, LXX attributes nine sons to Joseph (46:27 LXX). This is in keeping with LXX's propensity to adjust the text of the Pentateuch in order to ameliorate any perceived difficulties.[9] In this case, since Jacob mentioned the possibility of other sons

---

8. There is an interesting parallel to the adoption of a grandson as a son from ancient Ugarit (Mendelsohn [1959]). Westermann refers to this as a legitimation of Ephraim and Manasseh as heirs, not a complete adoption (Westermann [1986: 185]).

9. Larsson (1983) notes this with respect to the text's view of chronology, but it is true of LXX Pentateuch in general.

born to Joseph, LXX added another seven sons so that readers would not puzzle over Jacob's statement.

7. Finally, Jacob recalled Rachel's death, again demonstrating an incisive recall despite his weakening body. He remembered where she died – on the way to Ephrath (35:16), which the narrator notes is the same as Bethlehem. He also remembered that she was buried in the place where she died (35:19). This is not simply a remembrance of Joseph's mother, an old man continuing to look back wistfully to the loss of his favourite wife. Instead, it is part of his adopting Joseph's two sons. Now Rachel will be credited with four sons instead of only two.

8–12. Jacob next asked Joseph who the men with him were. Clearly, he was able to see them – the text says he saw them – but he was not able to recognize them. Thus, the text speaks of Jacob's blindness because of old age. However, this ought not to be taken in an absolute sense, since twice he is said to see Joseph's sons (vv. 8, 11). Many modern English versions understand the text this way.[10] This is similar to the modern notion of someone who is legally blind. Such persons are not necessarily suffering from complete blindness, but they have a severe reduction in visual acuity. Jacob's question, then, was probably meant to confirm that the two men were Ephraim and Manasseh. Thus, the notice of Jacob's blindness draws a contrast between Jacob's obtaining the blind Isaac's blessing by deceit (27:1–29) and Joseph's obtaining blessing for his sons without any duplicity. Joseph replied that they were his two sons, the ones God had given him. While he did not mention their names to Jacob – since his father already knew their names (v. 5) – his reference to them as God's gifts is an oblique reference to the names he had given them (see 41:51–52). Jacob's request to bring them near so that he could bless them did not immediately trigger the formal blessing. Instead, he gave them grandfatherly affection of hugs and kisses and was prompted to the emotional observation that he had never expected to see Joseph again, much less see his offspring. The Hebrew word for *offspring* (v. 11) is literally 'seed', a

---

10. See CSB, GW, NIV: 'he could hardly see'; NET, NRSV: 'he could not see well'; see also Hamilton (1995: 633).

key word in Genesis, especially in the patriarchal promises (12:7; 17:19; 22:17–18; 26:24; 28:13–14).[11] Then we are told that Joseph took his sons *from his father's knees*. This forms a play on words with *bless* (v. 9), since in Hebrew the words *bless* and *knees* both contain the same consonants in the same order. Moreover, it anticipates Joseph's concern for the blessing on his firstborn son (vv. 17–18), since the Hebrew word for *firstborn* also contains the same consonants, although in a different order. The narrative now depicts Jacob's sitting in his bed (v. 2), which most likely means that he was sitting on the edge of his bed with his legs hanging over the side. To receive a hug the young men would have literally been at Jacob's knees. With the area in front of Jacob now unoccupied, Joseph was able to demonstrate his respect for and gratitude to his father by prostrating himself before Jacob.

13–14. Next Joseph approached Jacob again with his younger son Ephraim on his right (Jacob's left) and the older son on his left (Jacob's right). When Jacob laid his hands on the men's heads, however, he crossed his arms, placing his right hand on the younger and his left hand on the older. In ancient Semitic culture the right hand was the favoured one, signifying power and preference. Then he began his blessing.

15–16. The text says that Jacob blessed Joseph – that is, by blessing Joseph's sons he was pronouncing a blessing on Joseph and his posterity (cf. 49:22–26).[12] Jacob's blessing is in three parts: a threefold invocation of God (vv. 15–16a), a blessing (16b) and the effects of that blessing (16c–d).

The invocation characterizes God as the same God before whom Abraham and Isaac walked, indicating their life of faith in the God of Israel (cf. 24:40).[13] God is also characterized as shepherding Jacob for his entire life. This is the first mention of God as

---

11. This word occurs sixty-five times in Genesis, the last two times in this chapter (vv. 11, 19).

12. Once again LXX's translators perceived a problem with saying Jacob blessed Joseph instead of his sons. Therefore, they removed this difficulty by translating v. 15 as 'he blessed them' (i.e. Ephraim and Manasseh).

13. Others who walked with God were Enoch (5:22–24) and Noah (6:9).

shepherd, though not the last mention of this in Genesis (see 49:24). Finally, God is called *the angel who has redeemed me from all harm* (v. 16a). This is the second time Jacob identified the Angel of God with God himself (cf. 31:11–13). While the Hebrew verb for *redeem* or 'rescue' is an important theological term in the Old Testament to describe God's gracious defence of his people, it is used only here in Genesis. God had rescued Jacob from Esau, from Laban, and even from the Canaanites after Simeon and Levi murdered the men of Shechem (35:5).

The consequences of the blessing are to be twofold. First, Joseph's sons will be *called by my name and the names of my fathers Abraham and Isaac* (v. 16c) – that is, they will be considered the sons of Jacob, grandsons of Isaac and the great-grandsons of Abraham, equal in standing with the other sons of Jacob. The second result of the blessing is that they will *grow to be numerous in the land* (v. 16d). This blessing of descendants will be repeated to Joseph (49:25).

17–18. When Joseph realized that Jacob had crossed his arms and put the greater blessing on the younger Ephraim, he *thought it was a mistake.*[14] Many commentators and English versions translate this phrase – literally, 'it was evil in his eyes' – as if Joseph was alarmed and disapproved of a deliberate act on Jacob's part.[15] However, in this context there is no hint that Joseph thought that his father had deliberately done anything wrong. He found Jacob's crossed arms disconcerting, but not necessarily an intentional act. In fact, considering Jacob's poor eyesight, Joseph's own action and words assumed that Jacob thought that Joseph had placed his older son Manasseh at his own right-hand side, thereby requiring Jacob to cross his arms to place the greater blessing on the firstborn son as would normally be expected. Therefore, he tried to uncross Jacob's arms and to identify which son was the firstborn: *Not that way, father! This one is the firstborn* (v. 18).

---

14. For a similar use of this phrase, see Jer. 40:4.

15. ESV, GW, NET, NRSV; Wenham (1994: 466). Some are less severe, translating 'it seemed wrong to him', which may indicate that Joseph was not upset but simply assumed his father had done something inappropriate, perhaps unintentionally. See TNK; Hamilton (1995: 640).

19–20. However, Jacob revealed that he had not made a mistake. He said, *I know, son, I know* (v. 19), indicating that he understood Joseph's words as a corrective for a mistaken, but well-meaning, old man. Jacob then explained that Manasseh was not deprived of a blessing: he would become a large tribe. However, Ephraim was to be more numerous. Then Jacob continued his blessing – with the narration emphasizing that Ephraim received a greater blessing, since he would be mentioned before his brother whenever the people of Israel invoked God's blessing of fecundity and fertility.

21–22. Although the blessing for Joseph was given primarily to his two sons, Jacob also spoke a blessing to Joseph. Jacob once again noted that he was near death (cf. 47:30). However, the God who had been with Jacob would also be with Joseph and would do for Joseph what he had promised to his father (cf. 46:4): bring him back to Canaan, *the land of your fathers* (v. 21). Then Jacob bequeathed property in the Promised Land to Joseph over and above the inheritance he was bestowing on his other sons. He referred to this plot of land as a *mountain slope* (v. 22), literally 'a shoulder'. He described it as property that he had seized by force – with sword and bow. In addition, he took it from *the Amorites*. Here this term must be a catch-all name applied to any native inhabitant of Canaan, since the inhabitants of Shechem (which means 'shoulder' in Hebrew) were identified ethnically as Hivites (34:2). No incident involving Jacob seizing land in Canaan is mentioned in Genesis, and this has led to much speculation as to what Jacob was referring to. Since *mountain slope* is also the name of the city of Shechem, and since Joseph was eventually interred there (Josh. 24:32), that appears to be the place in view in Jacob's bequest. He could have been referring to the land in Shechem he bought (33:18–19), but Jacob mentioned that it was attained through warfare. This suggests instead that the events of 34:25–29, when Simeon and Levi slaughtered the men of Shechem, are in view. At the time he denounced his sons' violence that took human lives (34:30). Thus, it appears that he was ensuring that neither Simeon nor Levi would profit from their brutality. Instead of either of those sons inheriting Shechem, it would be given to Joseph by placing it in Ephraim. However, paradoxically, it would become the Levitical city of refuge within

Ephraim that would serve to protect those who inadvertently took a human life (Josh. 20:7; 21:21).

Meaning

God favoured the younger Abel's sacrifice over the sacrifice of his older brother Cain. God favoured the younger Jacob over his older brother Esau. In the last of these reversals in Genesis, God showed his favour to the younger of Joseph's sons over his elder brother. However, in this case both sons received God's blessing through Jacob, a blessing that acknowledged their father Joseph's vital role in God's plan to preserve the elderly patriarch's family by bringing them to Egypt. This blessing prepares for Jacob's blessings for all of his sons in the next chapter, a prophecy of their futures that features Joseph and Judah as the most prominent heirs of Jacob.

C. Jacob's final acts (49:1–33)

i. Jacob's final blessing for his sons (49:1–28)

Context

1859 BC

The last words of Jacob, sometimes called the Testament of Jacob, form the first long poem in the Bible. It contains the final blessing pronounced by Jacob, who had blessed Pharaoh (47:7, 10) and Joseph and his sons (48:9, 15, 20). Now he would bless his twelve sons (v. 28). Not only does this poem prophesy about the future of the tribes produced by each of Jacob's sons, but it also recalls in poetic form the acts of four of them: Reuben's adultery (v. 4; 35:22), Simeon and Levi's murder of the Shechemites (vv. 5–6; 34:1–31), and Joseph's being sold into Egypt and his ascent to power there (vv. 23–24).

Two sons of Jacob are prominent in the last major section of Genesis, the account of Jacob's family (37:2 – 50:26): Joseph and Judah. These two sons receive the longest blessings among the twelve. Judah's blessing contains fifty-five words, while Joseph's blessing contains sixty-one words. Between the two of them, their blessings occupy almost half of the 253 words in this poem.

The order of the sons in the poem is unique. Leah's six sons occupy the first half of the poem. They are mainly presented in birth order except that Zebulun (Leah's sixth son) is blessed before Issachar (Leah's fifth son). Rachel's sons, Joseph and Benjamin, are last. Between the sons of Leah and Rachel are the sons of the concubines, but in a peculiar order: Bilhah's older son Dan is placed before the two sons of Zilpah (Gad and Asher), but Bilhah's younger son Naphtali is blessed after Zilpah's sons.

One striking feature of Jacob's prophecy is its use of animal imagery. At least twelve Hebrew words denoting animals are used a total of thirteen times in this poem.[16] In addition, three more words denoting animals may occur: one in Naphtali's blessing (v. 21, see comment below) and two in Joseph's blessing (v. 22, see comment below). There is also occasional agricultural imagery that occurs only in the blessings for the two principal sons, Judah and Joseph: wine and grapes (v. 11), wine and milk (v. 12) and perhaps vine and branches (v. 22, see comments below).

For well over a century many critical scholars have considered these words attributed here to Jacob to actually be sayings depicting later events and circumstances among the various Israelite tribes. Supposedly, they originally circulated independently until brought together by a later compiler.[17] However, there are a number of problems with this. First, some of the tribal sayings do not point to later situations. For instance, there is no subsequent offence of the tribe of Reuben that fits its condemnation in verse 4.[18] Second, some of the features of these sayings appear to contradict later Mosaic law, testifying to their very early dates. For example, the law

---

16. These are ox (v. 6), cub (v. 9), lion (v. 9, twice), lioness (v. 9), young donkey (v. 11), female donkey (v. 11), male donkey (v. 14), snake (v. 17), viper (v. 17), horse (v. 17), doe (v. 21) and wolf (v. 27).

17. Among these is Westermann. For a fairly comprehensive summary of this approach, see Seebass (1984).

18. As noted, for example, in Von Rad (1972: 423). In order to continue to maintain that this is a later tribal saying, Von Rad is then forced to declare that only a fragment of the original saying has been preserved. See also the comments in Hamilton (1995: 647).

in Deuteronomy 21:15-17 dictates that the firstborn son shall receive a double portion of his father's estate, and it forbids transferring that honour to the eldest son of a second wife. However, that is exactly what Jacob does in denying Reuben any significant inheritance (vv. 3-4) and granting it instead to Joseph (vv. 22-26). Overall, these sayings ought to be understood as genuine prophecies made by Jacob to his sons instead of later sayings produced by the Israelite tribes and reflecting their experience in the land of Canaan.

Finally, it ought to be noted that this first long poem in the Pentateuch is most similar in form to the last long poem in the Pentateuch: Moses' Blessing (Deut. 33:2-29). That poem pronounces blessing on the twelve tribes of Israel immediately before Moses' death, just as this poem pronounces blessing on Jacob's sons immediately before Jacob's death.

Comment

1-2. Jacob's summoning of his sons marks this as an oral version of his last will and testament to them, a recital of what will happen to them in the future. The phrase *in the latter/last days* (v. 1) occurs twelve more times in the Old Testament, always in prophetic contexts.[19] This phrase points to the coming of the promised Saviour, and these days commence with his coming (see Heb. 1:2). In Jacob's testament the messianic culmination of his words is indicated in his prophecy to Judah in verse 10. Although Jacob is not explicitly called a prophet here, it is clear that he is performing one of the functions of God's prophets: foretelling the future. In his opening exhortation to his sons he calls them *sons of Jacob* (v. 2) but calls himself *your father Israel*, forming a skilful contrast in parallel poetic lines.

3-4. The address to Reuben, which results in Reuben's condemnation by his father, is in two parts. The first part describes Jacob's eldest son with three synonymous terms: *my firstborn . . . my strength . . . the firstfruits of my virility* (v. 3). Eldest sons are described by the

---

19. Num. 24:14; Deut. 4:30; 31:29; Isa. 2:2; Jer. 23:20; 30:24; 48:47; 49:39; Ezek. 38:16; Dan. 10:14; Hos. 3:5; Mic. 4:1.

terms 'firstborn' and 'firstfruits of virility' also at Deuteronomy
21:17 and Psalms 78:51; 105:36. In the Ancient Near East firstborn
sons were especially favoured. Later, in the law given through
Moses, firstborn sons were to receive twice as large a share of their
father's estate as their brothers received (Deut. 21:15–17). However,
the use of the word *firstborn* (*bkr* in Hebrew) forms a bitterly ironic
play on words with the noun 'blessing' (*brk* in Hebrew). Because of
Reuben's sin against his father (35:22), his blessing as firstborn is
transformed into a reprimand.

Reuben is also described as *excelling in prominence, excelling in power*
because of his status as Jacob's firstborn. However, the second part
of this oracle describes the future of Reuben's tribe in negative
terms. Many versions translate the first phrase of verse 4 as
'unstable as water', though this does not capture the meaning well
for English readers. Words from this root are used elsewhere in the
Old Testament to depict wanton, reckless behaviour (Judg. 9:4;
Zeph. 3:4). Here the figure of speech appears to compare Reuben
to the destructive force of powerful but uncontrollable floodwaters.
It is because of this character flaw that Reuben will no longer excel.
Jacob, who had not commented on Reuben's sin when he learned
of it (35:22), now condemns him for it. The last line of the saying
switches from addressing Reuben in the second person (*you defiled
it*) to a third-person reference to Jacob's eldest son: *he got into my bed*
(v. 4). It would appear that Jacob turned from addressing Reuben to
speak to the rest of his sons about Reuben's indiscretion.[20] Nevertheless, since antiquity some have been bothered by the change
in grammatical persons.[21] However, such shifts in grammatical
persons are not unusual in biblical poetry, so any objections to the
change from *you* to *he* here are unpersuasive (cf. e.g. Song 1:2, as
well as the shift from second person to third person in v. 9 in
Jacob's address to Judah).[22] In addition, this shift prepares for

---

20. Gevirtz (1971).

21. Thus, LXX once again attempted to correct this perceived problem by
    translating 'you got into my bed'. See the footnotes at 49:4 in CSB and NRSV.

22. Berlin (1985: 40–41) labels these types of shifts in grammatical persons
    'morphological parallelism'.

Jacob's address concerning his next two sons, Simeon and Levi, whose oracle addresses them entirely in the third person.

This prophecy forecasts the lack of leaders for Israel from among the members of the tribe of Reuben. The only attempt at leadership among the Reubenites recorded in Scripture was the ill-advised rebellion against the authority of Moses with Dathan as one of its leaders (Num. 16:1–35; 26:9; Deut. 11:6; Ps. 106:17). After that incident the Reubenites fade from the history of ancient Israel, supplying no judge, prophet or king for Israel.

5–7. The next address groups together Simeon and Levi, Jacob's second and third sons. This pairing immediately recalls their role in the slaying of the Shechemites (34:1–31). The two men are called *brothers*, which of course they were in a literal sense. Here, however, the word probably takes on the meaning of equals in a venture or persons who share a common trait (1 Kgs 9:13; 20:32; Prov. 18:9).[23] Many versions translate the second line of verse 5 as 'their knives are weapons of violence'.[24] However, the word rendered 'knives' is unique to this verse, and its meaning is disputed.[25] Most likely it is a reference to knives, probably pointing to the circumcision that these two brothers of Dinah required of the men of the city of Shechem before they would allow the marriage of their sister to Shechem son of Hamor. Another often-cited interpretation is that the word means 'wedding feast', and that it indicates that the lure of a wedding involving Dinah and Shechem, and its associated feast, was used by these brothers as a ruse that enabled them to slay the Shechemites.

Next Jacob disavowed any complicity in their conspiracy: he was not part of their *council* or *assembly* (v. 6). Instead, it was their anger alone that led to the slaughter of the men of Shechem. The final poetic line of verse 6 mentions the brothers' act of hamstringing oxen. This has given rise to much discussion, since Genesis 34 notes only the capture of the Shechemites' cattle and does not mention

---

23. Wenham (1994: 473).

24. See CSB, ESV, GW, NET, NIV, NRSV.

25. For a fairly complete discussion of many of the proposed interpretations of this word, see Hamilton (1995: 648–649, n. 4).

any maiming of them. Therefore, some have sought to connect this
to the effect of their action on Jacob by means of a play on words.
It is noted that the word for *hamstring* (Hebrew *'iqēr*) is very similar
to the *ruin* (Hebrew *'ākar*) that Jacob had said they had brought
on him (34:30).[26] This, however, strains the parallelism with the
previous line, which says that *in their anger they kill men.* Therefore, it
is more likely that Jacob is referring to something that Simeon and
Levi did to the men of Shechem and not to himself. We should note
that all other animal imagery in this poem is figurative, not literal.
Thus, the parallel between *kill men* and *hamstring oxen* suggests that
these were both actions taken among the Shechemites. Since
hamstringing oxen partially disables them, this is probably a poetic
reference to the disabled state of the men of Shechem as they
recovered from their circumcision (34:25).

Finally, Jacob pronounced a curse on their anger. This is the
strongest condemnation in this poem, and it uses the same word
Noah used when he pronounced a curse on Ham (9:25), the only
other time in Genesis when a father is recorded as cursing a son.
The curse on Simeon and Levi would lead to these two tribes being
scattered in Israel. For the Levites this was fulfilled when, instead
of being granted a contiguous area as an inheritance in Canaan, they
were assigned forty-eight cities throughout the Promised Land
(Num. 18:23–24; 35:1–8; Josh. 21:1–45). The tribe of Simeon, on
the other hand, was granted cities within the boundaries of Judah
(Josh. 19:1–9; Judg. 1:3; 2 Chr. 15:9). This led to its eventual absorp-
tion into Judah, resulting in the loss of identity as a separate tribe.

8–12. Since antiquity Christians have understood this passage to
be a prophecy about the Messiah.[27] Many ancient Jewish interpretations also understood this as pointing to the Messiah.[28] As such, it

---

26. Carmichael (1969: 435–437).

27. See *ACCS* 2.325–335.

28. Josephus notes this messianic interpretation among his contemporaries.
    He calls this passage 'an ambiguous oracle that was also found in their
    [i.e. the Jews'] sacred writings, how, about that time [i.e. during the first
    century], one from their country should become governor of the
    inhabited earth' (*Jewish War* 6.312).

would be the last of the messianic promises in Genesis, tracing a path from Eve's promised descendant (3:15) through Noah's son Shem (9:26) to Abraham (12:2–3; 18:18; 22:18), Isaac (26:4) and Jacob (28:14), and finally now to Jacob's son Judah (vv. 10–12).

Jacob's words to Judah begin with a triple play on words: *Judah . . . praise you . . . your hand* (v. 8).[29] The opening verse depicts the brothers acknowledging Judah's leadership both in praise and by bowing before him. This sees a future where instead of bowing to Joseph and acknowledging his leadership (37:10; 50:18), the tribes of Israel will give that honour to Judah. The word for *praise* is seldom applied to humans in the Old Testament – perhaps only at Job 40:14 and Psalm 45:17; 49:18. Thus, there is already a hint of divine majesty connected with Judah. Between the two poetic lines describing the acceptance of Judah as the leading tribe of Israel is a description of Judah's defeat of his enemies with his hand on their necks, a portrayal of triumph over those who threaten his people.

After directly addressing Judah in the opening of this oracle, Jacob continues by speaking of Judah in the third person. Here Judah is compared to a young lion returning from the kill with his prey. Similar imagery will also describe the fierceness of the tribes of Gad and Dan in the Blessing of Moses (Deut. 33:20, 22). In his den Judah lies down like a lion or lioness. With the rhetorical question *who dares to rouse him?* (v. 9), Jacob states that it would be as foolish to oppose Judah as it would be to rouse a lion with its prey. This figure of Judah as a lion is employed by later Scripture passages. It is referred to twice in Balaam's prophecies (Num. 23:24; 24:9) where it is used to describe Israel as a whole – probably a type of synecdoche where Israel is described by reference to its chief part, the leading tribe of Judah. The figure of a lion that must not be roused is taken up by Isaiah (Isa. 31:4). There the lion is Yahweh, and he will come to defend Zion – perhaps a reference to the Messiah from Judah who is also depicted as divine. This theme is developed further at Revelation 5:5–14 where Jesus is depicted both as the Lion of the tribe of Judah and as one who is worthy to receive worship as God.

---

29. In Hebrew: *yĕhûdâ . . . yôdûkā . . . yādĕkā*.

Next Jacob turns to prophesy Judah's permanent place of leadership. He depicts Judah as having the signs of kingship: a sceptre and a leader's staff. The staff is said to be *between his feet* (v. 10). Since antiquity this reference to feet has been understood as a euphemism for the sexual organs, thereby describing Judah as providing royal leadership throughout coming generations (cf. Deut. 33:21; Mic. 5:2).[30] Nevertheless, several modern commentators have doubted this interpretation.[31]

The next line of verse 10 has been one of the most difficult passages to interpret in the entire Old Testament, and there has been no consensus among ancient or modern interpreters as to its meaning.[32] While there have been many suggestions, there are only a few that do not require radical emendations to the text. The most often discussed are the following:

1. The line could be taken as written to mean 'until he comes to Shiloh'. This apparently would be a prophecy of a Judean ruler coming to the city of Shiloh in the territory of Ephraim, perhaps to assert his control over all Israel. There are several problems with this interpretation, however. While Shiloh was an important Israelite centre for a while when the tabernacle was there (Josh. 18:1; 1 Sam. 1 – 4), it apparently was destroyed by the Philistines before David's day and never again became an important city in Israel. In addition, the name of the city is never spelled elsewhere in the Old Testament as it is here.

---

30. See 49:10, LXX: 'A ruler shall not be lacking from Judah and a leader from his thighs'; also Targum Pseudo-Jonathan XII: 'Kings or rulers shall not cease from the house of Judah, nor scribes teaching the law from his seed'; and Targum Onkelos XII: 'He who exercises dominion will not pass from the house of Judah, nor the scribes from his children's children forever.' See also Wenham (1994: 477); Good (1963: 429); Carmichael (1969: 439–440).

31. E.g. Hamilton (1995: 654, n. 10). Mathews (2005: 893) notes problems with the sexual interpretation, but does not dismiss it completely.

32. Westermann (1986: 231). For a complete survey of ancient and medieval interpretations, see Posnanski (1904). For a convenient survey of modern suggestions, see Frolov (2012), especially note 7.

2. Many of the versions take it to mean 'until he to whom it [i.e. the sceptre] belongs comes', which involves only a slight change in the Hebrew vowels.[33] This would be a messianic prophecy that the leadership of Judah among the people of Israel would last until the coming of the Messiah to claim it. This interpretation appears to be as old as LXX.[34] It is also found in several modern English versions.[35] There are various problems with this interpretation, not the least being that the spelling of 'whose it is' in Hebrew is invariably *lô*, not *lōh*, as it is in this verse.[36]

3. Another popular interpretation is to read the line as 'until tribute comes to him'.[37] This reading has the advantage of forming a nice parallel with the next line, which attributes obedience of the nations to the Messiah from Judah. Thus, the nations will bring tribute to him. However, once again, this interpretation involves a slight adjustment of the Hebrew vowels. In addition, it also divides the word *Shiloh* into two words – *šay lōh* – whereas all manuscripts record this as one word, not two.[38] Moreover, like the previous interpretation, *lōh* is again taken to be a variant of the usual Hebrew *lô*.

4. Finally, the Hebrew text can be read as it stands: 'until Shiloh comes'.[39] This would understand *Shiloh* not as a common noun, but as a proper noun naming the Messiah.[40] The name most likely

---

33. In antiquity, only Hebrew consonants were written. The vowels present in MT are a later, early medieval addition to the text.

34. LXX reads 'until the things stored for him come'.

35. CSB, NET, NIV; Hamilton (1995: 654); Mathews (2005; 895).

36. The normal spelling for 'whose it is' (i.e. *lô*) is found in the very next line, calling this interpretation into question. See Frolov (2012: 418).

37. ESV, NRSV, TNK; Steiner (2010: 219–226); Wenham (1994: 478).

38. Frolov (2012: 418).

39. See GW and the footnotes in CSB, ESV, NRSV.

40. An objection to this interpretation is that *Shiloh* would be a feminine noun but the verb *he comes* is masculine (e.g. Hamilton [1995: 659]). However, if *Shiloh* is understood to be a proper noun naming a man and not a common noun or a proper noun naming a city (which is always feminine in Hebrew), then that objection is moot.

ought to be derived from the Hebrew root *šlh*, meaning 'to be at ease', 'to rest', 'to be prosperous' (Job 3:26; 12:6; Ps. 122:6; Jer. 12:1; Lam. 1:5). Thus, it would picture the Messiah as a man coming from the tribe of Judah to bring rest and prosperity to Israel and the nations (see Matt. 11:28; Rev. 14:13). Several ancient Jewish interpretations of this passage simply substitute 'Messiah' for *Shiloh* here:

> until the coming of the Messiah of Righteousness, the Branch of David,
> for to him and to his descendants has been given the covenant of the
> kingship over his people for everlasting generations.
> (4Q Patriarchal Blessings)

> until the Messiah comes, whose is the kingdom, and unto whom shall
> be the obedience of the nations.
> (Targum Onkelos)

> until the time that the King the Messiah shall come, the youngest
> of his sons; and on account of him shall the peoples flow together.
> (Targum Pseudo-Jonathan)

> What is his [i.e. the Messiah's] name? – The School of Rabbi Shila said:
> His name is Shiloh, for it is written, until Shiloh comes.
> (Talmud, *baba Sanhedrin* 98b)

In addition, Christians have traditionally understood other Old Testament passages as giving descriptive names to the Messiah (e.g. Isa. 7:14 [Matt. 1:23]; 9:6; Jer. 23:6; Zech. 3:8), so this type of interpretation is neither unique nor unexpected.

The final line of verse 10 notes that *the obedience of the peoples belongs to him*. This is a reference to the Messiah's dominion over all peoples, an extension of the promise to Abraham, Isaac and Jacob that all peoples would be blessed through their descendant (12:3; 18:18; 22:18; 26:4; 28:14).

Verses 11–12 go on to depict in highly figurative terms the lush benefits of the Messiah's reign. He will tie his donkey to a vine. Later messianic passages associate the coming of the Messiah with a donkey (Zech. 9:9; Matt. 21:5; John 12:15). Normally one would not tie one's donkey to a valuable grapevine, since the donkey would eat it. However, here the picture is one of such abundance that the loss of a vine is seen as inconsequential. Moreover, the Messiah will wash his clothes in wine. Once again, the picture is that normally expensive wine will be as common as water so that the Messiah will not hesitate to use it to wash his clothes. Note that the expression *blood of grapes* (v. 11) refers to the juice used to make wine (Deut. 32:14). Finally, the Messiah's beauty is described as his having *eyes darker than wine* and *teeth whiter than milk* (v. 12).

13. The first son of Jacob addressed out of birth order is Zebulun, who is placed before his older brother Issachar. Zebulun is described as living by the sea and providing a harbour for ships. Based on the description of the cities allotted to Zebulun at Joshua 19:10–16, most modern maps illustrating the territories of the twelve tribes of Israel show Zebulun to be landlocked. However, in Moses' Blessing, the tribe of Zebulun along with the tribe of Asher is described as drawing wealth from the sea (Deut. 33:18–19). It may be that Zebulun had an outlet to the Mediterranean just south of Asher's territory. The southernmost coastal city in Asher was Aphek, so Zebulun may have possessed a corridor south of Aphek and north of the Wadi Kishon near Mount Carmel. This would also explain the reference to Sidon, the great Phoenician city. Located in the north of Canaan with an outlet to the sea, Zebulun could have been considered one of Sidon's neighbours. Note that Josephus described Zebulun's territory as bordering on two bodies of water: 'the land which reaches as far as the Lake of Gennesaret [i.e. the Sea of Galilee], and that which belonged to Carmel and the [Mediterranean] Sea'.[41]

14–15. The last of Leah's sons to be addressed by Jacob is Issachar. Many commentators understand this oracle to be negative in tone, mainly due to the end of verse 15 where Issachar is said to be a forced labourer.[42] However, there are reasons to believe that this is not a negative prophecy for Issachar.[43] First, it ought to be

---

41. *Jewish Antiquities* 5.84.

42. Kidner (1967: 230–231); Carmichael (1969); Gevirtz (1975); Wenham (1994: 480); Mathews (2005: 899).

43. Heck (1986); Hamilton (1995: 667–668).

noted that all of the other blessings on Jacob's sons that use animal imagery are positive. Second, the only clearly negative words of Jacob are directed to his sons who committed sins that affected their father (i.e. Reuben, Simeon and Levi, vv. 3–7). No such sin of Issachar is noted in Genesis. Finally, it is not necessary to view the forced labour in verse 15 as subjugation to Canaanites, as suggested by the negative view. Instead, Issacharites might be depicted as reliable workers, providing labour for public works projects during Israel's monarchy (2 Sam. 20:24; 1 Kgs 4:6; 5:13; 9:15; 12:18; 2 Chr. 10:18). This would harmonize well with the tribe's description as a sturdy donkey (v. 13). In exchange for being able to lie down and rest between the saddlebags that contained his burden, he was given good land. Another often-debated item in this prophecy is the meaning of the word usually translated *saddlebags*. Other meanings have been suggested, and it is often translated 'sheepfolds' in its two other occurrences at Judges 5:16 and Psalm 68:13.[44] Other suggestions include 'fireplaces' or 'trash heaps'.[45] However, in no instance in the Old Testament does the context preclude the concept of 'saddlebags', which is most appropriate here for a beast of burden. Furthermore, the Hebrew noun has a dual form, denoting two of something or something that comes in pairs, which is appropriate for saddlebags but not for the other proposed meanings.

16–17. Next Jacob turns to one of the sons of his concubines: Dan. This son is honoured by being the seventh one mentioned, and this is reinforced by the fact that only he and Judah are mentioned twice by name (cf. vv. 8, 9).[46] The oracle begins with a play on Dan's name: *Dan will judge his people* (v. 16). Not only does Dan's name mean 'judge', thereby creating wordplay, but also there is sound play in the Hebrew: *dān yādîn*. The concept of judging here emphasizes providing justice and vindication.[47] Dan will do this as

---

44. CSB, ESV, NET, NIV, NRSV, TNK. GW translates it as 'saddlebags' at Judg. 5:16 but 'sheep pens' at Ps. 68:13.
45. See the discussion in Heck (1986: 390–391).
46. On the importance of the seventh position in biblical genealogies, see Sasson (1978).
47. See NIV: 'Dan will provide justice for his people.'

one of the tribes of Israel, which perhaps notes that Dan, though a small tribe, will play an important role in Israel's history. The most notable Danite in the Bible is Samson, who was the beginning of the deliverance of Israel from the Philistines (Judg. 13:5). Another important Danite was Oholiab, whom God equipped as a skilled artisan to play a key role in the construction of the tabernacle (Exod. 31:6; 35:34; 36:1–2; 38:23). Dan is also described as a snake, a viper, who bites the unsuspecting heel of horses, causing their riders to be forcefully dismounted. Thus, although Dan would be a small tribe and easy prey for others, by stealth it would be more than able to hold its own. Dan's stealth was ably demonstrated later when some of the Danites moved north to conquer the unsuspecting city of Laish in the extreme north of the Promised Land and renamed it Dan (Judg. 18; the city was also called Leshem, Josh. 19:47). In this way they incorporated this city into Israel, even though it was outside the land apportioned to any of the twelve tribes by Joshua. Thus, Dan became a permanent reference point in Israel: 'from Dan to Beersheba' (Judg. 20:1; 1 Sam. 3:20; 2 Sam. 3:10; 17:11; 24:2, 15; 1 Kgs 4:25; 1 Chr. 21:2; 2 Chr. 30:5; Amos 8:14).

18. Abruptly Jacob turns from speaking about Dan to directly addressing God: *I wait for your salvation, Yahweh!* Because this appears to many to be an unexpected interjection, it has often been characterized as a later gloss inserted into this poem.[48] However, a closer look reveals that this is a strategically placed appeal to God for Israel's salvation. First, it ought to be noted that it comes after the important seventh son's oracle, highlighting the honour bestowed on Dan. Second, immediately before and after this short poetic line is the mention of tribes that will have to resort to attacking the heels of those who are stronger than they are. Jacob is confident of deliverance for God's people, though they are often seemingly confronted by stronger opponents. Interestingly, this verse joins the first and only use in Genesis of the word *salvation* with the last use in Genesis of God's name *Yahweh*.

19. Jacob's words to Zilpah's first son Gad form an elaborate pun on his name. Four of the six Hebrew words in this oracle play on

---

48. E.g. Westermann (1986: 235).

the sounds of the consonants *g* and *d*: *Gad will be raided* [*gĕdûd*] *by raiders* [*yĕgûdennû*], *but he will raid* [*yāgud*] *their heels.* The tribe of Gad would settle in Gilead east of the Jordan River. This would make them vulnerable to raiders (Judg. 11:1 – 12:7; 2 Kgs 10:32–33). Nevertheless, Gad would be able to strike back at the heels of the raiders as they retreated. Gadites became well-known warriors (1 Chr. 5:18; 12:8).

20. Asher's rich food that Jacob prophesied was due to the tribe's inheritance along the Mediterranean Sea in Galilee north of Mount Carmel (Josh. 19:24–31, 34). He is also depicted as producing royal delicacies. Many understand this to mean this tribe supplying their Canaanite and Phoenician neighbours with food for their royal courts (Judg. 1:32 notes that Asher was unable to drive out the Canaanites and so settled among them).

21. The last of the sons of Jacob's concubines to be addressed is Naphtali, the younger son of Bilhah. This tribe would settle in the attractive central upper Galilee west of the Sea of Galilee (Josh. 19:32–39).These words obviously praise Naphtali for its beauty. What is not obvious is the exact meaning of this prophecy.[49] Most English versions understand Naphtali as being compared to a wild doe.[50] However, LXX and some modern interpreters believe Naphtali is depicted as a tree – an oak or terebinth – based on a slight but questionable emendation of the Hebrew text.[51] Therefore, the first line of this verse is best read as it stands: *Naphtali is a doe that has been set free* – a reference to the tribe's beautiful land that was hospitable habitat for wild deer. The second line has also been variously translated. Some English versions understand it to say 'that bears beautiful fawns'.[52] There are at least two problems with this interpretation, however. One is that the word for 'that bears' is masculine in gender in Hebrew and therefore conflicts with the feminine *doe*. The other is that the word

---

49. Hamilton (1995: 676) notes at least six different understandings of this verse.

50. CSB, ESV, GW, NET, NIV, NRSV, TNK.

51. From *'ayyālâ* to *'ēlah.*

52. CSB, ESV, NIV, NRSV, TNK.

translated 'fawns' is based on a slightly different construal of the consonants of the text.[53] This proposal is aimed at producing a Hebrew word that occurs nowhere else in the Old Testament and that supposedly is a cognate of the Aramaic word that normally denotes lambs but is not known to denote fawns (Ezra 6:9, 17; 7:17). Instead, the line is probably best understood as it stands in MT: *He* [masculine, referring to Jacob's son, not the feminine doe] *brings forth beautiful words*. This probably refers to the tribe's reaction upon seeing the possession that it had inherited in the Promised Land.

22–26. Jacob's address to Joseph is the longest of all eleven of his oracles. It consists of three parts: Joseph compared to either a vine or a wild donkey (v. 22); Joseph's success and blessing in the face of difficulties (vv. 23–25); and the surpassing greatness of the blessings on Joseph (v. 26).

Most English versions follow a common ancient understanding of verse 22 as a comparison of Joseph to a fruitful vine.[54] However, some versions and many commentators believe that this verse compares Joseph to a wild donkey.[55] There are several reasons for this. First, Joseph is called a 'son of fruitfulness' in MT, which is often taken to mean that he is a fruitful vine. However, nowhere else in the Old Testament is 'son of' followed by a plant. Second, no other son of Jacob is compared to a plant. Instead, Judah, Issachar, Dan, Naphtali and Benjamin are compared to animals. Thus, it is proposed that Joseph is here pictured as 'son of a wild she-donkey' (v. 22). Instead of translating 'its branches climb over a wall' (literally, 'daughters a step upon a wall'), it is proposed that this phrase ought to be understood as 'daughters of a wild donkey next to a wall'. However, this depends on a conjectural meaning for the word translated 'wild donkey' based on a similar word in Arabic.[56] Thus, Joseph would be described this way:

---

53. From *'imrê* to *'immrê*.

54. CSB, ESV, GW, NET, NIV, NRSV.

55. TNK; Wenham (1994: 485); Hamilton (1995: 678–679; 683–684).

56. Gevirtz (1975: 37–38).

Joseph is a son of a she-donkey,
a son of a she-donkey beside a spring,
wild donkeys next to a wall.

No matter whether Joseph is compared to a vine or a donkey, a play on words is formed with 'Ephraim', the more populous of the two Joseph tribes.

Jacob next describes the difficulties faced by Joseph during his lifetime. Archers attacking him is a metaphor for those who exhibited hostility towards him, especially his brothers, but also perhaps Potiphar's wife. Despite these attacks, Joseph's own bow was steady, and his arms that held it were strengthened by God. God's strengthening him is indicated by mention of *the hands of the Mighty One of Jacob* (v. 24), which steadied Joseph's arms (literally, 'the arms of his hands'). The appellation *Mighty One of Jacob* occurs five times in Old Testament poetic texts (Ps. 132:2, 5; Isa. 49:26; 60:16).[57] Joseph is also strengthened by the *name of the Shepherd.* God is called shepherd only one other time in Genesis, when Jacob described God as his shepherd who had guided him throughout his life (48:15). Thus, this blessing on Joseph points to the strong connection between Jacob and Joseph depicted throughout the story of Joseph and his brothers. God is also called *the Rock of Israel,* an expression that occurs only here in the Old Testament.[58] The third and fourth ways in which Joseph was strengthened were *by the God of your father who helps you, and by the Almighty who blesses you* (v. 25). Yahweh is called *God Almighty* five times in Genesis in connection with Abraham, Isaac and Jacob (17:1; 28:3; 35:11; 43:14; 48:3). Here Jacob splits *God* and *Almighty* over two lines of poetry. God's blessings that strengthened Joseph are described by two merisms: *heavens above . . . the deep below* (i.e. all the blessings of the earth) and *the breasts and the womb* (i.e. the blessing of fertility).

Finally, Jacob describes the surpassing nature of the blessings that rest on Joseph: they exceed the most ancient of blessings

---

57. The equivalent 'Mighty One of Israel' occurs at Isa. 1:24.

58. A similar term using a different word for 'rock' occurs at 2 Sam. 23:3; Isa. 30:29.

associated with the hills (i.e. from the beginning of God's creation). Very similar language is used by Moses to pronounce a blessing on Ephraim and Manasseh at Deuteronomy 33:15. Jacob's final wish that these blessings remain on the head and brow of Joseph is almost identical to the language used in the Blessing of Moses concerning the Joseph tribes (Deut. 33:16).

27. Finally, Benjamin is depicted as a fierce wolf. The pair *in the morning . . . in the evening* is a merism that depicts the tribe's constant aggressive activity. This prophecy foretells the military exploits of Benjamin, from the activity of the judge Ehud (Judg. 3:15–30) to its participation in the battle against Sisera (Judg. 5:14) and its savagery at Gibeah that prompted an Israelite civil war in which this small tribe for a while was able to fend off the much larger forces of the other eleven tribes (Judg. 19 – 21). Warriors from Benjamin would become known for their skill as left-handed slingers (Judg. 20:15–16; 1 Chr. 12:2) and for their bravery as archers (1 Chr. 8:40).

28. This verse is the narrative summary of Jacob's testament. Three times it mentions blessing: *he blessed . . . according to his blessing he blessed*. By mentioning the twelve tribes and not simply Jacob's twelve sons, the author reinforces that this poem is not simply about Jacob's sons, but about what will happen to their descendants in the future (cf. v. 1).

ii. Jacob's final words and death (49:29–33)
1859 BC

29–32. Jacob's final concern was that he be buried in Canaan. This was the second time he had made this request (cf. 47:29–31), and it emphasized that Israel's future was not in Egypt but in the land promised to Abraham, Isaac and Jacob. Jacob was also careful to describe his ancestral tomb, three times mentioning it as a former Hethite holding that now belonged to him because of Abraham's purchase (23:1–20). He also emphasized that the family of God's chosen patriarchs and matriarchs were buried there. The listing of Abraham, Sarah, Isaac and Rebekah is not unexpected. Although Rebekah's death and burial is nowhere mentioned in Genesis, she had to have died in Canaan long before Jacob came to Egypt. However, the fact that Leah was buried there is somewhat of a surprise, since her death is never mentioned. Jacob's statement clarifies that Leah had died in Canaan sometime before Jacob came to Egypt.

33. The report of Jacob's death begins by mentioning that he drew his feet into his bed. Thus, it is implied that Jacob had been sitting on the side of his bed as he blessed his sons. Now he lay back down, never to stir himself again from that bed. The phrase *was gathered to his people* was also used to describe the deaths of Abraham (25:8), Ishmael (25:17) and Isaac (35:29). Thus, Jacob was now with his people, and his final wish was for his body to be interred with theirs.

Meaning

The emphasis of this part of the story of Jacob's family (47:28 – 49:33) is on Jacob's final acts. It is framed by Jacob's request – first to Joseph (47:28–31) and then to all of his sons (49:29–33) – that he be buried in Canaan. This focus on Canaan is a reminder of God's promises to the patriarchs: he would make them a great nation, give them the land of Canaan and use them to be a blessing to all peoples of the earth.

These promises are the point of Jacob's final acts. In his blessing on Joseph's sons (48:15–20) he bestowed on them God's promise of great increase, making them the most numerous of the twelve tribes of Israel, a pledge that was repeated in his blessing on Joseph (49:25–26). That blessing, however, was tied to the Promised Land: they were to be *numerous within the land* (48:16).

The promise of the land is especially emphasized in the testament of Jacob (49:1–27). There Jacob functions as a prophet, and his words predict aspects of the history of the tribes of Israel in the land of Canaan. For the most part Jacob's blessings on his sons were fulfilled from the time of the judges and into the time of the Israelite monarchy.

However, the promise of God to use the patriarchs to bless all nations looks beyond the history of God's Old Testament people, and so does Jacob's blessing on Judah. Though the kingdom would be taken from Israel when Judah was led into captivity in Babylon, the sceptre would not depart from Judah *until Shiloh* – the Messiah – *comes* (49:10). He would have *the obedience of the peoples* – not only Israel, but all the peoples of the earth.

In this way the last acts of Jacob in the book of Genesis set the agenda for the rest of Scripture: the making of a great nation that would leave Egypt by God's mighty hand and outstretched arm (Deut. 4:34; 5:15; 7:19; 26:8; Ps. 136:12); the granting of the land of Canaan to Israel, who would dwell there from the time of Joshua to the Babylonian conquest of Jerusalem, and then be graciously restored to the land by the command of Cyrus the Persian whom God would raise up for that purpose (2 Chr. 36:22–23; Ezra 1:1–4; Isa. 44:28); and, finally, the life, ministry, death and resurrection of Judah's great descendant, the Lion of the tribe of Judah, Jesus the Messiah, the Christ (Heb. 7:14; Rev. 5:5).

D. Joseph's final acts (50:1–26)

Context

With the death of Jacob, leadership of the family fell to Joseph. The final chapter of Genesis quickly summarizes Joseph's most important acts before his death. He and his brothers would carry out Jacob's wishes after first mourning his father, having him embalmed according to Egyptian custom and requesting permission to go to Canaan to bury their father.

In addition, there is another theme in the story of Jacob's sons that is resolved here: the tension between Joseph and his brothers that was introduced at the very beginning of their story (37:2–11). It had seemingly been settled when Joseph revealed himself to his brothers in Egypt (45:1–15). However, with the death of Jacob, Joseph's brothers were concerned that without the restraining presence of their father, Joseph might feel free to seek revenge for their reprehensible treatment of him. Joseph, however, demonstrated that he understood all that had happened to him to have been part of God's plan (50:19–20; cf. 45:4–8). Ultimately, since Joseph accepted God's will, he was able not only to forgive his brothers, but also to close the rift that threatened to divide the nation of Israel.

The book ends with Joseph's final words to his brothers (50:22–26; Heb. 11:22), a sort of parallel to Jacob's final words to his sons in Genesis 49. However, the completion of Joseph's wishes would wait four centuries (Exod. 13:19; Josh. 24:32).

Comment

i. Jacob's burial in Canaan (50:1–14)

1859 BC

1. Joseph's reaction to Jacob's death is unique in the Bible. Only here does someone kiss the deceased. The mention of Jacob's face recalls God's promise to Jacob that Joseph would close his eyes when he died (46:4).

2–3. We are told that Joseph used his own personal physicians to embalm his father. We are also informed that the forty days taken to embalm Jacob matched the normal time for this procedure, but that the total time that *the Egyptians* (v. 3) mourned Jacob was seventy days. This, no doubt, included the forty days needed to embalm the body. The seventy-day mourning period demonstrated the high regard in which the Egyptians held Joseph's father. The ancient Greek historian Diodorus noted that the period for mourning the death of a pharaoh was seventy-two days.[59]

4–6. At the end of the Egyptian mourning period Joseph indirectly asked Pharaoh for permission to bury his father in Canaan. No reason is given for Joseph communicating his request through *Pharaoh's household* (v. 4). Though Joseph was only second to Pharaoh in Egypt, he nevertheless used polite address when conveying his request: *If I have found favour with you* (plural – meaning the senior members of Pharaoh's court). Joseph's words to Pharaoh's household at the end of verse 5 correspond to the actual events: he wished to *go up* to Canaan (vv. 7–11), *bury* his father (vv. 12–13) and then *return* to Egypt (v. 14).[60]

Joseph's appeal to Pharaoh is a fair representation of Jacob's words, though it does not completely reproduce them. Joseph noted that Jacob had made him take an oath, but he omitted the custom of placing a hand under the thigh (47:29), perhaps because this custom may have been unfamiliar to the Egyptian king. In addition, Joseph diplomatically omitted Jacob's insistence that he not be buried in Egypt (47:29–30), though it was plain even from what Joseph did say that Jacob had not wanted to be buried in the land

---

59. *Histories* 1.72.

60. Westermann (1986: 200).

of the Nile. Instead, he quoted Jacob as requesting that he be buried *in the tomb that I cut for myself in the land of Canaan* (v. 5). This would have appealed to Pharaoh, since many Egyptian kings, priests and nobles prepared tombs for themselves while they were still living. Joseph saved the actual request to go and bury his father until the end of his plea and appended to it a promise to return to Egypt. Apparently the message was relayed to Pharaoh, whose permission was granted in the light of Joseph's oath to Jacob.

7–9. The retinue in Jacob's funeral cortège included Pharaoh's servants classified in two groups: the elders in Pharaoh's court and the elders of the land of Egypt – thus, court administrators as well as bureaucrats serving throughout the kingdom. Israelites who went to Canaan included the households of Joseph and his brothers, and his father's household. We are told that only the children, flocks and herds were left behind in Egypt – a sure sign that no-one expected to stay in Canaan after Jacob's interment. Moreover, this was an official Egyptian state procession, as the presence of horses and chariots attests. The procession left from *the land of Goshen* (v. 8), the same place from which the Israelites would leave Egypt four centuries later.

10–11. The next place mentioned in the itinerary is the threshing floor of Atad, which the text tells us was *across the Jordan* (v. 10). In the Old Testament this phrase often refers to the land east of the Jordan.[61] However, in a few cases it refers to land west of the Jordan River (Deut. 3:25; 11:30; Josh. 9:1; 12:7; 22:7). In this case the threshing floor was home to *the inhabitants of the land, the Canaanites* (v. 11). Since the term *Canaanite* is used in the Old Testament to refer only to ethnic groups who occupied the land west of the Jordan River, the location of the threshing floor must have been on the west side of the Jordan. The mourning at the threshing floor is described as loud lamenting and weeping. Moreover, we are told that Joseph mourned seven days for his father. This was the common Israelite period of mourning (1 Sam. 31:13; 1 Chr. 10:12; Job 2:13; Ezek. 3:15–16; Judith 16:24; Sirach 22:12), though exceptions were

---

61. Of the thirty-two times 'across the Jordan' occurs in the Old Testament, twenty-five refer to land east of the Jordan River.

later made for Moses (Deut. 34:8) and Aaron (Num. 20:29), each of whom were mourned for thirty days. The Canaanites who observed the mourning appear not to have known whom the mourning was for. However, they assumed that the mourners were all Egyptians, probably from the chariots and horses but perhaps also from their mode of dress. So the place also received the name Abel-mizraim. In most place names in the Old Testament *'ābēl* means 'brook, stream'.[62] Here it is a play on the word *'ēbel*, meaning 'mourning', implying the stream (*'ābēl*) of tears produced by the mourning (*'ēbel*) of the Egyptians (*miṣrayim*). Once again, we are told that it was located *across the Jordan* (v. 11).

12–13. The obedience of all of Jacob's sons is emphasized in that they all participated in his burial, just as the sons of Abraham and Isaac had participated in their burials (25:9; 35:29). Verse 13 appears to be a summary of the entire burial procession: they carried Jacob to Canaan, and they buried him in the place he had specified (cf. 49:30).

14. Finally, the narrative stresses that Joseph and everyone else who participated in the funeral procession returned to Egypt. Joseph kept his promise to his father (47:30–31) and his promise to Pharaoh (v. 5).

ii. Joseph forgives his brothers (50:15–21)
c.1859 BC

15. Back now in Egypt, Joseph's brothers realized that without the restraining presence of their father, Joseph was in the perfect position to exact revenge, should he seek to do so. In their own words they admitted that they had caused his suffering, and they were of the opinion that if he still held a grudge, he would not hesitate to repay them. The verb for *hold a grudge* is the same word used to describe Esau's hostility towards Jacob (27:41) and the word used by Jacob to describe the attacks that Joseph withstood because God had strengthened him (49:23–24).

---

62. See Abel-shittim (Num. 33:49); Abel-meholah (Judg. 7:22; 1 Kgs 4:12; 19:16); Abel-keramim (Judg. 11:33); Abel-Beth-Maacah (1 Kgs 15:20; 2 Kgs 15:29); Abel-Maim (2 Chr. 16:4).

16–17. The brothers first approached Joseph indirectly by sending him a message. They quoted Jacob's words before his death, saying, *your father gave a command* (v. 16). By calling Jacob *your father* and not 'our father', they were appealing to the special bond between Jacob and Joseph. Jacob's words to Joseph used two terms for what they had done to him: *transgression* and *sin*. These are further defined as *when they dealt you evil* (v. 17), which is equivalent to 'when they treated you badly' (NET, NIV; cf. TNK). Then Jacob pleaded for Joseph to forgive *the servants of the God of your father*. This last phrase invoked their common relationship with God who is gracious and forgiving (Exod. 34:6). It is God's forgiveness that moves those who trust in him to forgive each other (Col. 3:12–13).

Many modern interpreters believe that Joseph's brothers likely fabricated Jacob's appeal for forgiveness.[63] They note that Genesis never records these words of Jacob before he died, nor does Genesis explicitly say that Jacob knew of the brothers' actions that led to Joseph being enslaved in Egypt. However, it strains credulity that when Jacob was informed that Joseph was alive and in Egypt he did not enquire as to how that could be. Did he live for seventeen years in Egypt without once wondering how Joseph had come to be transported to the land of the Nile and rise to his high position? Moreover, in his blessing on Joseph, Jacob unambiguously mentioned attacks on Joseph (49:23). Genesis mentions only two wrongs purposely directed at Joseph: his brothers selling him into slavery (37:23–28) and the lies spoken by Potiphar's wife (39:17–18). It hardly seems credible that 49:23 is primarily concerned with Potiphar's wife and not with the crime perpetrated by Joseph's brothers. Therefore, Jacob may well have said the words quoted by Joseph's brothers.

Joseph's reaction to his brothers' words was to weep. This is the seventh and last time that Joseph is said to have wept (42:24; 43:30; 45:2, 14–15; 46:29; 50:1), though the reader is not told his reason for weeping. Since the narration does not say why he wept, the text is very powerful and poignant, allowing readers to explore the entire range of possibilities: Joseph may have been expressing

---

63. See the discussion in Wenham (1994: 490) and Hamilton (1995: 703).

disappointment in his brothers' lack of trust; he may have sympathized with their fears, remembering his fears from years earlier; or he may have been extremely moved by the mention of his father's appeal for mercy in the name of God.

18. After having approached Joseph indirectly, the brothers now came from Goshen and bowed before him – the last mention of the fulfilment of Joseph's dreams (37:5–11). The brothers also in effect offered their own punishment for Joseph to exact: *We are your slaves!*

19–21. Joseph's words, however, are immediately conciliatory. His brothers had nothing to fear. By asking the question *Am I in the place of God?* (v. 19), he was stating that exacting vengeance properly belongs to God (Lev. 19:18; Deut. 32:35; Rom. 12:19). While the Scriptures teach that God may choose to exact punishment for crimes through civil authorities (Rom. 13:3–4), Joseph, despite his great power in high office, was not placed in a position with the authority to judge and punish such misdeeds as his brothers had committed. Joseph then stated that he understood that his brothers had purposely conspired to commit an evil deed against him. Yet he had also come to understand that even in their wicked act, God was accomplishing a larger good, and God's goal was the survival of many people: the Egyptians and especially the family of Jacob. So Joseph pledged to continue the work of God by providing for his brothers and their children. Moreover, he reinforced this by offering them comfort and kind words.

iii. Joseph's death (50:22–26)
1806 BC

22–23. This verse begins by noting that Joseph and his father's family lived in Egypt. This matches the formula used at 37:1 to note that Jacob settled in Canaan. The notice of Joseph's lifespan of 110 years frames these last verses in Genesis (cf. v. 26). Since 110 years was considered by Egyptians to be the ideal lifespan, Joseph's 110 years, all but seventeen of them in Egypt, mark him as especially blessed by God to the very end of his days.[64]

---

64. E.g. *ANET* 414. See also Vergote (1959: 200–201).

24–25. Joseph's dying instructions to his brothers are similar to Jacob's earlier instructions to Joseph (47:29–31). That Joseph still had brothers implies that at least a few of them outlived him. Even as his last days drew near, Joseph expressed his confidence in God's promise to give Israel the Promised Land. This was the reason why he imposed an oath on *the sons of Israel* (v. 25) that they would carry his bones with them.

26. Once again, Joseph's age is stated. Like his father, he was embalmed. This was to preserve and prepare his body for later transport to the land given him by Jacob (48:21–22). The book ends with Joseph's body in a coffin in Egypt, enticing readers to learn the subsequent story of Israel in order to learn how the oath the Israelites swore to Joseph was kept.

Meaning
The last chapter in Genesis begins and ends with death, but not without hope. With the burial of Jacob in Canaan and the promised burial of Joseph's bones in the Promised Land, the narrative closes with unfinished business: the fulfilment of God's promise to grant the land of Canaan to the sons of Israel. Between these two events the story of Joseph's forgiveness of his brothers is related. That account finishes a theme that began with Abraham: the use of deception and trickery among God's chosen people. Abraham deceived Pharaoh (12:10–20) and also Abimelech (20:1–18). Isaac deceived another Abimelech (26:7–11), and Rebekah and Jacob tricked Isaac (27:1–40). Laban duped Jacob into marrying Leah (29:21–27), and Jacob's sons fooled their father into believing that Joseph had been killed by a wild animal (37:31–33). Would Joseph use the circumstances of the famine that had brought his brothers to Egypt as a ruse so that he could get his revenge? Joseph brought the trickery and dishonesty to an end. God's people would no longer be divided by roguish behaviour in Egypt as they waited for God's promise to be fulfilled.

With the placing of Joseph's body in a coffin, four centuries of the life of the people of Israel will be passed over in silence. The last word in Genesis – Egypt – reminds us that there is more to the story. Egypt is not the home of God's ancient people, but it is the place where the next book of the Bible will begin as the

Israelites move towards their Promised Land. Yet even that place
was not their ultimate goal, since like all of God's faithful people
they professed 'that they were foreigners and temporary residents
on the earth, that . . . they were seeking a homeland and . . . a better
place, a heavenly one. Therefore, God is not ashamed to be called
their God, for he has prepared a city for them' (Heb. 11:13–16, CSB).